European Navies and the Conduct of War

European Navies and the Conduct of War considers the different contexts within which European navies operated over a period of 500 years culminating in World War Two, the greatest war ever fought at sea.

Taking a predominantly continental point of view, the book moves away from the typically British-centric approach taken to naval history as it considers the role of European navies in the development of modern warfare, from its medieval origins to the large-scale, industrial, total war of the twentieth century. Along with this growth of navies as instruments of war, the book also explores the long rise of the political and popular appeal of navies, from the princes of late medieval Europe to the enthusiastic crowds that greeted the modern fleets of the great powers, followed by their reassessment through their great trial by combat, firmly placing the development of modern navies into the broader history of the period.

Chronological in structure, *European Navies and the Conduct of War* is an ideal resource for students and scholars of naval and military history.

Alan James is a Senior Lecturer in the Department of War Studies, King's College London, and a member of the Laughton Naval History Unit. He has written widely on France and its navy, including *The Navy and Government in Early Modern France, 1572–1661* (Boydell, 2004).

Carlos Alfaro Zaforteza is a Teaching Fellow in the Department of War Studies, King's College London. He is the author of a number of essays and articles on naval warfare and a member of the Strategic Leadership project, a joint venture of the Consejo Superior de Investigaciones Científicas (Madrid) and the Instituto Español de Estudios Estratégicos (Madrid).

Malcolm Murfett is a Visiting Professor in the Department of War Studies at King's College London and an Associate Editor of the *Oxford Dictionary of National Biography*. He has written a number of books on British foreign and defence policy in Asia and is the author of *Naval Warfare 1919–1945* (Routledge, 2013).

European Navies and the Conduct of War

Alan James, Carlos Alfaro Zaforteza, and Malcolm Murfett

Routledge
Taylor & Francis Group

LONDON AND NEW YORK

First published 2019
by Routledge
2 Park Square, Milton Park, Abingdon, Oxon OX14 4RN

and by Routledge
711 Third Avenue, New York, NY 10017

Routledge is an imprint of the Taylor & Francis Group, an informa business

British Library Cataloguing in Publication Data
A catalogue record for this book is available from the British Library

Library of Congress Cataloging in Publication Data
A catalog record for this book has been requested

ISBN: 978-0-415-67890-2 (hbk)
ISBN: 978-0-415-67891-9 (pbk)
ISBN: 978-0-429-46724-0 (ebk)

Typeset in Galliard
by Swales & Willis Ltd, Exeter, Devon, UK

For Penny, Luisa, and Ulrike.

Contents

Illustrations

Figures

Tables

Introduction

Alan James, Carlos Alfaro Zaforteza,
and Malcolm Murfett

In January 1945, as the Soviet Red Army pushed into East Prussia on three fronts, any remaining German illusions of avoiding a comprehensive defeat in World War Two were being swept away. The end of the greatest conflict in the history of the conduct of modern war was nearing. It had, of course, also been the greatest war ever fought at sea, and even in its final stages the need for naval power was as critical as ever. For the German Kriegsmarine in the Baltic, the aim was now only to delay the end so that it could retrieve as many German forces and civilians from the Eastern Front as possible. Waters had to be mined; enemy positions needed to be shelled by the guns of those heavy surface warships that had somehow previously avoided destruction; and a wholesale series of withdrawals and evacuations had to be undertaken. Despite what must have been a heart-wrenching experience for those involved, everyone had to exercise their duty to their fellow citizens, whether in uniform or not, and in the end something truly extraordinary occurred. Over the course of the next four months, over two million refugees were evacuated by the Germans from the Pomeranian coast and the ports in the Gulf of Danzig. Horrendous losses were suffered, such as the passenger liners and transport ships that were sunk en route, but the overall survival record is a tribute to the remarkable work of those responsible for planning and orchestrating this, the largest evacuation of its kind in history.[1]

Needless to say, this is not how German war planners had expected things to turn out. Whilst these heroic operations were being undertaken, RAF Bomber Command also attacked German cities and industrial infrastructure without restraint. By the end of March, German ports and naval bases were undergoing massive bombing attacks, and the deluge continued into April with the Luftwaffe powerless to do anything about it. Thousands of bombs caused colossal damage to the docks at Hamburg, Kiel, Bremen, and Wilhelmshaven and to the ships caught sheltering there.[2] In some respects, however, this dramatic collapse of German naval power is emblematic of the conduct of the entire war at sea, its colossal undertakings, shifting fortunes, and unpredictable outcomes. This is a story of the war that needs re-telling, and it is offered here in a way that captures the contingencies and the simultaneity of events as they played out on the global stage along with the immediate pressures under which decision makers were put by the many interlocking, and rapidly unfolding, events. It is a story, furthermore, which can only be told from the perspective, not just of the victorious Royal Navy or the US Navy, but of all of the navies that had a stake and made the war what it was.

A mass evacuation in the aftermath of calamitous military defeat might seem an unusual choice to hold up in this way as the pinnacle of a centuries-long history of modern naval warfare. Yet the sheer scale of these operations speaks of something genuinely exceptional. They also capture something of the very essence of naval power. They simultaneously demonstrate the indispensable role it plays in war as well as its limits and its essential subordination to fighting on land. They also illustrate that navies were never simply instruments of offensive war. Especially during this total, attritional struggle, which pitted the entire industrial and political might of nations against each other, they had been one of the principal keys to success or failure on the basis of the protection or predation of the essential sea lanes of supply and transportation upon which everyone depended to continue the fight. Yet the collapse of a European navy, and the end of the war itself, is also illustrative of another defining feature of navies. As attested by the lingering impression of the Dunkirk evacuation of 1940 on the popular memory and identity of Britain today, the military significance of such operations can be easily matched by the popular emotional responses they evoke and by their corresponding institutional and political impact. Mass evacuations occurred throughout the war, and it could be said that these and other high-profile operations, with their direct implications for domestic populations, represent the final throes of navies as popular expressions of national strength and identity, something that had been growing for many years and which had peaked in the decades just prior to World War One.

The operational flexibility of navies and the variety of uses to which they can be put has long been recognised. In addition to their military role, their important diplomatic and constabulary use has also been emphasised.[3] Their influence goes much further than this, however. They also played an important part in imperial or colonial enterprises, in the strategic thinking of governments, in the economic and maritime life of states, and even in the cultural relations of nations with the sea, all without the potentially menacing or disruptive presence sometimes associated with armies. This and the obvious, impressive visual effect of warships, and even of dockyards, always gave navies a peculiarly powerful potential political influence, projecting an image of national power abroad but also consolidating and contributing to the building of a political consensus at home. This political volatility is a consistent, though easily overlooked, element of the history of modern naval warfare, and its climax around the turn of the twentieth century was followed by the cataclysmic violence of global, industrial warfare.

An extended account of World War Two at sea sits rather prominently, therefore, as a peculiarly dramatic denouement to the long tale of escalation of modern war that is related in this book. Its distinctive, telescopic structure, with successive chapters focusing on ever narrower time frames, zeroes in on the events of the war themselves as the final resolution of the development of navies as powerful, technical instruments of war and of their evolution as representations of the political potency of states. This is not to present World War Two merely as an extended appendix nor to imply any kind of natural progression or simple historical inevitability. On the contrary, by bringing to light in some detail the contingencies and complexities of the fighting, along with the human element of naval command and the assumptions and even wishful thinking that was often applied during this war, the aim is to reinforce the need for the contextualisation and historicisation of the use of sea power and for ever greater sensitivity to the different political environments and contexts in which it was employed in the past. Throughout history, navies operated in different strategic environments, to different purposes, and reflected changing, historically- and culturally-conditioned ideas about the nature of war.[4] The challenge is to remember that World War Two, that most violent, organised use of sea power to political ends in history, cannot be understood in immediate, instrumental terms alone but also as a cultural, political phenomenon and that navies played an important role in both respects. Whilst Jeremy Black is certainly correct to detect in naval history to date an element of Euro-centrism and to suggest that naval power can only be properly understood by considering the experience of people on the sea globally, it was specifically European navies that evolved in step with the political evolution of states and western ideas of modern warfare, and it is on these grounds that they receive particular attention here.[5]

If, however, it is relatively easy to identify the end of the story, it is far harder to locate its beginning.[6] Violence at sea is nearly as old as human history itself, and modern naval warfare was always marked by a complex interdependence between public and private violence which makes it difficult to identify precise foundational moments for these formal institutions of state. Just over 500 years earlier, however, in August 1415, there were two nearly simultaneous campaigns of a different sort which may claim our attention. It was then that the Portuguese Prince Henrique, 'Henry the Navigator', began to build his reputation in the company of his father, King João I, at the conquest of Ceuta in North Africa.[7] Without doubt, this was an exceptional naval operation. The largest force ever assembled in Lisbon to date set sail with as many as 50,000 men and a fleet of sixty-three sailing ships, twenty-seven galleys, and over 150 smaller and support vessels. Initially encountering a well-defended position, the Portuguese force took the city and its riches at the second time of asking after a hard-fought but short clash on the beach. They left a garrison and established a legal presence which remains even today with Spain's continued ownership of the Moroccan enclave.[8] That same month another, larger and even more spectacular operation was underway to the north. The English king, Henry V, sailed to France with an unprecedented force, arriving at the mouth of the Seine with seven new, large warships (including three that were bigger than any ever previously built in England) and a total fleet of probably 700 ships.[9] The amphibious assault and successful siege of Harfleur that followed were the opening acts of a campaign that came to a head later that autumn with the celebrated Battle of Agincourt at which Henry V dramatically pressed his claim to the French throne, a claim Britain did not formally renounce until the nineteenth century.

It is tempting to represent the capture of Ceuta as an initial, tentative step by European powers to build overseas empires. Henry the Navigator, in particular, retains a popular reputation as one of the first visionaries of empire, overseeing the further Portuguese advance down the west coast of Africa as a prelude to the passing of the Cape of Good Hope and the penetration of the Indian Ocean by Vasco da Gama in 1498 and to the establishment of the first great European, maritime empire. Likewise, Henry V's fleet was remarkable not just for its scale but for the novelty of the direct royal investment in warships, a moment of insti-tutional growth, it could be said, linked to the strengthening of the monarchy. In this way, these events represent the two thematic threads that run through much of the writing on early modern navies.

Yet it is not enough to see navies simply as instruments of empire building or state building in this way; both events are also evidence of the growing domestic political value of naval power. Some time ago, Geoffrey Scammell argued that the capture of Ceuta, for example, was not in any meaningful sense an early sign of a determined, emerging naval power, and few current historians would date the early Portuguese imperial experiment to 1415. Likewise, the nature, and especially the timing, of this expansion cannot be explained fully by economic or commercial imperatives, much less by any advances in seafaring technologies, organisational capacity, or spirit of exploration. It can only be understood as part of a pattern of late-medieval politics and warfare.[10] It was a typical response for a new dynasty, the House of Aviz, finding itself at peace with Castile and seeking an opportunity for its nobility to pursue honour and reputation through 'just' conquest as part of a tradition of raids against the Muslim enemy. Medieval warfare was a means of building social bonds within the warrior elite of a soci-ety in this way and, at Ceuta, João I was able to offer the prospect of riches and reputation and thereby consolidate the strength of his dynasty.[11] Indeed most historians today are sceptical about Henry the Navigator's vision of over-seas empire, preferring to see him as firmly part of an older crusading tradition. To understand the conquest of Ceuta, therefore, we must take seriously the seemingly insincere motivations (to modern sensibilities, that is) of honour and reputation and the social function of medieval warfare. If chivalry profoundly affected the conduct of war in Europe, it should not be a surprise that it affected its corollary, overseas expansion.[12]

Much the same understanding of the nature of medieval warfare is required to understand Henry V's intervention in Normandy. To press his family's claim to the duchy, he not only prepared a fleet like no other, he brought an invading army accompanied by new and terrifying weapons in the form of four large siege guns which he directed against the walls of Harfleur. In this and other ways, the Hundred Years War, and the campaigns of Henry V in particular, are said to have marked an increased ferocity and ruthlessness, a key early step in the emergence of modern war-fare. In typical medieval fashion, however, Henry V was simply using war to claim an inheritance and, as Jan Willem Honig argues, the whole Agincourt campaign was characterised by the usual negotiation, ritual, and posturing in a long process of building the legal case for one's own rights and undermining the authority of the opponent.[13] If Henry V's campaigns mark a new departure in European warfare, it would seem to have been linked only to his audacity, for more than his predecessors he was willing to press his claim through conquest and occupation.[14] A huge, impressive fleet of modern ships made a perfect visual statement of this personal and legal confidence. A notable escalation in the use of navies occurred, then, in two quite different contexts in 1415 which need to be considered with care. In both cases, naval power was important for both practical reasons and as an eloquent statement of dynastic status and ambition.

All too often, however, this political context as a standard by which to evaluate navies is overlooked. Instead of relying upon the determination and aims of such leaders and their followers, strategic assumptions that are based upon British imperial and naval successes of the eighteenth or nineteenth century are often anachronistically and sometimes rather clumsily applied. It would, of course, be impossible and more than just faintly ridiculous to attempt to deny the long-term pre-eminence of the Royal Navy or Britain's influence on the aspirations of other countries.[15] Yet naval history cannot limit itself to a collective effort to explain relative British success. As N.A.M. Rodger reminds us, naval history is, by its very nature, international, and indeed, as some modern studies suggest, at different stages in history British pre-eminence was often far from guaranteed.[16] At the very least, smaller naval powers provided the foil to Britain as the leading actor in the play and had important roles of their own.

Fortunately, a much fuller picture of these other navies, and of their political purpose, is now possible. A generation of modern naval historians has been studying different national experiences, inspired to a large extent by Jan Glete's magisterial comparative study from 1993 of the histories of all European navies.[17] Many projects and working groups today explore the international character of naval warfare and make important, valuable comparisons, and in these we can certainly detect Glete's influence.[18] His notion of 'interest aggregation', the necessary alignment of the interests of government and of seafaring and trading populations as the key to relative national success, colours much of the best modern naval history. It is no longer enough for naval history simply to describe a growing monopoly of violence by the state. War at sea is complicated by the shifting alignments of potentially competing or shared interests between states, trading companies, merchants, coastal communities, privately-armed individuals, or others.[19] This perspective has not only ensured that the social history of navies and the relations of power that allowed navies to function remains essential to understanding the conduct of war, it has opened many other opportunities in what is becoming an increasingly rich and valuable field of research.[20] Even apparently once reliable and apparently clear national boundaries can be seen as conceptually limiting, or artificial, as the complexity of relations within or between coastal regions and across waterways is explored.[21] It is, therefore, not just the scale, cost, and technical complexity of navies that make them important subjects of academic study. Much more than just instruments of state policy, they were also enormous industrial, national undertakings and cultural reflections of the societies that supported them and which they served.

Currently, the practical challenges in guaranteeing the financial and political support necessary to build navies that could meet growing foreign policy needs is occupying much of the attention of naval historians. This is revealing creative and sometimes potentially even disruptive efforts by states to exploit their human, material, and financial resources. The eighteenth century, in particular, it has been shown, was a world of states which relied not just on their own organisational capacities but, in different ways and to different extents, on outside contractors to support their procurement, logistical, and even financial needs.[22] This growing interest in the 'contractor state' is bringing a tremendously important empirical and comparative perspective to bear that promises to transform the study of the early history of European navies. The only possible word of caution is that to the extent that, taken together, all of this serves to account for British successes, it still risks equating these successes with imperial or even political modernity itself. Indeed, it must be said that in most studies the British experience at sea, or in organising themselves to go to sea, is still held up, whether openly, implicitly, or even unwittingly, as a universal standard of success to be applied.

This approach to the history of navies is not just the inevitable effect of Britain's historical record but of the impact of the early historians and strategists who first wrote about it. For them, navies were indeed simply instruments of state, and they wrote their histories not for popular, nor even usually for academic, audiences but for a third group, the service industry. Originally, naval history was taught chiefly in naval academies, and lessons were to be drawn from the past for policy makers and practitioners about the importance of naval power and its development and deployment which could be applied to the international situations then being faced or anticipated.[23] The greatest influence on the practice of naval history came from the pen of the American strategist Alfred Thayer Mahan (1840–1914). His writing, notably *The Influence of Sea Power Upon History, 1660–1783* (1890), drew the lesson from the long experience of British naval and imperial pre-eminence that, to be a major power itself, the United States of the late nineteenth century needed sea power and specifically to invest in a powerful battle fleet with which to defeat any potential competition, to command the seas, and to protect the trade upon which its strength relied. This was certainly a compelling conclusion to draw, and Mahan seems almost to have single-handedly shaped both historical and strategic thought in Anglo-Saxon circles of the time. Though caricatured throughout much of the late twentieth century as deterministic and obsessed with battle, his reputation is currently enjoying something of a revival.[24] At no point, however, has there been a serious challenge to the narrative he did so much to sustain of the logical, triumphant rise of the modern British empire and state.

Thus, to borrow a phrase employed by John B. Hattendorf and James Goldrick, 'Mahan is not enough'.[25] Equally, however, it could be stressed that 'Britain is not enough' either. There were, of course, many other national experiences from which we can learn and continental theorists who can bring a different perspective to the past. This diversity is perhaps in most sharp relief with respect to the celebrated heroics of Admiral Nelson. His determined pursuit of victory which culminated in the iconic Battle of Trafalgar of 1805 and the destruction of the combined French and Spanish fleet had a profound impact which shaped the Royal Navy's very identity and, as Andrew Lambert argues, continued to affect its operational approach well into the twentieth century.[26] Accordingly, Trafalgar represents something of a high-water mark in English-language histories.[27] Perhaps not surprisingly, however, other national perspectives and traditions produce rather different assessments. Indeed, as Rodger points out, in France there had been a tradition of seeing victory in battle by a commander not even necessarily as something to celebrate, but potentially as 'something of a self-indulgence, a vulgar display by officers lacking self-discipline and moral fibre'.[28] Prior to Mahan's sudden rise to prominence in 1890, the most influential naval thinker in Europe was the French admiral Jurien de La Gravière (1812–1892), and he makes it quite clear, in his *Guerres maritimes sous la république et sous l'empire* (1847) and elsewhere, that in Europe, at least, the British experience of sea power was considered exceptional. It was not the norm, and the lesson for the historian, in his words, is that 'all' events which took place at sea in history become difficult to understand or to assess properly if one allows oneself to be 'blinded by the successes of Nelson which are all so regrettably and so easily explained'.[29]

A continental perspective on naval warfare seems especially important given how little impact British success at sea had on military thought more generally. Carl Von Clausewitz, whose classic text *On War* (1832) has established his reputation as the greatest theorist of war, was almost silent on naval warfare. When it was considered by others at all, it was neither British victories nor the nation's financial strength or the administrative system of the Royal Navy that was admired. For instance, Antoine-Henri de Jomini, who did take a direct interest in navies and was indeed the more influential military theorist in the nineteenth century itself, described a visceral resentment across Europe of Britain's strength in the wake of the dramatic victory over Napoleon. Jomini claimed that to the obviously dangerous, destabilising ambition of universal monarchy to which rogue European powers occasionally and unfortunately aspire in history must be added Britain's then current and equally deplorable 'absolute empire of the sea'. To denounce it and to contain it should be 'the rallying cry of European politics'.[30] It is important to keep in mind, therefore, that strategic thought in general, and naval strategy in particular, was not formed in slavish admiration of the British experience at sea and that Britain was not the only power to devise ways of using navies effectively.

On the continent, it had long been established that for navies, especially those less well-endowed with men and materials than Britain's, it was preferred to avoid battle and instead to contain an enemy, protect a merchant convoy, facilitate the landing of an army, or to use naval power in an even less direct fashion by turning it against an enemy's seaborne trade. The best naval history, therefore, takes seriously alternative perspectives such as that of the group of late nineteenth-century French strategists, referred to collectively as the *Jeune École*, who took a very different approach to that of Mahan. They responded to British pre-eminence by emphasising coastal defence and the value of exploiting modern technologies which could be used easily and effectively against a superior battle fleet whilst avoiding direct confrontation.[31] Writing later, in the inter-war years, the French admiral Raoul Castex (1878–1968) reacted in turn by arguing that strategy should not be based in this way directly on the technological means available. He accepted many of Mahan's conclusions, including the need for battleships, and felt that powers like France, which could not directly compete for naval mastery, could still use sea power positively against a dominant power, relying, for example, on manoeuvre to achieve minor, regional successes as part of a national 'general strategy'.[32] Arguably, one of Castex's greatest lasting contributions is the reminder that because of their operational flexibility, in many ways navies are actually especially well-suited to meeting the needs of medium and smaller powers.

Of course, Britain, too, exploited the flexibility of sea power, and this has not escaped the attention of Anglophone historians. Indeed it is the variety of uses to which naval power can be put that is usually celebrated, and it is for this reason that most historians would firmly reject being labelled 'Mahanian' with the narrowness of view that that can imply. Instead, flexibility is a key leitmotiv of a modern literature which emphasises the role of navies as dissuasive assets, the effectiveness of blockades, and the protection of overseas trade and lines of communication or, notably, which explores the relationship between state-run navies and private violence. Most often, this means the harnessing of private resources or the licensing of private violence to act against an enemy's trade or naval assets. Thus it is more usually the British naval strategist Sir Julian Corbett (1854–1922) who is fêted, in English at least. Corbett identified slightly different lessons to be drawn from history than Mahan's. Writing in the different international context prior to World War One, he advocated a more flexible approach to sea power for Britain, with less emphasis on the concentration of force and the need to seek decisive battle. His most famous work, *Some Principles of Maritime Strategy* (1911), has sealed his reputation as a giant of strategic thought, complementing Clausewitz by adding to the orthodoxy of the concentration of force and the strategy of overthrow an elaboration of the concept of limited war which navies by their nature are suited to wage.[33] Nevertheless, although Corbett's ideas certainly challenged some people's assumptions at the time and provoked controversy in Britain, it is all too easy to exaggerate their novelty. The vastly greater relative importance of armies on land, which he insisted upon, and the limited practical value of naval battle reflected already well-established principles held by European powers dating back at least to the eighteenth century and which were given full voice by continental theorists. Although it offers a more nuanced understanding of historical British success at sea and one that would be recognisable on the continent, Corbett's influence did little to loosen the thematic stranglehold on naval history of imperial or political modernity as embodied, mostly, by Britain.

It is, therefore, simply in an attempt to encourage this very thematic loosening that the authors of this book, each with a unique perspective and style, address the different contexts in which European navies operated. Although the book covers many centuries, it emphasises the changing political value of navies and the unique historical circumstances in which this occurred. In this respect, it stands in direct contrast to the 'long-cycle' approach adopted by Modelski and Thompson's comparative, quantitative analysis which was predicated on the un-historical assumption of a '500-year struggle for naval predominance' with clear, easily measurable winners and losers.[34] To do this properly, however, still requires some attention to quantitative detail, if for no other reason than that contemporaries themselves, particularly by the nineteenth century, also conceived of sea power in instrumental terms and measured it rather crudely by total tonnage or total guns. Figures 0.1 and 0.2, therefore, offer a very rough illustration tracking the results of the international competition between European navies between 1600 and 1937. It suggests, among other things, that national interest always demanded close attention to a state's relative standing in terms of naval capacity, and the marked peaks, which indicate periods of rapid naval construction, occurred in response to major European military crises. It seems, in other words, that the emergence of modern naval warfare can be mapped against moments of apparent destabilising aggression, whether by Louis XIV, Napoleon, Wilhelm II, or Hitler and Hirohito. Thus it is directly to the challenges to the international system, and to the basis on which states defined and identified themselves within it, that naval historians should turn their attention.

This book makes no claim, therefore, to encyclopaedic coverage of major events or of the history of different national navies. Nor is there any attempt to summarise the enormous literature on navies and warfare. It is an essay on the changing strategic context of European navies which helps, among other things, to contextualise and to aid an important re-telling of World War Two, the defining conflict at sea. For this, Clausewitz is a logical point of departure, for despite his own silence on sea power, his observation that political aims are the greatest of the influences affecting the character of war is just as valuable for understanding war at sea as on land.[35] In other words, although naval power consistently played a key role in the long-term development of the modern world, to appreciate it we must consider the roles navies played in the definition of national self-identity, both domestically and internationally, and thus in shaping or reflecting political aims in war. To our growing understanding of the instrumental value of navies in war or in the twin processes of empire building and the formation of the modern commercial, industrial, or militarised state, we must also add a sensitivity to their more intangible, political role. From the fifteenth century, when rulers and states began in their different ways to appropriate navies as part of their on-going political invention, they helped to shape political identity and define relative status and reputation in international affairs. This was beginning to be clear in 1415 and, by the time of the ideologically-charged, industrial wars of the twentieth century, navies were considered essential expressions of the vigour of the state and guarantors of national survival.

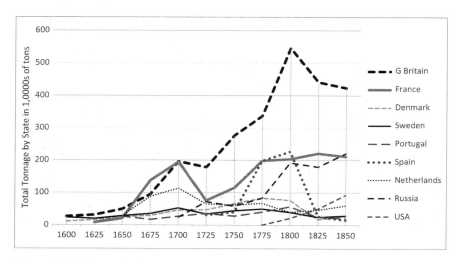

Figure 0.1 Total tonnage by state, 1600–1850[36]

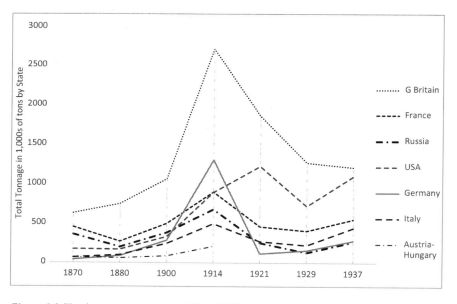

Figure 0.2 Total tonnage by state, 1870–1937[37]

Notes

1 Malcolm Murfett, *Naval Warfare 1919–45: an Operational History of the Volatile War at Sea* (London: Routledge, 2013); V.I. Achkasov and N.B. Pavlovich, *Soviet Naval Operations in the Great Patriotic War, 1941–1945* (Annapolis: Naval Institute Press, 1981).

2 Martin Middlebrook and Chris Everitt, *The Bomber Command War Diaries: an Operational Reference Book, 1939–1945* (Harmondsworth: Viking, 1985), pp.692–96; Jürgen Rohwer and G. Hummelchen, *Chronology of the War at Sea, 1939–1945: the Naval History of World War Two* (Annapolis: Naval Institute Press, 1992), pp.399, 404–10.

3 Ken Booth, 'Chap. 1, The Function of Navies', in *Navies and Foreign Policy* (London: Routledge, 2014), pp.15–25.

4 J.D. Davies, Alan James, and Gijs Rommelse (eds), *Ideologies of Western Naval Power* (Aldershot: Ashgate, 2019); Jeremy Black, *Naval Power: a History of Warfare and the Sea from 1500* (Basingstoke: Palgrave, 2009), p.229.

5 Jeremy Black, 'Naval Capability in the Early Modern Period: an Introduction', *Mariner's Mirror*, 97, 2 (2011), pp.21–31.

6 This point has been made by N.A.M. Rodger, *Safeguard of the Sea: a Naval History of Britain. Vol. 1, 660–1649* (London: HarperCollins, 1997), p.xxiv.

7 Compare with John Darwin's study of global empires which begins with Tamerlane's death in 1405. John Darwin, *After Tamerlane: the Global History of Empire* (London: Allen Lane, 2007).

8 Armando da Silva Saturnino Monteiro, *The First World Sea Power, 1139–1521, Portuguese Sea Battles* (Lisbon: Monteiro, 2010), p.86; Weston F. Cook, Jr., *The Hundred Years' War for Morocco: Gunpowder and the Military Revolution in the Early Modern Muslim World* (Boulder: Westview, 1994), pp.83ff.

9 Susan Rose, *Medieval Naval Warfare, 1000–1500* (London: Routledge, 2002), p.85; Craig Lambert, 'Henry V and the Crossing to France: Reconstructing Naval Operations for the Agincourt Campaign, 1415', *Journal of Medieval History*, 43, 1 (2017).

10 G.V. Scammell, *The First Imperial Age: European Overseas Expansion, c.1400–1715* (London: Routledge, 1992), pp.51–57.

11 Bernard Rosenberger, 'La Croisade africaine et le pouvoir royal au Portugal au XVe siècle', in *Genèse de l'état moderne en Méditerranée* (Rome: École Française de Rome, 1993), pp.332–36.

12 Jennifer R. Goodman, *Chivalry and Exploration, 1298–1630* (Woodbridge: Boydell, 1998).

13 Jan Willem Honig, 'Reappraising Late Medieval Strategy: the Example of the 1415 Agincourt Campaign', *War in History*, 19, 2 (2012); and, more generally, Jan Willem Honig, 'Warfare in the Middle Ages', in Hartman and Heuser (eds) *War, Peace and World Orders in European History* (London: Routledge, 2001).

14 Anne Curry, *The Hundred Years War* (Basingstoke: Palgrave, 1993), p.95.

15 Paul M. Kennedy, *The Rise and Fall of British Naval Mastery* (London: Penguin Books, 2017).

16 N.A.M. Rodger, 'Considerations on Writing a General Naval History', in John B. Hattendorf (ed.), *Doing Naval History: Essays Toward Improvement* (Newport: Naval War College Press, 1995), p.127; Bruce Lenman, *England's Colonial Wars, 1550–1688: Conflicts, Empire and National Identity* (Harlow: Longman, 2001); Bruce Lenman, *Britain's Colonial Wars, 1688–1783* (Harlow: Longman, 2001).

17 Jan Glete, *Navies and Nations: Warships, Navies, and State-Building in Europe and America, 1500–1860* (Stockholm: Almqvist & Wiksell, 1993); John B. Hattendorf, *Ubi sumus?: the State of Naval and Maritime History* (Newport: Naval War College Press, 1994).

18 A crowning example is the international co-operation that went into the valuable, four-volume collection of essays, Christian Buchet (ed.), *The Sea in History/La mer dans l'histoire*. 4 vols (Woodbridge: Boydell, 2017).

19 Richard Harding, *Modern Naval History: Debates and Prospects* (London: Bloomsbury, 2016), pp.109–129.
20 Evan Wilson, *A Social History of British Naval Officers, 1775–1815* (Woodbridge: Boydell, 2017).
21 Renaud Morieux, *The Channel: England, France and the Construction of a Maritime Border in the Eighteenth Century* (Cambridge: Cambridge University Press, 2016); Guy Chet, *The Ocean is a Wilderness: Atlantic Piracy and the Limits of State Authority, 1688–1856* (Amherst: University of Massachusetts Press, 2014).
22 H.V. Bowen et al., 'Forum: The Contractor State, c. 1650–1815', *International Journal of Maritime History*, 25, 1 (2013); David Plouviez, *La Marine française et ses réseaux économiques au XVIIIe siècle* (Paris: Rivages des Xantons, 2014); Rafael Torres Sánchez, *War, State and Development: Fiscal-Military States in the Eighteenth Century* (Pamplona: Universidad de Navarra, 2007); H.V. Bowen and A. González Enciso, *Mobilising Resources for War: Britain and Spain at Work during the Early Modern Period* (Pamplona: Universidad de Navarra, 2006).
23 A.D. Lambert, 'The Construction of Naval History 1815–1914', *Mariner's Mirror*, 97, 1 (2011).
24 Jon Tetsuro Sumida, *Inventing Grand Strategy and Teaching Command: the Classic Works of Alfred Thayer Mahan Reconsidered* (Washington, DC: Woodrow Wilson Center Press, 1999); Benjamin F. Armstrong (ed.), *21st-Century Mahan: Sound Military Conclusions for the Modern Era* (Annapolis: Naval Institute Press, 2013).
25 James Goldrick and John B. Hattendorf (eds), *Mahan is Not Enough: the Proceedings of a Conference on the Works of Sir Julian Corbett and Admiral Sir Herbert Richmond* (Newport: Naval War College Press, 1993).
26 'Chapter Seventeen: Nelson Revived, 1885–2005', in A.D. Lambert, *Nelson: Britannia's God of War* (London: Faber and Faber, 2004), pp.339–62; Jon Robb-Webb, 'Corbett and The Campaign of Trafalgar: Naval Operations in their Strategic Context', *Defence Studies*, 8, 2 (2008), pp.157–79.
27 David Cannadine (ed.), *Trafalgar in History: a Battle and Its Afterlife* (Basingstoke: Palgrave, 2006).
28 N.A.M. Rodger, 'The Nature of Victory at Sea', *Journal for Maritime Research*, 7, 1 (2005), p.115.
29 Jean Pierre Edmond Jurien de La Gravière, *Souvenirs d'un amiral*, vol. 2 (Paris: Hachette, 1860), pp.325–26.
30 Jomini, *Histoire critique et militaire des guerres de la Révolution*, vol. 1 (Paris: Anselin et Pochard, 1820), p.10.
31 Arne Roksund, *The Jeune École: the Strategy of the Weak* (Leiden: Brill, 2007); Martin Motte, *Une Education géostratégique: la pensée navale française de la jeune école à 1914* (Paris: Economica, 2004).
32 Hervé Coutau-Bégarie, *La Puissance maritime: Castex et la stratégie navale* (Paris: Fayard, 1985).
33 Jerker Widén, *Theorist of Maritime Strategy: Sir Julian Corbett and His Contribution to Military and Naval Thought* (Burlington: Ashgate, 2012); A.D. Lambert (ed.), *21st-Century Corbett: Maritime Strategy and Naval Policy for the Modern Era* (Annapolis: Naval Institute Press, 2017).
34 George Modelski and William R. Thompson, *Seapower in Global Politics, 1494–1994* (Basingstoke: Macmillan, 1988).
35 Beatrice Heuser, *Reading Clausewitz* (London: Pimlico, 2002).
36 Compiled from Jan Glete, *Navies and Nations: Warships, Navies, and State Building in Europe and America, 1500–1860*. 2 vols (Stockholm: Almqvist & Wiksell, 1993).
37 Compiled from Quincy Wright, *A Study of War*. 2 vols (Chicago: University of Chicago Press, 1942, vol. 1, pp.670–71).

1 European navies and princely power

Alan James

By the time the magnificent new 1,200-ton flagship of the Swedish navy, the *Vasa*, was launched in August 1628, the ambitious king, Gustav II Adolph, or Gustavus Adolphus as he is commonly known to history, had already been building the fearsome military reputation which would be so dramatically confirmed during his successful campaigns from 1630 in the Thirty Years War (1618–1648). Yet he was not just looking forward to the impressive tonnage that would be added to his navy or to the military effect that its sixty-four guns would have.[1] This ornate, gilded behemoth was designed to overawe his European counterparts. In this sense, it was intended to be a political statement, a reflection of the stature of the Swedish monarchy. When it took on water and sank on its maiden voyage, this was a serious political blow to the king, not just a military or financial one.

This had not been the first time that a monarch had tried to capitalise on the imposing visual effect of large warships. In 1511, Henry VIII famously launched his *Mary Rose* of 800 tons, whilst in Scotland, James IV launched his own gargantuan flagship, the French-designed, 1,000-ton *Michael*. Indeed right across Europe, the early sixteenth century was marked by the experimental construction of small numbers of very large warships.[2] Long before that, Henry V's 'great ships' of the early fifteenth century included the largest of all of these showpieces, the 1,400-ton *Gracedieu* of 1418. Thus rulers had long used naval power to such political effect, but this had been episodic and inconsistent. By the first decades of the seventeenth century, something quite fundamental seems to have changed, for there was a spate of such construction projects on the heels of a general escalation in the scale and organisation of naval warfare. To the *Vasa* should be added the Danish *Tre Kroner* of 1604, the French *La Couronne* of 1636, and the English *Sovereign of the Seas* of 1637.[3] Each of these over-sized giants made better expressions of royal prestige than effective weapons of war.[4] Power at sea was becoming a widely-accepted, and permanent, feature of the martial reputations which were the very foundation of royal authority and, by extension, of stable, prosperous societies.

Navies in sixteenth-century Europe

As Rodger warns in a survey of the many changes in sixteenth-century naval warfare internationally, there is a danger of anachronism in emphasising the role of 'states' at all. Contrary to the expectations of nineteenth-century observers and their followers, naval warfare was actually very common in late medieval Europe though it was mostly private and commercial. Monarchs participated, but often as individuals and for profit or simply to provide authorisation for private reprisals. When they did direct naval forces themselves, they relied largely on requisitioning, chartering, or otherwise exploiting private resources.[5] Spain, most conspicuously, did not even have a navy, as such, but a number of regional forces, and over the course of the sixteenth century any political inclination to impose bureaucratic, central control could not overcome a preference for local initiative.[6] For historians, therefore, an emphasis on embryonic, modern institutional developments and relative state power is perhaps not as relevant as an understanding of this political appropriation of naval power to the princely conduct of war.

The sixteenth century was a period of considerable escalation in warfare and, alongside the substantial growth in army size and in the scale and length of the conflicts that were fought at the sieges and on the battlefields of Europe, there was a parallel pressure to develop strength at sea. There is, of course, a developmental logic to the technical innovations which could explain this. Just as the appearance of heavy guns in the siege trains of the French king Charles VIII in the Italian Wars of the 1490s is said to have led to the design of the famously sturdy and defensible *trace italienne* fortifications in what Geoffrey Parker sees as the key to a Military Revolution in early modern Europe, so too did the introduction of heavy artillery lead to the redevelopment of warships and to a logical design process that produced heavily-gunned sailing ships with bristling broadsides. By mid-century, further refinements produced the galleon, which combined the manoeuvrability and movement of galley hull design with the gun-carrying capacity, rigging, and sea-worthiness of the sailing ship.[7] Naval historians, however, do not tend to restrict themselves to technologically determined explanations of historical change.[8] The motivation, they stress more typically, came from the evident commercial, imperial, and military advantages of sea power. It is implied that, for those monarchs and statesmen or even traders with the ability to appreciate these advantages, continuous investment and improvement were quite natural.

It was once possible to consider this foresight the monopoly of Europe's Protestants, with modernity and imperial verve the gift of the enterprising Dutch in the first instance, with the mantle being taken up by the English, later to find its full expression in the British Empire and even later in the United States. This could be usefully contrasted with a picture of steady decline in the lumbering, stultified empires of Catholic Spain and Portugal. There is certainly no denying that the landscape of naval warfare was changed by the Protestant Reformation which began in 1517 with Martin Luther's first public theological dispute with the church. Navies were embraced most enthusiastically by the northern monarchies which adopted Lutheranism and by England in its own split from Rome and its wars against France in the 1540s. Moreover, since the private violence of naval warfare particularly suited non-state actors, something of a 'Calvinist International' emerged between the so-called Elizabethan 'privateers', the Huguenots in France, and the rebellious Dutch 'Sea Beggars' in a large but loose European network of politicised violence.[9] Yet a simple division along confessional grounds is not an adequate approach to the escalation of naval warfare. The notion is seriously inconvenienced by the fact that by the dawn of the seventeenth century, Catholic Spain was still arguably the greatest power at sea. This had not been altered by England having withstood the famous attack by the Spanish Armada in 1588. Moreover, the Iberian overseas empires dwarfed their competition. Indeed, internationally, the Spanish example remained the international 'gold standard' of overseas empire well into the eighteenth century.[10]

It is, of course, quite natural to conceive of the changes in naval warfare as a progression, moving forward from humble origins to a powerful element of globalising modernity. Yet modernisation theory, in whatever form it takes, risks underplaying the values and motivations of people in the past, and it does not fully explain the sudden emergence of modern naval power. The Reformation was certainly the key, but not because it somehow created more able seamen. The Reformation created a new breed of political outsider to whom sea power offered not just certain obvious, immediate military opportunities, but an acceptable, alternative means of demonstrating the martial prowess needed to secure legitimacy, authority, or even survival in their struggle ultimately to join the inner circle of great powers. Thus rather than always seeing the escalation in naval warfare as the product of forces pushing 'forward', it could also be instructive to conceive of the motor forces of change pushing from the 'outside-in'.

From this perspective, the House of Habsburg unquestionably stood at the very centre of Europe. Not since the days of Charlemagne could anyone even approach the extraordinary inheritance which generations of warfare, careful dynastic planning, and some quite extraordinary luck all combined to bestow on Charles V, who was born in 1500. To the traditional Habsburg lands in Austria, the Spanish crowns of Castile and Aragon, including Naples and Sicily, and the Burgundian inheritance, which brought with it the many different provinces and territories of the Netherlands, was added in 1519 his most prestigious title, Holy Roman Emperor. The status of this title was not due to the direct authority it wielded but to the sheer scale of the empire which covered central Europe from northern Italy to the Baltic coast and to its lingering constitutional link to the Roman Empire making it, theoretically at least, the secular arm of the universal authority of the Catholic Church.

Open, violent competition characterised European affairs, as the Habsburg–Valois wars with France in the early sixteenth century reveal. Yet for a conflict which Charles V once suggested could be settled by a personal duel with Francis I of France, it is clear that questions of honour and stature and shared political values clearly mattered.[11] Throughout the century, the political invective of the day was full of woe over the threat, particularly from Spain, of 'universal monarchy' which would upset the natural political order to which all claimed to aspire. This jealousy of Spain, which in the latter half of the sixteenth century under Charles' son, Philip II, had become the main seat of Habsburg power, does not mean that the rest of Europe was always in direct conflict with them. Nor does it mean that they directly modelled themselves on Spanish institutions. Yet it does reveal something of this shared and evolving, cultural definition of 'greatness' which the Habsburgs embodied or abused, depending on one's perspective. In the late medieval tradition in which military reputation was the basis of social and political stability and standing, naval power gave new political actors who were desperate for legitimacy and stained by heresy in the eyes of the Papacy and the established Catholic monarchies another opportunity to compete with, and through military display to share, the imperial majesty dominated by Spain.

Late medieval naval warfare

It is easy to overlook this culturally conditioned 'outside-in' perspective because studies of early modern navies are invariably concerned, in one way or another, with the modernisation of states. Indeed it is even a defining theme of work on the earlier, late medieval period. At the outbreak of the Hundred Years War (1337–1453), for example, France could be said to have had the more developed, modern national navy, not England. Historians have long remarked that since the late thirteenth century there had been a permanent shipyard on the banks of the Seine at Rouen where the construction of galleys and their provisioning took place. The *clos des gallées*, as it is known, was founded in 1292 by Philip IV, an accomplishment for which he was once credited as the father of the modern French navy.

Further research into the administration of the yard, however, has tended to stress the modest scale of operations, the perennial lack of financial support and upkeep, and French reliance on Genoese shipwrights. As a first step in the development of a modern, permanent navy, therefore, it seems this had actually been rather tentative. Yet the strength of any longer-term institutional legacy was surely not the point. France had already long been conducting naval operations on the Mediterranean. With the growing tensions in northern waters, specifically with England, the *clos des gallées* was simply built to help extend its capabilities there. The few small galleys made and kept at Rouen could lead operations which would still be largely made up of hired merchantmen or dominated by borrowed Castilian or Genoese carracks.[12] In other words, it could provide a boost to what would remain a system of occasional hiring of fleets on a grand scale. The threat that even this posed was enough for Henry V to feel the need to destroy the yard in 1418, though French sea power was quite capable of recovering, as a large, punitive raid on Sandwich in 1457 later demonstrated.

Historical interest in the *clos des gallées*, therefore, seems to have been driven primarily by the mere fact that it was owned and financed by the French crown (not to mention by the relative wealth of surviving administrative documents available for historians to consult). There had been other shipyards in northern Europe, in Lübeck and Danzig, for example, but these were mostly private affairs and have, therefore, largely escaped the gaze of historians looking to trace institutional threads to modern navies.[13] Certainly in the years following the raid on Sandwich, the great powers stepped back from direct ownership and maintenance of navies, though this should not be considered a failure in a presumed, natural process of development. As historians of early modern warfare are increasingly making clear, the 'business of war' involved contracting out military responsi-bilities as an effective, flexible, and perfectly acceptable means of waging war.[14] Indeed an escalation of naval warfare in the Channel in the very early years of the fifteenth century has been noted, but this was not even an extension of the usual pattern of gathering occasional fleets by states but simply an attempt by the English and French monarchies to influence and to direct private violence to their own political ends.[15]

Thus it could be said that naval warfare in Europe was becoming more preva-lent and certainly more visible. However, despite the construction of the *clos des gallées* or the high-profile operations of Henry V or João I of 1415, the crowned heads of Europe never imagined that they would monopolise and direct all vio-lence at sea and certainly there was no temptation to try to establish a mastery of the seas for its own sake. On the Mediterranean, however, the state had a slightly different relationship with the sea. There, military traditions of naval warfare and the practical value of galleys were long-established. In addition to commerce raid-ing and general violence at sea, there was, most notably, a bitter military rivalry between Genoa and Venice who had long competed with each other and also with Iberian monarchs and North Africans as sea powers.[16]

Both city states had naval organisations with bureaucracies, reflecting the commercial interests of the citizens and the need to protect them. Venice, in particular, represents an early, formal navy with its large *arsenale* and its regular patrols at sea with its galley fleet. Technologically, too, there were advances. By the beginning of the fifteenth century, there was already some use of shipboard cannon in battle at sea, though guns were still used to best effect as land defences, as when Ottoman onshore guns stopped Venetian galleys from interfering effec-tively to prevent the capture of Constantinople in 1453.[17] Yet by far the most significant change in naval warfare on the Mediterranean in the fifteenth century was the rise of Ottoman power, and this did not translate into any sort of emerg-ing contest for supremacy. The Venetians did not seek a conflict at sea, preferring to defend their trade networks and to seek to maintain good relations. Even the loss of Negroponte to the Ottomans in 1470, during which the city was besieged by the Sultan's forces on land and supported by an enormous fleet of over 300 ships, did not signal a contest for naval supremacy in the eastern Mediterranean.

This essential continuity in Mediterranean naval warfare appears to have been broken when the Venetians challenged Ottoman naval strength at the Battle of Zonchio of 1499. That year, a siege of Lepanto by the Ottomans involved another huge mobilisation of naval strength which caused alarm for Venice and for the Knights of St John on Rhodes. This time, the Venetians prepared a large force of both galleys and sailing ships in response. Although over the four days of fighting there were no full, set-piece battles, the outcome was certainly a disappointment for Venice. Its big carracks ended up in flames, and the Ottomans had not been stopped in their primary aim of delivering artillery to their besieging army. For some people, there is a temptation to see this as a decisive turning point in his-tory. Jan Glete, for one, believed that Zonchio should have the same profile as the celebrated Battle of Lepanto of 1571 or the Spanish Armada campaign of 1588.[18]

There are two reasons for this. On one hand, it marks a significant shift in power, with the Ottomans now displacing Venice as the major force in the eastern Mediterranean. There were also new technologies in evidence signalling a long-term change in the conduct of naval warfare, including the construction of giant flagships on both sides and the widespread use of guns and armed sailing ships alongside the traditional galley. In many ways, then, Zonchio can act as a convenient marker for early modernity.

However, whilst it is certainly true that the use of heavy guns would very quickly become an essential feature of naval warfare with constant efforts made over the coming centuries to maximise their use, this was hardly due to the Battle of Zonchio. Moreover, despite the experiment with sailing ships here and elsewhere at the time, there was no shift to their general use in the sixteenth century. Galleys soon retained their place as the primary vessel for naval warfare on the Mediterranean. This suggests that purely instrumental explanations of change in naval warfare can be limited. Indeed far more telling in any battle than the technological innovations or the hardware used to meet existing operational ends are the political priorities it can reveal. In this case, for Venice, protection of coastal holdings as the basis of its trade and commercial interests was the key, and thus a naval threat as large as the one posed in 1499 simply could not have been ignored. For the Ottomans, whilst this display of might at sea certainly showcased their growing naval strength, it was an extraordinary support to an effort to consolidate what was and would remain essentially a land empire for which military conquest was the basis of the stature and power of the Sultan and therefore of political stability generally. Ottoman imperial interest in Muslim North Africa and the conquest of Egypt by 1517 were more significant in terms of the power balance in the Mediterranean. Thus in the years that followed, despite the perhaps inevitable clashes that would occur between the Ottomans and the Venetians, these were the priorities that the two powers continued to pursue.[19] As Glete himself observed, both still 'shared an interest in the maintenance of law and order in the Levant'.[20] They continued to pursue their interests on a Mediterranean sea that remained dominated by defensive fortifications, galleys, and piecemeal raiding.

Navies and northern European monarchies

More commonly, it is not just to growing state interest or to technological innovation that historians look for the impulse behind changes in sixteenth-century naval warfare, but rather to long-term economic trends which followed a fundamental shift in the primary centre of commercial activity from the Mediterranean to north-western Europe. Dutch fisheries and the carrying trade expanded the area's wealth and maritime industries, and Amsterdam and Antwerp eclipsed Genoa and Venice as the great commercial entrepôts in Europe.[21] Along with this eventually came the establishment of permanent navies which were largely designed to promote and protect commercial interests.

Commerce and trade alone did not drive this process, however. Indeed, far from it, for the greatest challenge facing monarchies in the sixteenth century was not the promotion of commerce but the pursuit of stability, security, and status, and thus it was the matter of protecting personal authority, or sovereignty, which mattered most. This was an enormous challenge. Since naval warfare was largely private and locally controlled, maritime government tended to be an extraordinarily complex medieval heritage of arcane legal traditions and privileges in the hands of countless local claimants often entirely beyond the legal reach of central authority. As Louis Sicking shows, the Burgundians began the fitful effort to impose some order and direction over maritime government in the Netherlands with an ordinance of 1488 based on earlier French legislation from the fourteenth century.[22] Yet the very difficult challenge of exercising meaningful influence over maritime affairs faced all governments throughout the sixteenth century. A lot was at stake. Royal authority, status, and legitimacy required this more than ever, for indeed some of the most direct challenges to the very political existence of many early modern monarchies would come from the sea.

Henry VIII was the first English monarch to make a concerted attempt to create a navy, with the administrative structures and support in place to maintain a permanent fighting force.[23] For him, only a spectacular show of force would do. It is not insignificant that it was his father, Henry VII, who established the first permanent, if modest, dockyard at Portsmouth, for both kings are known for their primary concern with securing the new Tudor dynasty, and their interest in naval power is undoubtedly linked. For Henry VIII, political survival, security, and success depended upon legitimacy, and his appetite for the imperial majesty that would shore it up was well and truly whetted when he acceded to the throne in 1509. His well-known dynastic insecurity subsequently nurtured considerable imperial ambitions, not in the sense of overseas expansion, but in the definition of his personal authority. In addition to extending his realm by incorporating Wales under the English crown, he famously rejected papal authority and established the Church of England. Perhaps not surprisingly, war with France was also a key part of his political ambitions. A formidable navy not only had practical benefits to this end, but for a monarch whose relations with his long-term foe, Francis I, were marked in 1520 by the meeting at the Field of the Cloth of Gold with lavish celebration and ceremony in a show of mutual respect and display of kingly virtue, it also provided another powerful statement of his military stature.[24]

Whilst the competition between these two is well documented, it is less often recalled that both coveted the prestigious imperial title that went to Charles V in 1519 and whose own interest in the sea is revealing. It might be assumed that Charles V would be most concerned with the early efforts of the conquistadores in Central America. Certainly, Habsburg Spain would always take the necessary steps to develop its lucrative new-world possessions, including the shipping and the defence of the overseas routes to and from America on which the riches of its silver mines were transported. Yet as J.H. Elliott describes, the early letters of Hernán Cortés to the court of Charles V, in which he described and tried to justify his conquests, appealed directly to the emperor's political self-perception which was shaped by his legal status in Europe; they did not play to ambitions for a global maritime empire as such. Indeed Cortés would not ever describe his adventures in the new world as Spanish imperial expansion because for Charles V there could only be one legal empire, the Holy Roman Empire in Europe. His empire, therefore, could not be extended by territory in the Americas. These were presented instead as 'just wars' of conquest, in the late medieval military tradition, which Cortés hoped Charles V would endorse and accept as his personal possessions as king of Castile.[25] For someone of the stature of Charles V, establishing a powerful standing navy or projecting power across the seas could never on its own have the same defining political effect that it could for Protestant powers. It could not define his imperial authority, which rested upon long-established and venerated legal traditions in Europe.

It is thus not in such dramatic episodes as the conquest across the Atlantic of Central America that we can discern Charles V's naval priorities, but in the more mundane, legal efforts to influence the government of local maritime affairs in the Netherlands, territories which were at the heart of his imperial identity. With the many established interests and legal traditions in place in this most diverse and constitutionally complex of regions, there was never any question of imposing a universal, recognised legal authority over maritime affairs in one fell constitutional swoop. It could only be through the personal efforts of someone with existing local standing that any central influence in maritime government could be exerted. Thus in 1540 Charles V introduced another reforming ordinance, creating a new office of admiral, but which he awarded to Maximilian of Burgundy, who was already Stadholder of a number of provinces, including Holland. This existing personal standing and influence offered the only hope of keeping the legislative creation of the new admiralty, which was designed to begin to unify maritime government, from being a dead letter.

Though limited in its immediate effect, this reforming initiative could still have a significant impact by focusing on those key elements of maritime government that, it was hoped, could be concentrated in the hands of the admiral without significant opposition: the authority to grant permissions for equipping warships and, through the establishment of a court of appeal, the adjudication of prizes taken at sea and other legal conflicts. Above all, it insisted on the admiral's authority to issue letters of marque, that is to say permissions to seek violent reprisals for losses suffered at sea which could only be done through him in the name of the emperor. As Sicking says, this attempt to legalise and to control private violence was never likely to have much real direct military utility.[26] The important thing, however, was to claim, and to try to enforce, authority over those elements of maritime affairs which touched on the dignity of the emperor in the essential matters of war and diplomacy. Eventually, of course, even this was a failure. The Calvinist nobility who rebelled against the Spanish monarchy had their first significant military success with their attack from the sea on Brill in 1572, and the complex, federal system of Dutch naval strength that evolved sustaining extensive local control over maritime affairs, overseen by five separate admiralties, played a key part in the long military struggle against the Spanish crown that ended with independence in 1648.[27]

France and Spain

For the French monarchy of the sixteenth century the effort to rationalise maritime government was a similar exercise in shoring up royal authority in the midst of civil war. Maritime government in France was also very fragmented. It, too, was marked by numerous entrenched local interests and legal traditions. Not least of the complications was that the office of admiral of France co-existed with the legally incorporated admiralties of Brittany, of Guyenne, and of the Levant (or Mediterranean). In France, the Calvinist minority, the Huguenots, were the most active seafarers, using the sea to help build a political identity, and the Calvinist nobility were eager to exploit the opportunity for sea power in the long-running Wars of Religion (1562–1598).[28] Indeed William of Orange would model the organisation of the Sea Beggars in the Dutch rebellion on the independent admiralty that the Huguenots operated at the French port of La Rochelle from where letters of marque were being issued in the name of the Huguenot admiral of Guyenne and by the rebellious prince de Condé.[29] Before the outbreak of the wars, even the admiral of France himself, Gaspard de Coligny, was a Huguenot, and it was the Huguenots who took the initiative overseas by trying to set up France's first colony in Florida.[30] The danger of a lack of royal authority along the important maritime frontier of the realm was made abundantly clear at the outset of the wars in 1562 when English forces briefly occupied Le Havre at the mouth of the Seine at the invitation of the Huguenots.[31] Such military support from the sea for the Huguenots from their co-religionists in England would be a feature of the wars well into the seventeenth century.

Heavy-handed attempts to impose royal authority had limited success in France. Coligny was stripped of his role as admiral in 1569 and, in the aftermath of his murder in Paris at the St Bartholomew's Day massacre of Huguenots in 1572, the crown mounted an unsuccessful naval operation employing the Mediterranean galleys to support a siege of La Rochelle.[32] Fortunes continued to dip for the French monarchy over the course of the long, complex civil wars, further complicated by the emergence of another militarised political force in opposition to the crown, the Catholic League. Yet, as has recently been shown, royal authority avoided the very real threat of dissolution and emerged by the early seventeenth century reaffirmed, not simply through military victories, but in large part by a long, tortuous process of legal negotiation and repeated legislative efforts to impose a peace settlement between the faiths.[33] Building the specifically maritime authority of the crown through a similarly difficult, pragmatic effort to enforce legislation in the ports and harbours of France was part of the same necessary process. Royal maritime authority was not recognised in Brittany, and by the 1580s, with the powerful League leader, the duc de Guise, coming to dominate government in Normandy, it was all but fully eclipsed there too. In response, the crown embarked on a two-pronged effort involving legislative reform which would be given teeth by the conduct of a large-scale military operation.

This ambition was linked to the anticipated death of the childless Portuguese king in 1580 and the international competition to secure the succession.

The strongest and the most determined legal claim came from the king of neighbouring Spain, Philip II. Spanish military preparations, therefore, began immediately to ensure the successful legal transition of authority by occupying the country and suppressing any resistance to the personal union of the two Iberian crowns. However, Catherine de Medici, the powerful Queen Mother in France, also had a legal claim to the Portuguese throne, though a much more distant one. For a late medieval monarch, it would be inconceivable not to at least assert such a legal claim and to give it some weight by backing it with military force. In order to protect her stature and legitimacy domestically and internationally and by association that of the Valois dynasty, she had to negotiate, through war, for concessions from Spain. Far from an act of pointless vanity or a distraction from the more important business of addressing the domestic wars, then, pressing her claim was at the very heart of what it meant to be a monarch and protecting royal authority in France. Since Portuguese resistance to the Spanish claim was focused upon the islands of the Azores, an opportunity arose for the Queen Mother and the King, Henri III, to mount a naval expedition to protect the islands which were rallying around a Portuguese pretender.[34]

Escalating naval warfare was, therefore, momentarily extended beyond European waters to the Azores because the key European issues were briefly located there. Preparations immediately began for the largest naval operation conducted by France in living memory, leading to the first ever deep-sea naval battle and long-distance amphibious operations by European powers. In a manner typical of late medieval monarchies, through purchase, hire, and pressing, mostly from the ports of Guyenne and of Normandy, and through the investment of speculators who hoped to profit from the conflict, a fleet of sixty ships with a force of as many as 7,000 men was gathered, setting sail for the Azores in June 1582. This was a considerable achievement and an indication of the continued ability of the French crown, when pressed, to gather and operate a significant fleet.

At the same time, there were ambitious legislative efforts to invigorate the office of admiral of France and to extend its legal jurisdiction over the whole Atlantic coast of France, overseeing a system of admiralty courts. Encountering fierce resistance, the crown again came to focus only on those rights that might have direct military or diplomatic significance, such as granting permits for overseas voyages and control over local militias in coastal areas. To have any success at all, the key was to award the office to a high-ranking noble in the court of Henri III and to insist on his authority to collect the lucrative income from the rights. This was no mere exercise in royal largesse or nepotism. It was part of an effort to claw some military and diplomatic influence from that complicated morass of medieval rights and traditions which governed maritime France. Only a self-interested and clearly already powerful individual would be able to confront local resistance. Again, the stakes were high. When in 1584 the king's younger brother died, leaving the Huguenot admiral of Guyenne, Henri de Navarre, as heir presumptive to the French crown, the wars were reignited, led by a resurgent Catholic League.

Unfortunately for France, the expedition to the Azores was a disaster as the fleet was heavily defeated in a rare and dramatic open battle off the island of São Miguel in July 1582. Still, this campaign had been an essential part of the effort to retain royal authority. It was a key priority, just as it had been for Spain, and in this respect, if any naval battle should compete with Lepanto and the Armada for historical attention it is this one. Indeed, one of the most notable features of Philip II's reign was the ruinous financial and military commitment to the ultimately hopeless task of merely hanging on to the authority he felt was his by right in the Netherlands. This determination to defend royal honour and to fight for what God and generations of his family's dynastic policies had determined should be his is unusual to a modern observer. To a late medieval monarch, however, it was simply the business of kingship and of being a sixteenth-century superpower. Historians have found it possible to question the ambition of Philip II's grand strategy.[35] Yet, for the head of the greatest royal household in Europe, whose recent dynastic successes had been unparalleled, there could have been no better prize than the final consolidation of his power base through the unification of the Iberian thrones. The sheer enormity of the naval power he deployed to guarantee the obedience of the islands and thus his legal title to Portugal reflects this priority. Over four years from 1580, Philip II sent increasingly impressive fleets with occupying armies to the islands until, following the sound defeat of the main French force in 1582, he sent in 1583 a force of over forty armed warships, twelve galleys, and up to 16,000 men in what can only be described as a final show of overwhelming strength. Of course, the Azores were also an important staging post on the route back from the Americas, and it was in Spain's interest, for this reason alone, to ensure that the islands did not fall under the influence of the French or to become a haven for pirates. Yet this does not fully account for the sudden determination by both the French and the Spanish monarchies to deploy military force on an unprecedented scale in the name of two rival dynastic claims.

In the euphoria of this unprecedented victory, the Spanish commander, the marquis of Santa-Cruz, famously suggested to his king that now was the time to attempt a similar operation against England. To that kingdom that had once been his by virtue of his brief marriage to Mary Tudor but which was now being ruled by the heretical Queen Elizabeth whose insult to his royal dignity was only matched by her effrontery in aiding the Calvinist rebels in the heart of his extensive personal empire, the Netherlands, Philip II would turn his naval attentions. Santa-Cruz had good reason to believe that Spain would be successful. He had just led Spain to victory in a long-distance operation and had been present, a few years earlier, at what was considered the greatest naval battle of all time: the victory of the Holy League of Spain, the Papacy, Venice, and others over the Ottoman Empire at the Battle of Lepanto.

The Battle of Lepanto, 1571

On 7 October 1571 a fleet of about 206 galleys and six oared-warships (or galleasses) under the command of Philip II's half-brother, Don Juan of Austria, had confronted an Ottoman force of up to 230 galleys with a number of small galleys in support. In the spectacular, bloody battle that followed, the Holy League lost only twelve galleys to the Ottomans' 180. The largest battle of the sixteenth century, on land or at sea, ended with an unambiguous, one-sided victory for the Holy League. At the time, the significance of the victory seemed to know no limits, as did the seriousness of the commemorations and the joy of the celebrations. Equally, historians once saw in this confrontation a key turning point in history, marking the end of the Muslim threat to Europe and the rise of the Christian west. Fought by the old-fashioned galley that was being replaced by the sailing warship, it also represented a last gasp of technological and geo-political significance for a Mediterranean in decline relative to a rising Atlantic economy.

It should not be forgotten, however, that galleys long remained a priority for states and an essential practical element of naval warfare on the Mediterranean as they did on the Baltic. Indeed, it is difficult to see the value of an emphasis on technological decline, given that Spain used galleys as late as 1800 in the Caribbean and oar-powered gunboats were still being built up to the mid-nineteenth century by Germany and Sweden. An important reassessment of the sixteenth-century galley was offered by John F. Guilmartin, who demonstrated that it had actually adapted well to the spread of heavy guns earlier in the century and had grown in size and strength. Far from being outdated technology, by the 1570s it was peaking as an instrument of offensive, destructive warfare.[36] Nevertheless, this sense of climax at the technological and operational level challenges only the detail and the timing of a broader narrative of decline of galley warfare and, worse, it potentially also reinforces and exaggerates the political significance of the battle itself.

Demonstrating a similar conceptual reliance on the political effect of technological change, Jan Glete described the lingering use of galleys, and the fact that the most active Mediterranean sea powers after 1580 were small ones, as a consequence of their 'inability' to adapt to organisational and technological changes in naval warfare occurring in northern Europe and of their apparent 'backwardness'. Tellingly, he lamented the missed opportunity that sea power seemed to be offering to the Ottoman and Spanish empires to become 'world powers'.[37] To assume, in this way, that being the leading imperial powers of the Muslim and Christian worlds respectively was not ambitious enough is potentially to ascribe late nineteenth-century territorial or imperial ambitions to sixteenth-century polities. The use or otherwise of galleys is neither a question simply of technological advances nor the result of tension between conservative strategic outlooks and forward-thinking innovation. It was an immediate and pragmatic response to particular political pressures and values.

Strategic assumptions about the potential effects of the Battle of Lepanto have left historians wondering why it is that after such a decisive victory the west could not have pressed for a more significant outcome. Yet far from being disabled, the Ottoman Empire retained Cyprus, which they had taken in 1570 from the Venetians who now paid tribute to them to protect their commercial interests. The Ottoman fleet was quickly rebuilt and their naval power fully re-established;

the expansion of their interests in North Africa continued apace with the recapture of Tunis in 1574, and by 1580 they had signed a truce with the Habsburgs.[38] Yet this assertion of Ottoman strength had little to do with any failing on the part of the western powers. It was simply a question of strategic priorities. In 1578, King Don Sebastian of Portugal died in Morocco at the Battle of Alcazarquivir, opening the succession crisis that would culminate with the Azores campaigns.[39] Rather than intervene on behalf of the Portuguese against the Ottomans, Philip II came to an accommodation because his greater priorities lay with his natural interests, that is to say in battling the Protestant heresy that was infecting his empire and in pursuing his dynastic interests. For the Ottomans, likewise, with influence in Muslim North Africa secure, they could turn to more pressing matters in Persia. Thus despite the undeniable significance of the Battle of Lepanto for contemporaries, it can best be considered in the words of Andrew Hess as a 'major frontier clash' between empires with different spheres of influence.[40] It was not a decisive confrontation, for neither side sought the destruction of the other. Though very serious fears were allayed and great prestige was undeniably won at Lepanto, a much bigger prize awaited in securing the Habsburg dream of unifying the Iberian peninsula, which involved the more straightforward process of subduing the opposition in the Azores. By 1583, with Portugal secure, and his naval resources now supplemented by a core of Portuguese galleons, the time was indeed ripe for the triumphant Philip II to turn to England.

The Spanish Armada and beyond

The Spanish Armada campaign of the autumn of 1588 occupies a special place in the popular memory of Britain, and much ink has been spilled on the subject. It was, of course, once seen in England as an act of God, with timely winds miraculously dispersing the Spanish force. Although modern historians leave less room for God in their accounts of the campaign, it still remains an extraordinary tale. The outline of events is well known. After many delays, organisational difficulties, and bad weather, the Duke of Medina Sidonia, who was given the command after the death of Santa-Cruz, finally led his fleet into the English Channel in July. In a tight, disciplined, traditional crescent-shaped formation, this force of 130 ships was a display of military strength like no other. Over the course of the week, the Armada slowly moved its way up the Channel, followed and harassed by the largely improvised English forces. Hoping to effect a meeting with the army of the Duke of Parma in Flanders and to transport it to England, it delayed in order to await news. Coming under attack by English fireships off Calais, the crews cut their cables before coming under attack in the famous Battle of Gravelines. Forced to the north-east by wind, the Armada then chose to return by the northerly route around Scotland and Ireland, where it was battered by fierce storms.

Nineteenth-century historians in Britain were inclined to credit the pluck and courage of the English seaman and traditions of English sea power over divine intervention.[41] Today, any apparent natural, national advantages that the English might have enjoyed have given way to more immediate explanations.

Instead, their guns, more numerous, lighter, and easier to reload, gave them a rate of fire which the Spanish simply could not match. The failure of the Armada, however, was primarily a strategic one. It would appear that Philip II's faith in God and the certainty of success led him to devise a plan that was beyond audacious. Transporting an entire army to conduct an amphibious landing and invasion so far from home was an extraordinarily difficult task, and it was made worse by the precision and inflexibility of the orders that Medina Sidonia was given. Without news of the whereabouts of Parma's army, he was forced to wait, making him vulnerable to English and Dutch predation and leaving him with little choice but to return home when the mission failed.[42]

It is possible, therefore, to see the campaign in a slightly different light. The very act of dreaming up, organising, and executing a naval action on this scale and at this distance from home is remarkable in itself. The show of Spanish strength was unparalleled. For Medina Sidonia, withstanding English attacks, maintaining cohesion, and progressing slowly up the Channel were his immediate aims, and he met them well. Even at Gravelines, the effect of the English guns was limited. The Spanish had not really been decisively outfought at all. Most of the damage was done by the storms on the return journey, and whilst it arrived in deplorable condition, most ships and most men of the Armada made it back home to Spain. The difficulty, however, with reconceptualising the Armada campaign in this way as a draw or even as a limited Spanish success is, as Rodger rather passionately insists, that 'nobody at the time imagined anything of the kind'.[43] There is no getting away from the fact that the Armada had failed and that, by surviving, England had indeed triumphed. That there can even be question marks over the very issue of winners and losers in a one-sided campaign such as this suggests that we need to reflect further on the nature of victory to the early modern mind.

As far as naval victory is concerned, it is at least as appropriate to credit the Dutch who fought the Spanish offshore and who disrupted the union of Parma's army with Medina Sidonia's fleet. For Spain, this failure had been a dramatic setback, but it was not one that could affect its longer-term naval strength, nor did it seriously affect its international standing. For contemporaries, however, success was not only measured in such instrumental ways but in terms of the political effect of fighting, and in this respect Tudor England had certainly won. For this reason, open battles, especially on a large scale like this, were often purposefully avoided in medieval warfare, not just because of the danger to which it exposed expensive and valuable armies, or navies, but because of God, upon whose unfathomable will the outcome ultimately depended and whose judgement on the justice of one's campaign could have enormous consequences.[44] In 1588, Philip II chose to take the risk. Elizabeth I had no such choice but, by surviving, her reward was all the greater. She had not only avoided the very serious threat of invasion and possible overthrow but had received a divine endorsement of her legitimacy. Thus it was not her navy, such as it was, that she celebrated afterward, but her authority, newly invigorated through battle, and, as the famous Armada portrait filled with nautical imagery and symbolism reveals, the sea could now be used to define and to represent her royal stature.

On a practical level, the victory over the Armada did not change very much. England remained a minor power with very little investment, or royal interest, in the navy. Spain continued to be a relative colossus, mounting another invasion attempt in 1598 (undone by storms), and the war with England continued until 1604. Yet to emphasise relative English weakness, or Elizabeth I's lack of financial support for the navy, is potentially to miss the wider significance of the Armada campaign. It reveals that although there was neither intention, desire, nor expectation on the part of early modern states to monopolise violence at sea, monarchs did wish to assume a monopoly of the military reputation, the glory, and the displays of political strength that naval warfare provided. Naval power was becoming part of the culture of war upon which European states and societies were built.

Just as Cortés had appealed to the traditions of 'just war' and imperial dignity in the hope of securing political endorsement from Charles V, so did many of the visionaries of popular imperial history in England appeal to the same military instinct. Walter Ralegh, for one, claimed that navies 'are markes of the greatness of an Estate'. By having built ships specifically for the purpose of war and achieving a measure of territorial integrity, England (along with Denmark and Sweden and more recently the Dutch) had built great reputations, he said. An opportunity therefore presented itself in the opening years of the seventeenth century. For whilst Spain, or more specifically Castile, had surpassed the Empire as the source of Habsburg status due to its sea power, it had no real navy to speak of; it relied on pressing ships for service, and what ships it had were better suited to trade than to war. This was a black mark, Ralegh claimed, on the majesty of the king of Spain.[45]

Thus naval history cannot just concern itself with how states organised themselves and how earnestly they set themselves to the administrative challenge of creating a permanent fleet, though that is clearly a serious challenge that all naval powers faced. It is also about how they assimilated the sea into the increasingly complex process of self-definition and the pursuit of greatness through war. Elizabethan England's brush with disaster and its dramatic, near miraculous survival in 1588 no doubt played a big part internationally in raising the profile of naval power.

The Baltic

As Ralegh suggested, in the Baltic the emergence of large, state-run navies had already occurred by the end of the sixteenth century. That this happened along with the early, formal adoption of the Lutheran Reformation is no coincidence. Historically, the area consisted of many small, regional powers, notably those northern German principalities that made up the Hanseatic League, which had traditionally been the greatest sea power in northern waters. Over the course of the century, it had come to be dominated by a small handful of more recognisably modern, relatively centralised monarchies. Specifically, Denmark (with Norway) and Sweden emerged out of the medieval Nordic Union, and both sported strong navies with heavily-armed, modern warships which played a key role both in their birth as distinct, Lutheran kingdoms and in their subsequent dynastic competition.[46] By the 1620s, Poland-Lithuania had also grown in influence and had a small fleet of its own. According to Jan Glete, this was due to the rise of Russian power in the eastern Baltic which led many smaller players to look for protection from the bigger regional powers. More than just the effect of armed competition, however, he insists that the growth of these navies was also economically driven and arose out of competition for the Sound tolls and control of the valuable Baltic trade in raw materials, and this required both state-building and the adoption of modern technologies of war.[47] It was clearly more than this, however, and in the case of Sigismund III of Poland (1566–1632) the hope was to capitalise on growing Spanish naval strength in the north and on imperial Habsburg plans then being entertained for a Baltic fleet of their own.[48] It was not the trade of Spain's principal foe, the Dutch, that he had his eye on, however, but reclaiming the now coveted Swedish throne from which he had been deposed in 1598. As elsewhere in Europe, naval warfare was intimately tied up with the process of defining royal, and thus national, identity in a time of great political change. Though accelerated by the international tension leading up to the Thirty Years War, sea power was a well-established feature of warfare in the Baltic region.

It is worth reminding ourselves that state-building was, of course, never an end in itself. It is a concept that can only ever be applied, with the benefit of considerable hindsight, and it merely describes what were essentially the political means by which rulers pursued existing aims like the consolidation of personal authority, dynastic security, and standing. From the late fifteenth century, the kings of Denmark were particularly active in this respect, as they attempted to assert their legal authority over Sweden within the Union. This necessarily required the threat and use of sea power. The ambitious Danish king Christian II (1481–1559) married the sister of the soon-to-be emperor, Charles V, in 1515 and tried to build an alliance of interest in this way between Denmark, the Habsburgs, and the Dutch, whose trading interest in the Baltic was growing. Yet he famously came up against organised resistance in Sweden led by Gustav Vasa, who had the support of Lübeck, a power which felt that the assertion of Danish strength at sea threatened its traditional role as the main middle-man for trade between the Baltic and the west.

Gustav Vasa needed sea power to defeat his Danish rival, who by 1523 was also deposed as king of Denmark, and it also played a part in the process of building the necessary legal consensus and justification for the new dynasty in Sweden, which he did in large part through the formal adoption of Lutheranism. The navy defended the political settlement from any Habsburg-backed military reaction and from internal opposition. Income from confiscated church property supported this process of political reinvention, and Sweden's new constitutional identity was reinforced when it sent its now considerable fleet in 1535 to intervene in Denmark on behalf of a Lutheran claimant to the Danish throne, Christian III, during the confessionally-driven succession crisis there. Therefore, both of these new Lutheran monarchies, fighting to survive against opposition at home and to consolidate their new positions within the international system, formed an alliance, and indeed by 1544, after a brief war with Emperor Charles V, Christian III won his formal recognition as king of Denmark.

In the years that followed, there were many clashes between the various powers, but the greatest came as Denmark, now in alliance with Lübeck and Poland, reacted to growing Swedish influence by embarking on a remarkable war that was fought over seven years (1563–1570). This war was unique, not just because of the use of large, modern warships but the frequency and scale of naval battles, one of which saw twenty-seven warships square up on each side.[49] Though Denmark and Lübeck had more developed maritime economies which provided an advantage in men and materials, Sweden had more purpose-built warships and was able to break allied blockades of Stockholm and put fleets of up to thirty large ships to sea. Both sides, in fact, concentrated on ship building, and by 1570, the year the peace was signed with neither Denmark nor Sweden establishing predominance, the Baltic navies were marked by some colossal showpiece ships.[50] Thereafter, the Swedish and Danish navies were the main players at sea, with Sweden concentrating on war with Russia to control the Gulf of Finland whilst Denmark was concerned with maintaining control over the Baltic in order to benefit from trade and from the Sound tolls and later with building its maritime power and influence through, among other things, Arctic whaling.[51]

Merchant traders, such as the Dutch, could take advantage of this short period of stability. The situation was later disrupted, but not due to commercial conditions at sea or by a competitive struggle for naval pre-eminence. It was, rather, a confessionally charged, dynastic struggle that threatened to upset international political order. The Reformation in Sweden had been very much a political decision, and for many years it was associated in the historical memory there more with the foundation of the Vasa dynasty than with any popular, confessional enthusiasm.[52] This made it no less significant, however. In 1592, the Catholic Sigismund III of Poland married a Habsburg princess, the sister of the future Holy Roman Emperor, Ferdinand II. This was clearly an alliance he was keen to cement, for when she soon died he quickly married her sister. To be sure, this Habsburg influence caused some disquiet in Poland, but in Sweden it caused a civil war for in 1592 he also inherited the Swedish crown. This was serious problem, for a union of the Swedish and Polish crowns would not only upset the balance of power in the Baltic but undermine the hard-fought identity of the Swedish monarchy itself. Sigismund III was duly deposed in Sweden in 1598, and the new king, Karl IX, embarked upon a retaliatory war against Poland.

In the naval conflicts that followed, Denmark, whose own naval power had been rapidly rising, inevitably became involved. In 1610, a Swedish blockade of Riga provoked the intervention of Christian IV of Denmark. By 1617, however, Sweden had got the upper hand in its struggle with Russia and by 1621 consolidated its position in the eastern Baltic with a large-scale amphibious operation which finally took Riga, followed by further conquests which challenged Danish power in the Baltic. Yet success for Sweden meant more than just territorial expansion. It meant legitimacy and status for the Vasa dynasty and, as Erik Ringmar has argued, these things depended upon honour and reputation. This, as much as anything else, is what motivated Gustavus Adolphus's intervention in the Thirty Years War.[53]

For the dynasties in this volatile region, competing to establish themselves, to secure their survival, and to ensure their longer-term stability and stature through the aggressive military pursuit of their rights and privileges, sea power was indispensable. This applied to big and small powers alike, as shown by the fascinating history of Scottish sea power, which at times relied on state-owned warships but more often on legal efforts to control privateering to political effect.[54] Yet if the Scottish experience demonstrates the ubiquity of sea power and reinforces its rising military and political utility for kingdoms of different sizes and stature (and future constitutional development), Denmark is in many ways most illustrative of the profound change by this time of the personal, political value of naval power as a demonstration of martial virtue for ambitious rulers. Christian IV, who briefly took up the international leadership of the Protestant cause in the Thirty Years War from 1627, took a very direct interest in the navy, building it into one of the biggest in Europe and treating it, according to Martin Bellamy, almost as his 'personal property' and a direct reflection of his own stature.[55] It was, of course, Sweden, however, that had the most impact internationally, not just in the Thirty Years War but by building an empire that helped to shape the political landscape of Europe well into the eighteenth century. Yet behind the growth of northern navies lay a recognition by all states not just of the military but of the growing political value of sea power.

The Dutch struggle with Spain

At the heart of the general escalation in shipbuilding and naval institutional structures in the 1620s was the longstanding struggle by the Dutch provinces against the Spanish monarchy (1568–1648). More than anything else, this made naval power a normal aspect of great-power politics and of war in Europe and indeed globally. Of course, the temptation is almost overwhelming to see the Dutch rebellion, their maritime trade and wealth, and their eventual independence from Spain in 1648 as a step in the political and economic modernisation of Europe. Much has been written about the Dutch miracle and on England's own growing reliance on the sea for its prosperity and influence, and the foundation of the English and Dutch East India Companies in 1600 and 1602 naturally figures prominently in histories of the period. The material interest in sea power is clear. Yet as important as early trading companies, technical innovations, and overseas commercial trading networks all clearly were, naval power was still primarily about imperial majesty and the competition for political legitimacy. It is difficult to exaggerate the determination with which Spain dedicated its wealth and its military and political energy to the reassertion of its authority in the Netherlands, even when that prospect became increasingly remote and the costs almost suicidally high. This was a contest to be fought at all costs, a position which inevitably feeds the impression among modern observers that Spain was simply a declining anachronism. For contemporaries, however, Spain's stature as both the greatest monarchy in Europe and as the greatest sea power was, for the moment, secure. The climax played out both on land and at sea.

By 1598, a full-scale embargo conducted out of Flemish ports was being imposed by Spain on Dutch trade in an effort to sever the economic lifeline that sustained the Dutch war effort. That it was from about this time that the Dutch pursued their East Asian trade in earnest seems no coincidence, as some compensation was sorely needed for their newly restricted activity in European waters if the struggle for independence was to continue. The Dutch were fighting, above all, for political survival in Europe, to be defined and to exist as a state with sufficient standing to survive.[56] In 1609, a twelve-year truce was signed, but this was simply a hiatus in the fighting between two exhausted powers. Indeed, in many ways, the truce, which did not explicitly cover the Indian Ocean, had simply exported the war there. At the same time, the Dutch East India Company (or the VOC) also commissioned a lawyer to write a treatise on the law of the sea. *Mare Liberum*, or *The Free Sea*, by Hugo Grotius is a classic of early modern political theory, and much ink has been spilled detailing its influence on the emergence of international law and modern ideas of statecraft. Be that as it may, *The Free Sea* clearly had a more immediate and directed purpose, to provide a legal operating basis for the Dutch not just in European waters but globally. This lengthy legal treatise culminates in the final assertion that 'the right of the Indian trade is to be retained of the Hollanders both by peace, truce or war'.[57] Relying on classical and secular authorities and on logical legal arguments, Grotius had built a case that, whether formally at war or not, the Dutch, via their primary instrument the VOC, could legitimately carry on the fight against the recently united Spanish and Portuguese crowns.

Not only was the fighting in Europe also expected to resume in 1621, at sea it was expected to resume with a vengeance. This could hardly have failed to affect neighbouring powers. Again, the international stakes were very high. For Spain, the very foundation of its authority as the defining political heart of Christendom was undermined by Dutch rebellion. Predictably, there was a resurgence of its naval strength in the north, with a new naval force, the Armada of Flanders, operating out of Dunkirk.[58] This not only attacked Dutch trade at sea, but it provided essential support to the armies operating out of the Spanish Netherlands. Notably, in a confident and menacing show of strength, in September 1639 forty-seven warships, gathered from Spain, Portugal, Naples, and Flanders, escorted thirty other ships carrying valuable treasure and over 20,000 troops for the fight on land against the Dutch. What followed was another turning point in history, no less significant than that of 1588. The Dutch under Admiral Tromp initially managed to stop this force from arriving in Dunkirk and to hold it in the Downs, off the English coast. A number of engagements followed, climaxing in a dramatic Dutch victory on 21 October 1639.

As in 1588, from a material point of view the Spanish losses were recoverable. The flagship escaped the carnage of the battle, and the bullion being carried made it to Dunkirk as did about one third of the troops. Moreover, from a

Dutch perspective, operating such a large fleet so late in the year was a serious financial strain. Again, however, such qualifications must not obscure what had unquestionably been a disastrous defeat for Spain. They lost two thirds of the warships of the fleet, with the Dutch managing to capture fourteen of them, but, more importantly, from this point it seemed that their fortunes had turned. It no longer looked like Spain would ever be able to defeat the Netherlands. Distracted by war at sea on the Mediterranean against a France that was eager to exploit its domestic troubles, particularly in rebellions against its diminished authority in Portugal and Catalonia in the 1640s, Spain was suffering a loss of reputation at sea from which it would never fully recover.[59]

Conclusion

The Battle of the Downs of 1639 marked the ascendency of the Dutch and secured their status as the leading naval power in Europe. The political, military, and economic ramifications of this were enormous, as confirmed by formal recognition of Dutch independence in 1648. Sea power had saved and thus to some extent had come to define the new state. By these first decades of the seventeenth century, then, naval power was playing a profoundly different role in the definition of political authority. The reason this took place primarily in northern European waters is not just an accident of geography or because states there were better able to adapt to change than Mediterranean ones. There was simply much more potential political capital in using naval power to meet their military needs.

Historically, big, accepted, traditional powers (like Spain, Portugal, the Papacy, or the Ottoman Empire) would use naval power unapologetically for instrumental purposes. Yet their status was not defined by it in any way. With the Reformation creating states and communities with confessional identities at odds with the traditional political structure of Europe, naval power was something that could therefore be exploited without shame when circumstances required it. It could become a remedy to apply by those who happened to lie outside the privileged inner circle of political pre-eminence in Europe. It was becoming something which could contribute to the consolidation of political standing and legitimacy, and it is no coincidence that the iconic, over-sized political showpieces such as the *Vasa* were launched in the early seventeenth century by Protestant powers Denmark, Sweden, and England.

There was another side to the story, too. The very political potency of naval power which could confer international and domestic reputation also made it a potentially radical, destabilising influence which states of all sorts needed to control. The Calvinists of the United Dutch Provinces, France, and England in the sixteenth century had used sea power imaginatively and aggressively to shore up political resilience in a hostile international environment with three quite different effects: fatally challenging the heart of the Spanish empire in Europe; animating the long, destructive Wars of Religion in France; and indirectly buttressing the Tudor state.

In many ways, however, the experience of France in the 1620s reinforces best the important thematic link between naval power, status, and domestic stability. The traditional, Catholic French crown also built a significant fleet in these years along with a colossal showpiece battleship of its own in 1636. This new French navy was used primarily for internal consolidation of royal power. Under the direction of the powerful cardinal de Richelieu, it initially blocked English support of the Huguenot city of La Rochelle, leading up to the famous siege of 1628. Subsequently, Richelieu associated himself with the navy very closely and celebrated his authority as the 'Grand Master of Navigation and Commerce', a new title created for him by the crown, with nautical imagery in his arms and in the decorations of the palaces he built for himself in Paris and the town of Richelieu itself. In this way, the symbolism of naval power and the visual imagery of the sea were recruited to the purpose of expressing noble and royal power in a way it had never done before in France.

Closely allied with the Dutch, and in truth very reliant upon them for maintaining their operational strength as they fought the Thirty Years War at sea primarily against Spain on the Mediterranean, France needed a navy of its own which reinforced and partly defined royal authority, for it competed for legitimacy and majesty both internally against the troublesome Huguenots and externally in war against Spain. By the early seventeenth century, for all powers it seems, navies had become a key part of domestic governance and a way to express and consolidate authority and to display the martial prowess upon which political reputations, social order, and national success depended.

Notes

1 Frederick M. Hocker, *Vasa: A Swedish Ship* (Stockholm: Medstroms Bokforlag, 2011).
2 'Such [very large] ships were built by Venice, the Ottomans, Portugal, Scotland, England, Denmark-Norway, France, the Order of St John and Sweden, and probably by mercantile interests in Genoa and Lübeck too'. Jan Glete, *Warfare at Sea, 1500–1650: Maritime Conflicts and the Transformation of Europe* (London: Routledge, 2000), p.26.
3 N.A.M. Rodger, *Safeguard of the Sea: A Naval History of Britain. Vol. 1, 660–1649* (London: HarperCollins, 1997), p.380.
4 Benjamin W.D. Redding, 'Divided by *La Manche*: Naval Enterprise and Maritime Revolution in Early Modern England and France, 1545–1642' (PhD thesis, University of Warwick, 2016), pp.175–93.
5 N.A.M. Rodger, 'The New Atlantic', in John B. Hattendorf and Richard W. Unger (eds), *War at Sea in the Middle Ages and the Renaissance* (Woodbridge: Boydell Press, 2003).
6 I.A.A. Thompson, *War and Government in Habsburg Spain, 1560–1620* (London: Athlone Press, 1976).
7 Geoffrey Parker, *The Military Revolution. Military Innovation and the Rise of the West, 1500–1800.* (Cambridge: Cambridge University Press, 1996); and see, N.A.M. Rodger, 'The Development of Broadside Gunnery, 1450–1650', *The Mariner's Mirror*, 82, 3 (1996).

8   See the special edition discussion by historians, Gijs A. Rommelse, 'Introduction: the Military Revolution at Sea', *Journal for Maritime Research*, 13, 2 (2011).

9   D.J.B. Trim, 'Transnational Calvinist Cooperation and "Mastery of the Sea" in the Late Sixteenth Century', in J.D. Davies, Alan James, and Gijs Rommelse (eds), *Ideologies of Western Naval Power, c.1500–1815* (Aldershot: Ashgate, 2019).

10 Jonathan Locke Hart, *Comparing Empires: European Colonialism from Portuguese Expansion to the Spanish-American War* (Basingstoke: Palgrave, 2003).

11 R.J. Knecht, *Renaissance Warrior and Patron: the Reign of Francis I* (Cambridge: Cambridge University Press, 1994), pp.278, 333.

12 Anne Merlin-Chazelas, *Documents relatifs au Clos des Galées de Rouen et aux armées de mer du roi de France de 1293 à 1418, vol. 1* (Paris: Bibliothèque nationale, 1977), pp.103–04; Susan Rose, *Medieval Naval Warfare, 1000–1500* (London: Routledge, 2002), p.16.

13 Rose, *Medieval Naval Warfare, 1000–1500*, p.19.

14 David Parrott, *Business of War: Military Enterprise and Military Revolution in Early Modern Europe* (Cambridge: Cambridge University Press, 2012).

15 C.J. Ford, 'Piracy or Policy: the Crisis in the Channel, 1400–1403', *Transactions of the Royal Historical Society*, 29 (1979), p.64; Rose, *Medieval Naval Warfare, 1000–1500*, p.83.

16 Maria Fusaro, *Political Economies of Empire in the Early Modern Mediterranean: the Decline of Venice and the Rise of England, 1450–1700* (Cambridge: Cambridge University Press, 2015).

17 Rose, *Medieval Naval Warfare, 1000–1500*, p.111.

18 Glete, *Warfare at Sea, 1500–1650: Maritime Conflicts and the Transformation of Europe*, p.95.

19 Molly Greene, *A Shared World: Christians and Muslims in the Early Modern Mediterranean* (Princeton: Princeton University Press, 2000).

20 Glete, *Warfare at Sea, 1500–1650: Maritime Conflicts and the Transformation of Europe*, p.94.

21 Jonathan I. Israel, *Dutch Primacy in World Trade, 1585–1740* (Oxford: Clarendon Press, 1989).

22 Louis Sicking, *Neptune and the Netherlands: State, Economy, and War at Sea in the Renaissance* (Leiden: Brill, 2004).

23 D.M. Loades, *The Making of the Elizabethan Navy, 1540–1590: from the Solent to the Armada* (Woodbridge: Boydell, 2009), pp.1–55.

24 Knecht, *Renaissance Warrior and Patron: the Reign of Francis I*, pp.170–75.

25 Anthony Pagden and J.H. Elliott (eds), *Hernán Cortés: Letters from Mexico* (New Haven: Yale University Press, 2001).

26 Sicking, *Neptune and the Netherlands*, p.479.

27 Jaap R. Bruijn, *The Dutch Navy of the Seventeenth and Eighteenth Centuries* (Columbia: University of South Carolina Press, 1993); Ivo Van Loo, 'For Freedom and Fortune: the Rise of Dutch Privateering in the First Half of the Dutch Revolt, 1568–1609', in Marco Van der Hoeven (ed.), *Exercise of Arms: Warfare in the Netherlands 1568–1648* (Leiden: Brill, 1997).

28 Mikaël Augeron, 'De la Cause au parti: Henri de Navarre et la course Protestante (1569–1589)', in Christian Hermann (ed.), *Enjeux maritimes des conflits européens, XVIe-XIXe siècles* (Nantes: Ouest Éditions, 2002).

29 A. Bardonnet, 'Registre de l'amirauté de Guyenne au siège de La Rochelle (1569–1570)', *Archives historiques de Poitou* 7 (1878).

30 Frank Lestringant, *Le Huguenot et le sauvage: l'Amérique et la controverse coloniale, en France, au temps des guerres de religion (1555–1589)* (Genève: Droz, 2004; 3rd edition), pp.52–53.

31 Tom Glasgow, 'The Navy in the Le Havre Expedition, 1562–1564', *The Mariner's Mirror*, 54, 3 (1968).

32 Alan James, *The Navy and Government in Early Modern France, 1572–1661* (Woodbridge: Boydell, 2004).

33 Penny Roberts, *Peace and Authority during the French Religious Wars, c.1560–1600* (Basingstoke: Palgrave, 2013).

34 Alan James, 'A French Armada? The Azores Campaigns, 1580–1583', *The Historical Journal*, 55, 1 (2012).

35 Geoffrey Parker, *The Grand Strategy of Philip II* (New Haven: Yale University Press, 1998), pp.67, 102.

36 John F. Guilmartin, Jr., *Gunpowder and Galleys* (Cambridge: Cambridge University Press, 1974).

37 Glete, *Warfare at Sea*, pp.110–11.

38 Daniel Panzac, *La Marine ottomane de l'apogée à la chute de l'Empire, 1572–1923* (Paris: CNRS, 2009), pp.15–54.

39 David Trim, 'Early-Modern Colonial Warfare and the Campaign of Alcazarquivir, 1578', *Small Wars and Insurgencies*, 8, 1 (1997).

40 Andrew C. Hess, 'The Battle of Lepanto and its Place in Mediterranean History', *Past and Present*, 57 (1972), p.72.

41 J.K. Laughton (ed.), *State Papers Relating to the Defeat of the Spanish Armada, Anno 1588* (London: Temple Smith, 1987).

42 Colin Martin and Geoffrey Parker, *The Spanish Armada* (Manchester: Mandolin, 1999; revised edition).

43 Rodger, *Safeguard of the Sea*, p.271.

44 Jan Willem Honig, 'Warfare in the Middle Ages', Hartmann and Heuser (eds), *War, Peace and World Orders in European History* (London: Routledge, 2001).

45 Sir Walter Rawleigh, 'A Discourse of the Invention of Ships, etc.', in *Judicious and Select Essayes and Observations, etc.* (London: Humphrey Moseley, 1650); see my essay in Richard Blakemore and James Davey (eds), *The Maritime World of Early Modern Britain* (London: Routledge, forthcoming).

46 Jan Glete, *Swedish Naval Administration, 1521–1721: Resource Flows and Organisational Capabilities* (Leiden: Brill, 2010).

47 Although the emphasis here is quite different, this section relies heavily on Jan Glete, 'Chapter Seven: Maritime State Formation and Empire Building in the Baltic', in Glete, *Warfare at Sea, 1500–1650* (London: Routledge, 2000), pp.112–30.

48 Michal Wanner, 'Albrecht of Wallenstein as "General of the Ocean and the Baltic Seas" and the Northern Maritime Plan', *Forum Navale*, 64 (2008).

49 Glete, *Warfare at Sea, 1500–1650*, p.122.

50 These included Sweden's *Mars*, reportedly of 1,800 tons, along with the Swedish *Röde Draken*, the Danish *Fortune*, and Lübeck's *Adler*, all of 2,000 tons. Note, however, that these large figures, provided by Glete, are calculations of displacement measured in metric tonnes. Usual estimates of size at the time relate to carrying capacity in tons. Ibid., p.viii.

51 Már Jónsson, 'Denmark-Norway as a Potential World Power in the Early Seventeenth Century', *Itinerario*, 33, 2 (2009).

52 Ole Peter Grell, 'Scandinavia', in Robert Scribner, Roy Porter, and Mikulas Teich (eds), *The Reformation in National Context* (Cambridge: Cambridge University Press, 1994), pp.111–12.

53 Erik Ringmar, *Identity, Interest and Action: A Cultural Explanation of Sweden's Intervention in the Thirty Years' War* (Cambridge: Cambridge University Press, 1996).

54 Steve Murdoch, *The Terror of the Seas? Scottish Maritime Warfare, 1513–1713* (Leiden: Brill, 2010).

55 Martin Bellamy, *Christian IV and his Navy: a Political and Administrative History of the Danish Navy 1596–1648* (Leiden: Brill, 2006).

56 J.R. Jones, 'The Dutch Navy and National Survival in the Seventeenth Century', *International History Review*, 10, 1 (1988).

57 David Armitage (ed.), *Hugo Grotius: The Free Sea* (Indianapolis: Liberty Fund, 2004), p.57.
58 R.A. Stradling, *The Armada of Flanders: Spanish Maritime Policy and European War, 1568–1668* (Cambridge: Cambridge University Press, 1992).
59 Though see the important qualification in Christopher Storrs, 'Chapter Two: Spanish Naval Power', in *The Resilience of the Spanish Monarchy 1665–1700* (Oxford: Oxford University Press, 2006), pp.63–105.

2 The seventeenth century

A first age of modern naval warfare

Alan James

From the middle of the seventeenth century, naval warfare underwent a profound transformation marked by three dramatic and violent wars fought entirely at sea between the two great maritime powers of the time, the Dutch and the English. A sudden and very steep increase in the size and number of specialised warships built by states and of the guns they carried during these three Anglo-Dutch wars (1652–1654, 1665–1667, 1672–1674) led to many lasting changes in naval warfare including the standardisation of 'line-ahead' battle tactics which aligned broadsides to maximise firepower.[1] The strict organisation and discipline and the extraordinary geometric and operational precision that this demanded were all captured by the French Jesuit Paul Hoste in his *Traité des évolutions navales* of 1697, which was translated into English and reissued on a number of occasions in the eighteenth century.[2] These expanded navies and tactical developments responded to immediate military needs,[3] of course, but from the middle of the seventeenth century, particularly for the new Dutch Republic and for the turbulent English state, they also acquired important symbolic, even ideological, value as potent expressions of national power and standing.[4] In England, the navy played a key role in the parliamentary victory in the Civil War (1642–1651). Thereafter, under successive new regimes, whether the Commonwealth and Protectorate of Oliver Cromwell (1649–1659), the restored Stuart monarchy of Charles II from 1660, or the reign of the Dutch king William III after the Glorious Revolution of 1688, the navy was seen as an essential prop, necessary to defend the islands from hostile reactions from abroad and to try to create a stable governing consensus at home.[5] It was, in other words, a key part of these successive political re-inventions.

Capitalising on the potential political impact of the navy, among other things, England rose in just a few decades from a collapsed, relatively marginal kingdom in the throes of civil war to become a significant European power. The measure of this success came at the apogee of this first age of modern naval warfare, when the Royal Navy helped to engineer the international effort to defeat the aggression of Louis XIV's France on the continent. More than anything else, it was this struggle which forever fixed in European minds the vital need for naval power and the permanent place of standing navies in European warfare. Certainly, the terms of the Peace of Utrecht of 1714, at the end of the long War of the Spanish

Succession (1701–1714), reflected Britain's strategic priorities. Gibraltar and Minorca on the Mediterranean along with Newfoundland, what is now Nova Scotia, and the lands around Hudson's Bay across the Atlantic in North America guaranteed Britain's lasting military influence in Europe based increasingly on its overseas assets. Britain was also granted the *asiento*, the monopoly over the slave-carrying trade to Spanish possessions in America. These unusual but valuable prizes of war did more than complement the military reputation of an aspiring, dynastic monarchy. They signalled the beginning of a successful shift in its very ambitions and the basis upon which it could seek legitimacy and security.

Bourbon France

It should be noted, however, that the pomp and courtly manners of Louis XIV (1638–1715) in France displayed legitimacy and stature on an altogether different scale. Indeed the dazzling rays of the Sun King penetrated all corners of seventeenth-century French life, though the metaphor can easily be extended to describe his impact on Europe more widely. This 'Most Christian' king of France felt it appropriate to try to occupy the gravitational centre around which would revolve the stellar dust and strewn debris of the cataclysmic Thirty Years War in Europe. Of course, this would not be without the chaos and violent collisions attendant at the birth of any new solar system, and the wars of Louis XIV brought a new scale and intensity to warfare. Indeed it is impossible to overstate the impact on European affairs more generally of a dynasty that under Louis XIV's grandfather held only the small kingdom of Navarre on the frontier between Spain and France but within just two generations threatened to eclipse the house of Habsburg entirely and to dominate Europe. Indeed the character of war itself was moulded by the emergence at this time of France as a military giant in line with these vaunted opportunities and by the equally determined international response it provoked. War at sea was really no exception. Until the end of the eighteenth century, throughout the 'age of sail', naval warfare would continue to be shaped by the lasting effects of this meteoric rise of the house of Bourbon and by its internal divisions and relations with other maritime powers.

In the tradition of late medieval kingship to which Louis XIV belonged, to aspire to such a shift in leadership, relative status, and power required not just shrewd dynastic politics but particularly remarkable military success. Thus although by 1648 Europe was famously exhausted by war, France would not back down, and its conflict with Spain continued until 1659. By extending this most costly and damaging of wars, France suffered internal disorder, open rebellion, and financial collapse and, from a modern perspective, the fruits of this extraordinary effort were very meagre indeed. Yet the young Louis XIV did win the hand in marriage of the daughter of Philip IV of Spain. From this came potential dynastic claims which in one way or another animated all of his wars culminating, toward the end of his life, in that which followed the Spanish Succession in 1701 and the accession of his grandson to the throne in Spain.

The choice of the Bourbon, Philip V, as king of Spain had been a compromise designed to avoid international conflict. What animated the long, exhausting war that followed was Louis XIV's refusal to allow him to renounce his legal right to the possible inheritance of the French throne as well. Although in practice there was only the remotest of chance of this ever happening, to allow the formal renunciation of his family's legal inheritance would have undermined the very principle of legitimate, God-given dynastic rights upon which Bourbon authority had grown and on the basis of which Louis XIV had been able to claim that all of his wars had been waged 'justly'. The merest prospect of both crowns, along with all of Spain's other European and overseas possessions, one day in the hands of a single Bourbon king was a potential upheaval that was unthinkable to the rest of Europe and for Louis XIV a dynastic prize, a tangible measure of success that would outshine that of Charles V himself, which was therefore irresistible.[6]

It is important, however, that we do not see in this some sort of aspiration for European hegemony. In essence, Louis XIV's aims were indistinguishable from any other dynastic monarch before him. Bourbon dynastic circumstances and successes had been such that they simply raised the international stakes, and with this naturally came an escalation of war. An enlarged and impressive French army, and navy, capable of meeting the military challenges Louis XIV faced and of both embodying and reinforcing the authority and international leadership to which he aspired were now required. Not surprisingly, then, at this time, right across Europe, national armies and navies grew enormously in size and in administrative sophistication. According to Jeremy Black, it was the size of these armed forces by the dawn of the eighteenth century which stand out as the most 'revolutionary' of all of the other, often widely trumpeted, early modern military developments, and it was the growth and organisational capacity of states which made them possible.[7] Yet behind these political and administrative changes necessarily lay a greater military urgency internationally, and this came from Louis XIV himself.[8] His reign was marked by the determined pursuit of his dynastic rights whilst encouraging a culture of noble military service and recognising and rewarding the ambitions of his most powerful subjects, fashioning what Guy Rowlands describes as 'the dynastic state'.[9] The result was that with the same demographic and economic base, Louis XIV was able to field armies that were far, far larger than his father had struggled to field earlier in the century.

It is certainly true that the commercial and military competition behind the three Anglo-Dutch wars provided the principal drivers of change in naval warfare. Yet with an historical interest in changes in the methods and means of fighting and in the commercial imperatives involved has come a neglect of the growing political value of navies and of the overweening influence of France. France, too, underwent a major political re-invention of sorts by 1661, and the construction of a navy, the largest in Europe, was seen as a necessary complement. It really should come as no surprise at all that the rise of European navies as a general and defining feature of the changing character of war occurred in parallel with the rise of *louis quatorzienne* France.

The first Anglo-Dutch war, 1652–1654

It is certainly tempting to see the outbreak of hostilities between England and the Dutch Republic in 1652 as the natural outcome of two rising competitive, modern, commercial powers whose reliance on the sea and overseas trade led them to an inevitable clash. There was plenty of competition and many obvious reasons for both sides to rely on sea power. After winning independence from the Spanish monarchy in 1648, the Dutch were free from crippling trade restrictions that had previously been imposed by Spain, and they seemed well-placed to continue to dominate, not just the herring fisheries of the North Sea, but the carrying trade of Europe and even that between England and its overseas possessions in North America. This was a challenge to England, which also had a strong merchant marine, an active fishing industry, and interests in North America, the Mediterranean, and increasingly in the Far East, where the Dutch presence was firmly established. The notion that the war was the calculated outcome of a commercially-minded government in England determined to push its interests to the point of war seems to be confirmed by the first of the Navigation Acts in 1651. This announced England's intention to cut the Dutch out of English trade with its colonies and in the Baltic, to protect English shipping from Dutch attack in the East Indies, and to limit and to tax Dutch fishing near English coasts.

Purely economic motives do not entirely explain the conflict, however. Merchants on neither side of the Channel pushed for war or expected to gain from it. The almost desperate reliance on sea power was due, rather, to recent momentous political changes in both countries. With the settlement of the eighty-year Dutch war with Spain in 1648, and in 1651 the end to the civil wars in the British Isles, two essentially new states had appeared. Both had been forged in large part by war at sea; both depended for their political existence and continued survival on naval power and, naturally, matters of politics, identity, and legitimacy also contributed to their close association with the sea and to the wars they fought against each other.[10] By mid-century, the Dutch were the leading sea power and could mobilise quickly for war against England with many fast, manoeuvrable ships. In England, however, the political commitment to developing a battle fleet had been especially sudden and profound, and a major programme of warship construction was underway. For the Commonwealth government, the navy continued to be seen as crucial to national political survival, because radical, republican England had many enemies, both internally and on the continent where the regicidal government had made itself an international pariah. Impressive, heavily-gunned warships, many named after parliamentary victories in the Civil War, which could command nearby waters were needed to protect England from Stuart sympathisers and royalist privateers, many of whom were living in, or harboured by, France. Defensive, then, but far from passive, the navy aggressively pursued a royalist fleet as far away as Portugal and in the Mediterranean, not to mention the role it played in subduing Scotland and Ireland.[11] It was, in other words, an expression of military desperation and political determination rather than of any desire to displace the Dutch as a global mercantile power as such.

The first Anglo-Dutch war can be seen as an aggressive act on the part of England against a wealthy and commercially dominant rival to further invent and consolidate the new regime. Tension had already been building due to heavy-handed English inspections of Dutch shipping during the struggles with the royalists and the French.[12] Yet the war, when it broke out in 1652, was evidence of a complex domestic struggle for national political identity as much as of commercial rivalry. Indeed, many people in England felt that, as fellow Calvinists and merchants, the Dutch were natural bedfellows, and serious overtures toward a political union had actually been made with the aim of facing the tyranny of Catholic Spain together. With their refusal to join, many of the religious radicals in government could indulge their view of the unrestrained ambition and unethical trade practices of the Dutch, who in their apparently lax and pluralistic ways represented a perversion of virtuous republicanism and of God's plan for England. More immediately, it was the support shown by the influential house of Orange with exiled Stuart sympathisers that was threatening. Indeed there was a general fear in England, which shaped foreign policy, of religious backsliding, either to Anglicanism or to popery, and of immorality and monarchy. For the Rump Parliament, the Dutch were 'an ungodly and ambitious tyranny'. Steven Pincus argues, therefore, that rather than hard-nosed commercial aggression the Navigation Act of 1651 was a punitive measure against a corrupt and uncooperative state.[13]

Though on balance England had the better of the results in the fighting and is widely held to have won the first Anglo-Dutch war, it was by no means an overwhelming military victory. The aim, in the end, was to cut off Dutch trade and to hold them in port and in this way to force a negotiated settlement. In the event, this proved rather difficult, and the Dutch admiral, Tromp, famously managed to escort many Dutch merchant convoys during the war. Somewhat less famously, the Dutch, along with the Danes, threatened England's ability to function at sea by closing the Baltic, reinforcing English vulnerability and the long-term strategic priority of maintaining this essential source of naval stores.[14] Still, there were many open battles in which the Dutch came off worse, and Tromp died in an unsuccessful attempt to break a blockade at the Battle of Schevingen in August 1653 which effectively ended the war. It was during this war that the line of battle was first systematically employed by the English.[15] Yet historical interest in battles and in the apparent implications of tactical developments has perhaps led to an exaggeration of their significance and indeed of the long-term political and economic effect of the war. The course of the first Anglo-Dutch war, it must be said, had not just been determined by fighting at sea but also by Oliver Cromwell's political inclinations. Seizing power as Lord Protector from December 1653, he was less willing to prolong a costly and divisive war with fellow Calvinists. For him, the navy was better used to consolidate his new regime and for use against the Barbary corsairs or what he considered to be the real enemies of religion and of the state, both Catholic France, with whom England had been fighting an undeclared war of sorts, and especially Spain.[16]

Cromwell, fearing enemies everywhere, pursued foreign war as a means of deflecting domestic pressure and building political authority with calculated determination. Not surprisingly, this had a lasting impact on naval power in Britain. In the few years of his Protectorate, and that of his successor and son, Richard, until 1659, there was an unprecedented expansion of the navy, though it was not until he came to an accommodation with France and the anti-Spanish foreign and naval policy of Louis XIV's principal minister, Cardinal Mazarin, in 1655 that it could have real effect. Settling for Jamaica as a permanent foothold in the heart of Spanish America, English forces under Robert Blake also managed to blockade Cadiz and to attack valuable Spanish convoys. It is possible to question the strategic benefits that resulted from this sustained and intense investment in naval power, especially given the direct role the navy played in bringing down the Protectorate and in the restoration of the Stuart monarchy.[17] Yet these years had unquestionably been an extraordinary display not just of the military potential of this new instrument of war, even on a global scale, but of its political potency. For good reason, then, Charles II carefully cultivated an especially close association with this new, powerful navy that he inherited and upon which the political future of the monarchy so evidently relied.

Thus, although in some ways the first Anglo-Dutch war marks the birth of the commitment to a permanent, standing navy in England, it is easy to exaggerate the extent to which this developed naturally as a result of technological or tactical innovations in naval warfare. Commercial competition seems an only slightly more likely source. In both countries, there was an unmistakeably defensive, yet boldly political aspect to naval growth. For the newly independent Dutch, protecting maritime commerce was essential, but naval strength meant more than just that. It had largely been the means toward the political ends of national survival.[18] Henceforth, it would remain an essential part of their attempt to gain acceptance as a secure and fully recognised player in European politics, something which could not simply be legislated in 1648. Rising Swedish power to the north was the immediate concern, and the Dutch intervened in their war with Denmark to ensure it was not over-run and with it the Sound and control of the entry into the Baltic. Though supporting different sides in this conflict, the English and Dutch mediated between the two sides and in the process restricted Swedish gains to one side of the now shared Sound, in Scania, which it had won in 1658.[19] Other challenges lay ahead for the Dutch, however. In particular, France would prove to be very dangerous neighbours for this new, republican state. For both the English and the Dutch then, to be a maritime power meant national political survival and the prospect of fully and securely belonging within a changing international order.

The second and third Anglo-Dutch wars, 1665–1667 and 1672–1674

The Second Anglo-Dutch War upon which the new king, Charles II, quickly embarked is another iconic naval conflict.[20] Of course, one could hardly find more different regimes than those of the radical Puritans of the Rump Parliament or of Cromwell and that of this restored, Anglican monarchy. That they both chose the same enemy might, therefore, seem to point to strictly naval or commercial motives for war, and certainly there were armed clashes in the Mediterranean, off the west coast of Africa, and in America. Yet for a newly established (or in this case newly restored) dynasty, the political opportunity for consolidation and legitimacy through the demonstration of fitness to rule was clear.[21] In the Dutch, Charles II had a perfect target, for it was relatively straightforward, not just to present their trading practices as violent and unscrupulous, but to portray them as a dangerous threat to the political nation. To Anglican royalists, the Dutch were seen as promoters of non-conformist republicanism.[22] Unfortunately for Charles II, this war would not bring the easy political rewards he sought, for his fortunes hinged not just on the performance of his navy but on his ability to sustain the idea that the Dutch were the natural enemy of England and, with the rise of absolutist, Catholic, and menacing France, this became increasingly difficult.

Far more significant from an international perspective than the Restoration in England, which was, after all, simply a return to a normal constitutional settlement, was the death of Cardinal Mazarin and the decision in 1661 by the young Louis XIV to lead his royal council himself. This began the period that has come to be known as his 'personal rule', which lasted until his death in 1715. The impact on the course of naval warfare was soon keenly felt by England. At first, all went well. Even before the formal declaration of war in March 1665, New Amsterdam in North America was taken and renamed New York in honour of the admiral, James, Duke of York, brother of Charles II, and in Europe there was muscle-flexing, too, as Dutch shipping was attacked. The war, when it came, however, was marked by classic, set-piece battles. The Dutch had rebuilt their fleet, and in England, for its part, there was a new determination and professionalism.[23] Although from a strictly logistical point of view it was difficult at this time to capitalise on any victory at sea by maintaining control of the seas or imposing an effective blockade, the English did come off better in the large Battle of Lowestoft of 1665.

Fortunes soon began to turn against England, however, when France initially joined on the side of the Dutch. Wary of a direct French attack or a landing in Ireland, the English divided their forces in 1666, leaving some to watch the Channel and an under-strength fleet to fight the 'Four Days Battle' against the Dutch in June.[24] Heavy losses were suffered on both sides, though English forces were eventually reinforced, and later in the summer England won a more evenly balanced battle. However, the great fire of London that year exacerbated crippling financial problems, and in 1667, with reassurances that the French were starting to turn against the Dutch and would not attack, the fleet was not even outfitted. This led to a great, national humiliation in which the Dutch admiral De Ruyter audaciously sailed right into the heart of England and attacked Chatham at the mouth of the Medway, taking the flagship, the *Royal Charles*, and burning a number of others. It is worth noting from this, therefore, that as much as it had been success in battle or the relative strength of standing forces that made the difference in this war, France was actually the key variable. Once France entered the war, Charles II had been in difficulty. Complaints about the conflict, its dangers and costs, grew. In addition to the economic disruption, however, there was the fundamental threat posed by Louis XIV, an evil tyrant who, it was feared, aspired to universal monarchy. For many in England, he posed the greater potential external threat and raised the spectre of the reintroduction of Catholicism under the distrusted Stuarts.

From this point onward, France was the main focus of international naval warfare. It built bigger warships with heavier guns and, after the war, Parliament in England overcame its suspicion of Charles II and voted money for ship construction in order to keep up with France.[25] Indeed it takes an almost wilful disregard of French influence even to refer to a third Anglo-Dutch war from 1672 at all, for this was quite clearly a Franco-Dutch war in which Charles II participated at sea as a junior ally to France. It could even be described as a Franco-Spanish war, in which the Dutch were dismissively treated by France as collateral damage, which lasted until 1679. At any rate, it began with a full-scale invasion of the Netherlands by the land armies of the greatest military power of the age. Politically, the Dutch were fighting to avoid extinction at the hands of Louis XIV and, surely, any conflict with the English at sea which involved such matters as trade conditions or niceties concerning the salute between passing ships was decidedly secondary. Of course, there was more at stake than just this, and there was intense fighting at sea, mostly between the English and the Dutch. The associated developments in naval warfare, moreover, were certainly remarkable. Nevertheless, they were very period and context-specific, occurring unusually in close narrow waters between relatively young regimes with no territorial dispute, both of which were reliant on their navies and their firepower for survival. The conditions were right for aggressive artillery duels between heavily-gunned, purpose-built warships which have so fascinated naval historians. It is, therefore, easy to overlook the fact that France's aggression, its continental interests, and Louis XIV's imperial world view had the most defining effect on naval warfare more broadly.

Charles II needed a quick victory in this war, because Parliament would not long tolerate the money it voted being used against the Dutch. Alas, this was not to be. In May 1672, a combined Anglo-French fleet suffered badly at Sole Bay at the hands of the Dutch. This stopped attacks on Dutch commerce and ended amphibious operations to hurt their land defences. Although this success was not enough on its own to avoid a domestic political crisis, when William of Orange later emerged from the turmoil and was reinstated as Stadtholder, the Dutch war effort was renewed with even more vigour. De Ruyter, was able, for the most part, to protect inbound shipping and to hold off enemy forces, thereby avoiding further collapse against the invading forces on land. At the same time, the Dutch raided New York and the Newfoundland fisheries. With his weaknesses at sea thus exposed, Charles II was forced by Parliament to step out of the war in 1674.

Despite the many difficulties faced, however, England did well out of the conflict. The Dutch were willing to concede the salute and to pay an indemnity, and they were formally blocked out of English trade. In some ways, it also seems to have set the stage for later English commercial growth which blossomed thereafter. Yet the direct link between the war and longer-term English financial strength is far from clear, and any benefits from this war were surely due to Dutch willingness to negotiate, given the almost existential threat they faced in the war with France. Although the English complained about the direct help they received from the French as allies at sea, the might of Louis XIV determined the nature and course of English involvement in the war, and in this sense it was this, as much as English shipbuilding, organisation, finance, or imaginative tactics which accounts for any benefits England reaped. From the French point of view, the war had been a success, and Louis XIV's reputation grew considerably. France made great gains against the Spanish Netherlands in the treaty of Nijmegen of 1678, and it was in this war that he earned the sobriquet Louis 'le grand'. True, the Dutch successfully resisted and defended themselves, but Louis XIV could console himself with knowing that this nation of heretical, republican merchants had at least been punished for affronting his majesty and 'daring to put limits to French conquest'.[26]

Colbert and the French navy

Dramatic change was not limited to Atlantic and northern waters; alongside traditional galley warfare, there was a marked rise of modern sailing fleets in the second half of the seventeenth century on the Mediterranean as well. English and Dutch competition for Mediterranean trade and influence certainly contributed to this change in the methods of war, though, again, the role of the French navy must not be overlooked. It is often forgotten that French naval interests lay primarily in the Mediterranean where longstanding military traditions made it a more attractive political theatre for Louis XIV. As with so many other aspects of French naval history, the difficulty appreciating this can be attributed to the extraordinarily close association of the French navy with its chief architect, Jean-Baptiste Colbert, who was named minister for the navy and the economy in 1665. Colbert, and *colbertisme*, are synonymous with state direction of the economy, the codification of maritime law, and colonial and mercantile projects such as the foundation of the French East India Company. Whilst there is no denying Colbert's responsibility for making France an Atlantic and global power and for the sudden and dramatic rise of its fleet in the 1660s to become the largest in Europe, what makes this association problematic is that his remarkable, and to some extent unrealised, ambitions have given the false impression that the French navy was his own personal project, as if it had been built to respond to his own economic vision in an attempt to ape the English and Dutch commercial miracles to the north for its own sake. In fact, there was no contradiction between Colbert's vision and that of the king he served, who was interested in sea power as a means of raising his profile among oriental monarchies and empires and, especially, in the dogged pursuit of his dynastic rights with respect to Spain.

The most immediate, formative influence on Mediterranean naval warfare was a renewed offensive by the Ottoman empire which attacked and occupied Venetian-held Crete in 1645. Sailing ships, many of which were hired from the Dutch, played a big part in the Venetian response, and in 1657 they defeated the Ottoman navy in battle.[27] It could be said that this marked the changing face of Mediterranean naval warfare. In 1650, the Ottomans had undertaken a building programme of sailing ships, or galleons, of their own, and by the 1680s the galleon had become the main vessel of their fleet. With this force, they could support the army conducting the long siege of the key fortress of Candia on the island which they eventually took in 1669. In its long, ultimately futile effort to defend Crete, Venice relied on support from its allies the Knights of Malta and the Papal States. It is worth remembering, however, that initially it was France who helped the most. In 1646, just before the outbreak of the mid-century civil wars in France, a small French fleet was sent out in support.[28] After the troubles, and a thawing of relations with the Papacy over a matter of doctrine within the French church, much more help was on offer. In 1669, the French galley fleet and a large expeditionary force of warships was brought to Candia by the then Grand-Master of Navigation, the Duke of Beaufort, who lost his life in the final, climactic stages of the war.

This episode is usually presented as a mere afterthought for the crown or, worse, as typical of the pointless ambition of independent noblemen, like Beaufort, who Louis XIV would soon tame in his efforts to modernise the state. In fact, the support given to Venice was quite substantial. It also occurred at the same time that another squadron of French warships was sent into the Indian Ocean, a sign of the growing tension preceding the Dutch war. This so-called Persian squadron clashed with Dutch forces off Ceylon and the Coromandel coast but to little lasting effect, and as soon as fighting in Europe formally broke out they were quickly recalled home. Predictably, this has been seen by historians as a wasted, rare opportunity for France to compete on an equal basis overseas and to modernise within a growing global economy. Colbert, who is inevitably credited with the initiative, was undermined, it is said, by the vain and pointless European war ordered by the king.[29] Yet by sending a fleet of warships in the first place, Louis XIV had made an effective statement in the Indian Ocean about his status as the leading monarch of Christendom and, as with the subsequent French embassies to Siam, which from a modern perspective seem not to have served long-term French commercial or strategic interests particularly well, he was very effectively trading on his status.[30] Whether in the eastern Mediterranean or the Indian Ocean, operations were undertaken not so much with relative Dutch mercantile success in mind but with the announcement of Louis XIV's stature.[31]

It might appear, therefore, that there is a fundamental contradiction at the heart of the French navy and one that was given full expression upon Beaufort's death. His title of Grand-Master of Navigation and Commerce, which had been created in 1626 for the cardinal de Richelieu, was suppressed and replaced by the re-established, traditional charge of Admiral of France, which was immediately given to Louis XIV's recently legitimised two-year old son, the comte de Vermandois. This carelessness seems to stand in stark contrast to the apparently more enlightened move of having put the navy into the safe administrative hands of the bureaucrat, Colbert, who could effectively oversee its growth.[32] Yet any distinction between modern bureaucratic state interest and an apparently anachronistic noble interest is false. Far from confirming his indifference to the navy by giving the admiralty to his infant son, Louis XIV was, in one respect, reinvigorating the office of Admiral of France. Granted, it would be some time before Vermandois could be expected to command in person, but the charge was being re-established as a proper military title worthy of the highest nobility. The point is that there was no tension between this and Colbert's ambitions. For his part, Colbert was a loyal servant of the crown whose personal interests were intimately tied to the dynastic ambitions of the king, and it was to serve these that he oversaw the growth of the navy. It is true that he was peculiarly successful, and indeed he has been criticised for personally dominating the navy, making a vast fortune from it, and for filling its hierarchy with family members and personal clients.[33] Colbert was unashamedly financially self-interested, but he shared this trait with every nobleman of his age and, like them, he was driven to build the influence of his family through service to the king. The fortunes of the French navy had always been tied to the personal interests of the nobility, and in this respect his differed very little from the naval careers of the Cardinals Mazarin and Richelieu before him. All of this was perfectly consistent with the broader military expansion of the state.

This is not how a successful naval power is normally expected to operate, however. Naval strength is usually presented as a natural extension of the wider commercial interests of a society and a reflection of the extent to which these insinuated themselves into, and shaped, the interests and policies of government. This is certainly seen to be the case with the Dutch and indeed with the English, especially after 1688 and the Glorious Revolution which saw the Catholic James II replaced by the Dutch William of Orange as king. Conversely, for many historians there is a sense of artificiality about the whole French experience. France, it is felt, was too *dirigiste* to be a successful naval power, the king and his interests too aloof to sustain the political and financial commitment required. This picture can be challenged in a number of ways. First, commercial activity in France was actually more vibrant and influential than the credit it normally receives would suggest. Moreover, in French port cities, too, there were enormous industrial undertakings in partnership with the hinterlands and even a certain shared interest with government in trade and its protection which informed the commercial invigoration that was a key part of Colbert's programme.[34] Yet this cannot be said to have been the main purpose of French naval expansion. The purpose was to serve the reputation of the king upon which depended the stability, order, and global influence that served the personal dynastic, political, and even the economic interests of anyone of any standing in French society.

The usually unspoken but still misguided assumption that Louis XIV sat in splendid cultural isolation from the rest of society and somehow contradicted or impeded the pursuit of France's real national interests can be sustained only through the application of standards of naval success that are tied to notions of fiscal modernity. From this perspective, it is easy to credit Colbert and his ambitions and achievements whilst bemoaning their ultimate failure. Yet great care must be taken when considering questions of motivation and purpose at this time. Certainly, 'power' and 'plenty' motivated people, as Jacob Viner argued in his classic statement on mercantilism of 1948 but, as a closer reading of it also reveals, 'honour', 'reputation', and even 'religion' played a role too. A possibly apocryphal comment that Viner himself attributed to Louis XIV in 1668 sums up the French position well: 'If the English wish to content themselves with being the greatest merchants of Europe and to leave for my part conquest through just war, then nothing could be easier than coming to an accommodation'.[35] The dramatic phase of large-scale, organised warfare witnessed in the second half of the seventeenth century was driven by many forces; armed competition for raw, relative power at sea was not alone, and it is not enough just to throw into the mix the pursuit of trade.

The French navy at war with Europe

From the perspective of Anglo-Dutch commercial or naval competition and of modern state-building, it is easy to see the French invasion of the Netherlands and the whole Dutch war (1672–1679) as an unfortunate self-indulgence on the part of Louis XIV. For those historians keen on tracing the rise, in order to emphasise a subsequent relative decline, of France, this had been a war born out of hubris, youthful aggression, and pride in which nothing much was achieved. Yet even as a sea power, for France meaningful political advantage in war could only come at the expense of Spain, and the greatest opportunity for the king's navy arose in 1674 when Sicily revolted against the Spanish monarchy. Without making a full military commitment to the conquest of the Kingdom of Naples, which anyway Louis XIV had not been trumpeting as a target of French 'reconquest', the navy could be used to demonstrate French strength at arms and secure an advantage over Spain in the context of the broader war. Thus it should be remembered that perhaps the greatest naval challenge to Colbert and the one to which he dedicated enormous energy was supporting the city of Messina. Six ships of the line and a number of supply ships were sent in 1674, slipping past the Spanish blockade of the city, providing relief and French protection. What followed was a series of dramatic naval battles in which France emerged victorious against combined Spanish and Dutch fleets and in which the famed Dutch admiral De Ruyter died. Further glory was then sought with an attack on the allied fleet in Palermo harbour in which fireships were used to devastating effect, destroying seven Dutch ships of the line. This very effectively demonstrated French mastery over both enemies in the Mediterranean and undoubtedly contributed to the successful negotiation of the peace in 1679.

There are, nevertheless, common assumptions about how navies in the past ought to have operated which can make it difficult to recognise these French successes. Indeed these operations in Sicily can be puzzling to historians who are struck by the lack of effort to capitalise on the victory either by pursuing the destruction of the allied fleet or by occupying Palermo. Instead, according to the incredulous E.H. Jenkins, we are told that Vivonne, the French 'vice-roy' in charge, was simply 'fat and lazy' whilst the 'fine work' of the French navy was allowed to be undone by the king who saw it as a mere 'sideshow'.[36] A similar sense of bewilderment greets the performance of the navy in the next major war, the Nine Years War (1688–1697). This was a defining period for the French navy although, as with all wars, the main focus was on land and on the aggressive assertion of sometimes quite spurious legal claims to territory at the expense of Spain or the Holy Roman Empire. In 1688, Louis XIV, still at the height of his powers, invaded the Rhineland in opposition to the recent election to the Archbishopric of Cologne. The ferocity and violence of this attack was shocking, even by the standards of the day, and it triggered an armed coalition against him. This, of course, involved the invasion of England by William of Orange, which then aligned England and the Netherlands very closely in opposition. Yet it was not the scale of naval forces that could now be arraigned against Louis XIV which was of particular concern, for he already had the strongest navy in Europe and his priorities were decidedly elsewhere. From his point of view, in England a legally constituted, Catholic monarch had been usurped by an heretical upstart. This was a challenge to the established order which, as God's representative on earth, he clearly felt it was his right to protect and even to some extent to shape. He immediately took James II under his protection and used his navy to land him and French troops in Ireland as the first step in the process of winning back his crown.

This was not to be, however, for the French navy was not able to prevent William III from beating James II at the Battle of the Boyne in 1690, which effectively ended any hope of his return. At about the very same time, however, the navy scored a spectacular victory in the Channel. The French admiral, the comte de Tourville, gathered a fleet of seventy French warships from the Mediterranean and Atlantic and pursued and defeated the combined Anglo-Dutch fleet off Beachy Head in July 1690. Tourville's fleet, though damaged in the fighting, continued to cruise the Channel, raiding the small port of Teignmouth before crossing over to Le Havre for much-needed relief and repairs on its way back to the main port of Brest. Critics have long pointed out that this had no direct effect on William III's grasp on power. No invasion of England had been attempted in the aftermath of the victory; again, there had been no attempt to pursue and to destroy the enemy fleet. Yet neither of these was practical under the circumstances, and neither had been planned. It is true that Seignelay, Colbert's son, was desperate for even more success from the navy which he now oversaw, but that had at least as much to do with a political rivalry with Louvois, who was successfully directing the king's army, as it did with any supposed failure on Tourville's part. From a broader point of view, although James II had not been restored to the throne, Louis XIV could feel that he had done his duty by him and, hard though it may be for modern sensibilities to accept, this would have gone a long way to satisfying his ambitions with respect to England. Much more significantly, Louis XIV could celebrate the nearly simultaneous success at the Battle of Fleurus in Flanders against an allied army of Dutch, Spanish, and German forces. Thus in 1690, his pre-eminence and stature had been loudly announced internationally in war on land and at sea, and in this way Tourville had certainly contributed at Beachy Head to the consolidation of Louis XIV's 'empire' in the original sense of the word, that is to say, of his personal authority and majesty.[37]

The difficulty for some in seeing Beachy Head as an important victory for France stems not just from the absence of any exploitation of the victory which could fit standard assumptions about the value and purpose of navies but that from this point forward there seems to have been a steady decline in French naval strength. Two years later, bolder plans were indeed laid against England, but the organisation of any sort of invasion force was disrupted and the French fleet was badly defeated at the Battle of La Hougue of 1692 off the Cotentin peninsula. This is sometimes said to have ended French pretensions for naval pre-eminence. Thereafter, the commitment to maintaining a battle fleet is said to have begun to wane, leading to a change in strategy from the bold, so-called 'guerre d'escadre', centred on the battle fleet, designed especially to command the narrow northern waters, to the cheaper, more piecemeal commerce-raiding strategy, the 'guerre de course'.[38] Yet the effect of this battle is easy to exaggerate, as is any stark distinction between the two approaches in subsequent French thinking.[39] On the day, Tourville had been vastly under-strength because the Toulon squadron had failed to appear in time. Outnumbered nearly two to one by the English fleet, he nevertheless held his own in open battle, including a ten-hour artillery duel between the two flagships, before retreating the following day. Most ships returned directly to Brest, whilst others were pursued by the English in the direction of Cherbourg, where they were pressed close to shore and destroyed. France lost fifteen major battleships in the ensuing carnage, which was a serious material blow. To be sure, it was a blow to French prestige as well, but like the defeat of the Armada for Spain in 1588, this had been an operational rather than a strategic loss. Shipbuilding soon made good the loss, and by 1695 the French navy was bigger than it had ever been.

Any immediate danger to England of a French-led re-imposition of a Catholic Stuart monarchy had passed. Yet in the same way that Beachy Head had provided mainly political benefits for France, a confirmation of the king's status and priorities, so too were the benefits to England of La Hougue similarly indirect. The drama of burning the French fleet could only have contributed to drawing the political elite more firmly behind the Glorious Revolution and its association with sea power. More ships were subsequently built in England, and by 1693 the ability to finance naval war was famously improved with the establishment of the Bank of England and of a national debt. With sounder, more committed financing, people were happier to invest, and with this alignment of interests any lingering support for the exiled Stuarts was eroded. Again, navies could be popular in England and could be used to build a governing consensus, as long as they were being used to fight a menacing Catholic enemy.[40]

The two battles of 1690 and 1692, therefore, did not so much establish naval preponderance one way or the other as carry the two political nations further along their diverging paths, with navies as instruments of the consolidation of the two increasingly different types of monarchy. For France, the navy played a more instrumental role in the pursuit of national success in the shape of Louis XIV's stature than the definitional role it played in an England that was yet again re-inventing itself constitutionally. The French navy was, therefore, simply an instrument of policy and therefore prone to changes in priorities or strategic calculations, and from 1695, bowing to the logic presented by the marshal, Vauban, who is better known to history for his engineering work and the modernisation of France's system of fortifications on land, France chose to concentrate its stretched financial resources on its armies and, at sea, to rely more on privateers.[41] In the final stages of the Nine Years War, contesting mastery of the Channel seemed a less valuable approach than leasing out many of its ships in a concerted effort to encourage attacks on the one evident strength that the English and Dutch shared, their commercial and financial strength.

It is curious that this shift is sometimes taken as a sign of weakness or decline or even as a means of questioning the wisdom or commitment of France to its navy in the first place.[42] Relying on the private resources and initiative of seafaring populations in times of war was completely normal. All trade at sea was violent, and war remained 'essentially private and commercial' in nature.[43] True, states traditionally participated, sometimes by buying and deploying ships, sometimes by requisitioning or hiring them, but most frequently they tried to influence and direct private violence through the courts and by licensing reprisal warfare. Despite the dramatic rise of state-owned battle fleets, private violence had become even more important to states by the middle of the seventeenth century. Indeed, as Rodger has argued, it is only by this time that we can begin to refer accurately to privateering at all, in the sense of commissions by the state to undertake attacks against an enemy, a systematic and targeted harnessing of private resources for war.[44] Since the cost, both material and financial, of naval battle was enormous, and its direct military value had shown itself to be limited, privateering was not merely second-best, a shadow of sound naval strategy. It was an integral part of it on which states came to rely. This is certainly true of France, and even Mahan, who located Britain's historical rise relative to France in their commitment to command of the sea, recognised that the damage done to Britain by French privateering attacks from the late 1690s was considerable. Warfare at sea was just as much an economic activity for the Dutch and English, too, as they sought to cut France off from the naval stores and grain it desperately needed from the Baltic. Indeed the need to cripple France economically in order to keep pace as naval powers undoubtedly shaped the wider character of European naval warfare for, in addition to spreading the fighting to the West Indies and North America, this brought them into conflict with Sweden and particularly Denmark, both of which were developing sizable fleets of their own to protect their merchant shipping.[45]

It is true that in his final years, Louis XIV pursued what he would have seen as his dynastic obligations with a seemingly suicidal tenacity against determined international opposition. The result was military defeat, financial disaster, and political compromise.[46] In the end, he was forced into accepting on behalf of his grandson, Philip V of Spain, an otherwise humiliating formal renunciation of his God-given right to the potential additional inheritance of the throne in France. As far as his navy is concerned, it had not been able to reverse French military fortunes, although it had won the day in the one major naval battle of the war against the English off Malaga in August 1704. In truth, the damage suffered on both sides was considerable, and France was subsequently unable to dislodge the English forces that had recently occupied Gibraltar. Still, the reaction of the French admiral, Toulouse, on the day is telling, for he felt it was unnecessary to pursue the matter any further because, as he put it, 'what we did . . . will suffice for the reputation of the Navy and the King's arms'.[47] An even greater challenge was soon faced in the home port of Toulon. In 1707, the city was attacked by land by the Duke of Savoy and by sea by the English navy. Against the odds, the French navy fought desperately and helped save the city, though in the process it was forced to scuttle many of its ships to keep them from falling into enemy hands, and it could do nothing to stop England from taking Minorca the following year and completing its domination of the western Mediterranean. This did not spell the end for French sea power, however. High-profile privateering operations continued overseas, in Brazil and elsewhere, and an attempt was made to put the Stuart pretender on the throne in Britain. It was primarily at the hands of the armies of the Duke of Marlborough or Eugene of Savoy that Louis XIV suffered, though for many in Britain this long, costly land war still seemed too great a commitment. A new Tory-led government was able to capitalise on the popularity of sea power and overseas opportunities to negotiate an end to the struggle, and the Peace of Utrecht, accordingly, reflected these priorities.

France for its part had made painful compromises, but this was in the name of greater priorities. Following on the heels of a failed British expedition to Quebec in 1711, it responded, not by bowing out of trans-Atlantic competition, but with a statement of grandeur worthy of Louis XIV in the foundation and construction of the fortress and city of Louisbourg on modern-day Cape Breton Island.[48] This imposing monument to French strength protected at once the remaining fishing grounds which provided an essential source of protein to French armies and the now threatened entry to the St Lawrence River and thus the approach, further inland, to New France itself. Indeed, so carefully did France protect its essential interests in the negotiation of the Peace of Utrecht of 1714 that one historian has been able to argue controversially that, despite the many military defeats it suffered, France had 'won the peace'.[49]

The rise of Russian naval power

Britain had not just established itself as the leading naval power on the Mediterranean and in Atlantic trade, but in the Baltic as well. Yet during the Great Northern War (1700–1721) from which Russia emerged as a major European power, Sweden and Denmark also re-established themselves as leading players, at least in terms of standing battleships. By 1709, their navies had about forty battleships each, almost the equivalent of the English and Dutch forces of the time, and most of the fighting at sea took place between them.[50] This war, in which Peter I's reputation, and Russian military fortunes more generally, were won was a war by a continental power with an interest in its security and status as a power in the eastern European landmass. Thus the celebrated reforms of the Russian army, its expansion, and notably its dramatic victory over the Swedish army of

Charles XII at the Battle of Poltova in 1709 were the keys to Russian success. Nevertheless, an essential part of the transformation of Russia into a major power involved its sudden rise as a sea power. Though it previously held Archangel on the White Sea, by 1703 it gained access to the Baltic, establishing a fortress and naval base at St Petersburg which would become the new state capital. Russian power on land, but also at sea, was a new fact of international life.[51] Indeed, its intentions to establish itself on the Black Sea were also very clear. This was a new, permanent power which would henceforth dominate eastern Europe and which would establish a maritime reach from the north and the south which, in theory at least, could threaten to envelope all of Europe.

Wishing to maintain order and open access to the Baltic, the Dutch and English contained Russian forces in the Gulf of Finland. They also initially helped Sweden against Danish aggression, even bombarding Copenhagen in 1700.[52] Yet after 1709, the balance in the war was tipped, and Sweden eventually lost its continental possessions with control of the Baltic states falling to Russian armies. The on-going struggle between Sweden and Denmark weakened both battle fleets and, with direct Russian trade with the West now open, Sweden's naval war against Russia was primarily directed against its trade toward the latter stages of the war. Thus the rise of Russian naval strength required the relative decline of its neighbours. What is more, without any maritime traditions on which to build, this growth owed much to outsiders. Dutch and Swedish expertise was brought in; used ships were bought from Britain, the Netherlands, and Hamburg. Yet this was more than just an acknowledgement of the practical value of a navy. In this war, Peter earned the moniker 'the Great', and far more audaciously from an international point of view he assumed an imperial title, 'emperor of all the Russias'. The cultural value of naval warfare was changing. Such a declaration of status would now be incomplete without a navy that reflected it, and there was a political determination to create one that was appropriate. From having no presence on the Baltic whatsoever, by 1720 Russia had a fleet of forty-six ships, fully thirty-three of which were battleships, which is more than either Sweden or Denmark had remaining by the end of the war.[53]

The rise of Russia is one of the most notable developments in early modern history. It was a fundamental and permanent change in European power politics. Its very suddenness, however, and its close association with Peter the Great, who very consciously and determinedly modelled a new Russia after the western powers he admired, makes it relatively easy to distil the standards and aspirations that drove the creation, *ex nihilo*, of Russian sea power. For very good reasons, historians have credited the so-called 'grand embassy' of 1697–1698, during which Peter I visited different countries, particularly the Netherlands, and also England, where he studied shipbuilding and many other related skills that he would so successfully import back home. Yet sea power was part of a broader re-invention of Russian society and indeed of himself as its embodiment in which the navy would be a statement of the stature of Peter the Great. Though the Dutch and the English were seen as a natural source of expertise and of hired help and were duly exploited as such, it was certainly not Dutch republicanism or a restricted, English-style monarchy that Peter I aspired to, no matter what fiscal advantages these constitutional aberrations brought to their emasculated leaders. It was, rather, to the greatest power of the age and to the palace of Versailles that he looked, if not for practical advice, then at least for inspiration.

Though trade and the obvious military advantages that naval power brought were certainly acknowledged in France, as they would be in Russia, Colbert had built a navy whose main purpose was to reflect and thereby reinforce the grandeur of Louis XIV. This was a broadly palatable message domestically and one which played well internationally, especially in Russia with its own autocratic traditions. Thus in the 1690s France not only had the largest navy but institutionally it had a well-developed administration, infrastructure, and hierarchy. Indeed an outstanding feature of modern, powerful monarchies of the time was the rationalisation of laws and the creation of grand, comprehensive ordonnances covering all aspects of government. In France, Colbert had been responsible for the great reforming edicts that provided the framework for the rise of the French navy, and a similar exercise was undertaken in Russia.

Standing as the preface to the Sea Regulations, and claiming to have been written by Peter himself, is a story that confirms similar priorities. This 'Account of the Rise of Naval Power', subtitled 'The Story of the Little Boat', was clearly an exercise in creating a national naval tradition. Russian naval power, it was claimed, had not been inspired by the spectacle of powerful foreign navies, but had a native origin which was necessarily built around the figure of Peter himself. The story told of a young Peter happening across a sight that was entirely new to him, a small boat that was among the belongings of his great uncle. Against the wishes of his fearful mother, he insisted on sailing it and some others that he then had built. Later, in military operations against the Tatars, he recognised the need for a proper force and sent for Dutch experts, and indeed a fleet of thirty ships eventually helped to capture Azov from the Ottomans in 1696.

This was also the year that his half-brother died, leaving Peter with sole authority as czar, and in a manner reminiscent of the start of the personal reign of Louis XIV in 1661, he too would use the sudden expansion and modernisation of the navy as a statement of his growing personal authority. There is an interesting parallel with the experience in France of Peter's attempt to fix this association. Colbert had claimed, slightly disingenuously, that he built the French navy from virtually nothing, just a few neglected hulks. The navy, in other words, was to be the creation of the new reign. Significantly, however, he made a point of stressing the inspiration that he got from the ambitious but largely futile attempt by the cardinal de Richelieu earlier in the century to endow France with a navy. In a similar way, the story of the little boat in Russia credited divine providence for choosing Peter to bring to life the seed that had been sown by the designs his father had entertained earlier in the century, as if each navy was to have its own John the Baptist figure.[54]

Conclusions

With its new-found naval power, Russia was able to subdue Finland, mostly through the use of galleys that operated well in the shallow Baltic waters, and even to take the fight to the Swedes at sea. In 1716, Peter himself commanded the Russian fleet and a proposed combined operation against them which he hoped would involve Hanover, Prussia, Britain, and Denmark.[55] This extraordinary rise of Russian sea power was celebrated; the little boat was brought from Moscow to St Petersburg, 'repair'd and beautify'd' to give her a 'most glorious appearance', and used for fleet reviews, and it has remained as a lasting symbol of the emergence of Russian naval power.[56] This small detail must be considered alongside the extraordinary changes that make the seventeenth century truly a first age of modern naval warfare. As is well known, by the dawn of the eighteenth century large, standing, state-run navies along with the systematic application of private violence at sea had both become permanent features of European warfare more generally. However, among the many well-documented changes in the nature of fighting at sea, the technologies, and the necessary support structures which affected the functioning and even the constitutional shape of states to some extent, one should not neglect to consider the increased cultural value naval power now had to build political reputation and legitimacy. As the leading power in Europe, France influenced this change in ways that are not always credited.

Notes

1 Jaap R. Bruijn, 'States and their Navies from the Late Sixteenth to the End of the Eighteenth Centuries', in Philippe Contamine (ed.), *War and Competition between States* (Oxford: Clarendon Press, 2000); Jan Glete, *Warfare at Sea, 1500–1650: Maritime Conflicts and the Transformation of Europe* (London: Routledge, 2000), p.27; J.R. Jones, *The Anglo-Dutch Wars of the Seventeenth Century* (Harlow: Longman, 1996); N.A.M. Rodger, 'The Development of Broadside Gunnery, 1450–1650', *The Mariner's Mirror*, 82, 3 (1996).

2 P. Paul Hoste, *L'art des armées navales, ou Traité des évolutions navales, etc.* (Paris: Anisson et Posuel, 1697). Most writing on naval warfare in the eighteenth century came from France; see, Hubert Granier, 'La Pensée navale française au XVIIIe siècle', in Hervé Coutau-Begarie (ed.), *L'Évolution de la pensée navale* (Paris: Fondation pour les Études de Défense Nationale, 1993).

3 M.A.J. Palmer, 'The "Military Revolution" Afloat: The Era of the Anglo-Dutch Wars and the Transition to Modern Warfare at Sea', *War in History*, 4, 2 (1997).

4 Gijs Rommelse and Roger Downing, 'The Fleet as an Ideological Pillar of Dutch Radical Republicanism, 1650–1672', *International Journal of Maritime History*, 27, 3 (2015). See also the ideological context of naval war in Steven C. Pincus, 'Popery, Trade and Universal Monarchy: the Ideological Context of the Outbreak of the Second Anglo-Dutch War', *The English Historical Review*, 107, 422 (1992).

5 J.D. Davies, *Kings of the Sea: Charles II, James II, and the Royal Navy* (Barnsley: Seaforth Publishing, 2017); Bernard Capp, *Cromwell's Navy: the Fleet and the English Revolution, 1648–1660* (Oxford: Clarendon Press, 1989).

6 As Brendan Simms points out, there was an alternative prospect. A reunited Habsburg empire rivalling that of Charles V was at least equally abhorrent, hence the need for a compromise. Brendan Simms, *Europe: the Struggle for Supremacy, 1453 to the Present* (London: Allen Lane, 2013).

7 Jeremy Black, *A Military Revolution? Military Change and European Society, 1550–1800* (Atlantic Highlands, NJ: Humanities Press, 1991); Jeremy Black, *European Warfare, 1660–1815* (New Haven: Yale University Press, 1994).

8   Jean-Philippe Cénat, *Le Roi stratège: Louis XIV et la direction de la guerre, 1661–1715* (Rennes: Presses Universitaires de Rennes, 2010).

9   Guy Rowlands, *The Dynastic State and the Army under Louis XIV: Royal Service and Private Interest, 1661–1701* (Cambridge: Cambridge University Press, 2002).

10 Rommelse and Downing, 'The Fleet as an Ideological Pillar of Dutch Radical Republicanism, 1650–1672'.

11 Elaine Murphy, *Ireland and the War at Sea, 1641–1653* (Woodbridge: Boydell, 2012); M. Baumber, *General-at-Sea: Robert Blake and the Seventeenth-century Revolution in Naval Warfare* (London: Murray, 1989).

12 N.A.M. Rodger, *The Command of the Ocean: A Naval History of Great Britain. Vol. 2, 1649–1815* (London: Allen Lane, 2004), p.7; Robert Brenner, *Merchants and Revolution: Commercial Change, Political Conflict, and London's Overseas Traders, 1550–1653* (Princeton: Princeton University Press, 1993).

13 Stephen C.A. Pincus, *Protestantism and Patriotism: Ideologies and the Making of English Foreign Policy, 1650–1668* (Cambridge: Cambridge University Press, 2002).

14 R.C. Anderson, 'Denmark and the First Anglo-Ducth War', *The Mariner's Mirror*, 53, 1 (1967).

15 Brian Lavery, 'The Revolution in Naval Tactics', in Acerra, Merino, et al. (eds), *Les Marines de guerre européennes XVIIe-XVIIIe siècles* (Paris: Presses Universitaires de Paris-Sorbonne, 1985); N.A.M. Rodger, 'The Development of Broadside Gunnery, 1450–1650'.

16 Capp, *Cromwell's Navy: the Fleet and the English Revolution, 1648–1660*, pp.83–84.

17 See, Rodger, *The Command of the Ocean*, pp.20–32.

18 J.R. Jones, 'The Dutch Navy and National Survival in the Seventeenth Century', *International History Review*, 10, 1 (1988).

19 Capp, *Cromwell's Navy*, pp.106–09.

20 Gijs Rommelse, *The Second Anglo-Dutch War (1665–1667): Raison d'État, Mercantilism and Maritime Strife* (Hilversum: Verloren, 2006).

21 Davies notes the pursuit of 'honour' and 'reputation' as a defining purpose of English naval strength. J. David Davies, 'The Birth of the Imperial Navy? Aspects of English Naval Strategy c.1650–90', in Michael Duffy (ed.), *Parameters of British Naval Power, 1650–1850* (Exeter: Exeter University Press, 1992), p.22.

22 Pincus, 'Popery, Trade and Universal Monarchy: The Ideological Context of the Outbreak of the Second Anglo-Dutch War'.

23 J.D. Davies, *Gentlemen and Tarpaulins: the Officers and Men of the Restoration Navy* (Oxford: Clarendon Press, 1991).

24 J.D. Davies, 'The Birth of the Imperial Navy?', p.25.

25 Ibid., pp.26–28; French ships were certainly not of better quality, however. Daniel Dessert, *La Royale: vaisseaux et marins du Roi-Soleil* (Paris: Fayard, 1996), pp.123–38.

26 Louis-Aimé Martin, *Oeuvres complètes de Jean Racine. Avec les notes de tous les commentateurs, Vol. 5* (Paris: Lefèvre, 1820), p.405.

27 Louis Sicking, 'Selling and Buying Protection: Dutch War Fleets at the Service of Venice (1617–1667)', *Studi Veneziani*, 67 (2013).

28 Jérome Cras and Geraud Poumarède, 'Entre finance et diplomatie: les armements du commandeur François de Neuchèze pour le secours de Candie', in Daniel Tollett (ed.), *Guerres et paix en Europe Centrale aux époques moderne et contemporaine* (Paris: Presses Universitaires de Paris-Sorbonne, 2003).

29 Glenn J. Ames, 'Colbert's Indian Ocean Strategy of 1664–74: A Reappraisal', *French Historical Studies*, 16, 3 (1990).

30 Ronald S. Love, 'Monarchs, Merchants, and Missionaries in Early Modern Asia: the Missions Étrangères in Siam, 1662–1684', *The International History Review*, 21, 1 (1999).

31 Alan James, 'Raising the Profile of Naval History: an International Perspective on Early Modern Navies', *The Mariner's Mirror*, 97, 1 (2011).

32 Bernard Lutun, *La Marine de Colbert études d'organisation* (Paris: Economica, 2003).

33 Dessert, *La Royale*; Daniel Dessert, C. Giry-Delaison, and R. Mettam, 'La Marine royale, une filiale Colbert', *Patronages et clientèlismes* (London: Institut Français, 1995).

34 Caroline Le Mao, *Les Villes portuaires maritimes dans la France moderne, XVIe-XVIIIe-siècle* (Paris: Armand Colin, 2015); Caroline Le Mao and Philippe Meyzie, *L'Approvisionnement des villes portuaires en Europe du XVIe siècle à nos jours* (Paris: Presses Universitaires Paris-Sorbonne, 2015).

35 Camille-Georges Picavet, *La Diplomatie française au temps de Louis XIV (1661–1715): institutions, moeurs et coutumes* (Paris: F. Alcan, 1930); Jacob Viner, 'Power Versus Plenty as Objectives of Foreign Policy in the Seventeenth and Eighteenth Centuries', *World Politics*, 1, 1 (1948).

36 Ernest Harold Jenkins, *A History of the French Navy: from its Beginnings to the Present Day* (London: Macdonald and Jane's, 1973), p.60.

37 Alan James, 'La Bataille du Cap Béveziers (1690): Une glorieuse victoire pour le roi stratège', in Bolanski, Lagadec and Mercier (eds), *La Bataille: du fait d'armes au combat idéologique XIe-XIXe siècle* (Rennes: Presses Universitaires de Rennes, 2015).

38 Geoffrey Walter Symcox, *The Crisis of French Sea Power, 1688–1697: from the Guerre d'Escadre to the Guerre de Course* (The Hague: Martinus Nijhoff, 1974).

39 Benjamin Darnell, 'Reconsidering the Guerre de Course under Louis XIV: Naval Policy and Strategic Downsizing in an Era of Fiscal Overextension', in Rodger et al. (eds), *Strategy and the Sea: Essays in Honour of John B. Hattendorf* (Woodbridge: Boydell, 2016).

40 David Armitage, 'The Elizabethan Idea of Empire', *Transactions of the Royal Historical Society*, 14, 1 (2004).

41 Martin Motte, *Les Larmes de nos souverains. La pensée stratégique navale française* (Paris: Centre d'études stratégiques de la Marine, 2014).

42 Jan Glete, *Navies and Nations: Warships, Navies, and State Building in Europe and America, Vol. 1, 1500–1860* (Stockholm: Almqvist & Wiksell, 1993), p.221.

43 N.A.M. Rodger, 'The Law and Language of Private Naval Warfare', *The Mariner's Mirror*, 100, 1 (2014).

44 Ibid.

45 Rodger, *The Command of the Ocean*, p.157.

46 Guy Rowlands, *The Financial Decline of a Great Power: War, Influence, and Money in Louis XIV's France* (Oxford: Oxford University Press, 2012); the most stinging criticism of the navy's overall performance and its administration is in Dessert, *La Royale: vaisseaux et marins du Roi-Soleil*; for a detailed analysis of the navy's structural weakness, Benjamin Darnell, 'The Financial Administration of the French Navy during the War of the Spanish Succession' (DPhil, University of Oxford, 2015).

47 Quoted in N.A.M. Rodger, 'The Nature of Victory at Sea', *Journal for Maritime Research*, 7, 1 (2005), p.114.

48 Adam Lyons, *The Expedition to Quebec: Politics and the Limitations of British Global Strategy* (London: Bloomsbury, 2013).

49 Jean-François Brière, 'Pêche et politique à Terre-Neuve au XVIIIe siècle: La France véritable gagnante du Traité d'Utrecht?', *Canadian Historical Review*, 64, 2 (1983).

50 Glete, *Navies and Nations, Vol.* 1, p.233.

51 E.J. Phillips, *The Founding of Russia's Navy: Peter the Great and the Azov Fleet, 1688–1714* (Westport: Greenwood Press, 1995).

52 Rodger, *The Command of the Ocean*, p.163; R.C. Anderson, *Naval Wars in the Baltic, 1522–1850* (London: Francis Edwards, 1969), pp.133–36.

53 Glete, *Navies and Nations*, Vol. 1, p.234–35.

54 Collis stresses the importance of religion and Peter's image, although he develops the theme of Peter as Noah. Robert Collis, *The Petrine Instauration: Religion, Esotericism and Science at the Court of Peter the Great, 1689–1725* (Leiden: Brill, 2012).

55 Rodger, *The Command of the Ocean*, pp.229–30.

56 Thomas Consett, *The present state and regulations of the church of Russia. Establish'd by the late tsar's royal edict. Also in a second volume a collection of several tracts relating to his fleets, expedition to Derbent, &c* (London: S. Holt, 1729), p.218.

3 Globalisation and escalation, 1715–1815

Alan James

If the reign of Louis XIV provided a backdrop to a period of profound and lasting escalation in naval warfare, this was utterly eclipsed by another, far more dramatic growth a century later associated with the political rupture of the French Revolutionary and Napoleonic wars (1792–1815). For Britain, France had always provided the main competition and represented the principal threat that drove naval growth. Yet this was a unique moment in the history of naval warfare. Despite the internal, existential turmoil suffered by Revolutionary France, the material neglect of its naval infrastructure, widespread mutinies, and the loss of almost its entire officer class, the fighting at sea was still conducted on an unprecedented scale that would not be matched until the modern industrial age, and it was marked by many of the most memorable naval battles of all time. There is some debate about how directly victories at sea contributed to the eventual military defeat of Napoleon, yet there is no disputing the longer-term outcome.[1] Britain established itself not just as a major power, but arguably as the leading power of Europe and a guarantor of sorts of the new international system that emerged from the Congress of Vienna of 1815. As a result, naval power and its corollary, overseas trade, were now held as an alternative political ideal in Europe, widely accepted as central, and now potentially even defining, elements of international standing and influence. This change could not have occurred without popular engagement, and the effect was that, now, in addition to being expressions of martial reputations and of the legitimacy and security of states, navies were also reflections of popular political opinion and so could embody new, emerging national ideals in Europe.

Throughout the eighteenth century, Britain's rivalry with Bourbon Europe had dominated conflict at sea, and this began to alter the very landscape of international politics. Europe's wars were now fought on a global scale, and the material pressures this created are difficult to exaggerate. States of all sizes had to respond to the changing circumstances in which Britain eventually came to dominate the seas and international trade. At its most acute, war at sea came to be seen as an attritional contest of relative national economic and military endurance, and the chances of survival were largely measured in straightforward, material terms. The eighteenth century, therefore, was marked by the financially exhausting competitive construction of large numbers of ships of the line, particularly by rivals

Britain and France.[2] It is often pointed out that in what was essentially a battle between national economies, Britain enjoyed most of the advantages, and by the time of the iconic Battle of Trafalgar of 1805 these, along with years of technical, organisational, and logistical developments, all came to a head.[3]

On their own, however, any institutional or fiscal advantages the eighteenth-century British state had accrued were not enough to defeat Napoleonic France. Europe had never faced a threat like the one imposed by the radicalism of French revolutionary fervour or, especially, by the sweeping military successes of Napoleon, whose voracious imperial ambitions were backed by enormous citizen armies and an offensive strategy of annihilation which appeared to be overturning the old order. Those who argue that war with Napoleon was not just on another scale, therefore, but of an altogether different kind are unmoved by evidence of various continuities in the practical conduct of war between the late eighteenth and early nineteenth centuries. Instead, they point to these two more fundamental, related changes, that is to say to the seeming unlimited strategic ambition of Napoleon with his disregard for the laws, or norms, of war and to the involvement in war of active, politically committed populations which both enabled and drove this escalation.[4] On both counts, the extraordinary expansion of European navies and the sudden intensity and scale of fighting at sea does indeed add weight to the broader argument that, at this time, there was a profound, even revolutionary, change in the character of war more generally.

Andrew Lambert has described the necessary strategic response to Napoleon at sea which was embodied by Admiral Nelson's determination and by his relentless pursuit of comprehensive victory in battle.[5] Of course, victory was also something that had to be 'organised' and, as the work of Roger Knight, Martin Wilcox, and many others makes abundantly clear, this was the result of a wider, national effort.[6] In this sense, too, Britain had an advantage. The popularity of the navy in Britain had long made it an effective tool in building legitimacy and security and in defining the political reputation of the nation. This had been a large part of Britain's relative strength in the eighteenth century, and it is for this reason that much of the best naval history of the period has become an exploration of how well different states could compete on these grounds and tap into the financial resources of their populations or contract out essential services to them.[7] More than just financially or militarily interesting then, the alignment of interests within states around naval power and the popularity of navies themselves was a crucial aspect of the consolidation of a broader political consensus.

Navies rely upon, and can in turn reinforce, popular political goodwill. Ships of the line are visually impressive, even awe-inspiring, and, since the fighting is usually out of sight of populations who are shielded from its direct effects, reports of dramatic action at sea could have a significant effect. Among the many immediate strategic advantages of Nelson's victories, therefore, the often timely fillip they provided for a sometimes beleaguered and desperate domestic audience might well have been the most important, for this was a new, ideological struggle against an implacable enemy which required an unprecedented sense of common purpose and the mobilisation of much of the domestic economy for war. [8]

Certainly, victory in the Napoleonic wars confirmed the essential, instrumental value of navies as weapons of war and as tools of economic protection and predation. It did much more than this, however. It marked an alteration in the very definition of the international political ideal for which states competed.

Navies in a Europe of dynastic states

Although Britain and France had by no means been constantly at war, it was once fashionable to consider the long eighteenth century, from 1688 to 1815, as a second Hundred Years War which, of course, Britain won.[9] Naval warfare was largely shaped by this rivalry, and it is easy to see a pattern of French failure measured against British success. The navy, therefore, is often prominent in the many critical assessments of France as an eighteenth-century power. Its failures are seen as a symptom of an atrophied financial system and, more broadly still, of the impossible balance that needed to be struck between the contradictory demands of being both a continental and a maritime power. Yet, in many ways, this last distinction is largely artificial. French naval and colonial interests were tied every bit as intimately as its continental military ambitions were to the same single, integrated goal: the consolidation of the Bourbon monarchy's new status and its attempt to occupy the political centre of Europe in place of traditional Habsburg, imperial power.

This ambition was neither anachronistic nor a trivial matter of vain dynastic competition. Even less, however, was it symptomatic of any sort of new system of 'balance of power' politics which is often said to have been ushered in by the Peace of Utrecht.[10] Indeed by ending a complex war through a negotiated settlement that recognised rival dynastic claims, if Utrecht had done anything at all, it merely confirmed an unequal international system defined by central leadership. The prospect of Louis XIV's fullest success, if left unchecked, might have been unbearable for the rest of Europe, but no one had wished to challenge the basis on which the international system operated. All players would continue the pursuit, through negotiation and through war, of reflected stature, because from this pursuit came legitimacy, social order, prosperity, and indeed power.[11] The eighteenth century would see more international competition from new, rising powers, but as the senior branch of the Bourbon dynasty and the self-styled greatest monarchy in Christendom with unparalleled stature and traditional land-based wealth, France remained the greatest of these powers, with an unmatched cultural and military influence throughout the century.[12]

Naval power, it is true, had developed a domestic political significance in Britain that was simply not matched in France, but a navy was still a necessary accessory in the wardrobe of any French king. It was used to protect the periphery of the realm, its trade, and to support its overseas presence, as well as being a means of menacing Britain and disrupting its interests in Europe and around the world. In these different ways, it served the greater purpose of protecting France's status as the pre-eminent power in Europe and the guarantor of European peace. Thus, although Britain had the largest navy in Europe in 1714, both Spain and France rebuilt their own and not necessarily to create a mirror-image of their British equivalent. The Spanish monarchy invested heavily in dockyards both in Spain and in Havana and in the large, sturdy warships needed to protect its American empire and to help strengthen its grip on Sicily and Naples.[13] Though historians have recently tarnished the French reputation for building high-quality ships,[14] the standardisation of design in the eighteenth century and the lighter, faster ships that were produced speak of a formal commitment and of a navy that could protect overseas interests even if it was less suited to direct confrontation.

Initially, Britain and France co-existed reasonably well, as the new Hanoverian dynasty in Britain under George I, all too aware of its vulnerabilities, sought to protect itself from internal 'Jacobite' rebellion, to defend its obvious continental interests, and to send fleets to guarantee access to the Baltic. France, too, was undergoing something of a political re-invention under the new king, Louis XV, who was just five years old in 1715 when he succeeded his grandfather to the throne of the militarily and financially exhausted kingdom. Much of the time in the early decades of the century the two powers were even in alliance, for both had an interest, along with Austria, the Netherlands, and Savoy, in enforcing the terms of the Peace of Utrecht which came under threat from the aggrieved Philip V of Spain. In 1718, for example, a fleet of twenty ships commanded by the British admiral, Byng, chased and defeated a fleet that had been sent to support the Spanish occupation of Sicily, though it took French armies crossing the Pyrenees to force Spain to return the island to Austria.[15]

In the Baltic, the long-term threat was Russian power, though it was against Sweden, which along with Spain tried to support Scottish rebellion in Britain, that George I, the Hanoverian prince, found himself at war. Indeed, at sea, by far the greatest concern was with Spain, and in 1727 a Spanish attempt to recapture Gibraltar was successfully beaten back. There was no domestic, political consensus, however, about how Britain should respond. In parallel with the defence of Gibraltar had been a failed attempt to disrupt Spanish treasure ships in Cadiz and in the West Indies which fuelled domestic debate about priorities and the appropriate use of sea power. Motivated by a mixture of extraordinary confidence in British naval strength based to some extent on a favourable, almost 'mythical', historical memory of Elizabethan seafarers, a desire for a financial return on investment in the navy, and a mistrust of the continental interests of the Hanoverian monarchy, many in Britain felt that the navy should be expanded and dedicated to an aggressive assault on the Spanish empire and its riches.[16] This was Britain's only hope, it was said, to protect itself and to compete with the major powers. In October 1739, these debates came to a head with a declaration of war against Spain, the emotive case for which came from the allegedly rough treatment received by British interlopers in Spanish Caribbean trade at the hands of its *gardacostas*.

A number of highlights in this war helped build popular enthusiasm for the navy in Britain and to give weight to those who argued for a more robust or determined pursuit of empire and naval warfare. Early on, Admiral Vernon captured Porto-Bello on the Panamanian isthmus, which triggered an outpouring of national pride and confidence.[17] Perhaps more famously, Anson's difficult circumnavigation of the globe included the capture of the Spanish Acapulco–Manila treasure ship, which led to his extraordinary celebrity and later to his commitment to improving and professionalising the navy. British success was far from unmitigated, however. The conspicuous failure to capture Cartagena on the Spanish Main in 1740, for example, laid bare British limitations. Indeed, the war at sea with Spain had failed to bring the quick victory some anticipated, and it embroiled Britain in the wider War of the Austrian Succession (1740–1748) against France, which raised the stakes for the Royal Navy. At first, results were not encouraging. Notably, the indecisive Battle of Toulon in 1744 saw a Franco-Spanish fleet break out of the port and force a blockading British fleet back to Minorca. In the end, however, the navy proved its essential value to Britain by disrupting French activity. It did this by dominating the Western Approaches to the Channel and covering the main French port of Brest, and in 1747 two dramatic battles off Cape Finisterre, the western tip of the Breton peninsula, secured the navy's reputation by disrupting French convoys and providing welcome, encouraging news back home.

The navy had not been decisive, however. Indeed the naval war failed to affect Spanish policy significantly or to strengthen Britain's international hand. As Richard Harding argues, the war was a disappointment, a failure to be explained, though he demonstrates how valuable for future conflicts the experience of amphibious and deep-sea operations, commercial warfare, and blockade would be.[18] There were also lessons to be learned about the leverage of overseas assets, such as the capture of Louisbourg in 1745 and its return to France at the negotiating table. There was certainly an economic case for naval war, too. Although French privateers took as many as 3,000 British merchant ships in this war, the economic damage inflicted by Britain was greater still. This affected the conduct of war more generally, for increasingly in the eighteenth century economic wealth came to be seen as a foundation of national strength, and in such ways navies were confirmed as essential weapons of economic warfare. More concretely, there were also broader political advantages from the war for Britain, as Brendan Simms argues. It had successfully limited the French hand on the continent and settled an arguably much more important matter by stopping French invasion attempts aimed at fomenting rebellion in support of Charles Edward Stuart's claim to the British throne.[19] More than just ensuring the survival of the Hanoverian dynasty, this had a profound effect on the wider political nation, animated since the days of Louis XIV by often vague but nevertheless real fears of popery and tyranny from across the Channel.[20]

British policy is sometimes presented as divided between the continental interests of the Hanoverian kings and their, mostly Whig, supporters and the Tories, those who advocated this more ambitious 'blue water' policy. It is certainly true that there was no set naval strategy, as such, and the navy remained a divisive political issue throughout the century. Yet whatever its record, the navy was now widely held by everyone as a key to the defence of British interests.[21] Despite the variety of opinions, most people could share the vision of an emerging Protestant,

British nation, whose security was guaranteed by its rising international standing, and accept that this was augmented by the wealth and political or military influence generated by its historical reliance on sea power.

Naval power was, therefore, at the heart of political debate in Britain and was acquiring ever greater significance, whereas in France, which did not have dramatic victories at sea to celebrate, it simply did not have the same potential. In 1746, for example, there had been a disastrous French expedition to relieve Louisbourg, which had fallen to British forces, leading to embarrassment and widespread disruption for the navy more generally.[22] Yet this did not initiate a broader debate about national priorities. Any equivalent debate about pursuing either continental interests or overseas or maritime ones simply would have had no meaning in France, which for years had stood transfixed by the obvious priority of the storm clouds that were gathering over the longstanding succession crisis in Austria.

It would be difficult to exaggerate the wider significance of the lack of male heirs to the Habsburg Emperor, Charles VI. The status of the Habsburg dynasty and with it a recognisable, ordered Europe depended upon a solution, and the stakes were revealed in 1740. That year, the Elector of Brandenburg, later to be known as Frederick the Great, invaded the rich Austrian province of Silesia in an unusually decisive act of expansionist aggression. This opening act of the wider War of the Austrian Succession is a pivotal event in the history of modern warfare, destabilising Europe for decades and marking a significant step in the territorial organisation of the militarised Prussian state. Frederick had never accepted the terms of the famous Pragmatic Sanction of 1713 that had been negotiated internationally to allow the emperor to circumvent the usual laws of inheritance and protect the integrity of the Habsburg inheritance, and he seized the opportunity when the emperor's daughter, Maria-Theresa, inherited the traditional Austrian lands in 1740.

In a manner reminiscent of the Thirty Years War in the previous century, France, as the greatest European power and self-styled arbiter of European peace, could not remain indifferent to war in the Empire. This was especially so since Maria-Theresa's husband, chosen to exercise the role of Holy Roman Emperor whilst maintaining a Habsburg connection to the title, was duke of Lorraine and thus threatened to bring the French province under the imperial sway. Thus, in what would inevitably be a war that would have to be fought on land and at sea, France turned against Austria. It is true that Prussia had acted precipitously and dangerously in seizing Silesia and that Austria had the backing of its aggressive British ally, which was keen to protect Hanover, but it was Austria that had altered the rules of the international system to its own advantage and thus posed the greater threat to the order upon which French status depended. Though France did little to disguise the fact that it was pursuing its own selfish interests, this still required a foreign policy dedicated to defending the principles of international law and dynastic rights. It had to be seen to be securing a settlement that reflected its dignity and standing as the legal, military, and moral head of Europe.

Typically, this war was settled, not just by military operations in the field, but by negotiations and by the dynastic vagaries of the courts of Europe. Militarily, French armies did well, almost over-running the Austrian Netherlands and earning the lasting military reputation of the maréchal de Saxe in the process. Yet negotiation only became possible upon the death in 1745 of the elector of Bavaria who, with French support, had briefly held the title of Holy Roman Emperor as Charles VII, interrupting the centuries-long Habsburg monopoly. Austria thereupon withdrew occupying troops from Bavaria in exchange for the election of Maria-Theresa's husband, Francis-Stephen, now prince of Tuscany, the first of the Habsburg-Lorraine dynasty to be emperor.

France's priority in these years was clearly not given over to the pursuit of overseas maritime strength for its own sake or to territorial expansion. To the bewilderment of many French people at the time, and to historians since, in the peace negotiations the Austrian Netherlands were simply handed back and a precarious, European settlement, not unlike the status quo ante, though with Silesia still in Prussian hands, was agreed to end the war in 1748. Though it might seem like very little, as Jonathan Dull suggests, there were material advantages to France. '[T]he very moderation of the peace treaty was an act of statesmanship' to add to the tangible benefit of breaking the threatening Austro-British alliance and the establishment of a balance in Europe between Prussia and Austria.[23] At sea, the war had gone less well for France, but through success in war in Europe and by such things as negotiating the return of the fortress of Louisbourg, it protected its essential interests and maintained the presence of the crown overseas.

The Seven Years War, 1756–1763

By 1756, there was little to suggest that naval power could have a determining influence on the outcome of a major European war. Despite many advances internationally, navies were still largely seen as ancillary to, or even compensation for the lack of, the traditional expression of national strength, a large army. Nor was it by any means clear that Britain even held an advantage at sea relative, in particular, to France and to Spain, who had both been building their fleets and professionalising their organisations too.[24] By this time, no longer trusting Austria's willingness to protect Hanover, Britain had accepted Prussian reassurances and come to an accommodation. This galvanised hostility to Prussia on the continent and led to a major realignment of European alliances. A restive Russia joined Austria in hoping to be able to return Prussia to its rightful station and to recover Silesia in the process. The alignment of all three great continental powers against Prussia was completed when, in what is often considered a 'diplomatic revolution', France allied with its traditional foe, Austria, against the aggressive-but-threatened Prussia, which pre-emptively occupied Bavaria in 1756.

In this way, Britain had come to find itself relatively isolated and vulnerable in Europe. Of course, France was the most direct threat to British interests not just in Hanover but in North America, and indeed in Britain itself, and this meant that navies would necessarily play a big role in the next war.[25] Already by 1754 fighting

had broken out in North America. Against attempted incursions by British coloni-
als, France with her Indian allies had begun to re-assert its claim to the interior by
constructing fortifications there and defeating British expeditionary forces, notably one led by Edward Braddock in 1755. Though at sea Britain was disruptive,
capturing a number of French ships in North American waters, the eruption of
formal hostilities in 1756 did not bode well, following as it did the French capture
of Minorca. The failure by Admiral Byng to retake the island and his subsequent
execution for 'failing to do his utmost' to bring the French to battle speaks not just
of a confident doctrinal commitment in Britain to offensive action but of an almost
desperate reliance on sea power. Indeed, these early years of the war were quite
difficult.[26] Britain's new ally, Frederick, expected naval support in the Baltic as protection from Russia. However, there was neither the spare capacity nor the desire
to challenge Russia or to antagonise Sweden or Denmark, who could jeopardise
access to naval stores there. The priority for Britain was to protect its beleaguered
army in Hanover and to distract France with raids on the Norman and Breton
coasts, an effort which also included a failed attempt on the port of Rochefort.

From 1758, however, there was a dramatic change in British fortunes which
did as much as anything to secure the popular perception of the navy. In a concerted effort at sea, Britain exploited improvements in supply and organisation
from the previous war and thus could pursue longer and more effective blockades of Brest and other French ports. It also targeted New France, and the first
step in its fall was a large amphibious operation which re-took the fortress of
Louisbourg in 1758. This was followed in 1759 by the fall of Quebec and in 1760
by Montréal. 1759 also saw Britain take Guadeloupe in the West Indies, where
French privateers had been disruptive, and, with some East India Company ships,
naval support also helped in the struggle against France in India, leading eventually to the surrender of Pondicherry and the loss of France's main possession
there. Faced with such heavy losses, France responded with a naval offensive of its
own by attempting an audacious final knock-out blow through invasion of Britain
itself. In the late summer of 1759, the Brest squadron, on its way to Quiberon
Bay, where it was hoping to effect a difficult union with the Toulon squadron,
was pursued in stormy weather by an audacious Admiral Edward Hawke. The
damage that was subsequently inflicted was not as great in physical terms as is
sometimes assumed of a battle that is often said to have been decisive. Two ships
were sunk, and on the next day one was taken whilst six others were scuttled or
burned. The effect, however, was complete. It put an end to a French attempt at
invasion of Britain. It confirmed France's financial exhaustion and accelerated the
series of defeats globally that led to the difficult Peace of Paris by which France
lost many of its overseas possessions including, of course, all of New France.

As with all early modern wars, the course and even the outcome of the
Seven Years War was affected as much by dynastic changes as by military vic-
tory. The death of George II in 1760 brought a greater willingness by his son
George III to seek peace. In Russia, the accession in 1762 of the new tsar,
Peter III, led directly to Russian withdrawal and peace with Prussia. However,
a global and naval climax seems almost to have been made inevitable by the

death of Ferdinand VI of Spain in 1759 and the commitment to sea power and personal hatred of Britain by the new king, Carlos III. Although Spain thereupon entered the war on behalf of their troubled Bourbon cousins, this help came too late and was, in fact, disastrous. In 1762, after a brief but difficult campaign, Britain took Havana, overcoming the defensive fortifications and challenging conditions there. East India Company ships were then used in forcing the surrender of Manila.[27] These were the two keys to global Spanish power in the Americas and the Pacific. Suddenly, therefore, and on the back of a largely improvised strategy, Britain found itself in a very strong bargaining position with respect to both France and Spain.

In some ways, this victory and the manner of its achievement came as something of a surprise, the effect of which was that the Royal Navy was more firmly than ever associated in Britain with the nation's defence and with its present and prospective future greatness. As Rodger expressed it, the many victories in the Seven Years War 'turned the old national myth of sea power into reality'.[28] In other words, success seemed to vindicate those who had long argued that Britain had a unique history and a special role to play as a sea power. It also helped crystallise a growing sense of the value of expanding Britain's various interests around the world and of linking them ever more closely as part of a coherent, mutually supporting, economic and military imperial system.[29] In contrast, for historians at least, the associations of the French navy are invariably negative, linked to common themes that colour eighteenth-century French history of fiscal difficulties, serial financial mismanagement, structural dysfunction and, by further extension, of the collapse of the state in the Revolution from 1789. For Spain, similarly, it seems to confirm a picture of long-term decline.

A slightly different light is cast on this picture of these two widely divergent paths, however, by the different national perspectives revealed in the extraordinary Peace of Paris of 1763. Britain might appear to have held all the cards and to have been in a position to dictate terms, but the war had been expensive for Britain, too, and domestic weariness with the expense and disruption of fighting meant there was a real need for negotiation.[30] In a typical pattern, its overseas trophies were used as bargaining chips in order to secure a settlement which was concerned above all with guaranteeing Britain's security vis-à-vis its European rivals France and Spain. Cuba and the Philippines were returned in exchange for Florida and Minorca and for guarantees of Portuguese independence, in other words for a limitation to Spanish power and for corresponding British influence in the port of Lisbon. Spain gained Louisiana from France, that is to say the territory west of the Mississippi, a reflection of the broader British priority of addressing the security threat from France, whilst Canada itself was kept by Britain, all but eliminating the French presence in North America. Finally, of course, Britain insisted on the evacuation of French forces from all European territories held by George III.

Control of all of North America and strengthened influence in India and over African slaving stations and sugar-producing Caribbean islands all certainly represent an extraordinary step in the long-term growth of Britain's imperial and naval pre-eminence. Yet it could be said that the redefinition and expansion of Britain's global empire was as much an effect as the main purpose of the negotiations, which was simply to protect Britain's operational naval capabilities in Europe and to limit the French threat everywhere. In other words, it is tempting to think solely in terms of global or of naval winners and losers, but this is to play down the extent to which, from the British perspective, security fears with respect to France animated the war and the subsequent peace negotiations and to risk over-looking the rapid recovery of the French navy after 1763 and its role in defeating Britain in the next major war.[31] It also has a whiff of anachronism about it, for it ignores the nature of eighteenth-century warfare, which, despite important mod-ernising trends, remained a process of violent negotiation played out in a world of litigious, though mutually recognised, dynastic states. It plays down the broader comparative context in which Britain was acutely aware of its own relative 'small-ness', its lack of status, and its vulnerability to both internal rebellion and to foreign invasion. British identity was to a large extent being shaped by the effects of invasion scares from France and a recognition of French military strength.[32] Indeed a growing imperial swagger was not the only effect of the Seven Years War. Many people in Britain also felt distinctly uneasy about territorial expansion and imperial over-reach, with many feeling that governing a French-speaking, Catholic population in the relatively unproductive Canada should not have been negotiated and that Guadeloupe, for example, which was returned to France, would have been a better acquisition.[33] Territorial growth and the government of alien peoples, it was said, was more typically a feature of Iberian empires or worse of Oriental despotism, not the extension of the commercial, maritime activity which had so far been the source of British identity and strength.[34]

France had undoubtedly been humbled in the Seven Years War and its threat to British interests had been comprehensively addressed, but its position in Europe was respected, and it was able to celebrate the peace, for its main priori-ties had been recognised and protected. With the return of Belle-Isle across from Quiberon Bay, which had been taken by Britain in 1761, metropolitan French ter-ritorial integrity was completely unmolested. Since the Peace of Utrecht in 1714 the French priority in North America had been maintaining a visible royal pres-ence and access to the rich fishing grounds of the grand banks off Newfoundland. By negotiating the maintenance of the islands of St Pierre and Miquelon, France at least maintained the latter, valuable for their own sake and for keeping alive the deep-sea activities of its population which could in the future be used to man its warships. Retaining Guadeloupe, Martinique, and a few other sugar-producing Caribbean islands, slaving stations in West Africa, and its factories in India, France managed, despite its much-reduced colonial holdings, to maintain an active, lucrative global presence. Again, it seems, territorial expansion, as such, was not valued by France as the measure of global imperial success.

The bold modernising process that we tend to identify with Britain, based on the integration of popular and political interest and the corresponding flexibility of the political and financial system, certainly makes sense as a way of understanding naval competition in the eighteenth century. Yet it was neither this nor the associated global territorial reach that animated international relations but rather the competition for relative status, and this is the key to understanding military change. France was not a signatory to the parallel Treaty of Hubertusburg between Austria and Prussia which, when compared to the situation in 1648, can be interpreted as a sign of the decline of French influence over central European affairs. The overall settlement of 1763, however, did not greatly affect its position in Europe. Of course, there was much soul-searching due to the extent of the military losses, but rather than ushering in a period of decline it was the start of a process of modernisation and military renewal in France. It has been said that France lost the war but won the peace in 1763, as if its diplomacy was so extraordinary that it was able to secure a peace settlement that the outcome of the fighting would suggest it did not deserve. Certainly there were critics of the British negotiations who felt that a better deal should have been secured on the back of its comprehensive military victory, but it is important to bear in mind the relative stature of the two states within a fundamentally unchanged Europe.

The expansion of European navies

After the Seven Years War, there was a general, steady expansion of navies across Europe, although, as Richard Harding says, this phenomenon remains 'poorly understood'.[35] Britain's demonstrable and obvious success in the war at sea and its increased commitment to naval power thereafter, however, is certain to have played a significant role. Put simply, to compete with Britain all powers large and small would need naval strength for defence and to protect their own maritime and commercial interests. Yet the impact was more profound than any dispassionate calculation of relative power and national security interests. National political survival in the early modern period was not merely a question of the militarily weak defending themselves against the predatory strong. As Fredrick Spruyt has argued for earlier centuries, the very rise of powerful, centralised states in Europe with large military institutions had been at least as much a matter of 'institutional mimicry' as it had been the outcome of direct armed conflict.[36] It would seem that, by the late eighteenth century, navies had acquired much of the cultural value that armed strength on land had always had. They had become objects of emulation and thus key parts of this ongoing process of national self-definition and mutual recognition. This was due in no small part to the domestic political and commercial advantages that Britain enjoyed which did not go any more unnoticed internationally than Britain's dramatic feats of arms at sea.

Navies, therefore, had become an important expression of legitimacy and national pride in Europe, and not just for their incontrovertible utility in war but for the political message they carried domestically and internationally. Their technological and organisational sophistication alone made them evidence of national strength and vigour. Also, and perhaps more importantly now, navies had the potential to promote exploration and scientific enquiry, which appealed to the political instincts of this age of Enlightenment and rationality. Thus it was that the first major test of Britain's post-war settlement and its naval power soon came with the crisis of 1770 over the Falkland Islands, which were a key step in the opening of the Pacific to European guns, ships, and scientists. Wishing to protect its monopoly of European interest in the Pacific, Spain reacted furiously to the establishment of a British settlement on the western island and sent a squadron to expel them. France, however, was not yet in a strong enough position to resist, and in any case Louis XV had no interest in another open naval war with Britain. The potentially reckless enthusiasm of the duc de Choiseul, who had been the French naval minister during the Seven Years War, and his desire to seek revenge against the British, was a concern at the time and no doubt led to his dismissal later that year. The French settlement on the eastern island therefore was withdrawn, and France refused to support the Spanish, who were then forced to back down and allow the British to re-establish themselves.[37]

The crisis demonstrated beyond any doubt that British sea power was now dominant and could, by the very threat of its use, influence international relations globally. The next year, in 1771, British threats prevented the French from sending a squadron to the Baltic to help Sweden.[38] Later, at Nookta Sound on the west coast of Vancouver Island, a Spanish squadron stepped down in a confrontation over British incursions into the north-eastern Pacific. Again, however, the conclusion should not be that French policy was simply moribund. Although forced to back down during the Falklands crisis, for example, much higher priorities and far more valued prizes had come with the formal annexation of Lorraine in 1766 and the occupation of Corsica in 1768, which were kept as permanent acquisitions of metropolitan France. Averting open war at sea in 1770 had been more than a desperate act of self-preservation then. It permitted the energetic assertion of French pre-eminence in Europe.

As a leading force in the Enlightenment, France hoped to remain at the forefront not just of philosophy and letters but of medicine and science, although, as notable developments in artillery technology made clear, it was most determined to remain a major military power. Advances in French military thought were encapsulated by Guibert, who in many ways prefigured Napoleon by promoting a divisional system in the army, the use of columns to overcome the rigidity of traditional linear infantry formations, and generally the mobile, bold pursuit of war.[39] Even the evocation of nationalist fervour and its exploitation on the battlefield began to take hold as France confidently attempted to re-assert its place at the top of the military hierarchy.[40]

All the while, and as a necessary complement to its ambitions, France also rebuilt its navy, and a huge expansion was a consistent theme for the rest of the century.[41] Even Spain, despite its traditional reputation for maintaining a timid, defensive, and protective stance, pursued an offensive strategy at sea.[42] Yet from the perspective of 'mimicry' in international politics, the expansion of European navies might have been due not just to British success but to French investment. Bold plans were laid at the end of the Seven Years War to build up France's total ships of the line in just five years from the immediate post-war figure of forty-seven to eighty, with a similarly ambitious building programme in Spain with a target of sixty.[43] This growth included the modernisation of Brest and Toulon and the establishment of a school of naval medicine. French warship design was standardised. Lorient and Cherbourg had arsenals built.[44] Significantly, too, under Louis XV there was a concerted effort to control public finances by reducing the debt and reforming the administration. Although he did not manage to permanently suppress the obstructive *parlements*, there was even a popular element to the resurgence of French naval power, with port cities more willing to build ships and merchants more willing to co-operate.[45] Eighty ships of the line had always been an unrealistic ambition, but after Louis XV's death in 1774 there was a renewed commitment to the navy, and French and Spanish shipbuilding, taken together, threatened to eclipse Britain's.[46] Britain had certainly won the war of 1756–1763, but it had not brought France to its knees.[47] The ideological, military, and even naval threat it posed had not been eliminated.

It is important to bear in mind that French naval power did not just grow in the context of its rivalry with Britain. It had been part of the longer-term competition to occupy the central ground against imperial Habsburg power since the seventeenth century and now, arguably even more importantly, in trying to sustain its wider international status in the eighteenth. Indeed in some respects French policy remained remarkably consistent within an international system that was changing more quickly in its size and complexity than in the basic principles that governed it. Though warfare in eighteenth-century Europe remained fundamentally dynastic, or at least fought over dynastic pretences and matters of international precedence and relative legitimacy, there were, simply put, more competitors now, and navies helped to feed a more frenzied aspirational competition. Sweden and the Ottoman Empire were considerable powers in eighteenth-century European politics. In central Europe, too, the rise of Prussia most notably, but also Saxony and Hanover, augmented by the British crown, and to an extent also Bavaria, all contributed to the growing competition for security and standing. It is plausible to suggest that this was largely responsible for the general escalation of war, which was marked by the large, professional armies in disciplined formations and well-drilled in the use of artillery with which we associate the eighteenth century and, by extension, by the professionalisation of navies and the systemisation of war at sea.[48] The appearance of Dutch and Swedish naval colleges is but one reflection of this. Yet nothing better illustrates the changing complexion of Europe and the parallel role of navies in defining political ideals than the rise of Russia to great power status.

Neither Russia's merchant fleet nor its navy ever approached the size of Britain's. It nevertheless adopted naval power with some determination and readily associated its national identity with it. As seen above, by 1721 and the end of the Great Northern War, Russia had beaten back Swedish expansion and established itself as the major power in eastern Europe.[49] In many ways, Russia was emblematic of a new, modern Europe in which successful states and economies developed as colossal war-waging machines and policy makers increasingly pursued the pragmatic, determined pursuit of power with fixed, principled purpose. In this way, naval power was becoming part of the very definition of modernity itself for it had shaped a war which, in the militarisation of the combatant states and in its scale and intensity, foreshadowed to some extent modern wars of political survival.

Thereafter Russian trade with the west grew quickly. However, it was the Russian war with the Ottomans from 1768 to 1774 and specifically the naval battle of Chesme of June 1770 which, as Tim Blanning puts it, announced Russia's arrival 'as a maritime power'. [50] Although it was done with British connivance and support, the Russians managed to send their Baltic fleet, which included at least nine significant ships of the line, to the Mediterranean. Off the western Anatolian coast they encountered a stronger Ottoman fleet and though deep within enemy waters inflicted a dramatic, one-sided defeat.[51] This was that most rare of occurrences: a large, set-piece naval battle between major powers with a clear outcome. Of course, it could be argued that little direct benefit came from this, that it was not a strategic victory in the broader sense.[52] Yet it was clearly an important moment in terms of political invention. It was a powerful statement of Russian ambitions and relative strength in the area which was echoed by the construction in Russia of elaborate monuments marking the victory.

Elsewhere in Europe, very real fears of Russian expansion at Ottoman expense, which included the prospect of Russian control of the Balkans, led to truly extraordinary measures. Rather than facing the risks of taking up arms to stop them, a proposal was raised by Frederick the Great in 1772 to try to satisfy the Russian appetite by sharing Polish territory between Prussia, Russia, and Austria.[53] This first partition of Poland was one of the most momentous developments of the century. It is, on one hand, a clear demonstration of the politics of the age based on the calculation of naked national self-interest and, according to some, indicative of a growing cynical power-driven system that would culminate in the wars of Napoleon.[54] It could also be seen, however, as exceptional and simply an attempt to maintain order and stability in the region as recognisably as possible by satisfying Russian ambitions whilst ensuring Prussia and Austria would not lose relative standing. In the event, however, Russian ambition and pride would not be satisfied until its status as a sea power able to contain the Turks was secured. By the terms of the peace in 1774, Russia secured access to the Black Sea and freedom of navigation for its growing merchant marine. Greater Russian pretensions were announced loudly and clearly to the rest of Europe with the formal annexation of Crimea in 1783 and the expansion of its Black Sea Fleet over the rest of the century.

There was little France or anyone else could do about the shifting power of eastern Europe.[55] In the conflict between Russia and the Ottoman Empire, France had not been able to provide effective support to its ally, and Britain later forced the French to abandon the mobilisation of its Mediterranean fleet.[56] In this light, the French decision in 1778 to embark on a naval war with Britain on behalf of American rebels might, therefore, appear to have been rather short-sighted, motivated by pique and a simple desire for vengeance or as evidence of a lack of options and of France's declining relative influence in central and eastern Europe. It could, on the other hand, also simply be an indication of the extent to which naval warfare had become a source of legitimacy and international leadership. This would certainly have seemed to be the case by 1783 with two great powers, Russia and France, ensconced in Crimea and victorious at sea over Britain respectively.

American Independence

For France, the War of American Independence (1776–1783) was unique. It would not be a war in which it would be distracted by British naval power. It would, instead, inevitably be a direct, head-to-head challenge to Britain at sea.[57] The opportunity certainly seemed ripe. Britain faced considerable challenges that it was never able fully to resolve. Almost as soon as the logic of an integrated global imperial system had begun to present itself, it began to unravel. The Royal Navy, the key to the proper functioning of this imperial system, also necessarily became an instrument of commercial policing, which led to the famous Boston Tea Party in 1773. Soon it was occupied with suppressing an open rebellion. This was an entirely new strategic challenge. Whereas British strength had relied heavily on the colonies in the past, with American reinforcements making the capture of Louisbourg and Havana in the Seven Years War possible, for example, now they were the enemy. Operations would have to take place at long distances with troops and supplies transported across the Atlantic. It was, moreover, far harder to find a centre of gravity to attack and immeasurably harder still to impose an effective blockade along the entire North American coast.[58]

There was some initial success as the Royal Navy helped to take New York in 1776. The Battle of Saratoga the next year, however, made the prospect of beating the British seem realisable to the rebels. French intervention in 1778 was also an important turning point.[59] Britain made the understandable, though most likely fatal, decision to send a fleet to America in pursuit, which not only could not defeat the French there but allowed an opportunity to challenge Britain's advantage in the Western Approaches.[60] Worse was to come, however, as Spain joined the French side in 1779. Britain's warships were now significantly outnumbered. Gibraltar and Minorca came under a direct threat, and another invasion of Britain itself was attempted. This combined Bourbon invasion failed, due mostly to problems of co-ordination and disease, but Britain could not contain France and Spain like it had in the past, and it would therefore have to face large French expeditionary forces overseas. In this way, the Caribbean became an important theatre of this European war. In 1780, for example, after defeating a Spanish squadron and relieving Gibraltar, Admiral Rodney sailed to the West Indies, where he had indecisive encounters with the French whilst the Spanish successfully attacked a British West Indian convoy. The next year, the French admiral de Grasse captured Tobago before sailing north, isolating the British army at Yorktown and effectively ending British hopes in the war.[61]

In contrast, Britain won a victory in the large, set-piece Battle of the Saintes between Guadeloupe and Dominica in April 1782. It would be too much to argue that this had no broader strategic effect and was just the exception that proved the rule of overall British inability to overcome the disciplined defensive formations of the Bourbons and to affect the outcome of a major war through the projection of sea power. It was, after all, the product of an intense building programme, the refinement of offensive tactics, and a determined pursuit on the day. Indeed, the failure of another Spanish attempt at Gibraltar later that year only confirmed a menacing rise in British sea power. Nevertheless, it is part of a bigger picture in which, from 1782–1783, France also scored victories against Britain in dramatic deep-sea battles of its own in the East Indies under the bailli de Suffren. His successes there were cut short by the formal cessation of hostilities, although it is unlikely that British power in India could have been seriously challenged by this French offensive at sea, and in this respect perhaps a general rule had been established. Despite the vastly improved ability of European navies to project their power globally, they were most effective in European waters.

Defeat in war to France and the loss of the American colonies affected British strategy, which had been developing not out of clear-sighted principles and careful, long-term calculations, but in a piecemeal approach to changing circumstances. Now, there was a conservative return to the approach to sea power that had previously served Britain so well. In other words, deep-sea power projection was largely abandoned for a concentration of effort on the defence of the home islands and operations in European waters which could disrupt the overseas projects of its European rivals. Guarding the Western Approaches to the Channel, defending against foreign invasion, and blockading or otherwise disrupting European rivals was accepted as the most effective use of naval power just as it had proven to be in the past.[62] In India, for example, where naval power had played a big role in extending British influence at the expense of the French, this was largely the effect of interests in place, that is to say of the ships of the East India Company and local alliances, rather than of the Royal Navy itself.

The humbling of Britain and the failure of its navy to win the war by 1783 had what seems to be a rather paradoxical effect. The 1780s witnessed what can only be described as a European naval arms race. This reinforces the point that one should not dismiss too readily the effect that the enthusiastic French embrace of naval power might also have had on a Europe which emulated such displays of military strength by its leading powers. Naples built a small fleet. The Dutch nearly doubled their number of battleships. More significantly, by 1785 the French had sixty-two major ships of the line whilst the Spanish had sixty-one. By 1790, these numbers had risen to seventy-three and seventy-two. Though Britain was committed to maintaining a two-power standard and also built significantly, by 1790 taken together French and Spanish totals matched its own.[63]

Beyond the immediate impact of British successes and the effect of mutual emulation between states, there is a third, more direct and possibly more significant explanation for the expansion of European navies: the ripple effect of Britain's growing dependency on sea power and the associated need to police neutral shipping to support it. Throughout the eighteenth century, Britain's effectiveness at sea depended on its ability to deprive opponents of necessary materials and trade. Britain's difficulties in the War of American Independence exacerbated the situation and drove a cyclical, escalatory pattern. Its growing commitments deepened its dependence on its naval strength. This brought exponentially expanding demands, and the cost of maintaining its naval power was increasing tension and potential conflict with smaller powers such as the Netherlands, Denmark, or Sweden.

During the war, in addition to trying to intercept French commerce at sea, British trade had to be protected and not just from attacks by French privateers but from the two to three thousand American privateers that put to sea during the war as well.[64] In addition, British heavy-handedness in policing neutral shipping for contraband items that could help the enemy created serious international tensions. Concerned, too, about maintaining access to the Baltic, an essential source not just of naval stores but of grain, Britain initially hoped to maintain good relations with Russia, though it was soon clear that its maritime interests would have to be defended by force. The nature of the privateering war changed by 1780, when Russia formed the first League of Armed Neutrality to protect neutral shipping. Russian squadrons were sent to sea to enforce this freedom against Royal Navy ships and soon the League was joined by Denmark and also by Sweden, which had itself been encouraged by France to organise such resistance. By 1783, they had been joined by Prussia, Portugal, Naples, and the Ottoman Empire.

Dutch merchants, in particular, flouted British rules and traded with the American rebels during the war. The Dutch also supplied France with materials essential to its naval war effort. Naturally, they wished to protect their right as a neutral power to transport goods to belligerents, which became a rallying cry of sorts for the other maritime powers of the time. It had been in a vain attempt to stop the Dutch from joining the League that Britain declared war in December 1780, beginning a so-called 'fourth' Anglo-Dutch war. Britain pressed its advantage quickly and forcefully. The Dutch, with only twenty ships of the line to begin with, had been caught unprepared. Attempts to capture British convoys were mostly unsuccessful. Conversely, Britain was able to contain the Dutch and to pick off French convoys. It is a measure of the extent to which Britain needed to protect its naval strength and to use the sea to defeat France that it ran roughshod over Europe's other naval powers which all ranged against it in this way. In a further reverberation of the titanic clash with France, this struggle was inevitably extended globally, with a number of successful operations against Dutch colonial holdings in the West Indies, Africa, and India.

British warships might have been most effective in European waters, but colonial assets remained valuable targets in Britain's efforts to cripple an enemy, either as pawns or for furthering its own economic interests and extending control of global sea lanes. Richard Harding has noted that, against the trend of rising numbers of privateers at this time, the numbers from France and Spain actually declined.[65] The reasons for this are undoubtedly complex, though it may in part be a reflection of the extent to which the build-up of their navies had been intended as statements of royal power, attempts to retain the status upon which their national interests depended and which direct control of a national navy could now afford. In contrast, Britain's political and military identity was tied almost entirely to the sea, creating a far greater imperative to monopolise trade and violence at all levels on the world's seas.

The French Revolutionary wars, 1792–1802

The French Revolution from 1789 caused untold disorder in the French navy. Political divisions alienated the traditional officer corps, almost all of whom were nobles, and central authority on the maritime periphery collapsed.[66] Due to financial crises, the neglect of its ships and the critical lack of supplies and men, the French initially could only put to sea around forty of the seventy-two ships of the line that they had on paper.[67] With many cities in open rebellion, including Bordeaux, Marseille, and then Toulon, the situation looked very bleak. This desperation fed the radicalisation of the Revolution, and by late 1793 the government was in the hands of Robespierre and the infamous Committee of Public Safety. Britain was able to take advantage of French disruption, sending a major fleet to the West Indies to destroy essential French economic interests there. Over the next few years, Britain also scored two of its most memorable victories in battle at sea. The Glorious First of June of 1794 was a one-sided deep-sea battle in which seven of twenty-six French warships were taken and an enormous loss of life was inflicted. In February 1797 Spain, recently allied to France, suffered a dramatic loss to an outnumbered British fleet at the Battle of Cape St Vincent off the south coast of Portugal. Previously, rebellious Toulon, fearing the Revolutionary army that had just brought Marseille to obedience, invited the British Mediterranean fleet to provide protection, later joined by seventeen Spanish ships. The city could not be defended on land, however, and it fell to French government forces in December but not before the fleeing British forces destroyed valuable naval supplies, burning nine ships and capturing four others. There were other disappointments at sea for the battered and under-manned French navy. With far more ships at its disposal, the British were able to contain the French Mediterranean fleet, and attempts to relieve it with ships from Brest were consistently foiled.

What is more remarkable than the complete collapse of French sea power, however, was the extraordinary capacity of the French Revolutionary state to rebuild it and indeed to escalate naval war beyond recognition. Once the authority of the monarchy had been challenged beyond repair by the reformers who wished to restore France as a great power with influence over continental Europe, the state immediately fell into an extraordinarily rapid downward spiral of violence and increasing radicalism.[68] The extreme political rhetoric and bloodshed was a sign of the sheer desperation to re-establish some kind of effective political legitimacy. Although the situation was quite simply unparalleled, this new state turned to the same source of political legitimacy upon which uncertain states had always relied, war. Coupled with the potentially existential military threat that France faced from neighbouring continental armies, the state quite naturally and thoroughly turned into what was effectively a colossal war machine with its entire population theoretically at arms. This frantic political re-invention through war would now necessarily also include the creation of a navy to match.

As the Toulon episode reveals, perhaps the greatest challenge to the state was internal rebellion. This it famously dealt with with ruthless and deadly efficiency in the Vendée and also in Brittany. Commissioners were sent to different French ports to force through a programme of naval construction and reform led by the feared André Jeanbon Saint-André at Brest. The effect was extraordinary. By May 1794, France had made good its losses of the previous year and had as many as fifty ships of the line in service. Although it famously lost at the Glorious First of June, France had been able to oppose the British with an equivalent fleet, fight valiantly, and more importantly meet its strategic purpose of covering for a large and desperately needed convoy of supplies and grain for a hungry population.[69]

This likely brought more political than material relief, especially as the battle coincided with other important and emotionally charged successes. After having suffered a number of reverses in the West Indies earlier in the year, on 2 June a French force arrived at Guadeloupe and began the recapture of the island. Much more importantly, victory against the Austrian army at the Battle of Fleurus of 26 June marked a military turning point that led to the French conquest of the Austrian Netherlands and the United Provinces and the evacuation of British forces from the continent by 1795.

Thus, the overall picture of chaos in the French navy and of British victories at sea should not be allowed to obscure either the extraordinary military achievements of the French government or its ability to impose order and to push through a remarkable programme of naval rearmament and reorganisation. French fortunes were not fatally damaged by the war at sea. Indeed, the opposite seems to be true, as the international alliances against it quickly unravelled. The newly established Batavian republic was a French puppet state which put much of the Dutch navy of twenty-eight smaller ships of the line to French use. The Prussians declared themselves neutral, and Spain made peace with France. The British took advantage of the Dutch situation to occupy the Cape of Good Hope and other colonies in the Caribbean and the Far East, leaving only Austria and Sardinia actively fighting France on the continent. When a French army led by a young Napoleon defeated Sardinia and took Milan by April 1797, France controlled all of northern Italy, and an accommodation was signed with Austria. This gave France a number of Venetian warships, though it was Spain's alliance with France in August 1796 that had the most effect on naval warfare, putting over ten large warships and sixty-five smaller ones into French service. In response, the British left Corsica and were forced to withdraw their Mediterranean fleet.

Russian support for Britain in the North Sea and Mediterranean was withdrawn by the new tsar, Paul I, in November 1796. Between them, the Dutch, French, and Spanish forces could put about ninety ships to sea, though Britain still had overall numerical superiority and got some help from Naples and Portugal. Yet British commitments in North America, the Caribbean, South Africa, the East Indies, and the Mediterranean also meant that it was difficult to apply sufficient pressure in European waters. France could take advantage with invasion threats, sparking and exacerbating a financial crisis in Britain that led to worrying mutinies in the navy in 1797.

After a coup by the French army in September 1797, the political rise of Napoleon was marked by renewed French confidence at sea.[70] He signed a peace with Austria, and another invasion of Britain was planned. Of course Britain was not about to roll over.[71] To some extent it was saved by the timely blow to Spanish naval confidence that had been struck by Cape St Vincent in February and then in October 1797 by victory against a Dutch fleet in the North Sea at the Battle of Camperdown. Both confirmed in Britain a popular faith in the navy. More significantly, Napoleon then decided that an invasion was not practical at this time and turned his attention to Egypt in a bold, if curious, extension of French power and a threat to British communications with India.

A familiar pattern unfolded of emphatic British naval successes which built confidence and sustained the war effort but played out against the broader backdrop of ominous French military expansion. Most dramatic in this sense was Nelson's victory at the Battle of the Nile of August 1798. Luckily missing Nelson's squadron that had been sent to monitor it, a French fleet captured Malta before arriving in Egypt in July and landing a huge army. After initial difficulties tracking and locating it, in one of the most famous incidents in naval history Nelson took advantage of the exposed French ships at anchor. The surprised and unprepared French fleet was enveloped and annihilated; only two ships survived. Though the French army could continue its conquest of Egypt, it was stranded.

This victory had an extraordinary impact, especially with respect to the international reaction against France. British sea power had landed a serious blow to French prestige, and like Quiberon Bay in 1759 it seemed to open the floodgates. The Ottomans declared war on France and even co-operated with the Russians, who were permitted to send forces from the Black Sea through the straits. Britain had captured Minorca from Spain in 1798 and by 1800 the Ottomans and Russians captured the Ionian Islands whilst Britain also re-captured Malta. Naples, or the Kingdom of the Two Sicilies, was most relieved by the French defeat and went on the offensive. Most importantly, however, by 1799 Russia and Austria were also at war with France.

Of course, fighting Napoleon was an entirely different prospect than fighting Louis XV had ever been. As First Consul of France from late 1799, Napoleon concentrated his efforts on his principal enemy, Austria, knocking it out of the war and securing in the process French claims west of the Rhine and setting up a client state in northern Italy. At sea, Britain was able to maintain a particularly effective, close blockade of Brest which reinforced international confidence, though it had its failures, too, in its attempts at combined operations in the north of Holland, the Quiberon peninsula, Ferrol, and Cadiz, which it was also blockading.[72] Once again, Britain's reliance on the uncertain effectiveness of its sea power to defeat France created a cycle of ever greater dependence and of exponentially inflating commitments which inevitably alienated other powers, and this contributed to the unravelling of the alliance against France.

The Russian Tsar, Paul I, was also Grand-Master of the Knights of Malta and naturally expected to share in the capture of that island. Partly out of feelings of personal injury by Britain, he also organised another League of Armed Neutrality in December 1800 with Sweden, Denmark, and Prussia. Thirty ships of the line would be deployed to block British access to the Baltic. This required a firm response, and a British fleet of twenty ships was despatched and destroyed an anchored Danish fleet in April 1801 and threatened Copenhagen itself. Following this effective display of force, no further action against the Swedes or Russians was even needed. The recent death of Paul I had, anyway, already prepared the demise of this threat to British naval strength.

Nevertheless, and although France capitulated in Syria and Egypt, its military successes in Europe had been extraordinary. By the Peace of Amiens of March 1802, Britain conceded the enormous gains in Europe made by France and returned most of its conquests abroad, including Malta, which was put back into the hands of the Knights of Malta, gaining in the process relatively little, mostly in the form of Ceylon and Trinidad. France remained a military giant and a very threatening one at that. This had been an exhausting war, and it soon turned out to be no more than a brief hiatus in an escalating European crisis. Britain's utter reliance on sea power was obvious, and facing the dangers ahead the emotional and political effect of the heroism that Nelson displayed at the Nile, Copenhagen, and elsewhere would be more crucial than ever.

Napoleonic wars, 1803–1815

War was the very life-blood of the new French state. It is no surprise, therefore, that its most successful general emerged out of the chaos to lead and to rebuild it and that the only means by which to do so was the aggressive and successful conduct of war. By naming himself emperor in 1804, Napoleon revealed more than just unhinged, personal ambition. Warfare on a normal scale toward a negotiated, balanced settlement offered insufficient security. This new, resurrected France would simply have to establish an empire in Europe through the force of arms, on land and at sea, or be defeated fatally.

By the time of the Peace of Amiens, although the French navy was still vastly outnumbered by the British, the recapture of the colony of Saint-Domingue, where a slave uprising had led to independence, was initially the priority at sea. Although Martinique and Guadeloupe were re-captured in the process, this had been costly in terms of men and ships. Very quickly, however, formal war erupted with Britain after its refusal to relinquish Malta according to the terms of the Amiens treaty. British sea power and the prospect of another international coalition pushed Napoleon to plan a full-scale invasion, and he built a huge fleet of landing craft and gathered an army of over 100,000 men to this end. To cross the Channel successfully, however, France needed a strong escorting fleet. The effort to gather such a fleet, and Britain's attempts to disrupt it, dominated naval warfare leading up to the Battle of Trafalgar. Britain had between forty-five and fifty warships dedicated to blockading Brest, Rochefort, and Ferrol, of which thirty-seven were always at sea. Overall, eighty-three ships of the line and ten of fifty guns were available to Britain by 1805 versus forty-five French ships and the small number of remaining Dutch ships. These were supplemented late in 1804 by the fifty or so ships that Spain had on paper when it was driven into an alliance with France following a successful attack by Britain on its four returning treasure ships that year. Yet nowhere could these forces be successfully gathered in the face of British disruptions and eventually the invasion idea was dropped by Napoleon.

Far more important to Napoleon was the threat from Russian and Austrian armies and it was toward them that he directed the army that had been gathered for the invasion of Britain. Villeneuve, who commanded the French and Spanish fleet, was sent to Naples to counter a joint British and Russian operation there. He was also to disrupt the British blockading forces if the opportunity arose. It was to this end that Villeneuve, with eighteen French and fifteen Spanish ships, challenged Nelson's fleet of twenty-seven off Trafalgar. The story is as well-known as the defeat was complete for Villeneuve. One French ship was destroyed whilst eight French and nine Spanish ships were taken. No British ships were lost, and in the aftermath further French and Spanish ships were wrecked or captured.

The war was not over, of course, but what followed demonstrated both Britain's ability to make its now undisputed dominance of the sea count and the almost disproportionate effort needed to sustain it.[73] Napoleon hoped to exploit the potential vulnerability of Britain's need for constant vigilance and the control over trade and violence at sea. On its own, neither direct invasion attempts, set-piece battles at sea, nor even a programme of targeted commerce raiding was likely to bring Britain to its knees, but if the demands on the state could be stretched beyond sustainability that could be its Achilles' heel. Thus, Napoleon aimed to exploit his imperial conquests on the continent and to pool naval resources. More ominously, he tried to impose a continental economic zone that would exclude all British trade. This combination of economic strangulation and military provocation, it was hoped, would apply unbearable pressure to an unbalanced system and send it crashing down.

It must be said that historians tend not to be impressed with Napoleon's plan which, it would seem, was doomed from the very start. There is plenty written on the relative health of the British economic and political systems and on the elaboration of a strategy for victory. Yet it would be impossible to exaggerate the seriousness with which this threat was taken and the effect it had on British sea power. Essentially Britain again had to be at war with neutral shipping and any trade at sea in French goods, and the lengths to which it went to deny other sea powers of any freedom of action lends at least some credibility to Napoleon's judgement. Forbidding all trade in French goods whilst helping British trade to overcome the embargo required an enormous investment in warships and the maintenance of continuous blockades. It also meant taking other extraordinary measures. When Denmark refused to join with Britain in 1807 and thus threatened to crumble under French pressure, Copenhagen was bombarded and its small navy was simply confiscated, creating lasting hostility between the two countries. The Portuguese fleet was likewise seized, and Turkey was threatened by a British squadron, though Constantinople escaped the same devastation. Russia soon joined France and an invasion of Sweden from one direction and the threat of a Franco-Danish one from the other posed a direct threat to British hopes.

This was only contained by the fleet of Admiral Saumarez, who managed to maintain informal relations and to keep British trade flowing even after Sweden, too, was formally absorbed into the French empire in 1809.[74]

All aspects of the British military and diplomatic machine needed to go into overdrive. Most alarmingly, they had to watch an aggressive shipbuilding programme of the French empire itself. Britain was forced to invest heavily and in 1809 mounted an unsuccessful campaign to destroy the ships being built in the mouth of the Scheldt. Its overseas strength was needed more than ever, and up to 1815 French and Dutch colonies fell, including Martinique, Guadeloupe, and the Cape of Good Hope. The capture of Reunion and Mauritius in 1810 also ended the French threat to British East Indian interests.[75] In many ways, in its now unlimited commitment to warships, to dominating neutral shipping, to maintaining essential clandestine trade with the continent, and to using overseas assets to apply diplomatic pressure it could be said that Napoleon had pushed Britain to the fullest logic of its dependence on naval strength. A new form of monopolistic and global naval super power was forged in the furnaces of modern war.

In comparison, the War of 1812 against another important neutral shipping power, the United States, was a decidedly minor conflict. Nevertheless, it is a very clear indication both of the role that navies now had in defining a military or political culture in the modern world and, more specifically, of how this giant would operate within it. Initial American victories in single-ship battles did a lot to boost American morale in a difficult war, and indeed this continued thereafter to provide a shared point of pride that fed the development of American naval power and national identity. For Britain, locked in the most intense, costly, and dangerous war of its history against a France that had become less a state, as the familiar international system had understood them to be, and more a lawless military machine, the American conflict could only ever have been a distraction or damaging sideshow. For this very reason, however, it was absolutely essential to maintain dominance at sea. Britain went to extraordinary lengths to stop attacks on British commerce, to protect its merchant convoys, to insist on its right to inspect neutral shipping, to attempt to blockade and restrict American freedom of action, and to insist on victory in war and its increasing share of the world's trade.[76] The greater war against Napoleon permitted no less.

Conclusions

Once again, a major escalation of naval warfare was being driven by the imperial world view of a French leader, though in the case of Emperor Napoleon I, quite literally so, and the violence required to repair France by returning it to the heart of Europe was on a scale that simply eclipsed that unleashed by Louis XIV before him. Developments in British sea power had always been driven very directly by the fears and pressures that arose from war on the continent, and the Napoleonic wars raised the stakes significantly. In doing so, they brought naval warfare in the age of sail to its apogee and laid the path for more than a century to come of British pre-eminence at sea. To be sure, Britain had not been able to cripple the

French economy, and the Royal Navy on its own could not defeat Napoleon. He was, of course, defeated in a continental land war, and British armies played a more direct role in this. Sea power was nevertheless indispensable. It limited French colonial and commercial ambitions; it provided the essential financial 'sinews' of war, and militarily it helped, not least in maintaining the British army on the Iberian peninsula, for example. Not just victory but Britain's status and its place in the international system depended to an extraordinary extent on its naval power and wealth. This required an uncommon commitment and far more than just the large warships, well-drilled gun crews, and the famous leadership and command in war for which it is known.

The success of the eighteenth-century British state is a common historical theme. Thanks largely to work on the relative fiscal resilience of the British and French monarchies, it seems clear that British success was due not simply to the development of a 'fiscal-military' state as John Brewer described it, but to what Rodger refers to via Patrick O'Brien as a 'fiscal-naval' state whereby British success was the effect of a state that was, in effect, actually built upon huge investment in naval power.[77] The benefit for the economy of such investment was as striking as the fighting capacity of the navy itself. Many lessons are often implied from all of this work regarding constitutional and economic modernity. Yet the enormity of this financial and political commitment suggests less a self-consciously bold state than one caught in the spiralling demands of is dependence on the sea which effectively required the ability to police and dominate the world's seas. This had a great effect on the conduct of modern war, for Napoleon's fate was tied up in the struggle against maritime Britain. His Continental System required control of the whole continent, and it was Russian impatience and the opening of their ports to trade that led to Napoleon's overextension and his ill-fated Russian campaign in 1812. According to Rodger, 'had there been no economic warfare against Britain there would have been no need to make an enemy of Russia'.[78]

Britain's dependence on the sea could hardly have failed to affect international relations either, for the Royal Navy's many dramatic victories had helped to galvanise both domestic and international resolve to defeat Napoleon. Perhaps the greatest change, therefore, was not just due to the fact of British power but to its wider political effect. The popularity of naval power had fed a growing national identity in the eighteenth century, and as strategy and policy was increasingly influenced by public opinion it became woven into the very fabric of the British state.[79] This popularity, however, was not confined to Britain, and the influences that affected the growth of European navies ran in different directions. This is a measure of the extent to which navies and the trade, wealth, and even political strength with which they are intimately associated had become a new standard of political legitimacy.

There was an inevitable post-war decommissioning in the Royal Navy that was economically and socially disruptive, but Britain took no risks and made certain that it retained a greater total tonnage of large warships than France, Spain, Russia, the Netherlands, and the United States combined.[80] It was poised, therefore, to take full advantage of its position and the status and legitimacy it offered, as the nineteenth century came to be shaped by this new power. Maritime Britain now defined and occupied a new, alternative sort of political centre in Europe which other powers would compete to occupy or from which, at least, they could receive reflected status through imitation. Over the next century, Britain would cling as tenaciously to this source of legitimacy, security, and identity as the emperors and kings of late medieval Europe did to theirs.

Notes

1 Patrick Villiers, 'Et si Trafalgar n'avait jamais existé? Ou le mythe de la victoire décisive', *La Revue Maritime*, 472 (2005).
2 Jonathan R. Dull, *The Age of the Ship of the Line: The British and French Navies, 1650–1815* (Lincoln: University of Nebraska Press, 2009).
3 Roger Morriss, *The Foundations of British Maritime Ascendancy: Resources, Logistics and the State, 1755–1815* (Cambridge: Cambridge University Press, 2011); Leandro Prados De La Escosura (ed.), *Exceptionalism and Industrialisation: Britain and its European Rivals, 1688–1815* (Cambridge: Cambridge University Press, 2004); Christian Buchet, *The British Navy, Economy and Society in the Seven Years War*, trans. Anita Higgie and Michael Duffy (Woodbridge: Boydell, 2013).
4 On the general character of war at the time, John Stone, *Military Strategy: the Politics and Technique of War* (London: Continuum, 2011).
5 Andrew D. Lambert, *Nelson: Britannia's God of War* (London: Faber and Faber, 2004).
6 R.J.B. Knight, *Britain Against Napoleon: the Organization of Victory, 1793–1815* (London: Allen Lane, 2013); Roger Knight and Martin Wilcox, *Sustaining the Fleet, 1793–1815: War, the British Navy and the Contractor State* (Woodbridge: Boydell, 2010); James Davey, *The Transformation of British Naval Strategy: Seapower and Supply in Northern Europe*, 1808–1812 (Woodbridge: Boydell, 2012).
7 Rafael Torres Sánchez, *War, State and Development: Fiscal-Military States in the Eighteenth Century* (Pamplona: Ediciones Universidad de Navarra, 2007); H.V. Bowen and Agustín González Enciso, *Mobilising Resources for War: Britain and Spain at Work during the Early Modern Period* (Pamplona: Ediciones Universidad de Navarra, 2006); Jürgen G. Backhaus, *Navies and State Formation: the Schumpeter Hypothesis Revisited and Reflected* (Zurich: Lit Verlag, 2012).
8 N.A.M. Rodger, 'The Nature of Victory at Sea', *Journal for Maritime Research*, 7, 1 (2005).
9 François Crouzet, 'The Second Hundred Years War: Some Reflections', *French History*, 10, 4 (1996).
10 Philip Bobbitt, *The Shield of Achilles: War, Peace, and the Course of History* (New York: Knopf, 2002).
11 On the value of prestige and 'gloire', see Jeremy Black, *War in Europe: 1450 to the Present* (London: Bloomsbury, 2016), pp.67–70, 198.
12 N.A.M. Rodger, *The Command of the Ocean: A Naval History of Great Britain. Vol. 2, 1649–1815* (London: Allen Lane, 2004), p.261; Colin Jones, *The Great Nation: France from Louis XV to Napoleon, 1715–99* (New York: Columbia University Press, 2002).
13 Pablo Emilio Pérez-Mallaína Bueno, *Política naval española en el Atlántico, 1700–1715* (Sevilla: Consejo Superior de Investigaciones Científicas, 1982), pp.42–43, 397–407.
14 Rodger, *The Command of the Ocean*, pp.408–25.
15 Ibid., pp.226–28.
16 Shinsuke Satsuma, *Britain and Colonial Maritime War in the Early Eighteenth Century: Silver, Seapower and the Atlantic* (Woodbridge: Boydell, 2013); Philip Woodfine, 'Ideas

of Naval Power and the Conflict with Spain, 1737–1742', in Jeremy Black and Philip Woodfine (eds), *The British Navy and the Use of Naval Power in the Eighteenth Century* (Leicester: Leicester University Press, 1988); N.A.M. Rodger, 'Queen Elizabeth and the Myth of Sea-Power in English History', *Transactions of the Royal Historical Society*, 14 (2004).

17 Kathleen Wilson, 'Empire, Trade and Popular Politics in Mid-Hanoverian Britain: the Case of Admiral Vernon', *Past and Present*, 121 (1988).

18 Richard Harding, *The Emergence of Britain's Global Naval Supremacy: the War of 1739–1748* (Woodbridge: Boydell, 2010).

19 Brendan Simms, *Three Victories and a Defeat: the Rise and Fall of the First British Empire, 1714–1783* (London: Allen Lane, 2007).

20 Linda Colley, *Britons: Forging the Nation, 1707–1837* (New Haven: Yale University Press, 1992), p.368; Stephen Conway, *War, State, and Society in Mid-Eighteenth Century Britain and Ireland* (Oxford: Oxford University Press, 2006).

21 Rodger, *The Command of the Ocean*, p.178.

22 James Pritchard, *Anatomy of a Naval Disaster: the 1746 French Expedition to North America* (Montreal and Kingston: McGill-Queen's University Press, 1995).

23 Dull, *The Age of the Ship of the Line*, p.61.

24 Catherine Scheybeler, 'A Study of Spanish Naval Policy during the Reign of Ferdinand VI' (PhD, King's College London, 2014); Jonathan R. Dull, *The French Navy and the Seven Years' War* (Lincoln: University of Nebraska Press, 2005), pp.11–12.

25 On the wider war in Europe and its significance, see Franz A.J. Szabo, *The Seven Years War in Europe, 1756–1763* (London: Routledge, 2015); on the Franco-British rivalry and its global context, Daniel A. Baugh, *The Global Seven Years War, 1754–1763: Britain and France in a Great Power Contest* (Harlow: Longman, 2011).

26 George Yagi, *The Struggle for North America, 1754–1758: Britannia's Tarnished Laurels* (London: Bloomsbury, 2016), pp.159–86.

27 Nicholas Tracy, *Manila Ransomed: the British Assault on Manila in the Seven Years War* (Exeter: University of Exeter Press, 1995).

28 Rodger, *The Command of the Ocean*, p.290.

29 H.V. Bowen, 'British Conceptions of Global Empire, 1756–1783', *Journal of Imperial and Commonwealth History*, 26 (1998).

30 H.M. Scott, *The Birth of a Great Power System, 1740–1815* (London: Routledge, 2013), pp.115–16.

31 Jonathan R. Dull, *The French Navy and American Independence: a Study of Arms and Diplomacy, 1774–1787* (Princeton: Princeton University Press, 1975).

32 Stephen Conway, 'War and National Identity in the Mid-Eighteenth-Century British Isles', *English Historical Review*, 116, 468 (2001), pp.882–86.

33 Helen Dewar, 'Canada or Guadeloupe? French and British Perceptions of Empire, 1760–1763', *Canadian Historical Review*, 91, 4 (2010).

34 Jack P. Greene, *Evaluating Empire and Confronting Colonialism in Eighteenth-Century Britain* (Cambridge: Cambridge University Press, 2013).

35 Richard Harding, *Seapower and Naval Warfare, 1650–1830* (Annapolis: Naval Institute Press, 1999), p.220.

36 Hendrik Spruyt, The *Sovereign State and its Competitors: an Analysis of Systems Change* (Princeton: Princeton University Press, 1994).

37 Nicholas Tracy, 'The Falklands Crisis of 1770: Use of Naval Force', *The English Historical Review*, 90, 354 (1975).

38 Harding, *Seapower and Naval Warfare, 1650–1830*, p.236.

39 Azar Gat, *A History of Military Thought: from the Enlightenment to the Cold War* (Oxford: Oxford University Press, 2001), pp.45–55.

40 Alan Forrest, 'French Revolutionary and Napoleonic Wars', in Geoff Mortimer (ed.), *Early Modern Military History, 1450–1815* (London: Palgrave, 2004).

41 Olivier Chaline, 'Franco-British Naval Rivalry and the Crisis of the Monarchy, 1759–1789', in Swann and Félix (eds), *The Crisis of the Absolute Monarchy: France from Old Regime to Revolution* (Oxford: Oxford University Press, 2013).

42 Agustín Guimerá, 'The Offensive Strategy of the Spanish Navy, 1763–1808', in Rodger, et al. (eds), *Strategy and the Sea* (Woodbridge: Boydell, 2016).

43 Hamish Scott, 'The Importance of Bourbon Naval Reconstruction to the Strategy of Choiseul after the Seven Years' War', *International History Review*, 1(1979).

44 Dull, *The French Navy and the Seven Years' War*, p.245; Harding, *Seapower and Naval Warfare, 1650–1830*, p.231.

45 J.F. Bosher, *French Finances, 1770–1795: from Business to Bureaucracy* (Cambridge: Cambridge University Press, 1970), pp.142–65.

46 Harding, *Seapower and Naval Warfare*, p.219.

47 Patrick Villiers, 'Le Commerce colonial au fondement du financement de la Guerre d'Indépendence Américaine', in *La France sur mer: de Louis XIII à Napoléon Ier* (Paris: Pluriel, 2015).

48 Sam Willis, *Fighting at Sea in the Eighteenth Century: the Art of Sailing Warfare* (Woodbridge: Boydell, 2008).

49 Robert I. Frost, *The Northern Wars: War, State and Society in Northeastern Europe, 1558–1721* (London: Longman, 2000).

50 Brian L. Davies, *The Russo-Turkish War, 1768–1774: Catherine II and the Ottoman Empire* (London: Bloomsbury, 2016), pp.155–60; T.C.W. Blanning, *The Pursuit of Glory: Europe, 1648–1815* (London: Allen Lane, 2007), p.104.

51 Daniel Panzac, *La Marine ottomane de l'apogée à la chute de l'Empire, 1572–1923* (Paris: CNRS, 2009), pp.204–12.

52 Harding, *Seapower and Naval Warfare, 1650–1830*.

53 H.M. Scott, *The Birth of a Great Power System, 1740–1815* (Abingdon: Routledge, 2013), pp.161–62.

54 Paul W. Schroeder, *The Transformation of European politics, 1763–1848* (Oxford: Clarendon Press, 1994).

55 Blanning, *The Pursuit of Glory*, pp.588–91.

56 Hamish Scott, *British Foreign Policy in the Age of the American Revolution* (Oxford: Oxford University Press, 1990), pp.181–91.

57 For the naval dimension of the war, Sam Willis, *The Struggle for Sea Power: a Naval History of American Independence* (London: Atlantic Books, 2015).

58 Nicholas Tracy, *Navies, Deterrence, and American Independence: Britain and Sea Power in the 1760s and 1770s* (Vancouver: University of British Columbia Press, 1988); on British challenges, David Syrett, *The Royal Navy in American Waters, 1775–1783* (Aldershot: Scolar Press, 1989); Stephen Conway, *The British Isles and the War of American Independence* (Oxford: Oxford University Press, 2000).

59 Dull, *The French Navy and American Independence*.

60 N.A.M. Rodger, 'Sea-Power and Empire, 1688–1793', in P.J. Marshall (ed.), *The Oxford History of the British Empire, vol. 2, The Eighteenth Century* (Oxford: Oxford University Press, 1998); David Syrett, 'Home Waters or America? The Dilemma of British Naval Strategy in 1778', *The Mariner's Mirror*, 77, 4 (1991).

61 Villiers, 'La Chesapeake, la bataille qui a gagné la guerre d'Indépendence', in *La France sur mer* (Paris: Pluriel, 2014), pp.231–40.

62 Rodger, 'Sea-Power and Empire, 1688–1793'.

63 Rodger, *The Command of the Ocean*, p.361.

64 Harding, *Seapower and Naval Warfare, 1650–1830*, p.238.

65 Ibid., p.246.

66 William S. Cormack, *Revolution and Political Conflict in the French Navy, 1789–1794* (Cambridge: Cambridge University Press, 1995).

67 Dull, *The Age of the Ship of the Line*, p.130; Martine Acerra and Jean Meyer, *Marines et révolution* (Rennes: Ouest-France, 1988).

68 Brendan Simms, *Europe: the Struggle for Supremacy, 1453 to the Present* (London: Allen Lane, 2013), p.143.
69 Michael Duffy and Roger Morriss, *The Glorious First of June 1794: a Naval Battle and its Aftermath* (Exeter: University of Exeter Press, 2001).
70 Jean-Marcel Humbert and Bruno Ponsonnet, *Napoléon et la mer, un rêve d'empire* (Paris: Seuil, 2004).
71 Sam Willis, *In the Hour of Victory: the Royal Navy at War in the Age of Nelson* (London: Atlantic Books, 2013).
72 Dull, *The Age of the Ship of the Line*, p.157.
73 James Davey, *In Nelson's Wake: the Navy and the Napoleonic Wars* (New Haven: Yale University Press, 2015).
74 Davey, *The Transformation of British Naval Strategy*.
75 Harding, *Seapower and Naval Warfare*, p.275.
76 Andrew D. Lambert, *The Challenge: America, Britain and the War of 1812* (London: Faber and Faber, 2012); John B. Hattendorf, 'The Naval War of 1812 in International Perspective', *The Mariner's Mirror*, 99, 1 (2013).
77 N.A.M. Rodger, 'From the "Military Revolution" to the "Fiscal-Naval State"', *Journal for Maritime Research*, 13, 2 (2011); Patrick O'Brien, 'The Nature and Historical Evolution of an Exceptional Fiscal State and its Possible Significance for the Precocious Commercialization and Industrialization of the British Economy from Cromwell to Nelson', *The Economic History Review*, 64, 2 (2011), pp.438–39.
78 Rodger, *The Command of the Ocean*, p.563.
79 Jeremy Black, *The English Press in the Eighteenth Century* (London: Croom Helm, 1987); Jeremy Black, 'British Foreign Policy in the Eighteenth Century: a Survey', *The Journal of British Studies*, 26, 1 (1987), p.45.
80 Knight, *Britain Against Napoleon*, p.468.

4 The Vienna Settlement, 1815–1854

Carlos Alfaro Zaforteza

The dramatic war at sea to defeat Napoleon paralleled the rapid escalation in warfare on land that was witnessed by Clausewitz, whose thinking has done so much to shape conceptions of modern war. Yet the transition from this to the industrial, 'total' wars of the twentieth century was far from direct. The Congress of Vienna of 1815 brought much-needed stability and balance to the European system, whilst, at sea, unchallenged, and indeed largely unchallengeable, British superiority for most of the century meant that a remarkable expansion of the global economy took place under a general *Pax Britannica*. Unlike the periods of frequent, intense warfare that Europe experienced in the eighteenth century and again during the first half of the twentieth, this was an age primarily of gunboat diplomacy in which diplomatic and policing duties predominated over the strictly military function of navies.[1] In this policing of the seas, carried out chiefly but not exclusively by the British navy, the villains were pirates, slave traders, or recalcitrant protectionists; small cruisers and gunboats, rather than battleships, did most of the actual fighting. Nevertheless, national navies assumed ever greater importance, for they were particularly visible symbols of the military and industrial might of the nation-state, and they appealed to an increasingly influential public opinion. Whether singly or in fleets, in this period, warships were exhibited and paraded more than ever before. Naval affairs were a significant feature of public debate and of party politics in a way that simply was not possible in the early modern period or following a general shift of political priorities after World War One. In many ways, therefore, the nineteenth century was the golden age of European navies, despite the relative lack of dramatic sea battles. It was the apogee of naval strategic thought, naval diplomacy, and the use of navies for nation-building.

This was also an age of Industrial Revolution which transformed the maritime world and escalated naval warfare. Technological developments removed dependence on wind and tide along with the limitations of timber for shipbuilding, and they enabled efficient long-distance trade and global communications. Although Britain's industrial capacity was unmatched, giving it an undeniable advantage in this respect, it would be a mistake to reduce the nineteenth century to an account of a British-imposed peace. Indeed, it could be argued that the net effect of mass politics, industrialisation, and changes to the international system after 1815 was actually the diffusion of naval power and the steady erosion of British hegemony. It should be remembered that the Napoleonic wars had not only emphatically demonstrated British strength at sea but, more broadly, the invaluable role that naval power could play for all powers, big and small. Thus, during the nineteenth century, there was a curious combination of tacit, if still somewhat begrudging, acceptance of Britain's predominance from which everyone derived some advantage and a defiant determination to employ naval power to one's own ends. Indeed, other states retained a jealously guarded, if sometimes modest, freedom of action, and in the first half of the century Britain faced real challenges to its three main priorities: maintaining its maritime rights, such as the right of search and blockade; the right to enforce the abolition of the slave-carrying trade in West African waters; and the ability to enforce its imperial will through gunboat diplomacy. Even the introduction of steam power was problematic, for such new technologies opened opportunities to others, as well, and could make asymmetric warfare a viable strategy. Indeed prior to the outbreak of the Crimean War (1853–1856), in which a coalition of states successfully checked Russian expansion, Britain faced a Europe of navies that was far from simply prostrate. Without openly challenging Britain, other navies protected an important role for themselves internationally and consolidated their domestic political significance. In the end, a number of key legal concessions protecting neutral shipping were extracted and later enshrined into international law by the Declaration of Paris of 1856.

Maritime interests and the Congress system

The chief aims of the Congress of Vienna were to contain France and to ensure collective security through a balance of power. Britain's specific priority, however, was to exclude extra-European affairs from the settlement altogether.[2] From the outset of the peace talks, its position was firm; Foreign Secretary Lord Castlereagh insisted on 'peremptorily excluding from the general negotiations every maritime question', to the extent, he argued, that 'Great Britain may be driven out of a Congress, but not out of her maritime rights'.[3] In this way, Britain secured an unspoken acceptance of its longstanding right of search at sea and of the many imperial interests it had won during the war. Britain had conquered Ceylon, the Cape, and British Guiana from the Netherlands; Mauritius from France; and Trinidad from Spain. In Europe, bases from which it could carry on the surveillance of the continent's coasts and trade routes, and the lucrative business of smuggling, included Helgoland, Malta, and the Ionian Islands. Although Lisbon was not officially under direct British control, for all practical purposes it was an existing imperial outpost and, like Gibraltar, a British naval base.

For defensive or deterrent purposes alone, a relatively modest force would have sufficed after 1815. For Britain, however, with its comparatively tiny army, the function of the navy was now to maintain Britain's great-power status and extend its global reach, and the sheer scale of the material superiority over its rivals that was maintained is striking. The navy's core strength consisted of approximately 125 serviceable ships of the line. The next two powers, France and Russia, with around fifty and forty respectively, followed far behind.[4] Table 4.1 provides an approximate idea of the hierarchy of sea powers around 1830, organised by the total number of guns available, which puts Britain's lead into even sharper focus. Although counting guns might seem a crude way of assessing naval strength, diplomats and statesmen at the time frequently used this standard in their own calculations. Yet mere numbers still do not reveal the full extent of British superiority. Unlike its European counterparts whose status and security depended upon maintaining large standing armies, Britain did not need them to guard against invasion. The army in India, for example, was financed entirely with local resources, was remote, and did not greatly affect European politics. The financial power of the British state, the capability of its maritime industries, and the supply of experienced sailors were, on the other hand, essential factors that made it immensely superior to its potential rivals. Likewise, the navy enjoyed a unique status in British society as the senior service and an essential aspect of national identity. Contrary to the experience elsewhere at times, it never lacked political support, nor was its role ever called into question.[5]

Outside Europe, the United States expanded its influence into the Gulf-Caribbean area whilst its merchant shipping expanded worldwide. Owing to the lack of powerful continental neighbours and the country's political culture, the American navy was held as 'the only arm by which the power of this Confederacy can be estimated or felt by foreign nations and the only standing military force which can never be dangerous to our own liberties at home'.[7] Elsewhere, the picture was rather different. Of the European powers, initially only Russia, with its extensive possessions in Asia and America, was interested in checking British power. Tsar Alexander I even briefly toyed with the idea of creating an international maritime balance of power.[8] Russia could certainly not achieve this on its own. Its naval resources were always split between its two main areas of interest, the Black and Baltic seas. Furthermore, until the introduction of icebreakers at the end of the century, the Baltic Fleet lay disarmed, blocked by ice in Kronstadt

Table 4.1 Naval powers, 1830[6]

		Guns
Superpower	Great Britain	23,000
Great	France	7,200
	Russia	6,000
	Turkey–Egypt	4,400
Medium	United States	2,500
	Sweden	2,200
	Netherlands	1,400
	Austria, Brazil, Denmark, Spain	900
Small	Naples, Portugal, Sardinia	500
	Greece	200
	Prussia	10

for five months a year. As a major continental power, Russia's army was the chief defence priority and placed a heavy burden on the national budget.

Austria actually came out of the Congress with considerable maritime assets: the short coastal strip that included the port of Trieste was supplemented with the Venetian and the Dalmatian coasts. Additionally, lying in Venice dockyard was the fleet of the former Napoleonic Kingdom of Italy, which included ten ships of the line and eight frigates, either ready for sea or in advanced stages of construction. The Austrian government was not interested in a big navy, however. Indeed, despite the considerable development of Austrian maritime trade, there were good reasons to keep the navy small. Foreign Minister Metternich was well aware, for example, that a substantial navy would jeopardise the British alliance on which Austria relied. Its needs were covered with the commission of three frigates and some minor vessels. The rest were duly scrapped after several unsuccessful attempts to sell them. Still, during the Near Eastern crisis of 1840, Austria sent a squadron of two frigates, two corvettes, and some other minor ships to co-operate with the British fleet.[9] Considering Austria's great-power status, this was a tiny contribution, but it nevertheless signalled its interest in Middle Eastern politics.

Prussia's interest in sea power was even more limited. Even Greece, with its negligible military power, was vastly more powerful at sea. The government simply chose not to have a standing navy. Three armed merchant ships and five customs cutters, briefly used during the war, were sold as soon as hostilities ended. By 1848, at the outbreak of war against Denmark, the only Prussian warships in existence were a small training sloop, dependent on the Finance Ministry, and six small, oared gunboats. Other members of the new German Confederation with maritime interests, such as Oldenburg and Mecklenburg, or the Hanseatic cities of Hamburg, Bremen, and Lübeck, practised strict neutrality policies and eschewed the use of armed force.[10] Although the Netherlands and Spain had to deploy significant forces to police their still substantial colonial empires, they were too weak to effectively defend their overseas interests themselves.

In the aftermath of the Napoleonic wars, the French government's priorities were the payment of war reparations and the rebuilding of the army. Overseas interests had a low priority. All colonies and related trade had been lost during the war, and the centres of economic activity moved inland, to northern and eastern France. Saint-Domingue, the jewel of the empire, was lost for good, but France still managed to retain key overseas assets at the peace table. Britain returned a number of places, including Guadeloupe, Martinique, and Sainte-Lucie, which the French government considered the most valuable. As a protected market, they were deemed essential to the recovery of the oceanic shipping business, which was the source of skilled seamen for the navy. The country's chief maritime interest lay, however, in the Mediterranean and, although the French navy retained most of its naval materiel, for some time a lack of properly-trained personnel and low budgets kept the service in a poor state of readiness.

For Britain, there was no such post-war decline. Between 1815 and 1830 many ships of the line were replaced by new, more powerful types. The former had been hastily built during the war, with unseasoned timber, and their hulls were now rotten. The whole effort amply surpassed the avowed two-power stand-ard established in 1817 to match the combined forces of France and Russia.[11] Certainly, Britain's position as a European great power required a large, visible battle fleet, which could go some way to offsetting the lack of a strong army. Overseas, too, Britain was determined not just to protect what had been won, but to extend its influence even further, seizing key spots along the world's oce-anic routes: Singapore (1819), the Falklands (1833), Aden (1839), Hong Kong (1841), etc. Simultaneously, it occupied or laid claim to vast expanses of territory in South Africa, Australia, Burma, and India, and opened up new markets (the 'informal empire') in Latin America, West Africa, and the Far East. The vigorous activity of British traders, missionaries, and soldiers 'served notice that the rest of the world', in the words of Ronald Hyam, 'was not to be left in peace, slumbering in what they often regarded as its "pathetic contentment"'.[12]

Nevertheless, there were limits to Britain's influence, particularly within the European states system. Most notably, it could set strict limits to French overseas influence, but not to its great-power status in Europe.[13] In 1823, only eight years after the Battle of Waterloo, and despite British protests, France again invaded the Iberian Peninsula. This time it was to restore Absolutist rule in Spain, in co-operation with other continental powers. This resulted in increased French influence, which went against British interests. For Foreign Secretary Canning, this move was 'an affront to the pride . . . of England'. Decision making within the Vienna system, however, was virtually impervious to sea power; Canning's diplomacy could be backed by neither a large army nor a continental ally. In such a situation, he could not avoid the loss of face, but he could certainly limit the damage. He knew that British commerce with Spanish America would be threat-ened if Spain recovered its rebellious colonies. So, he let it be known that he was determined to prevent French forces from helping Spain this way. The navy certainly could do this, and the French knew it. Thus, Britain secured a French commitment to respect British influence in Portugal and to abstain from help-ing Spain in America but had to put up with the overthrow of the constitutional regime in Madrid.

In general, the colossal growth of the British navy and the flurry of overseas expansion after 1815 was met with grudging acquiescence or even indifference from other great powers.[14] Unilateral action and heavy-handed use of naval power did, however, also create some ambivalence. Whilst it brought an element of order and stability that enabled commerce on the world's oceans, it was also resented as an unchecked instrument of coercion in support of British interests. This seemed evident in the British intervention on behalf of Greek independence from the Ottoman Empire which led to the Battle of Navarino of 1827 when the Ottoman and Egyptian navies were defeated and soon thereafter to the first Opium War (1839) and the *Don Pacifico* affair in Greece (1850).[15] However, it should not be assumed that Britain's was the only active navy in this period. The French navy, notably, intervened in a number of places, not just in Spain and later Algeria (1830), but also alongside the British at Navarino. Two particularly illustrative examples of the successful deployment of smaller navies in the first half of the nineteenth century, however, are the rise of the Russian Black Sea Fleet and the Egyptian navy.

Two new navies: Egypt and Russia

In the first decades of the nineteenth century, the Eastern Question sparked four wars in quick succession: the Greek War of Independence (1821–1829), followed by the Russo-Turkish War (1828–1829) and the Turco-Egyptian wars (1832–1833, 1839–1840). Though never intended to challenge the British or French navies, the often-overlooked naval forces involved in these conflicts had important roles to play. They affected the fate of the Ottoman Empire and the balance of power in the Middle East. The Ottoman Empire managed to contain Russia until the destruction of its fleet at Navarino removed one of the chief obstacles to Russian expansion. Constantinople now lay vulnerable to attack by an army advancing along the coast, with its logistics well covered by maritime transport, and Russia seized the opportunity. Although no great battles took place in the ensuing war, the fleet provided sterling service in traditional support duties.[16] Victory by 1829 gave Russia the eastern shore of the Black Sea and increased influence in the Balkan Peninsula; only the Anatolian coast remained firmly in Turkish hands. Russia also secured free navigation through the Straits, the natural outlet for exports from the rich grain-producing region of Ukraine.

Tsar Nicolas I (1825–1855) valued the navy as an effective instrument of the state, and he endowed it with special status by appointing one of his most trusted aides, Prince Menshikov, as Navy Minister,[17] and by having his second son, Grand Duke Konstantin, trained as a naval officer. This consolidated the political profile of the navy and ensured adequate funding.[18] Useful in support of Russian expansion against Muslim resistance in the Caucasus, the primary focus, however, remained Constantinople. To seize the opportunity when it came, a fleet and an army were kept primed at Sevastopol ready to sail and occupy the Straits before British and French forces could arrive. Even before the introduction of steam power, this strategic manoeuvre could be performed in less than forty-eight hours by taking advantage of the prevailing northerly winds. Indeed this occurred in 1833, during the First Turco-Egyptian War, when an Egyptian army advancing through Anatolia got disturbingly close to Constantinople. After suffering several defeats, and unsuccessfully requesting British assistance, the Sultan was left with no alternative but to resort to his traditional enemy for help. Soon, a Russian Fleet anchored in the Bosporus and Russian troops encamped on the Asiatic shore. This deterred any further Egyptian advance but caused alarm among British and French statesmen.[19] The price of Russian aid was a formal Turkish promise to close the Straits to foreign warships and a notable increase of influence in Constantinople, to the detriment of Britain and France.

The Black Sea Fleet had clearly become a significant instrument of Russian power. Accordingly, it also contributed to the development of national identity. Between 1825 and 1853, the Nikolayev naval shipyard built most of the fleet's units, including twenty-five ships of the line. Sevastopol became a first-class dockyard and naval base, with impregnable fortifications and all the required facilities to support a fleet, including a costly special basin with seven dry docks capable of accommodating the largest vessels. The force that operated from this base had an average strength of fifteen ships of the line and eight frigates, supplemented in the 1840s by a substantial steam component. Although still smaller than the Baltic Fleet, it was qualitatively superior in both ships and personnel and, despite its reputation among historians, largely successful against its Turkish rival. Indeed, when the Crimean War broke out, the destruction of this fleet and its base was the chief objective of the enemy. Once the ships were scuttled, naval personnel and guns played a key role in the defence of the city. Its leaders, admirals Nakhimov, whom the contemporary press dubbed 'the soul of the defence of Sevastopol', Kornilov, and Istomin, emerged as the heroes of the siege. The three were killed in action and their names have been perpetuated in the national memory. They constitute a major component of the national myth of Sevastopol, 'the city of Russian glory'.[20]

A similar political investment shaped the experience in Egypt and, given the purpose for which it was built, the Egyptian navy must also be considered a success. Unlike the Ottoman Empire or the North African regencies, Egypt had no maritime tradition at all. It lacked all the necessary resources, such as timber, a shipbuilding industry, or seamen. At first, the navy was composed of frigates and smaller craft, built in European shipyards, and manned by French officers and Algerian seamen. They proved their worth, however, by helping to suppress the Greek rebellion, which the Sultan's navy had been unable to do. Unfortunately, this very success helped trigger the intervention of the great powers in favour of the Greek insurgents. The Egyptian army was rescued, but the navy lost most of its materiel at the Battle of Navarino.

This was not the end, however. Mohamed Ali, the energetic, modernising Pasha of Egypt (1805–1848), realised that a navy was an essential instrument to achieve his political aims and set out to rebuild it on a larger scale. Having seized power instead of being appointed by the Sultan, he needed to defend what he hoped would become a new de facto independent, hereditary state. Efficient armed forces would enable him to expand his sovereignty, defend him from his overlord, and eventually confer him recognition and legitimacy. This ambition was the cause of the two Turco-Egyptian wars. He frequently visited the ships and the dockyard at Alexandria himself and directly intervened to solve difficulties which might arise. In Egypt, the army was more popular with the elites. To raise the profile of the navy, like Nicolas I in Russia, Mohamed Ali had one of his sons trained as a naval officer.[21] French expertise was brought in to help build a domestic shipbuilding industry, and work on the Alexandria naval dockyard was begun in 1829. France was interested in a potential ally in the Eastern Mediterranean that could deploy a significant naval force. What was a mere stretch of beach was soon transformed into a large shipbuilding complex. The labour force was made up of locals, directed and trained by a member of the French navy's corps of naval constructors and a team of workers from Toulon dockyard. In January 1831, the first ship of the line was launched, the first such vessel built on the African continent. By mid-1832, three 100-gun ships had been completed and were fully operational. Up to 1840, the dockyard completed a total of twelve battleships, in addition to frigates and smaller craft.[22] It was difficult to balance the heavy cost of operating a fleet and providing the comprehensive dockyard facilities to maintain it, however, and some essential work, such as the dredging of Alexandria harbour, was sacrificed. Yet the ships themselves were reasonably well-built and equipped and competently manned. If not quite up to European standards, the quality of the Egyptian navy was certainly up to its objectives: to both support the Pasha's land campaigns and stand up to the numerically superior Ottoman navy.

Mohamed Ali was fully aware of the Western powers' qualitative and quantitative superiority and never meant to confront them.[23] Nevertheless, the sudden creation of a new fleet and its creditable performance[24] destabilised the balance of power in the Eastern Mediterranean and caused uneasiness in Britain. In 1839, when the Sultan attempted to subdue the Pasha by force, he caused a major crisis. The Ottoman army was routed; the Sultan himself died, and the Ottoman fleet defected to Alexandria. Mohamed Ali seemed all powerful. His army was victorious, and his navy now included no fewer than twenty ships of the line and fifteen frigates, making it the largest naval force in the Mediterranean. The way to Constantinople lay open. The denouement came when the powers intervened to prevent the collapse of the Ottoman Empire or a take-over by Mohamed Ali. A British fleet cut off the Egyptian army from its base in Alexandria and harassed its logistics. Although his force was far more powerful than the one destroyed at Navarino, the Pasha was a pragmatic statesman and chose not to fight. In exchange for retaining his governorship of Egypt, he renounced his conquests and returned the Turkish fleet. He was also forced to disarm. His army was reduced to 18,000 men, and he was banned from building or acquiring warships without express permission from Constantinople.[25] This meant a rapid decline of the navy. His ships had been built of unseasoned timber for expediency and were unlikely to last more than ten years. Only a sustained shipbuilding effort to replace them could maintain his naval strength. Another clause in the Sultan's decree directly struck at the Egyptian 'sinews of war'. The Anglo-Ottoman commercial treaty of 1838 was to be implemented in Egypt, just like in any other province of the Empire. The state monopolies that financed the armed forces, and kept British business from interfering, were thus eliminated. When the Crimean War broke out, Egypt's military power was much diminished. The Pasha then was able to send only 20,000 troops and a squadron of two ships of the line, three frigates, and two steamers.[26]

In exchange, however, Mohamed Ali had met his political objective: he was recognised as the legitimate, hereditary ruler of Egypt. His navy had been short-lived, and its operations were largely confined to supporting the army and to deterring Ottoman naval intervention, yet it had achieved precisely what its creator had striven for. Neither the Russian nor the Egyptian navies fit the Mahanian paradigm of an independent, ocean-going force in a quest for decisive battle. Their function was to support land operations and back their states' diplomacy. Although they grew in parallel with the commercial vitality of Odessa and Alexandria respectively, they were not meant to protect maritime trade. Skilful diplomacy was the complement to these naval forces, which were designed as army auxiliaries against a particular enemy within a restricted geographical area. As long as they were used within these limits, they could be successful. Once conflict escalated and threatened the regional balance of power, Britain and France stepped in. Yet what better evidence could there be of the effectiveness of these navies than the need that was felt to neutralise them?

The idea of a maritime coalition against a hegemon

This fate could only be avoided by a state if it formed part of a coalition that could confront the naval hegemon. The Franco-Spanish family compacts of 1733, 1743, and 1761, the armed neutralities of 1780 and 1800, and the Napoleonic attempts to unite the continental navies had all been designed to balance British naval power. Although it only materialised into policy late in the century, this idea lingered after the Napoleonic wars. To be effective, however, a coalition required at least one major navy at its heart to give it the necessary leadership and strength. The Abbé Pradt, a prominent contemporary international affairs analyst, argued that the French navy should take this role, and the idea became commonplace in the French press.[27] Honoré de Balzac, when he worked as a journalist for the *Chronique de Paris*, for example, argued that it was in France's interest 'to encourage the Russian navy, the Egyptian navy, [along with] the Danish and Swedish navies'.[28] A slight variation was proposed by the German economist Friedrich List. He was one of the intellectual forces behind the establishment of the *Zollverein* customs union and the 1848 movement for the creation of a German navy. In his influential book *Das nationale System der politischen Ökonomie* (the national system of political economy) (1841),[29] he also proposed a maritime coalition to defend the interests of small and medium powers engaged in overseas enterprise. Should they 'find their efforts obstructed by a nation assuming supremacy in manufactures, commerce, and shipping, they can only resort to an alliance among themselves to destroy or nullify such unwarrantable pretensions'.[30] The allusion to Britain is clear enough. To achieve this, he proposed incorporating Denmark and the Netherlands within a unified Germany 'which would thus obtain all it wants at present; that is, fisheries, naval power, with maritime and colonial commerce'. Liberated from the burden of maintaining costly armies, these two countries would then be able to further contribute to the common maritime and colonial assets.[31]

There were even echoes of this wider concern about naval imbalance in Britain. In 1827, the Prussian government imposed punitive duties on foreign shipping, and a member of parliament derisively complained of 'the insolent dictation of a petty German prince to which our rejoinder should have been from the mouths of our cannon'. Yet some British statesmen were aware of the need to restrain free-trade imperialism. The response to this bellicose attitude came from the Secretary of War, William Huskisson, who warned against unprincipled unilateralism:

To act as if there were one rule of international law for ourselves, and a different rule for other states, would be not only monstrous injustice, but the only course, I verily believe, by which our maritime power could be brought into jeopardy. Such a pretension would call for and warrant a combination of all the world to defeat it; and it is only in such a combination, acting together in a just cause, that this Country can have anything to apprehend.[32]

The Duke of Wellington, prime minister in the succeeding cabinet, also felt uneasy and privately expressed the same reservations to his Secretary of War:

We have possession of nearly every valuable post and colony in the world, and I confess that I am anxious to avoid exciting the attention and jealousy of other Powers by extending our possessions and setting the example of the gratification of a desire to seize upon new territories.[33]

In 1846, the marriage of the sister of the Queen of Spain, Isabel II, to a son of the French king seemed to confirm British fears that France was planning an alliance with Naples and Spain, also ruled by Bourbon monarchs.[34] In the 1840s, these two countries created substantial steam forces, which proved capable of independent action in the Mediterranean and rendered good service during the revolutionary events of 1848 and 1849. Yet maritime states with substantial interests overseas, such as Spain and Holland, strove to stay neutral, fearing the terrible prospect of either French invasion or the loss of overseas colonies to Britain. The greatest prospect for France came after the Crimean War. In 1857, Napoleon III let Bismarck know that he favoured the naval development of Prussia and other states as part of a plan to establish a balance of power at sea.[35]

Neutrality: the Declaration of Paris, 1856

Apart from its support for Mohamed Ali's Egyptian navy, however, it seems that France made no serious effort to organise a maritime coalition. Despite the lack of any balance to British hegemony, there was nevertheless still opposition around the principle of neutrality and specifically the exercise of what Britain considered to be its 'maritime rights'. Such was Britain's sense of entitlement that it felt it could declare a formal blockade even if the necessary naval forces to enforce it were not, in fact, present. This was known as a paper blockade, which provided a pretence for capturing enemy property on the high seas, regardless of the carrying ship's flag, on the dubious grounds that it was technically running the blockade. The British considered such tactics among their chief tools of economic warfare, highly valued because they were believed to have saved the country during the Revolutionary and Napoleonic wars.[36] Yet they ran counter to the majority interpretation of international law. Most states advocated the 'freedom of the seas' doctrine. According to it, neutral ships were entitled to carry enemy goods ('free ships, free goods'), except for those declared contraband of war.[37] This argument was a major concern in international relations; it had provoked the armed neutralities of 1780 and 1800, was a cause of war with the United States in 1812, and constituted an underlying theme in the nineteenth-century debates over sea power and international law.

British abuses during the wars of the French Revolution and empire left a bitter taste, and this was widely reflected in French propaganda.[38] Hostile reactions were certainly not limited to the French though. On the eve of the Crimean War, Denmark, Sweden, and the United States in particular could retaliate if their shipping was subjected to search by British warships by supporting privateers, something that would win international sympathy. If they chose to, the Scandinavian states could allow privateers access to their ports and deny the same to belligerent warships.[39] Prior to the outbreak of the war, Russia, of course, was the biggest threat. Taking advantage of strained Anglo-American relations and the precedent of American privateers conducting hostilities on behalf of Latin American states during their struggle for independence, Russia could issue letters of marque in the United States.[40] Therefore, Britain could not afford to alienate neutrals if it wanted to keep Russia diplomatically isolated. Moreover, maintaining the French alliance was crucial to winning the war, and this meant agreeing to the doctrine of 'free ships, free goods'. In exchange, neutrals agreed to deny privateers access to their ports and to ban their citizens from privateering.[41]

Britain had agreed to this concession only for the duration of hostilities. Yet at the end of the war, French diplomacy managed to enshrine these principles in the Declaration of Paris of 1856, the first major international agreement regulated by multilateral treaty.[42] There were several reasons for this sea change in British policy. Despite its logistical capabilities, Britain struggled to maintain its military strength during the conflict. It was the French army which played the leading role in the fall of Sevastopol, the pivotal event of the war. For all the usefulness of navies, the yardstick of power in European politics was still land power. The British Army proved too small, and an attempt to recruit additional troops in the United States triggered a diplomatic crisis. Anglo-American relations deteriorated to the extent that there was even talk of war, which in turn further weakened the British position in Europe. To reject the French initiative would only have made the British situation worse.

Moreover, many British statesmen and some public opinion advocated the end of the 'old mercantilist system'. The abolition of the 'maritime rights' was a logical step after the repeal of the Corn Laws (1846) and of the Navigation Acts (1849) which had long restricted the carrying of goods to British colonies to British ships. The Foreign Secretary, Lord Clarendon, convinced his boss Lord Palmerston that:

> it is clear that we can never again re-establish our ancient doctrine respecting neutrals, and that we must in any future war adhere to the exception to our rule which we admitted at the beginning of the present war, under pain of having all mankind against us.[43]

The Economist, the leading free-trade journal, also supported the abolition of the 'maritime rights':

the mode of carrying out the claim by British men-of-war stopping and examining every neutral ship on the high seas was most vexatious . . . Their captains and crews were exposed to much overbearing and even insolent treatment . . . Our mode of carrying out the right of search therefore tended to bring us in every place, wherever we had a ship of war, into angry collision with the subjects of every neutral nation, and provoke an extension of the hostilities in which we were engaged.

It was necessary, then, the article continued, to 'remove from ourselves sources of annoyance, and make us more friendly neighbours to all maritime nations'.[44] Though forced to make concessions and facing fierce opposition, in the end the government did manage to defend British prestige and to protect its shipping industry by negotiating the abolition of privateering as a form of warfare in exchange.[45]

Slave trade: the right of search controversy in the 1840s

There was also effective international opposition to Britain's determined efforts to enforce the abolition of the slave trade. To many, this was just another way for Britain to try to maintain naval supremacy, and much of the opposition it faced was actually focused on the controversial, related issue of the right of search and the affront to national pride that it represented. In 1841, British diplomacy seemed to have achieved a great success by persuading Russia, Austria, Prussia, and France to sign the Quintuple Treaty granting each other the right of search in West African waters and treating slave trading as piracy. Yet this was never ratified because, in practice, it meant the monopoly of enforcement to the British navy, since no other naval force existed in the area. This prospect caused particular alarm in France and the United States. Although they did not abolish slavery until 1848 and 1862 respectively, the outcry was about the defence of the 'freedom of the seas' against so-called British 'maritime rights'. British policy in the Egyptian crisis of 1840, Anglo-American tension over the Maine boundary issue, and the *Caroline* affair were still raw issues in France and the United States. Violent episodes also lived in popular memory, such as the attack on the Danish frigate *Freya* and the capture of the convoy that she escorted in 1800, or the controversial attack by the *Leopard* on the American *Chesapeake* in 1807. Such aggression against neutrals, and the impressment into the British navy of sailors on American ships, had been major causes of the War of 1812. French propaganda and British intransigence ensured that these outrages were widely known and lingered in the collective memory. In antebellum United States, this was reflected through the traditional condemnation of British maritime 'tyranny' in Fourth-of-July public addresses.[46]

This was a serious concern for Britain because a Franco-American alliance could have seriously constrained its imperial policies. There were further complications, too, because the same ships, trade networks, and suppliers were being used for both the slave trade and the growing palm oil trade.[47] Distinguishing between a slaver and an ordinary ship at sea became difficult, and this led to many abuses. The numerous wooden casks, generally carried disassembled, could be seen as evidence of slaving, because they were needed to provide water on the long passage, but they could also well be used in the oil trade. Innocent or not, captured vessels would usually be taken to Sierra Leone, the site of the mixed court. By the time a verdict was issued, the crew's health, the cargo, and the ship had usually deteriorated beyond recovery. Abolitionist zeal, national prejudice, or lust for prize money led to the capture and ulterior condemnation of many innocent ships.[48] To those with a stake in the West Africa trade, this all seemed designed to preserve the privileged position of the Liverpool merchants. The British navy not only protected them but also frightened away foreign competitors.[49]

These concerns all came to a head around 1840, with the escalation of British efforts against the slave trade and negotiations for the Quintuple Treaty the following year. The British government increased the West Africa squadron, concluded treaties with the chiefs of the regional states, promoted commercial agriculture, and sent steam gunboats up the River Niger. At the same time, the navy increased its attacks against slave factories ashore.[50] Although these measures were implemented largely out of genuine abolitionist concern, they caused alarm among the oil traders. They looked like a concerted effort at British imperial expansion, with the right of search being used as an instrument of intimidation. Even abolitionists in France and the United States, the only powers capable of challenging Britain, seemed more concerned with checking British sea power than the moral duty to curb the slave trade.

In the United States, the southern slave-holding lobby saw the British as a direct threat. Yet American attitudes toward the right of search are perhaps best illustrated by Secretary of State, and future president, John Quincy Adams in 1822. Asked by the British minister in Washington if he could think of anything more wicked than the slave trade, he replied: 'Yes, admitting the right of search by foreign officers of our vessels upon the seas in time of peace; for that would be making slaves of ourselves'.[51] The crisis was triggered by an American diplomat. Lewis Cass, the American ambassador in Paris, was an ambitious politician and a 'slave power' representative. As soon as the Quintuple Treaty was signed, off his own back Cass protested strongly to the French government and wrote a pamphlet denouncing British policy. This was initially published in French, but it was soon translated into English and German and widely circulated on both sides of the Atlantic. Its effect on French and American public opinion was considerable. He argued that the treaty made the British navy the 'police of the seas . . . who may be harsh or lenient, as her prejudices or interest may dictate'.[52] Cass was forced to resign because he became an obstacle to Anglo-American negotiations, though his popularity back home soared, and this contributed significantly to his nomination as the Democratic Party presidential candidate for the 1848 election.[53]

In August 1842, Anglo-American negotiators reached an agreement. Britain did not officially renounce impressment, and the United States government did not grant the right of search, but it did agree to deploy a naval force of a total of eighty guns in West Africa, ostensibly to co-operate in the suppression of the slave trade. The chief reason, however, was the protection of American trade, against both the British navy and other Africans. The instructions to Commodore Matthew C. Perry, commander of the four-ship squadron deployed, explicitly stated that the United States 'meant to give to England and all the world an assurance of her determination and ability to protect her own flag against abuse, and thus to remove all pretext for any interference with it by other nations'.[54] Given the small number of ships and the large patrol area, slave traders continued to use the American flag, confident that the chances of meeting an American warship were virtually non-existent. Yet the main aim was achieved: the force was sufficient to protect American national honour and trade. In his 1842 State of the Union message, President Tyler announced the end of the British practice of

> subjecting to visitation ships sailing under the American flag, which, while it seriously involved our maritime rights,[55] would subject to vexation a branch of our trade which was daily increasing, and which required the fostering care of Government.[56]

An agreement between France and Britain took longer to reach.

Both governments did have reciprocal right of search by treaties concluded in 1831 and 1833. Thereafter, French slave trade practically ceased to exist, whereas French legitimate trade with West Africa increased. Just prior to the signing of the Quintuple Treaty, news of the seizure of two French ships appeared in the press, enflaming French public opinion. The result was a cross-party consensus over the need to check British power; national honour and interests were threatened, and the *chambre des députés* refused ratification.[57] Adolphe Billaut, the opposition leader in the *chambre*, a man closely connected to the shipping business, argued that Britain's persistent efforts to get the right of search was patent evidence of its determination to achieve the sovereignty of the seas. The three treaties that France had signed with respect to the slave trade, he claimed, undermined French sea power, the country's alliance policy, and the development of trade.[58] Even Alexis de Tocqueville, a noted anglophile and abolitionist, upheld French national honour. In a famous speech at the *chambre*, he argued for the end of the right of search. The treaties, he said, were unlike any other because they 'confer to the armed forces of one nation the extraordinary right to seize criminals from another, and where? In the seclusion of the ocean; where anything can be done; where anything might be assumed'.[59] As a consequence, Tocqueville's reputation in Britain sharply deteriorated, even among intellectuals; John Stuart Mill's correspondence with him was discontinued precisely from this date.[60] All of the treaties were repudiated, and a new agreement was not finally reached until 1845.

Like its American counterpart, it entailed a French naval presence and negated the right of search. By March 1846 the French West Africa station comprised twenty-nine ships, including seven steamers, with a total of 180 guns. This was a major deployment, surpassed only by the 1830 expedition to Algeria, and much larger than the US squadron. Its real purpose was not to hunt down non-existent French slavers. It was even too large for deterring British abuses and supporting

French trade. The main purpose was to balance British presence in the area and uphold France's ranking as the second strongest naval power.[61] It was no coincidence that that same year the government had a bill approved for a large increase in naval strength. By the mid-1840s, therefore, a considerable international naval force had gathered in West Africa, which included a Portuguese squadron based in Angola and Spanish ships based at Fernando Poo.[62] The main reason for this international display of naval force was the alarm caused by British high-handed assertion of the right of search. The practical monopoly of British naval presence in the area had been broken, yet British imperialism in other areas went largely unchallenged.

Gunboat diplomacy and 'free trade'

The Anglo-Chinese wars of the mid-nineteenth century are a classic example of free-trade imperialism.[63] The second of these wars (1856–1860) provides a particularly interesting illustration of the limits of gunboat diplomacy because, in this case, it met with determined resistance, and it took escalation to full-scale hostilities to bring China to terms. The 'Canton City Question' was at the heart of the matter. Foreigners whose factories lay outside the walls legally had access to the inner city, but they were routinely denied this access in practice. In China, this was seen as an important act of resistance to British imperialism, and by 1856 the issue had become a matter of national honour for both sides. The British consul, Harry Parkes, and his superior, the Governor of Hong Kong, Sir John Bowring, had been spoiling for a fight, and they found their opportunity in October 1856 when the Chinese police captured the British-registered ship *Arrow* before Canton. Owned by a Chinese trader resident in Hong Kong, the vessel was engaged in dubious business, and its British papers had expired. Parkes demanded the return of the crew along with an apology, and he requested some warships to be sent from Hong Kong. Chinese resistance forced a steady escalation, however. The four forts that guarded the access to the city from the sea were silenced by the overwhelming firepower of the British squadron and were occupied by landing parties. Yet this was not enough to make the Chinese authorities yield. Next came an attack on the forts defending the city's waterfront. These were also taken without much resistance, and landing parties took positions in the factories. The final step was an attack on the city itself. Although by European standards it was an almost defenceless city, the naval landing parties were insufficient for the task of investing and occupying Canton. Only the army could have provided a sufficient number of troops. As an alternative, Parkes chose to bombard the city. Since it was densely populated, loss of life and property was heavy.[64]

When the news arrived in London it caused acrimonious controversy. The press, sympathetic to the government, justified the bombardment on the grounds of national honour and the security of trade. *The Times* justified the use of naval force to defend the 'liberty and security for our commerce'.[65] The opposition used the bombardment to attack the government of Lord Palmerston. It complained about the frequent resort to force for allaying difficulties. Richard Cobden, in particular, criticised British merchants for being over-dependent on the guns of the Royal Navy. Palmerston lost his case in Parliament, but won it in the subsequent election, which pivoted around this issue. He knew that his bellicose, patriotic policies were popular with a large portion of the electorate. Thus, he got ample support for his policies to 'persuade' unwilling governments to accept free trade. His electoral victory enabled him to send more ships to cope with the war that his deputies had started in China.[66]

Britain was not the only power to use gunboat diplomacy. A combined Anglo-French force attempted to open the navigation and trade of the enormous la Plata basin to foreign ships. Buenos Aires was blockaded from the sea, and in 1845 a combined squadron escorted a convoy of more than a hundred merchant ships up river to the province of Corrientes and Paraguay. However, river batteries harassed the convoy at various points, and the attempt was not repeated. The blockade was maintained for some years, but it failed to coerce the Buenos Aires government, led by Juan Manuel Rosas, and was finally abandoned.[67] Blockade and naval operations had not been enough. It took the intervention of a regional power, Brazil, along with the local land forces of the governor of Corrientes, to finally overthrow Rosas in 1852.

Brazil was keen to uphold Uruguay's independence and keep Mato Grosso's access to the sea via the Paraguay River. Its modern, efficient navy was instrumental in achieving control of the Rio de la Plata. It ensured the use of the river for troop movements, simultaneously denying it to the enemy.[68] This is an important reminder that such medium powers could also be involved in the expansion of their own trade, and some had the capability and the political will to intervene. Resistance to western imperialism was possible, as Rosas proved, and China, too, would eventually succeed. New technologies, such as the introduction of steam power, also allowed European powers to undermine British naval hegemony somewhat.

The introduction of steam power

In 1807, the first commercial steamboat, the *Clermont*, started plying the waters between New York and Albany. It was built by the American inventor Robert Fulton and equipped with a British-made engine. Soon, steam navigation became widespread in the coastal and inland waters of the United States and western Europe. If the usefulness of steam power for transport and communications was self-evident, in its early stages of development it was considered inappropriate for fighting at sea; naval experts were not impressed by the early attempts to build effective fighting ships.[69] Many difficulties had to be overcome. A boiler explosion, caused by either cannon shot or accident, was the most dreaded disaster on board a steamer. Enemy fire could, likewise, easily immobilise a ship by damaging either the engines or the paddlewheels. Furthermore, the weight and space taken up by the engines, boilers, and coal precluded these vessels from carrying an adequate armament. Early steam engines were prone to break down and consumed large amounts of coal. Steamers frequently had to enter a dry dock to have their hull cleaned. Otherwise, they would suffer undue loss of speed and increase their coal consumption. For many years, engine repair facilities, a large supply of coal, and dry docks were difficult to find outside certain areas in the United States and Europe. Engineers were scarce and not subject to military discipline, which meant they did not fit into the command structure.

In contrast, the sailing ship represented a mature technology, which reached its zenith precisely in the decades after the Napoleonic wars. The last ships of the line were substantially larger, better designed, and more powerfully armed than those present at Trafalgar. Only by the 1850s did marine engineering developments finally enable the fitting of screw propellers and lighter, less bulky engines that did not seriously interfere with their endurance, seaworthiness, or firepower. Until then, both naval officers and statesmen continued to regard the sailing ship of the line as the yardstick of sea power.[70]

Transatlantic navigation, however, benefited from a combination of private investment in the development of the necessary technology and government financial help. In 1838, the first crossing of the Atlantic under steam took place, but the building and running of large steamers across the ocean was still too risky for the private sector. The loss of a single ship, not infrequent at the time, represented a heavy loss of life and capital and could cause the bankruptcy of the ship owner. But the benefit of fast transatlantic communications was too tempting, and these only grew with increased political control of overseas territories and new business opportunities. Around 1840, the British government subsidised the first transatlantic steam packet lines, the Cunard and Royal Mail, which covered the North and South Atlantic respectively, and the Peninsular and Oriental, which covered the route to India. In compensation, the vessels were built with a heavier scantling, so that in a national emergency they could be used as either warships or troop transports.

A similar project was attempted in France, but its private sector had neither the required capital nor the industrial capacity to build the ships. Naval yards, therefore, had to be used to build the eighteen large steamers that were planned, but only a few of these ever saw commercial use. Yet the programme was a success in other respects: French naval yards developed their ability to build steam vessels, a marine engineering industry was created, and the navy acquired a fleet of fine steamers.[71] This force provided the army with increased strategic mobility, lent credibility to the threat of an invasion of Britain, and proved its worth in various interventions in the Mediterranean. French strategists had been quick to see the usefulness of steam power. General Henri-Joseph Paixhans (1783–1854) inaugurated the material school of strategy, which took advantage of the accelerated pace of technological development. In his book *Nouvelle force maritime* (1822) he proposed an alternative solution to France's chronic naval inferiority vis-à-vis Britain: a naval force composed of steamers armed with shell guns. The vessels would be smaller, with smaller crews, than a ship of the line. These fast, manoeuvrable vessels would destroy the enemy battle fleet with their powerful shell guns.[72] This revolutionary concept of asymmetric warfare would result in much-reduced costs of materiel and personnel and alleviate France's structural lack of experienced seamen.

Unfortunately, these ideas were not translated into policy. In a peaceful context, the French navy had other priorities. Still, the fleet that conducted the amphibious expedition against Algiers in 1830 already included seven steamers, which proved to be extremely useful.

Two decades later, a French naval officer set forth his ideas in more volatile political circumstances. In 1844, François d'Orléans, Prince de Joinville (1818–1900), a naval officer and the third son of King Louis Philippe, published a famous article, 'Note sur l'état des forces navales de la France', which was widely circulated and sparked an invasion scare in Britain.[73] His ideas were even more radical than Paixhans's, since they bypassed the concept of battle. He argued that a fleet of steamers could cross the Channel in a matter of hours, dodge the British fleet, and land 30,000 troops. Given the small British homeland army, this invasion force would have little difficulty in occupying London. This knock-out strategy made the traditional sailing battle fleet irrelevant. It was not clear among naval experts whether it would succeed in practice, but what really mattered was that statesmen and public opinion believed it was possible. The risk of invasion, however small, existed. Lord Palmerston conceded in the House of Commons that 'the Channel is no longer a barrier. Steam navigation has rendered that which was before impassable by a military force nothing more than a river passable by a steam bridge'.[74] The press echoed this and similar declarations by other leading public figures. Even the proliferation of steamers in the Brazilian, Sardinian, and Neapolitan navies caused concern and fears of a 'maritime federation' against Britain. Some of these statements were disingenuous, meant to increase the naval budget. Yet the net effect was that continental powers no longer considered Britain's position invulnerable, and the confidence of the British people in security from invasion was undermined.

The *Note* had essentially been a disgruntled officer's effort to call domestic attention to the weaknesses of the French navy, but Joinville's status gave it a certain ominous authority. Additionally, public opinion in both countries had been enflamed by the press over relatively minor issues relating to Anglo-French rivalry overseas. Britain's international status and identity as the first maritime power was a sensitive issue for the British public; any perceived undermining of this position caused general anxiety. The possibility of the deployment of a *force de frappe* of troop-carrying steamers across the Channel, poised for invasion, simply brought such feelings to a boil. The consequence was the mid-century invasion panics of 1844, 1851–1853, and 1859–1861. Although the government of Louis Philippe had no hostile intention, with the steamers mostly deployed in the Mediterranean, an overreaction of sorts was probably required to reassure the British public.[75]

What followed was a naval armaments race which only ended in the mid-1860s.[76] France attempted to shorten the gap in naval capacity by taking advantage of rapidly changing technology. Yet it had to cope with British industrial might, at a time when the United Kingdom was effectively the workshop of the world. Its maritime industries could build the largest, most advanced warships, faster and cheaper than any other country. The greatest asset to somehow offset this disadvantage was the corps of naval constructors. The superb scientific education received at the *École Polythechnique* had no match and enabled technological innovation. Yet France never intended to achieve quantitative parity with Britain. As in other continental states, the navy came second to the army, the real basis of great-power status and national security on the continent. Admiral Jurien de La Gravière cogently explained the objective of French sea power to his British friend Admiral Mends in 1860:

> [You] wish to be incontestably masters of the sea, and to fear neither us nor any maritime coalition; [we] do not object to this pretension up to a certain point. We should not wish, however, that your security should be such, that you could imagine yourselves able to treat us in any way you like.[77]

Although steam power had not yet been introduced into battle fleets by mid-century, three examples of its use, by the British to deter rebellion in Ireland, by Spain to suppress a Carlist revolt, and the improvisation of a German navy against Denmark, all reveal its growing value and reinforce the role of navies as expressions of national identity and guarantors of internal order and stability. Britain's greatest domestic security problem was Ireland. The early development of steam navigation in the country enabled the small army in the British Isles to better cope with its commitments on both sides of the Irish Sea. The ability to transport troops quickly, routinely carried out by the Dublin Steam Packet Company since the 1820s, no longer required large garrisons on both islands. Nevertheless, in 1831–1832 the army was stretched almost beyond its resources. The Reform Bill riots required the deployment of 19,000 troops in the London area. Simultaneously, the so-called Tithe War in Ireland demanded substantial military presence. Catholic Irish peasants resisted paying taxes to finance the Anglican Church. Thus the navy sent two of its precious few steamers. They could enter or leave harbours at any time and quickly turn up at any point required, either to use their guns or land troops. Their ubiquitous presence deterred populations in coastal areas from resorting to violence. In 1848, the threat of a full-fledged rebellion again required a heavy deployment of troops. Admiral Sir Charles Napier commanded a fleet that patrolled the Irish coast. It included no fewer than nineteen steamers, chiefly based at Dublin and Cork, ready to transport troops to any trouble spot. Others operated close inshore or on rivers, where sailing ships had limited mobility. Notably, HMS *Rhadamanthus* anchored before Waterford with its guns trained on the city to deter a possible popular revolt.[78]

The mobility provided by mechanical propulsion was essential in the civil conflict in Spain, too. For a considerable period, the Liberal government had to cope with the Absolutist threat. The mountains of Catalonia were a hotbed of Carlism and the base of active guerrilla forces. In October 1848, after the threat of revolution had been dealt with, the Spanish government concentrated its efforts on ending the two-year conflict. The army in Catalonia had to be reinforced as soon as possible, but the country's difficult land communications precluded this. No railway network existed yet, and private steamers were few and small. Fortunately, the Spanish navy was building up a strong steam component. In less than a month, a dozen navy steamers, most of them built in British shipyards, supplemented by five chartered mail packets, managed to transport 12,000 soldiers to the seat of war. These troops came from places as diverse as Corunna, Cadiz, Malaga, and the African enclaves. With increased strength, the army of Catalonia was at last able to defeat the Carlist guerrillas. The navy steamers thus proved invaluable in ending a conflict that had been festering and threating to spread to the whole country.[79] This was neither the first nor the last occasion in which steamers were used to deal with civil unrest. Similarly, the Neapolitan navy also used its steamers to put down the revolt of 1848 in Sicily. During this period of revolution, other navies, such as those of Sardinia, Austria, the Sicilian Republic, and the Frankfurt Parliament desperately struggled to purchase any available steam vessel on the market that could either be converted into a warship or was large enough for troop transport.

At the start of the First Schleswig-Holstein War (1848–1851), the Frankfurt Parliament also felt the urgent need for a fleet. The Danish blockade of the German coast outraged public opinion all over Germany and caused a clamour for a national navy. This would be composed entirely of steamers, which could come out at any time and attack the blockading force. Steamers could easily be converted into useful warships, and they required fewer experienced sailors than sailing ships. Even with these moderate demands on human resources, however, it was difficult to find adequate personnel, hence the cosmopolitan character of the crews; they included British, American, and Belgian officers and seamen. Command of the fleet was eventually given to Rudolf Brommy, a German who started his career as a merchant seaman and afterwards served in the Chilean and Greek navies. The next fourteen posts down the command ladder, however, were all held by foreigners.[80]

Ships were also difficult to acquire. As mentioned above, the market for sizeable steamers was still scarce. Only three were available domestically, provided by the Hamburg-based shipping company *Hanseatische Dampfschifffarts Gessellschaft*. A further three, *Der Königliche Ernst August, Grossherzog von Oldenburg*, and *Frankfurt*, were bought from the British shipyard Patterson, Bristol, under the misleading cover names of *Cora, Inca*, and *Cacique* to circumvent British neutrality laws. They were most likely under construction for other customers and were bought at much higher cost than in normal circumstances. Finally, a search for larger ships during the armistice yielded three transatlantic steamers, *Barbarossa, Erzherzog Johan*, and *Hansa*. These were bought from the Cunard, Royal Mail (British), and Black Ball (American) lines respectively.[81] Coming from subsidised companies, they were designed so that they could be easily converted into warships; their hulls and decks were prepared to mount heavy guns. The origins of the ships reflect the predominance of the British shipbuilding and shipping industries. Out of nine units, six, including two of the largest, were British-built and British-owned. Only two of the small ones were built in Germany. The *Hansa* was built in the United States, the country with the most developed maritime industries after Britain. The great demand and versatility of steamers, and the vitality of the British marketplace, is further demonstrated by the liquidation of the fleet after the war. Six vessels were sold to the British General Steam Navigation Company. In contrast, sailing ships proved useless. The former Danish frigate *Eckernförde*, captured at the battle of the same name, was a purpose-built warship. But like all sailing ships it demanded a large crew of experienced officers and seamen, which was beyond the resources of the Reichsmarine.

Despite the lack of a domestic shipbuilding industry and other difficulties, this new navy had tremendous political impact and symbolic significance. As with most navies in history, this is most clearly reflected in the names given to the ships, which evoked German economic and political power and even, by naming some after liberal German monarchs, German liberal constitutionalism. This attempt to improvise a fleet is particularly relevant because it boldly played on national sentiment and the collective memory of a unified Germany. It certainly won the support of German public opinion and was later used as a precedent for the Imperial navy. It was also an attempt at asymmetrical warfare. With the acquisition of steamships, the Frankfurt Parliament got around the difficulties of setting up a traditional naval force: the time and expense which would have meant the construction of sailing ships of the line and frigates, the large numbers of experienced officers and seamen required, and the heavy running costs. Instead, it applied Paixhans's theories. The Reichsmarine did not have time to prove itself, and it was disbanded shortly after the war. It nevertheless shows that by mid-century the idea that technology provided new, alternative solutions to the standard instruments of sea power was commonplace. Whether putting down a rebellion or breaking a blockade, by 1848 both naval officers and statesmen saw a valid military instrument in those frail-looking paddle-wheel steamers, which were already revolutionising maritime transport and communications. The operations discussed here are perhaps not as compelling as traditional naval battles, but their political effects were more relevant, and the German experience foreshadowed more ambitious national naval projects to come.

Conclusions

British naval hegemony in the decades following the Congress of Vienna was largely undisputed. However, in different ways other powers, large and small, were able to operate effectively in the maritime environment to further their own interests and could, to some extent, limit British freedom of action. These policies fed the perception that navies were essential policy tools as well as popular expressions of national identity and of political coherence. Similarly, whilst industrial Britain enjoyed many obvious technical advantages, in other countries the advent of steam reinforced the value of navies in military thought and provided important new opportunities.

Notes

1   Ken Booth, *Navies and Foreign Policy* (London: Croom Helm, 1979), pp.15–25.
2   Paul W. Schroeder, *The Transformation of European Politics, 1763–1848* (Oxford: Oxford University Press, 1994), pp.514–15, 73–75.
3   Castlereagh to Lord Cathcart, British Ambassador to Russia, 14 July 1813, in Marquis of Londonderry (ed.), *Correspondence, Despatches, and other Papers, of Viscount Castlereagh, vol. 9* (London: John Murray, 1853), pp.34–35.
4   Jan Glete, *Navies and Nations: Warships, Navies and State Building in Europe and America, 1500–1860, vol. 2* (Stockholm: Almqvist & Wiksell International, 1993), pp.554, 80, 656–69.
5   C.J. Bartlett, *Great Britain and Sea Power: 1815–1853* (Oxford: Clarendon Press, 1963); Andrew D. Lambert, *The Last Sailing Battlefleet: Maintaining Naval Mastery, 1815–1850* (London: Conway Maritime Press, 1991).
6   Jérôme Louis, 'La question d'Orient sous Louis-Philippe' (PhD thesis, École Practique des Hautes Études, Paris, 2004), pp.63–64. Figures rounded off. Brazil added for completeness. Categorisation as in original document.
7   John Quincy Adams, 'First Annual Message, 5 Dec. 1825', in Gehard Peters and John T. Woolley, 'The American Presidency Project', University of California, www.presidency.ucsb.edu/index.php. Accessed 20 December 2013.
8   Jacques-Henri Pirenne, *La Sainte-Alliance: organisation européenne de la paix mondiale*, 2 vols (Neuchâtel: Éditions de la Baconnière, 1946–1949), pp.I, 265–266, and II, 2, 9, 16–17, 220–23.
9   Lawrence Sondhaus, *The Habsburg Empire and the Sea: Austrian Naval Policy, 1797–1866* (West Lafayette: Purdue University Press, 1989), pp.35–52, 101–04, 275.
10 Walter Hubatsch, 'Die deutsche Reichsflotte 1848 und der Deutsche Bund', in Walter Hubatsch (ed.), *Die erste Deutsche Flotte 1848–1853* (Herford: E.S. Mittler & Sohn, 1981), pp.30–31.
11 Andrew D. Lambert, 'Preparing for the Long Peace: the Reconstruction of the Royal Navy, 1815–1830', *The Mariner's Mirror*, 82 (1996), p.49.
12 Ronald Hyam, *Britain's Imperial Century, 1815–1914: a Study of Empire and Expansion* (Basingstoke: Palgrave, 2002), pp.8–15, quoted on p.9.
13 Bartlett, *Great Britain and Sea Power*, pp.65–68; Roger Bullen, 'The Great Powers and the Iberian Peninsula, 1815–48', in Alan Sked (ed.), *Europe's Balance of Power, 1815–1848* (Basingstoke: Macmillan, 1979), pp.62–66; Jacques Droz, *Histoire diplomatique de 1848 à 1919* (Paris: Dalloz, 1952), pp.299–302.
14 C.J. Bartlett, *Defence and Diplomacy: Britain and the Great Powers 1815–1914* (Manchester: Manchester University Press, 1993), pp.9–10; C.A. Bayly, *Imperial Meridian: the British Empire and the World, 1780–1830* (London: Longman, 1989), pp.227–28.
15 C.J. Bartlett, 'Statecraft, Power and Influence', in C.J. Bartlett (ed.), *Britain Pre-eminent: Studies in British World Influence in the Nineteenth Century* (London: Macmillan, 1969), pp.183–84, 86; C.A. Bayly, *The Birth of the Modern World, 1780–1914: Global Connections and Comparisons* (Oxford: Blackwell, 2004), pp.137–38; F.R. Bridge and Roger Bullen, *The Great Powers and the European States System, 1815–1914* (London: Longman, 1980), p.31.
16 John C.K. Daly, *Russian Seapower and 'The Eastern Question', 1827–41* (Annapolis: Naval Institute Press, 1991), pp.18–34.
17 Jacob W. Kipp, 'The Grand Duke Konstantin Nikolaevic: the Making of a Tsarist Reformer, 1827–1853', *Jahrbücher für die Geschichte Osteuropas*, 34 (1986), pp.6, 7.
18 Ibid., pp.12, 13.
19 Daly, *Russian Seapower*, pp.82–99.

20 Orlando Figes, *Crimea: the Last Crusade* (London: Allen Lane, 2010), pp.489–92; Serhii Plokhy, 'The City of Glory: Sevastopol in Russian Historical Mythology', *Journal of Contemporary History*, 35, 3 (2000), pp.369–83.

21 Henry Dodwell, *The Founder of Modern Egypt: a Study of Muhammad Ali* (Cambridge: Cambridge University Press, 1931), p.225.

22 *Annales Maritimes et Coloniales* 1 (1832), pp.281–82. Ibid., 2 (1840), p.185. Louis, 'La question d'Orient sous Louis-Philippe', ibid., 2, pp.214–16.

23 Kahled Fahmy, 'The Era of Muhammad Ali Pasha, 1805–1848', in M.W. Daly (ed.), *The Cambridge History of Egypt, vol.2* (Cambridge: Cambridge University Press, 1998), p.159.

24 For naval operations during these wars see Charles E. Callwell, *The Effect of Maritime Command on Land Campaigns Since Waterloo* (London: William Blackwood and Sons, 1897), pp.120–38.

25 Andrew McGregor, *A Military History of Modern Egypt: From the Ottoman Conquest to the Ramadan War* (Westport: Praeger, 2006), p.118.

26 Candan Badem, *The Ottoman Crimean War (1853–1856)* (Leiden: Brill, 2010), pp.81, 112; Hyam, *Britain's Imperial Century*, pp.100–02.

27 Dominique Dufour de Pradt, *Du Congrès de Vienne*, 2 vols (Paris: Delaunay, 1815), pp. I, 126–27, and II, 20, 24–25.

28 Honoré de Balzac, 'La France et l'étranger', *Chronique de Paris* (16 April 1836); reprinted in Honoré de Balzac, *Oeuvres Completes*, vol. 23 (Paris: Calmann Lévy, 1879), p.449.

29 Friedrich List, *Das nationale System der politischen Ökonomie* (Stuttgart: F.C. Kotta'scher Verlag, 1841). All quotations are from the first English edition (1856).

30 Friedrich List, *National System of Political Economy* (Philadelphia: J.B. Lippincott & Co., 1856), p.352.

31 Ibid., p.265; Rolf Hobson, 'Prussia, Germany and Maritime Law from Armed Neutrality to Unlimited Submarine Warfare, 1780–1917', in Rolf Hobson and Tom Kristiansen (eds), *Navies in Northern Waters 1721–2000* (London: Frank Cass, 2004), pp.102–04.

32 Albert H. Imlah, *Economic Elements in the Pax Britannica: Studies in British Foreign Trade in the Nineteenth Century* (Cambridge: Harvard University Press, 1958), p.13.

33 Quoted in M.S. Anderson, *The Ascendancy of Europe: Aspects of European history, 1815–1914* (Harlow: Longman, 1972), p.193.

34 Bartlett, *Great Britain and Sea Power*, pp.167, 88.

35 Quoted in James P. Baxter, *The Introduction of the Ironclad Warship* (Cambridge: Harvard University Press, 1933), pp.149–50.

36 Henry Kissinger, *A World Restored: Metternich, Castlereagh and the Problem of Peace, 1812–1822* (London: Phoenix Press, 2000), pp.33–34, 39, 92–93; Charles K. Webster, *The Foreign Policy of Castlereagh, 1815–1822: Britain and the European Alliance* (London: G. Bell and Sons, 1934), pp.48–49.

37 Harold Nicholson, *The Congress of Vienna: a Study in Allied Unity, 1812–1822* (London: Constable & Co., 1946), p.289; Wilhelm G. Grewe, *The Epochs of International Law* (Berlin: Walter de Gruyter, 2000), pp.551–54.

38 Grewe, *The Epochs of International Law*, pp.410–12; A.D. Harvey, 'European Attitudes to Britain during the French Revolutionary and Napoleonic Era', *History*, 63 (1978), pp.358–62; Koen Stapelbroek, 'The Rights of Neutral Trade and its Forgotten History', in Koen Stapelbroek (ed.), *Trade and War: the Neutrality of Commerce in the Inter-State System* (Helsinki: Helsinki Collegium for Advanced Studies, 2011), pp.3–10.

39 H.W. Malkin, 'The Inner History of the Declaration of Paris', *British Yearbook of International Law*, 8 (1927), pp.3–7; Jan Martin Lemnitzer, *Power, Law and the End of Privateering* (Basingstoke: Palgrave, 2014).

40 Francis Piggott, *The Declaration of Paris 1856* (London: University of London Press, 1919), pp.8–9.

41 C.I. Hamilton, 'Anglo-French Seapower and the Declaration of Paris', *The International History Review*, 4, 2 (1982), pp.171–72.

42 Stephen C. Neff, *War and the Law of Nations: a General History* (Cambridge: Cambridge University Press, 2005), p.188.

43 Clarendon to Palmerston, 6 April 1856, in Nicholas Tracy (ed.), *Sea Power and the Control of Trade: Belligerent Rights from the Russian War to the Beira Patrol, 1854–1970* (London: Ashgate, 2005), p.32.

44 'Improvement in the Laws of Nations', *The Economist* (3 May 1856), pp.476–477.

45 Hamilton, 'Anglo-French Seapower and the Declaration of Paris', pp.182–90; Bernard Semmel, *Liberalism and Naval Strategy: Ideology, Interest, and Sea Power during Pax Britannica* (London: Allen & Unwin, 1986), pp.53–64.

46 John W. Coogan, *The End of Neutrality: the United States, Britain, and Maritime Rights 1899–1915* (Ithaca: Cornell University Press, 1981), p.22.

47 Martin Lynn, *Commerce and Economic Change in West Africa: the Palm Oil Trade in the Nineteenth Century* (Cambridge: Cambridge University Press, 1997), pp.60–61.

48 Foreign and Commonwealth Office Historians, *Slavery in Diplomacy: the Foreign Office and the Suppression of the Transatlantic Slave Trade* (London: Foreign and Commonwealth Office, 2007), pp.13–15; Marika Sherwood, *After Abolition: Britain and the Slave Trade since 1807* (London: I.B. Tauris, 2007), pp.117–20.

49 Lawrence C. Jennings, *French Reaction to British Slave Emancipation* (Baton Rouge: Louisiana State University Press, 1988), pp.145–47; Hugh G. Soulsby, *The Right of Search and the Slave Trade in Anglo-American Relations, 1814–1862* (Baltimore: Johns Hopkins University Press, 1933), pp.119–23.

50 J. Gallagher, 'Fowell Buxton and the New African Policy, 1838–1842', *Cambridge Historical Journal*, 10, 1 (1950), pp.43, 47–48; Christopher Lloyd, *The Navy and the Slave Trade: the Suppression of the African Slave Trade in the Nineteenth Century* (London: Longmans, Green and Co., 1949), pp.94–99.

51 Quoted in Soulsby, The Right of Search and the Slave Trade in Anglo-American Relations, p.18.

52 Lewis Cass, *An Examination of the Question, Now in Discussion, between the American and British Governments, Concerning the Right of Search* (Paris: n.p., 1842), p.22.

53 D. Jones and A. Rakestraw, *Prologue to Manifest Destiny: Anglo-American Relations in the 1840s* (Wilmington: SR Books, 1997), pp.78–79; Willard C. Klunder, *Lewis Cass and the Politics of Moderation* (Kent: Kent State University Press, 1996), pp.111, 218.

54 J. Scott Harmon, 'The United States and the Suppression of the Illegal Slave Trade, 1830–1850', in Craig L. Symmonds (ed.), *New Aspects of Naval History* (Annapolis: Naval Institute Press, 1981), pp.214–15.

55 Here it refers to the right of sailing unmolested.

56 John Tyler, 'Second Annual Message, 6 Dec. 1842', in Gerhard Peters and John T. Woolley, *The American Presidency Project*, www.presidency.ucsb.edu/ws/?pid=29484. Accessed 20 August 2012.

57 Jennings, *French Reaction to British Slave Emancipation*, pp.144–48; Servane Marzin, 'La France, l'Angleterre et la répression de la traite des noirs sous le ministère Guizot (1840–1848)', in Sylvie Aprile and Fabrice Bensimon (eds), *La France et l'Angleterre au XIXe siècle: échanges, représentations, comparaisons* (Paris: Créaphis, 2006), pp.243–49.

58 *Annales du Parlement Français, 1842 legislature, vol. 4, Chamber of Deputies* (22 January 1842), pp.95, 106.

59 Alexis de Tocqueville, *Oeuvres completes, vol. 9* (Paris: Michel Lèvy Frères, 1866), pp.399, 401, 404.

60 Edward Beasley, *Empire as the Triumph of Theory: Imperialism, Information, and the Colonial Society of 1868* (London: Routledge, 2005), p.80.

61 Serge Daget, 'France, Suppression of the Illegal Trade, and England, 1817–1850', in David Eltis and James Walvin (eds), *The Abolition of the Atlantic Slave Trade* (Madison: University of Wisconsin Press, 1981), pp.208–09.

62 David Eltis, *Economic Growth and the Ending of the Transatlantic Slave Trade* (New York: Oxford University Press, 1987), pp.87–88, 94–95.

63 For the first of these conflicts see Rebeca B. Matzke, *Deterrence through Force: British Naval Power and Foreign Policy under Pax Britannica* (Lincoln: University of Nebraska Press, 2011), pp.105–53.

64 J.Y. Wong, *Deadly Dreams: Opium, Imperialism, and the Arrow War (1856–1860) in China* (Cambridge: Cambridge University Press, 1998), pp.78–79.

65 David Brown, *Palmerston: a Biography* (New Haven: Yale University Press, 2010), pp.400–01.

66 Ibid., pp.402–05; Gerald S. Graham, *The China Station: War and Diplomacy 1830–1860* (Oxford: Clarendon Press, 1978), pp.318–21.

67 Jean-David Avenel, *L'Affaire du Rio de la Plata (1838–1852)* (Paris: Economica, 1998); David McLean, *War, Diplomacy and Informal Empire: Britain and the Republics of La Plata 1836–1853* (London: British Academic Press, 1995).

68 Francisco Fernando Monteoliva Doratioto, 'Poder naval e política externa do Império do Brasil no Rio da Prata (1822–1852)', *Navigator*, 12 (2010), pp.19–20.

69 Wallace S. Hutcheon, *Robert Fulton: Pioneer of Undersea Warfare* (Annapolis: Naval Institute Press, 1981), pp.127–48; Douglas Dakin, 'Lord Cochrane's Greek Steam Fleet', *Mariner's Mirror*, 39 (1953), pp.211–19.

70 Jean Boudriot, 'Vaisseaux et frégates sous la Restauration et la Monarchie de Juillet', in *Marine et technique au XIXe siècle* (Paris: Service Historique de la Marine, 1988), pp.65–83; Lambert, *The Last Sailing Battlefleet*.

71 Stephen S. Roberts, 'The French Transatlantic Steam Packet Programme of 1840', *Mariner's Mirror*, 73 (1987), pp.273–86; David B. Tyler, *Steam Conquers the Atlantic* (New York: D. Appleton-Century Company, 1939).

72 Henri-Joseph Paixhans, *Nouvelle force maritime* (Paris: Bachelier, 1822).

73 François Ferdinand Philippe Louis Marie d'Orléans, Prince de Joinville, 'Note sur l'état des forces navales de la France', *Revue des Deux Mondes* (15 May 1844), pp.708–46. Reprinted in several media and as a pamphlet in several editions.

74 *Hansard's Parliamentary Debates*, Ser. 3, Vol. lxxxii, col. 1224, 30 July 1845.

75 Bernard Brodie, *Sea Power in the Machine Age* (Princeton: Princeton University Press, 1943; repr., Greenwood Press, New York, 1969), pp.48, 59, 63–64, 69; David Brown, 'Palmerston and Anglo-French Relations, 1846–1865', *Diplomacy & Statecraft*, 17 (2006), pp.681–87.

76 Bartlett, *Great Britain and Sea Power*, pp.155–64, 277–93; C.I. Hamilton, 'The Diplomatic and Naval Effects of the Prince de Joinville's *Note sur l'etat des forces navales de la France* of 1844', *The Historical Journal*, 32 (1989), pp.675–87; C.I. Hamilton, *Anglo-French Naval Rivalry, 1840–1870* (Oxford: Clarendon Press, 1993), pp.15–105.

77 Jurien de La Gravière to Admiral Sir William R. Mends, 8 November 1860, in B.S. Mends, *Life of Admiral Sir William Robert Mends* (London: John Murray, 1899), p.331, cited in Baxter, *The Introduction of the Ironclad Warship*, p.149.

78 *Annual Register for 1848*, p.93; Bartlett, *Great Britain and Sea Power*, pp.89–90, 207, 70; Geoffrey Best, *War and Society in Revolutionary Europe, 1770–1870* (Leicester: Leicester University Press, 1982), pp.242–43; Jerome Devitt, 'The "Navalization" of Ireland: the Royal Navy and Irish Insurrection in the 1840s', *Mariner's Mirror*, 101, 4 (2015), pp.388–409; Edward M. Spiers, *The Army and Society, 1815–1914* (London: Longman, 1980), pp.77, 82.

79 Carlos Alfaro Zaforteza, 'Sea Power, State and Society in Liberal Spain, 1833–1868' (PhD thesis, King's College London, 2011), pp.152–53.
80 Lawrence Sondhaus, *Preparing for Weltpolitik: German Sea Power before the Tirpitz Era* (Annapolis: Naval Institute Press, 1997), pp.22–26.
81 Arnold Kludas, 'Die Kriegsschiffe des Deutschen Bundes 1848 bis 1851', in Hubatsch (ed), *Die erste Deutsche Flotte 1848–1853*, pp.54–60.

5 The collapse of the Congress System, 1854–1870

Carlos Alfaro Zaforteza

Europe was beset by chronic instability in the years following the Crimean War (1853–1856) and was violently reshaped by the convulsions of the German and Italian wars of unification (1859, 1864, 1866, and 1870). These short but extraordinarily intense wars were mirrored by longer, but by no means any less intense, conflicts globally, notably the American Civil War (1861–1865), the Paraguayan War (1865–1870), and the Tai Ping War in China (1850–1864). Along with this escalation in the scale and lethality of war was the general adoption of steam power in naval warfare, its wide use, and the inevitable effect this had on Britain's relative standing. Previously, a combination of Britain's indisputable naval superiority and the priority given over to domestic affairs by most European powers had largely removed the imperative for any meaningful, competitive struggle for command of the sea. Yet the independence from wind and tides that steam power afforded enabled other navies to play more prominent roles as auxiliaries to their respective armies. Other technical innovations in shipbuilding and design, particularly the ironclad warship, the modern commerce-destroying cruiser, and later the torpedo boat, also gave states a viable deterrent against the naval hegemon. Thus, the 1860s witnessed a generalised naval arms race and the creation of new navies that went some way to restricting British foreign policy options, and this is a pattern that would recur in the 1880s, as will be discussed in the next chapter. Although British industrial capacity eclipsed that of its rivals and was well equipped, therefore, to deal quickly with such challenges, it is still the case that innovation in naval warfare largely came from elsewhere, particularly from the French and US navies. The American Civil War, in particular, had a very marked effect. It was here that many new techniques in naval warfare were introduced, or developed, and laid before an international audience. This shaped public debates and, by extension, strategic thought right up to the outbreak of World War One.

The Crimean War and its lessons

The Crimean War was remarkable for the unprecedented engagement of public opinion, and navies played a big part in this. From the very outset, at the Battle of Sinope in November 1853, navies proved more visible and more emotive than armies. Here, an Ottoman squadron suffered a terribly one-sided defeat at the hands of the Russian fleet, which was equipped with modern shell guns. This was the first large-scale use of explosive projectiles at sea, and the Turkish ships were quite literally blown out of the water with massive loss of life. Although there was heavy fighting on the land fronts of the Balkan Peninsula and in the Caucasus, it was this dramatic naval action that triggered French and British intervention in the war. When the news reached Paris and London, it caused outrage for two main reasons. First, a largely Russo-phobic audience saw the 'massacre of Sinope', as the press dubbed it, as proof of Russian ruthlessness and barbarism. Secondly, the attack on the Turkish squadron was perceived as a direct affront to France and Britain, whose fleets lay at anchor in the Bosporus. They had been sent there to deter a Russian attack on Constantinople and to restrain Russian bellicosity and had conspicuously failed in this last respect. The media used the consequent indignation to pressure statesmen, who had so far advocated restraint, to declare war on Russia.[1]

As the Russians soon discovered, the allies would soon prove to be very different adversaries, and the war at sea that followed was shaped by a marked disparity in naval strength between the two sides. The main units of the Russian Black Sea Fleet were sailing ships, whilst the allied navies had steam battleships in the face of which the Russians simply retreated, scuttling their ships to block the Sevastopol harbour entrance. Nevertheless, the men and guns of the Russian fleet still played a prominent role in the defence of the city.[2] That the names of Admirals Nakhimov, Kornilov, and Istomin, who all died at Sevastopol, were given to warships of the modern Russian navy indicates the extent to which they were enshrined in national memory.

This allied expedition to Crimea had been the first large-scale use of steam in naval operations in history, and it confirmed two essential features of sea power. Once the Russian Black Sea Fleet had been neutralised, these navies supported the main military objective, the destruction of the naval base of Sevastopol, and in this way demonstrated that they were indispensable adjuncts of armies. The war also showed that in the new steam era the role of merchant shipping as an essential component of sea power was more important than ever. Sending a large army and keeping it supplied for an extended period at such a long distance (Sevastopol lies 2,000 sea miles from Toulon and 4,000 from Portsmouth) was possible only through regularly scheduled deliveries, an impossible feat in the age of sail. The Anglo-French army initially consisted of around 55,000 men, but it eventually reached a peak of about 150,000. Over a period of almost two years, everything, from replacement troops to food, coal, or horses, had to be sent by sea. The consequent demand on shipping affected trade worldwide. Freight costs and coal prices significantly increased, and some trades suffered from scarce shipping, due to the high profits in the service of these armies. Likewise, mail and passenger traffic were disrupted as French- and British-subsidised lines ceded their large steamers as troop transports.

The ability of France and Britain to cope with these logistical demands was a direct function of their relative industrial strength. Stores, ammunition, and food could be carried in sailing ships, but the large-scale transport of troops and horses had to be conducted by steamships. The health hazards of a long journey in cramped conditions would, otherwise, have had potentially catastrophic consequences. At the time, however, large steamers were costly and difficult to build, and consumed an enormous amount of coal. Only the British shipbuilding and shipping industry could provide this type of ship in any numbers. Indeed, most vessels of the contemporary continental lines, such as the *Compagnie Générale Transatlantique* or the *Hamburg-Amerika Linie*, were British-built, and only the very large subsidised lines, such as the British Cunard or Peninsular and Oriental, or the French *Messageries Impériales*, operated suitably-sized ships at all. British yards were also already building iron-hulled merchant ships, and in this respect a good illustration of the relative industrial imbalance internationally is the *Himalaya*, the largest merchant ship afloat when launched for the Peninsular and Oriental line in 1853. Although iron hulls were still too thin for warships because they created dangerous shrapnel when hit by enemy shells and were difficult to repair, the *Himalaya* was nonetheless an impressive industrial achievement, and only British shipyards were capable of building such a ship. Moreover, only British shipping companies had enough capital to own and operate it. When the sudden need for transport capacity arose, she was purchased by the British navy and converted into a troopship. In her inaugural journey, she carried no fewer than 3,000 men and their equipment from Southampton to Turkey in just eleven days.

The French navy attempted to compensate for the relative lack of shipbuilding capacity and shipping resources of the French private sector by building a force of large steamers in its own dockyards in the 1840s.[3] Unfortunately, this was not enough to meet the requirements of the fleet and the army's demands for both operations in Algeria and for the expedition to Crimea. The French government, therefore, also had to rely on scarce French-flagged merchant shipping, including the steamers from the *Messageries Impériales*, a large number of foreign merchant vessels, mostly British registered, and fifteen ships of the line from the navy commissioned as transports. When the two fleets entered the Black Sea, the French vessels were packed with troops. Only the British fleet was ready for combat, a clear indication of the wide gap in resources that underpinned British maritime superiority.[4]

Technological developments also changed the nature of coastal warfare. In the sail era, the danger of a lee shore always haunted mariners. Only oared or steampowered ships could operate close to the coast without such concerns about wind and tide. Naval operations in the Baltic and Black seas, therefore, required diverse types of steam gunboats that could comfortably operate in shallow, coastal waters. This need accelerated the widespread adoption of the screw propeller, which allowed for a better distribution of firepower than a paddle wheel and maximised the benefits of a full rig.[5] The sudden rise in demand for these gunboats could not be met by the naval dockyards, which were already busy with ongoing construction and the maintenance of the fleet at wartime strength. So most of the work, in France as well as in Britain, was done by private shipyards.

Although France built twenty-eight such gunboats, Britain managed to build a total of 156, and if ever it could be said that Britain was the 'workshop of the world', it was during the 1850s and 1860s.

The carefully planned and effective collaboration that was needed between royal dockyards and the private sector operated in three broad stages. First, private shipyards built the bare hulls. Power-plant contractors then fitted the engines, and the royal dockyards did the rest, which included coppering the hulls, providing the rigging, and fitting out the ships. The most extraordinary aspect, however, was the construction of large numbers of engines, which represents the first instance of mass production in marine engineering, only possible by the introduction of standardisation. The Admiralty specified the use of Joseph Whitworth's screw thread standards, making bolts interchangeable regardless of manufacturer, which was quite simply a revolutionary change. There were also constraints, however. The increased demand for timber, for example, on top of that already required for large ships, meant that only the first boats could be built of properly seasoned wood. Many others which were built of green wood soon suffered rotten hulls and proved unfit for service.[6] Their engines and boilers, on the other hand, were brand new and could certainly be re-used in new hulls.

After the war, the capabilities of the British shipping industry were soon on full display in defence of the Empire. Above all, the great rebellion of India in 1857 required the movement of European troops over even longer distances, and reinforcements were urgently needed. The only shipping company with steam ships capable of sailing around the Cape was the Peninsular and Oriental, which had a British government contract to carry the mail to India. The contract provided for government use of the ships in a national emergency, and thus it was possible to send 6,000 soldiers just at the moment when they were most needed. Soon a transport service was organised, which entailed not only the charter of ships, but also the provision of coal to the various ports of call. This, too, was a service which only British industry could provide, for only Britain benefited from good-quality, cheaply-mined coal carried at cheap freight rates. By December 1857, more than sixty troopships could be seen anchored off Cape Town, one of the main stops on the route to India.[7] Here again the private sector proved its ability to provide the required shipping in a national emergency, providing essential carrying capacity and preventing the diversion of warships from their main duties.

A period of French leadership

The disparity in industrial capacity did not prevent the French government from learning lessons from the Crimean War, and it implemented its own solutions which reflected the new capabilities of steam fleets. A programme for the transformation of the fleet in 1857 envisaged the construction, over a thirteen-year period, of a fleet of forty screw ships of the line. It also included, for the first time, seventy-two purpose-built troop transports and twenty littoral warfare ships.[8] This new force structure gave the French army an unequalled strategic mobility, significantly enhancing the efficiency of the French armed forces as an instrument of foreign policy. Indeed, France was the only European power of the time with both a first-class army and a first-class navy. It should be no surprise, therefore, that France was recognised as the dominant power in post-Crimean Europe and was a close collaborator of Britain overseas.

Although there was little naval combat during the German and Italian wars of unification that followed, navies still offered essential support to armies, and with its new force structure the French navy was able to play the leading role in this respect. Comprised entirely of steam-powered vessels, the main French battle fleet was made up of fast screw battleships only. Moreover, with the construction of its transport fleet, it was capable of delivering an expeditionary force of 40,000 troops, complete with horses and equipment. The small French merchant marine had been incapable of supporting anything on this scale, and in the Crimean War France had had to rely on British shipping. Chartering and gathering merchant steamers also took time. Now, however, its naval transports could be available at short notice for surprise attacks.

In many respects this was the stuff of nightmares for Britain, as Joinville's menacing ideas seemed to have been given real teeth. France had always had the soldiers, but now it also had the naval materiel to do the job: the paddle frigates of the 1840s, still in good condition; the purpose-built screw transports of the 1857 programme; plus, fast battleships of the *Napoleon* class to escort and support them. A naval arms race was the inevitable result, and when the Franco-Austrian war (or Second Italian War of Independence) erupted in 1859 and threatened to spread into a general European conflict, an invasion panic gripped Britain.

It has long been a staple of British historical writing on this period to argue that Napoleon III had an ambitious, if ultimately misguided, wish to challenge the superiority of the British navy in this way. In practice, the French navy built only to a certain predetermined strength, well below Britain's. Its naval deployments were not particularly threatening either. Indeed, the nucleus of the battle fleet and most of the transports were based in the Mediterranean. Furthermore, many Britons seemed to forget, or were at least uncomfortable with the idea, that France was actually a British ally and that Napoleon III himself was an Anglophile. In addition to the Crimean War, the Anglo-French alliance had, in fact, operated in places as far away as China and Mexico, and both countries concluded a free-trade treaty in 1860. Indeed, despite rampant Anglophobia in the French media, which was duly reciprocated in Britain, Napoleon III actually went to war with all of the European great powers except for Britain. Nevertheless, the fear of invasion in Britain still ran very deep. A famous pamphlet by Richard Cobden that tried to allay these anxieties which were being whipped up in the press went through no less than six editions. Other contemporaries in Britain and beyond, and indeed many historians since, also derided these panics.[9]

Even so, the new French *force de frappe* proved its worth from 1859. French transports prevented the Austrian army from defeating in detail the French and Sardinian forces. Compensating for the insufficient railway system, they achieved the required troop concentration through the port of Genoa. Shortly thereafter, a French expedition into the Adriatic threatened a landing near Venice, to take the defences of the Austrian Quadrilateral from the rear.[10] This strategic manoeuvre was essential in forcing Austria to make peace. Accordingly, when the Franco-Prussian war broke out in 1870, French plans logically included a landing on the Baltic coast, to pin down Prussian troops.

Unfortunately for the French, their plans were overtaken by events. First, there were rumours that a combined Prussian and Spanish force, based in Cartagena, would attack the troopships plying the waters between Algeria and Southern France. This required the deployment of the battle fleet in the Mediterranean and delayed its sailing to the North Sea. More immediately, the Prussian invasion was unexpectedly rapid and devastating. The troops allocated to the expedition had to be sent to defend the threatened capital.[11] This expedition was a failure, therefore, and in this respect it certainly reinforces the case that in European politics and war, armies still counted for far more than navies. Nevertheless, taken together, these two case studies both still illustrate how a mobile naval force could make a flanking manoeuvre with potentially decisive effect.

Perhaps the most momentous development to come out of the Crimean War, however, was the armour that had been on these Prussian and Spanish ships. A new type of warship, the ironclad, had very effective protection for its wooden hulls from enemy fire, and this changed naval warfare almost overnight. The attack of the allied fleets on the Sevastopol seaward defences had confirmed the experience of Sinope, that is to say that wooden ships simply could not cope with the devastating effects of explosive shells, whilst their own fire had failed to inflict any noticeable damage on Russia's granite forts. The French navy came up with the solution. New armoured batteries had proven invulnerable to shell fire, but they were unseaworthy and fit only for coastal warfare, and this spurred French naval architects on. Masterminded by Charles Dupuy de Lôme, generally held to be the greatest naval architect of the nineteenth century, the French developed a larger, seagoing version; and, in 1858 they launched the *Gloire*, the greatest ship of the age. Although rated as a frigate because of its single gun battery, she was superior to any wooden screw battleship. She was also expensive, however, and difficult to build, with iron armour plating on the sides and a significant increase of iron components in the hull. This development pushed at the very limits of the country's industrial capability, but at once the ongoing Anglo-French naval race was focused on such ironclads, and although British industrial might ensured that it could respond quickly, it was the French, with their excellent corps of naval constructors, who led this innovation.[12]

The introduction of these armoured ships changed the force structure of navies with far-reaching consequences. First, existing screw battleships became almost useless as combat units. Major and medium navies alike, which were engaged in building screw ships of the line and fitting engines to some of the existing sailing ships, realised that the transition to steam power had to go hand in hand with the introduction of armour. They found themselves saddled with brand-new, or still incomplete, screw ships of the line and frigates which with their lack of armour were rendered obsolete almost at once. To salvage at least a fraction of the heavy investment already made, many ships were converted and some several times. The four British ships of the *Royal Sovereign* class are a case in point. They were originally ordered in 1841 as 116-gun, three-deck sailing ships of the line. Whilst still under construction, their design was modified to fit them with steam engines. In April 1862, the *Royal Sovereign* herself was subjected to a second conversion, this time to an ironclad turret ship. She was cut down to the lower deck, her masts were removed, her sides were armoured with iron plates, and her new armament was made up of four gun turrets. Her sister ship *Prince of Wales*, launched in 1860 as a screw ship of the line, was not even commissioned. As soon as she was completed, her machinery was removed and fitted to the ironclad *Repulse*, which itself had been originally built as a screw ship of the line.[13] All of this was designed to cope with the rapidly changing technology, by making the most of the available materiel. In the midst of an arms race with France, with a large number of ships already under construction, Britain strove to save a part of the huge capital already invested and to strike a balance between quality and quantity. Other navies, such as the Italian, Russian, and Spanish, found themselves in the same situation and adopted the same solution of converting wooden vessels to ironclads. Only the French navy, who started ironclad building and stuck to a carefully planned construction programme, did not resort to such conversions and enjoyed all the advantages of setting the pace, rather than reacting to others.

Innovation and escalation

The introduction of the ironclad warship and the rapid obsolescence of the still relatively new screw ships of the line has been well covered in the historical literature.[14] Yet this was more than just a remarkable technical innovation. It was part of a wider pattern of the determined expansion of military strength and the escalation of war. The quantum leap in offensive and defensive power that the ironclad represents came at a moment in European international relations when the Vienna system was being challenged by revisionist statesmen such as Bismarck, Cavour, and Napoleon III. The consequence was the intense violence of the wars of unification of Germany and Italy and the fear that these might expand into a general European war. In this tense atmosphere of instability, and in the midst of an economic boom, governments naturally paid particular attention to ensuring that they had the means, including the necessary technologically-advanced hardware, to survive any major war.

In laying down the first seagoing ironclad in 1857, the French government had also introduced a new type of armament: breech-loading, rifled guns, more powerful and faster-firing than the standard muzzle-loading, smooth-bore artillery then in use. The *Gloire*, therefore, represented a significant, qualitative escalation of the ongoing armaments race with Britain. The response, based upon Britain's far more developed maritime industry, was the frigate HMS *Warrior* (1860), now preserved as a museum ship at Portsmouth dockyard. *Warrior* still exists primarily because it was simply too large to have been built of wood. Uniquely, she was constructed entirely of iron, whereas the *Gloire*, though an armoured ship, was still chiefly built of perishable wood. Yet the assumption that *Warrior* was therefore necessarily a much better ship is due not just to this, and to its larger hull, but also to the efforts of British nationalist historiography over the years. Again, the reality is more complex.

French naval constructors benefited from scientific training which enabled them to better explore and implement innovative ideas. In the design and construction of the *Gloire*, it was not just size but cost and making the most of available resources that was the key to a carefully planned programme of the transformation of the fleet. Limited size ensured limited cost and good manoeuvrability, and it obviated the need to build larger, expensive dry docks. Wooden hulls also still had advantages. The first was that they constituted an existing, mature technology, for which it was easy to find skilled labour. Wood continued to be the standard shipbuilding material worldwide, as it would remain for at least another decade. Moreover, in contrast with iron hulls, they were not subject to heavy fouling, so that wooden ships did not lose speed as fast and did not need to enter dry dock so often.

Of course, French constructors were certainly aware that there could be clear advantages to iron hulls, just as they were of the limitations of French industry to produce them. To gain experience with the new material, therefore, the French navy established experimental iron-building facilities at Lorient dockyard. A similar ship to the *Gloire*, but with an iron hull, was built, and all subsequent classes of ironclads included a unit that was built there of iron. In many respects, however, the *Gloire* and *Warrior* remain emblematic of the respective industrial infrastructures and technical cultures of the two countries. In addition to the iron merchant ships that private British dockyards had been building for years, they built many ironclad screw battleships with wooden hulls. Yet by mastering a technique to produce cheaper, stronger hulls in less time in this way, Britain could now take fullest advantage of the advantages that iron offered. Above all, it did not require the time-consuming seasoning of timber, and it was not subject to rotting.

Warrior was built by Thames Iron Works, a shipyard on the Thames, at the time the main shipbuilding centre in the United Kingdom. It was a very handsome ship, fifty percent larger and a hundred percent more expensive than the *Gloire*. Although it effectively reflected the unrivalled capabilities of contemporary British shipyards, it was a very costly experiment. Indeed, a total of six such giant ironclads were built, which were all widely criticised for their excessive size and cost. Sir Edward J. Reed, Director of Naval Construction from 1863 to 1870 and one of the outstanding naval constructors of the century, argued against building these very long, unwieldy, and tremendously expensive ships and for returning to more sensible designs.[15] What is more, the coal capacity of those ships was disproportionately small for their size and engines, and they could only use specially-built, extra-large dry docks, only available in Britain. Consequently, their operation was mostly restricted to the waters around the British Isles. Arguably, the French responded in a more measured, successful way. They followed up the *Gloire* with homogeneous classes that incorporated gradual improvements and moderate increases in size and cost. This policy kept costs relatively low and brought tactical uniformity to the fleet. The British, less concerned with costs, experimented with diverse designs, but ended up with a motley collection – very much as the French themselves would later do in the 1890s – that neither significantly increased the navy's fighting power nor resulted in an entirely satisfactory type. Indeed despite British industrial and financial superiority, by the end of 1864 British expert opinion still could not see a clear-cut advantage over the French ironclad fleet.[16]

The situation was also complicated by the fact that those states unwilling, or unable, to invest in the first-class seagoing ships that had replaced wooden battleships had the possibility of acquiring smaller, cheaper coast-defence ships. Generally also built of iron, which allowed for virtually any shape and distribution of weights, these vessels could comfortably confront conventional wooden ships in coastal waters.[17] Procurement, on the other hand, was not necessarily straightforward. As a prominent illustration, in March 1862 James Bulloch, the Confederate agent in Europe responsible for the acquisition of naval armaments, secretly ordered two small ironclads from John Laird & Co. of Liverpool. This yard was renowned for building state-of-the-art warships and doing undercover business with the Confederacy. Bulloch counted on widespread sympathy for the Southern cause and had a personal rapport with Laird, who he hoped would help disguise the vessels as merchantmen and thereby flout the Foreign Enlistment Act of 1819. Ultimately, however, this was not possible, for even a lay observer could tell that they were really warships, equipped with four heavy guns in twin turrets and a ram at the bow. Not just that, they were manifestly superior to the 'monitors', that is to say to the Union's equivalent ships, and were clearly quite capable of lifting the blockade then being imposed on them and of attacking Northern coastal cities. The moral and propaganda effect of this would have been enormous. A Confederate newspaper stated that 'the destruction of Boston alone would be worth a hundred victories in the field'. Union statesmen fully agreed. Secretary of State William H. Seward feared that the 'rams', as the ships were called, would 'enter Portland, Boston, New York, or, if they prefer, . . . attempt to break the blockade at Charleston, or ascend the Mississippi to New Orleans'. If this threat had materialised, it would have been an effective counter to the recent Union victories at Gettysburg and Vicksburg. As one of these 'rams' was almost ready to sail, the US government put maximum diplomatic pressure on the British. On 5 September 1863, Charles F. Adams, US minister in London, delivered an ultimatum. If the ships were allowed to leave Britain, he said, 'it would be superfluous of me to point out to your lordship that this is war'.[18] Indeed the previous day, the British government had realised that it could no longer sustain its position and had chosen to act. This time, it did not rely on any legal arguments; it simply sent a detachment of royal marines and a battleship to the mouth of the River Mersey and purchased the two vessels for the British navy.[19] The blow to Confederate morale was significant. Just as the blockade was becoming more effective, European industry, it seemed, could not be counted on for the warships it needed to survive.

As this episode suggests, the skills and facilities to build these highly technical vessels were scarce and limited to the very few industrialised countries that
could produce iron hulls, steam engines, armour, and rifled guns. In practice, this
meant France, the United States, and, above all, Britain. Despite the diffusion of
sea power and the specific, direct challenges posed by France, Britain was in an
unassailable position because of its industrial capacity, a position of strength that
was self-reinforcing. The British shipbuilding industry reaped the benefits of the
1860s boom in naval construction, not only to supplement the royal dockyards,
but also to meet the heavy demand of ironclads from foreign navies. At the time,
it had virtually no competitors in quality, cost, and delivery times. Countries
as diverse as Peru, Prussia, Spain, or Turkey ordered ships in Britain, either for
lack of domestic industry or to supplement their own shipbuilding capacity.[20]
Crucially, this dependency on industrialised economies did not subside once a
sufficient number of the new ships had been completed, because there was a rapidly escalating cycle of innovation. Striking that impossible balance between more
powerful guns and sufficiently defensive armour meant that the development of
one necessarily led to the further development of the other. Bigger guns that
could pierce the armour of ironclads could lead quite quickly to their obsolescence.[21] Only great powers had the financial means to keep up. Be that as it may,
the clearest illustration of the accelerated pace of technology, and its profound
effect on the tactics and force structure of navies, are the efforts of the Union and
Confederate navies in the American Civil War.

The American Civil War and its legacy

The influence of the Civil War was manifested in a number of ways. First,
American innovations in naval technology attracted the attention of Europeans
who soon adopted them, forming the basis for the theories of the material school
of strategic thought, better known as the *Jeune École*. Not to be overlooked
is the enormous military power that was mobilised by the Union government
and the commercial relations with European countries of both the Union and
the Confederacy that substantially affected European interests especially in the
Western hemisphere. Britain, the great power with the highest stakes in North
America, now had to cope with a state whose strength had increased by leaps and
bounds since 1812. Probably the most disruptive factor in Anglo-American relations of this period was the naval activities of the belligerents. Notably, the *Trent*
Affair of 1861, in which the Union navy captured two Confederate diplomats
from the British ship *Trent*, threatened to escalate to war. More broadly, relations
were complicated by the blockade of Confederate ports and the construction of
Confederate warships in British shipyards.[22] Last, but not least, even more than
the Crimean War, the American Civil War was a conflict that was widely reported
in the media. In a country with a high literacy rate, the press was able to play a
crucial role in shaping political attitudes, expectations, and decisions, and this
effectively cemented the growing relationship between public opinion and the
conduct of naval warfare.

It is not surprising, therefore, that the two most significant naval battles of the war were also the most publicised. The combat between the two iron-clads, the *Monitor* and the *Virginia*, at Hampton Roads, Virginia, in 1862, and that between the famous Confederate cruiser *Alabama* and the *Kearsarge* off Cherbourg in 1864, were unlike most engagements that take place at sea where only the combatants are present. These were quite literally public events, with all the allure and drama of a personal duel. Indeed the geography of Hampton Roads effectively made it a 'naval amphitheater' where tens of thousands of troops from both armies, the crews of Union, British, and French warships, and of course journalists could all be present and watch the combat unfold.[23] The battle at Cherbourg had even been arranged in advance by the respective commanders and was duly publicised to ensure a large number of spectators.[24] In addition to many engravings for the illustrated press, French painters, notably Edouard Manet, also immortalised this contest. Raphael Semmes, the *Alabama*'s commander, who managed to escape to Britain, was fêted as a public celebrity and published a personal narrative of his exploits. The book ran through several editions, first in France then in Britain and the United States.[25] Both episodes were clearly early cases of mass entertainment reflecting the public fascination with technology and power. Just as significant as the major breakthroughs in the conduct of naval war itself, therefore, was the fact that these were not just appreciated by a small elite group of experts, but by a wider public audience. Debates on technology and strategy had become matters of public interest and even partisan issues in domestic politics.

The *Virginia* was an armoured ship that had been converted from a frigate, the *Merrimack*, and is an example of the resourcefulness and innovation with limited means that was making naval warfare more effective. It also demonstrates the growing moral effect of navies and the fear that they could cause among an enemy. It was one of the ships at Gosport Navy Yard, close to Norfolk, that was burned by Union forces as they abandoned the place to prevent them falling into the hands of the Confederates. The *Merrimack*, however, was salvaged. The engines were repaired, the hull was cut down to the waterline, an armoured case-mate was fitted on top of it, and the bow was equipped with a ram. Unfortunately for the Confederacy, however, it was difficult to acquire the armour plate needed. Only the Tredegar Iron Works, of Richmond, was capable of producing it, but it had to combine the job with the production of heavy ordnance and munitions for the army. Nevertheless, as soon as it was finished, this makeshift warship came out to attack the blockading squadron.[26] The results of its appearance, newly relaunched as the *Virginia* on 8 March 1862, are well known and caused a panic in Washington. Only hours after the engagement, an anxious, frightened Edwin S. Stanton, the Attorney General, walked into Lincoln's office with the news, having summoned the other cabinet members to an urgent meeting. Initially, they were concerned that the ship might sail along the coast, attack coastal cities, and even reach Washington. These concerns proved far-fetched, but the *Virginia* had shown that a single armoured ship had the potential to destroy a whole squadron and raise the blockade.

The following day the *Virginia* came out to complete the destruction of the blockading squadron, but by this time the armoured Union ship, the *Monitor*, had arrived and was ready for combat. The result of the duel was tactically indecisive; neither ship inflicted significant damage. True, the *Virginia* had not met its objective, but her mere existence was a major factor in thwarting General McClellan's Peninsular Campaign, the Union offensive to capture Richmond. McClellan's left flank remained exposed as long as Union vessels were barred from sailing up the James and Chickahominy rivers. This situation only changed with the destruction of the Confederate ironclad.[27] The implications of this were not just strategic but international. The *Virginia* had directly affected ship construction and refits in Britain for the Royal Navy. Most other European navies had already started acquiring ironclads, but the Battle of Hampton Roads removed any lingering doubts about their merits and convinced both statesmen and the general public alike of the need to spend the hefty sums required to keep abreast.

The cost, however, was absolutely staggering. An armoured frigate similar to the *Gloire* cost roughly twice as much as a wooden frigate, which in turn cost about twice as much as an equivalent sailing frigate. On top of this came the costs of building new facilities and finding the required skilled labour to work them efficiently. For medium and smaller powers, it became almost impossible to preserve a domestic armaments industry. Only great powers with their large resource base and economies of scale could invest heavily in new technologies and industrial plant. This posed a dilemma for others who had to weigh up the relative merits of the short-term solution of spending on ships or the long-term solution of spending on industrial infrastructure and research and development, but which could not meet present needs. Small powers opted for the former; most medium powers opted for a combination of both. The main beneficiaries of all of this were French and British industries.[28] For smaller powers emphasising coastal defence, the reconstruction of the *Merrimack*, and especially the *Monitor*, which had a more advanced design, provided the model. For them and even for larger powers, the low-cost ironclad equipped with gun turrets provided a cheap, cost-effective alternative to the conventional battleship.

Technology, it seems, had allowed a weak state to conduct asymmetric warfare against a strong enemy, and this led to the further diffusion of sea power. Initially, ironclads had been built only in Europe, but now European powers with interests in the Americas would have to include this type of ship in their overseas deployments with the inevitably dramatic increase in the cost of maintaining a naval presence that this entailed. The Confederacy had started the war with no naval force at all and a limited ability to build one, though it, too, was soon building ironclads.[29] The Union, in contrast, enjoyed plentiful material and human resources to quickly build up its navy to meet the demands of the war. Not a formal signatory to the Declaration of Paris, the Union government still accepted the abolition of privateering, but found that inexpensive, fast steam cruisers, legally recognised as proper warships, could equally wreak havoc on enemy trade. At the same time, small, cheap ironclad rams, and submarine mines, could effectively defend a country's coasts and make blockade by enemy forces a hazardous affair.

This new kind of low-cost naval force, pioneered by the Confederacy, could not achieve command of the sea, but it constituted an effective instrument for a strictly defensive strategy. Small states were no longer helpless against the gunboat diplomacy of stronger powers, and in the 1860s several navies were built along these lines. Besides the Confederate navy, others such as the Union and Russian navies did away with the traditional battle fleet composed of seagoing battleships and heavily invested, instead, in the much cheaper coast-defence ironclads and commerce-raiding cruisers. The United States and Russia faced the threat of war with Britain and France, the former over Anglo-French neutrality, the second over the Polish uprising of 1863. They needed cheap vessels that could be quickly built as deterrents.

In the United States, the North's industrial predominance, and its greater material and human resources, were evident in the production of greater numbers of ironclads, which were both faster and more advanced than those from the South. Still, it was only possible because of the existence of capable private shipyards, which took on most of the building. Most notably, the quick delivery of the *Monitor* to counter the *Merrimack* that was being rebuilt at Norfolk was essential. Thus started one of the most famous naval armaments races in naval history, which consisted of just two ships. The contract specified no more than a hundred days from signature. To achieve this, the designer and project manager, the engineer and inventor of Swedish origin John Ericsson, subcontracted the components to different manufacturers in the New York area. Continental Iron Works built the hull, Albany Iron Works produced most of the armour, Delamater & Co. manufactured the engines, and Novelty Iron Works was responsible for the turret.[30] Practically all the monitors were built by private yards, which were more flexible in switching over to iron construction, whilst navy yards continued building wooden vessels.[31]

Despite the unusual prominence of the *Monitor* and *Virginia*, the most famous ship of the war was actually a small, relatively unassuming, wooden warship, the Confederate cruiser *Alabama*. Built in Birkenhead in 1862 by John Laird of Liverpool as a fast sloop of war, she became the prototype of the modern commerce raider. *Alabama* featured regularly in the news, and her short career of less than two years exemplifies most of the naval issues of the American Civil War. Indeed, the analysis of her achievements was central to the theories of the *Jeune École*, and it was the forerunner of the surface raiders that featured so prominently until well after World War Two. Again, in order to circumvent British neutrality laws, which prevented the building of warships for belligerents, *Alabama* posed as a merchantman contracted by a private businessman. Despite the protests of US diplomats and the fact that the ship's true nature was evident to any expert observer, the ship was duly completed without government interference. Only days before she sailed, the British government gave the order to detain it. But it was too late. Under the pretence of conducting sea trials, she went to sea and never returned. She met with another ship chartered by James Bulloch in the Azores, and there she received her armament, also British manufactured, and was officially commissioned as a unit of the Confederate navy, with a British crew.

Although, as noted above, it was already getting harder to procure ships in this way, the British government's lax interpretation of neutrality, widespread sympathies for the Confederacy, and the great profits of the arms trade had made this affair relatively straightforward.

In less than two years, the *Alabama* destroyed sixty-five Union merchant ships, which made her the most successful of the Confederate raiders. This was, of course, a tiny fraction of the total tonnage under the US flag, but the subsequent panic led to increased insurance premiums and a notable decrease of business for US-flagged vessels, as traders started using neutral shipping to avoid the risks. By the end of 1863, Confederate raiders had managed to provoke a massive flight from the flag, significantly reducing the prosperous American merchant navy. James Gordon Bennett, the editor of the *New York Herald*, the newspaper with the highest circulation, complained that it was 'galling to the national pride that four or five fleet [*sic*] Anglo-rebel cruisers should be allowed to drive our commerce from the seas' and criticised the government for 'the neglect, the carelessness, the incompetency, and the utter imbecility of the Navy Department'.[32] The indignation against Britain, evident in the wording, was based on a solid foundation. The *Florida*, another successful raider, and the *Alabama* were British-built, like the Laird rams, and more raiders were known to be under construction in British shipyards. The *Alabama* ended her career off the port of Cherbourg in June 1864. Semmes challenged the commander of the *Kearsarge* to a duel. The superior armament of the *Kearsarge* decided the issue, and the *Alabama* ceased to be a threat. Shortly after this contest, *The Economist* expressed relief as well as uneasiness about how simple it had been for a small power to hurt the interests of a great trading nation:

> The history of the Alabama . . . is not a pleasant one for mercantile men. It seems to show that the advance of naval science has given to maritime armaments a dangerous or even fatal advantage over maritime commerce – that any country possessed of a port, or not possessed, can send out a steam man-of-war which, if built for speed, well supplied with money, and commanded by an adventurous man, may harass trade for months with almost perfect impunity . . . The Alabama has been able for many months to traverse the ocean, seizing or burning American merchant ships with such frequency and impunity that shippers have avoided them, shipowners have commenced selling them, and the trade of a very great country has been most seriously impaired.[33]

As soon as the war ended, the US government demanded compensation for the damage caused by the British-built raiders. The US merchant marine, which had come a close second to the British at the beginning of the war, was greatly diminished and declined until World War One. The *Alabama* was so prominent that the whole affair came to be known as the '*Alabama* claims'. One of the American coercive actions was the building of other fast commerce raiders similar to the *Alabama*, in anticipation of the eventuality of an Anglo-American war.

These tensions continued until 1872, when the issue was finally settled. The British government finally recognised its responsibility for the damage to US interests and agreed to pay an indemnity. This went a long way toward convincing French strategists of the *Jeune École* that the policy of building of super-*Alabamas*, though they might remain technically flawed, was an effective coercive means.[34]

Conclusions

These middle decades of the nineteenth century witnessed a period of profound escalation in the conduct of war and of technological innovation in military hardware.[35] This was mirrored, not surprisingly, by equally profound changes in the strategic outlook and physical make-up of navies. Britain, as the leading naval power and as the most advanced industrial economy was best placed to cope with the changes of scale and with the technical challenges that were now faced. Indeed, Britain benefited quite handsomely from the diffusion of sea power, as the growth of different national navies, and their need to keep abreast of these advances, further stimulated its shipbuilding industry. Yet this escalation was not solely of Britain's design, nor was Britain solely in control. In Europe, France, in particular, embraced opportunities opened by steam and armour, and the experience of the American Civil War had the most direct impact on European navies more generally. The configuration of the rapidly rebuilt Russian navy in light of the Polish uprising of 1863 and the threat of wider war is a clear illustration. The value of its new coastal ironclads and commerce-raiding cruisers was not in any doubt. A decade later, the introduction of torpedo boats completed a triptych of changes that marks what for European navies was nothing short of a revolution in military affairs. At least as significant for the longer-term future, and escalation, of naval warfare, it must not be forgotten, was the extent to which these developments had been enabled or even driven by public engagement in political debates about the construction and deployment of navies.

Notes

1 Andrew D. Lambert, *The Crimean War: British Grand Strategy, 1853–56* (Manchester: Manchester University Press, 1990), pp.56–66; Orlando Figes, *Crimea: the Last Crusade* (London: Allen Lane, 2010), pp.52, 144–47.

2 Figes, *Crimea*, pp.489–92; Serhii Plokhy, 'The City of Glory: Sevastopol in Russian Historical Mythology', *Journal of Contemporary History*, 35, 3 (2000), pp.369–83.

3 Stephen S. Roberts, 'The French Transatlantic Steam Packet Programme of 1840', *Mariner's Mirror*, 73 (1987), pp.273–86.

4 Michèle Battesti, *La Marine de Napoléon III: une politique navale*, vol. 1 (Vincennes: Service Historique de la Marine, 1997), pp.80–84.

5 Antony Preston and John Major, *Send a Gunboat: the Victorian Navy and Supremacy at Sea, 1854–1907* (London: Conway), pp.9–31, 194, 196–205.

6 G.A. Osbon, 'The Crimean Gunboats, I', *Mariner's Mirror*, 51 (1965).

7 H.C.B. Rogers, *Troopships and their History* (London: Seely Service, 1963), p.122.

8 Battesti, *La Marine de Napoléon III*, p.1224.

9 Richard Cobden, *The Three Panics: an Historical Episode* (London: Ward & Co., 1862).

10 Battesti, *La marine de Napoléon III*, pp.798–813.

11 Ibid., pp.1025–80.

12 James P. Baxter, *The Introduction of the Ironclad Warship* (Cambridge: Harvard University Press, 1933), p.99.

13 Andrew D. Lambert, *Battleships in Transition: the Creation of the Steam Battlefleet, 1815–1860* (London: Conway, 1984); Andrew D. Lambert, 'Duke of Wellington Class Steam Battleships', *Warship*, 32 (1984), pp.239–43.

14 Baxter, *Ironclad Warship*; Howard J. Fuller, *Clad in Iron: the American Civil War and the Challenge of British Naval Power* (Westport: Praeger, 2008); C.I. Hamilton, *Anglo-French Naval Rivalry, 1840–1870* (Oxford: Clarendon Press, 1993); Andrew D. Lambert, 'Politics, Technology and Policy-Making, 1859–1865: Palmerston, Gladstone and the Management of the Ironclad Naval Race', *Northern Mariner*, 8 (1998), pp.9–38.

15 Fuller, *Clad in Iron*, pp.5–7; Edward J. Reed, 'On Long and Short Iron-Clads', *Transactions of the Institution of Naval Architects*, 10 (1869), p.60; Stanley Sandler, *The Emergence of the Modern Capital Ship* (Newark: University of Delaware Press, 1979), pp.21–23.

16 Howard J. Fuller, '"Seagoing Purposes Indispensable to the Defence of this Country": Policy Pitfalls of Great Britain's Early Ironclads', *Northern Mariner*, 13 (2003), pp.35–36; M.S. Partridge, 'British Naval Power in the 1860's', *Mariner's Mirror*, 75 (1989), p.90.

17 William Hovgaard, *Modern History of Warships* (London: Conway, 1971), pp.20–27.

18 Adams to Russell, 5 September 1863, in Ruhl J. Bartlett, *The Record of American Diplomacy: Documents and Readings in the History of American Foreign Relations* (New York: Alfred A. Knopf, 1954), p.294; Brooks Adams, 'The Seizure of the Laird Rams', *Proceedings, Massachusetts Historical Society*, 45 (1912), p.291.

19 Raimondo Luraghi, *A History of the Confederate Navy* (London: Chatham, 1996), p.271.

20 Sandler, *The Emergence of the Modern Capital Ship*, pp.71–77.

21 Bernard Brodie, *Sea Power in the Machine Age* (New York: Greenwood Press, 1969), pp.171–257.

22 James M. McPherson, *War on the Waters: the Union and Confederate Navies, 1861–1865* (Chapel Hill: University of North Carolina Press, 2012).

23 David A. Mindell, *War, Technology, and Experience aboard the USS Monitor* (Baltimore: Johns Hopkins University Press, 2000), pp.72–73, 78–80.

24 Farid Ameur, 'La Guerre de Sécession au large de Cherbourg. La France impériale et l'affaire du *CSS Alabama* (juin 1864)', *Relations Internationales*, 150 (2012), p.17.

25 Raphael Semmes, *Croisières de l'Alabama et du Sumter* (Paris: E. Dentu, 1864); Juliet Wilson-Bareau and David C. Degener, *Manet and the American Civil War: the Battle of U.S.S. Kearsage and C.S.S. Alabama* (New Haven: Yale University Press, 2003), pp.34–39.

26 For a global view of the naval war see McPherson, *War on the Waters: the Union and Confederate Navies, 1861–1865*; and, Craig L. Symonds, *The Civil War at Sea* (Santa Barbara: Praeger, 2009). For the *Merrimack*, see William N. Still, *Iron Afloat: the Story of the Confederate Armorclads* (Columbia: University of South Carolina Press, 1985), pp.18–25.

27 Craig L. Symonds, *Lincoln and his Admirals: Abraham Lincoln, the U.S. Navy, and the Civil War* (New York: Oxford University Press, 2008), pp.136–39.

28 Carlos Alfaro Zaforteza, 'Medium Powers and Ironclad Construction: the Spanish Case, 1861–1868', in Craig C. Felker and Marcus O. Jones (eds), *New Interpretations in Naval History* (Newport: Naval War College Press, 2012), pp.11–21.

29 Still, *Iron Afloat: the Story of the Confederate Armorclads*.

30 W.H. Cracknell, *United States Navy Monitors of the Civil War* (Windsor: Profile Publications, 1973), p.277.

31 William H. Roberts, *Civil War Ironclads: the U.S. Navy and Industrial Mobilization* (Baltimore: Johns Hopkins University Press, 2002).

32 Symonds, *Lincoln and his Admirals*, pp.258–59.
33 'The Protection of Maritime Commerce', *The Economist*, 25 June 1864, p.798.
34 David H. Olivier, 'Two Sides of the Same Coin: German and French Maritime Strategies in the Late Nineteenth Century', in Bruce A. Elleman and S.C.M. Paine (eds), *Commerce Raiding: Historical Case Studies, 1755–2009* (Newport: Naval War College, 2013), *passim*.
35 Hew Strachan, *European Armies and the Conduct of War* (London: Routledge, 1983), pp.90–129.

6   The age of empire, 1870–1914

Carlos Alfaro Zaforteza

Introduction

The Franco-Prussian War (1870–1871) not only changed the European balance of power, but the very conduct of war itself. The stunning German victory left no doubt that an effective defence against invasion depended upon mass armies and railway networks. For years, therefore, the enormous cost of building these up absorbed the bulk of European defence budgets. Little was left for navies. For a while, their potential role in any such short, intense conflict seemed almost irrelevant by comparison. In the 1880s, however, when colonial rivalry erupted between the great powers so, too, did a renewed interest in navies. The spread of industrialisation, the consequent division between manufacturing countries on one side and food and raw material producers on the other, and the integration of the world economy multiplied those links between Europe and the rest of the world which only navies could securely forge. It was the great armaments race from 1905, however, that finally confirmed unambiguously the now simply indispensable role that navies were seen to play, both as instruments of imperialism and as effective weapons of industrial warfare.

The reassertion of the importance of naval affairs in public life in the three decades leading up to World War One was both rapid and profound. Neither before nor since have navies appealed so much to both elites and the wider public. As Eric Hobsbawm observed, at this time, 'naval scares had political sex appeal, unlike army reforms'.[1] Nationalism, imperialism, militarism, and Social Darwinism all fed, and in turn were further fuelled by, an active promotion of sea power, an outlook which came to be known as 'navalism'. These all played on similar emotions and led to heavy expenditure on navies which would be otherwise difficult to justify or explain on military grounds alone. Mass politics demanded constant efforts at nation-building to which navies lent themselves particularly well. Since military might and industrialisation were inextricably linked, the battleship, in particular, conveyed an image of power and technological prowess like no other piece of military equipment. In the words of Sir Michael Howard, it

> was indeed a symbol of national pride and power of a unique kind; one even
> more appropriate to the industrial age than armies. It embodied at once the

technological achievement of the nation as a whole, its world-wide reach and, with its huge guns, immense destructive power. It was a status symbol of universal validity, one that no nation conscious of its destiny could afford to do without.[2]

The result was intense competition. Consequently, naval races abounded. The Anglo-German (1905–1912) is the best known, but others, such as the Anglo-French (1884–1904), Franco-Italian (1885–1899), and Austro-Italian (1909–1914) races also had momentous political consequences.[3] Almost prophetically, the rapidly hardening assumptions about naval power were borne out by contemporary naval conflicts. The Sino-Japanese (1894–1895), Spanish–American (1898), and Russo-Japanese (1904–1905) wars all seemed to confirm the essential value of an efficient navy for the winners and the grave risks of not having an adequate one for the losers.

The decline of sea power after 1870

The maritime aspects of the Franco-Prussian War rarely merit more than a mention in general histories of the conflict, because sea power did not materially affect the outcome. Nevertheless, although the French navy was unable to avert disaster, the war still marks a watershed in the history of sea power. For now, navies, it seemed, had proven themselves ineffective in continental warfare against rich, industrialised countries. It was assumed that any future war would be similarly brief and that mass armies, strategic railways, and mobilisation plans, not sea power, would be the key to survival. Even the landing of a 40,000-man army behind enemy lines was less of a threat to a state which could quickly and efficiently deploy its troops through a network of railways. Equally, without sufficient time for their effect to tell, blockades, too, would be less effective. Finally, the sense that any losses in shipping or overseas colonies could be recouped at the peace table contributed to the general neglect of navies.

With the notable exception of Britain, all European powers, therefore, set out to create mass armies on the Prussian model. The transition from small, professional forces to mass conscript armies meant a quantum leap in the military power of the state, but also in defence expenditure. The increased costs of food, clothing, accommodation, large stocks of state-of-the-art armaments, and strategic railways were so high that even the great powers struggled.[4] France, for example, attained a minimum degree of security against its northern neighbour only by 1882. The army was rebuilt at a staggering cost, but naval expenditure significantly diminished as a result. Between 1872 and 1886, it amounted to less than 8.5 per cent of the army's budget.[5]

The German Empire, now Europe's pre-eminent military power, and on the road to economic and industrial supremacy, was content with a medium-sized navy, basically composed of coast-defence ironclads and cruisers. The two major navies created *ex novo* in the 1860s, the US Navy and the Russian Baltic Fleet, also did without battleships. The former was quickly demobilised at the end of the Civil War, returning to its antebellum force structure and trade-protection duties. Even the British navy was run down somewhat in the absence of rivals. Not surprisingly, the period between 1868 and 1884 has been referred to as the 'dark ages of the Admiralty' or by US Navy historians as a period of 'material decline and intellectual stagnation'.[6] Whilst reduced commitments might have reflected a more general peace, from the perspective of naval officers they also led to reduced budgets and poor career prospects. A stable Europe controlled from Berlin and the absence of overseas rivalries meant that naval force was required for little more than policing the seas.

Battleship construction was also affected by technical issues. By the early 1870s, developments in guns and armour had created a difficult problem. Put simply, it was relatively easy and cheap to build bigger guns but not to produce ships with the corresponding armour needed to protect them. The only way to combine mammoth guns, extremely thick armour, sufficient speed, and seaworthiness in the same hull was through an inordinate increase in size and cost. A brief comparison between the first sea-going ship to incorporate these features, the Italian *Duilio* (1876), and the first sea-going ironclad, the French *Gloire* (1859), in Table 6.1 conveys an idea of the dramatic changes that took place in less than two decades. Whilst size doubled, cost increased more than four-fold. The smaller crew of the *Duilio* reflected the great reductions in manpower enabled by the omission of sail rigging and the mechanical operation of guns.[7] The building times, not directly proportional to size, also reflect the tranquil, parsimonious 1870s, in the case of the *Duilio*, as compared with the shorter period for the *Gloire*, built in the midst of an arms race, with a large budget. The result was a concentration of resources in fewer, more costly hulls. Fleets operating in coastal waters, however, now faced a new threat against which no effective protection existed. Though still crude and unreliable, underwater weapons had already shown their potential and posed

Table 6.1 Early evolution of the battleship[9]

	Gloire	*Duilio*
Country	France	Italy
Launched	1859	1876
Building time (years)	2.5	7
Hull material	Wood	Iron
Displacement (tons)	5,500	10,900
Cost (French francs)	4.7 million	22 million
Number of guns	36	4
Calibre (cm)	16	45
Weight (tons)	3.6	100
Armour thickness (cm)	12	55
Sails	Full rig	None
Crew	570	420

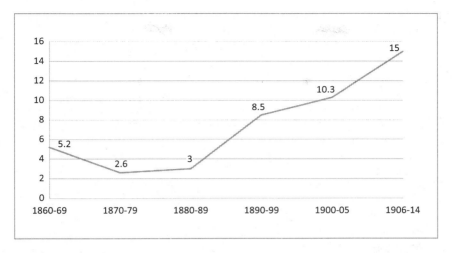

Figure 6.1 Great-power first-class battleship construction, 1860–1914. Number of hulls laid down, mean annual rate[10]

considerable risks to these expensive, scarce units, so that the loss of just one could be crippling, both materially and morally.

All of these doubts about the role of battleships and their cost resulted in a considerable decrease in construction rates for nearly two decades (see Figure 6.1), as attention turned to cheaper alternatives: coast-defence ships and cruisers.[8] Yet this decline in their status and of navies generally, such as it was, was only temporary and would very soon be reversed in the most emphatic fashion imaginable.

Causes and consequences of recovery

On 23 August 1884, a French fleet commanded by Admiral Courbet destroyed a Chinese force anchored before Foochow dockyard (Fujian Province). The action took place during the Sino-French War (1884–1885) to assert French claims to Indochina and get special conditions for French trade in the Chinese bordering provinces. This unilateral display of power, the professionalism displayed by French sailors, and the disruption of British trade along the Chinese coast caused alarm in London. To further pressure the Chinese government to make peace, France declared rice contraband of war. It was being shipped along the coast from the mouth of the Yang Tse to the northern region around Peking and used not just as essential food but even as a means of paying taxes in kind. Britain protested; like China, it depended on maritime transport to feed its population. Yet the German and Russian governments, which were self-sufficient in food production, quickly recognised the French declaration, which set a dangerous precedent.[11] The Chinese government, confronted with the prospect of financial failure and civil unrest, yielded to French demands. For France, the army's operations in Tonkin had been indecisive. The navy played the leading role, and for the first time since the Franco-Prussian War it was praised by the media. This time, it had lived up to the country's expectations, and Courbet and his officers became household names.[12] The French navy had regained its lost prestige.

Comparable acts of imperial expansion also took place in other parts of the world. In June 1884, Chancellor Bismarck, who temporarily abandoned his anti-colonial views, announced the acquisition of German South-West Africa, modern Namibia, in response to the request of Bremen businessman Adolf Lüderitz. He then sent a squadron of four ships to assert German rule in the area, where German missionaries and traders had been active for years. Shortly thereafter, another squadron was sent to East Africa to impose a protectorate on Zanzibar. The Sultan initially challenged this claim but was eventually 'persuaded' by the presence of the German warships, which anchored before his capital with their guns pointing to his palace.[13] Further north, Italian colonial activity also developed. On 5 February 1885, an Italian fleet landed an expeditionary corps and began the occupation of Eritrea.[14] Such displays of naval power, hitherto restricted to the established colonial powers, reveal the now widespread use of navies as instruments of empire and status symbols.

The diffusion of naval power, and the consequent capacity to project power overseas, stoked the 'scramble for Africa' and the general quest for overseas colonies. The 1880s saw an outburst of such expansion involving not only Britain and France, but also Italy, Germany, and smaller powers. One of the chief results of the Berlin Conference of 1884–1885 was the establishment of a fledgling German colonial empire and French expansion in the Far East. Bismarck and French prime minister Jules Ferry, a follower of Paul Leroy-Beaulieu's ideas, set up a temporary alliance to advance their overseas interests. The window of opportunity had been opened when the British government was discredited by the news of the fall of Khartoum and the Russian advance in Central Asia. For a short period, Bismarck and Ferry managed to isolate Britain diplomatically and raise again the idea of a maritime balance of power to achieve their objectives.[15] Apart from the economic benefit and political control implied, prestige was a major motive. Indeed, it was Ferry's main argument for an increase in the naval budget at the end of the Berlin conference:

> Since the policy of colonial expansion is the general objective that drives European powers today, we must take action, otherwise what will happen is . . . what has happened to other nations which played a very great role three centuries ago, and which have descended . . . to the third or fourth rank.[16]

The links between imperialism, prestige, and sea power are evident in this early formulation of *Weltpolitik*. It is no wonder that British opposition politicians became concerned. Since the government seemed complacent, they chose to appeal directly to public opinion with the help of powerful journalists and disgruntled naval officers. To state their case, they enlisted the services of

W.T. Stead, who had converted the sensationalist *Pall Mall Gazette* into a leading political journal. H.O. Arnold-Forster, a fellow journalist specialised in defence affairs, and Captain (future Admiral) John Fisher supplied him with the necessary information. Stead skilfully exploited British nationalism in a series of articles entitled 'The Truth about the Navy'.[17] The opening phrase of the first of these, published only three weeks after the Battle of Foochow, stated that '[t]he scramble for the world has begun in earnest'. He then called into question the condition of the navy and set forth his expectations of it:

> A system by which two-thirds of all the bread eaten in England has come to be grown over the sea can only be defended on the assumption that the ocean highway is as secure as the Great Northern railway . . . It is, therefore, an axiom of the Liberal free traders that our superiority at sea must be 'absolutely irresistible', and that our hundred millions sterling must, if needs be, be spent cheerfully rather than that our irresistible superiority should be challenged by any possible combination of hostile Powers.[18]

The articles caused public uproar and led to demands for increased naval expenditure. The government had to bow to popular pressure, even though it was confident that British naval supremacy was not threatened.[19] The resulting five-year building plan, generally known as the Northbrook Programme, included two battleships and five cruisers.[20] Two further five-year programmes followed: the Naval Defence Act of 1889, made up of no less than ten battleships and thirty-seven cruisers, and the Spencer Programme of 1894, which authorised seven battleships and twenty cruisers.[21] These were acts of rampant navalism, in the sense that they enjoyed a surprising extent of popular support. They also constituted milestones of the Anglo-French naval arms race and competition for empire.

Thus 1884 marks the beginning of mass public awareness of naval affairs in Britain. It is no coincidence that it came only months after the Third Reform Act, which considerably extended suffrage. This was a period of economic depression. The steel and armaments industries were strategic sectors that needed government support. Steel, in particular, faced stiff competition from Germany and the United States, which had lower production costs. Since the newly-enfranchised workers were not subject to direct taxes, as the landed classes were, they had no incentive to oppose heavy government expenditure. Indeed, the working classes benefited from the resulting creation of jobs and came to take pride in the navy, which played an entertainment and identity-building role similar to today's football league. Thus, significant interest groups from British society came to have a stake in naval development.

Some Liberals considered this expenditure extravagant, to the extent that Prime Minister Gladstone resigned over the Spencer Programme, rather than accept 'the greatest and richest sacrifice ever made on the altar of militarism'.[22] Nevertheless, the international effect of the 'Truth about the Navy' scare was the start of a two-decade-long naval race with France, later joined by Russia. 'Absolutely irresistible' naval superiority had certainly ensured security for Britain, and also absolute freedom to act unilaterally. Hitherto, most powers had grudgingly accepted this as a fact of life, but now many had the capability and the political will to join in the competition for overseas empire.

The second stage of the industrial revolution, characterised by the large-scale use of steel and significant advances in chemistry and electricity, enabled great strides in naval architecture, armaments, and marine engineering. Its spread also enabled the production of military hardware in other countries, however. British manufacturers no longer enjoyed the virtual monopoly of technologically advanced products. British maritime industries continued to be by far the largest, but French and German armaments now competed in quality. In the 1880s, it was German shipyards that provided the Chinese fleet with modern warships.[23] This is all the more remarkable when considering that less than a decade before, the German navy was still ordering battleships from British shipyards. French industrialisation was also taking great strides, and this was noticeable in the French navy's materiel.[24] Gun manufacturers such as Krupp and Canet started to compete successfully with Armstrong and Vickers. Among the torpedo-boat-building shipyards, a highly-specialised business, Normand, of Le Havre, and Schichau, of Elbing, built more and better boats than their British counterparts. The lucrative naval armaments market was no longer a British monopoly.[25] On the other side of the Atlantic, the US Navy, which for years relied on obsolete wooden, full-rigged ships, equipped with old muzzle-loading, smooth-bore guns, was at last modernised. In 1883, Congress authorised the first four ships of the 'new navy', with steel hulls and modern guns. The requirement to have the ships built and equipped entirely by domestic industry led to the introduction of steel plating manufacture and other modern technologies in the United States.[26] Industrialisation and the diffusion of naval power went hand in hand.

Technological development also decisively affected maritime trade. By the 1880s, advances in metallurgy and marine engineering gave birth to the steel-hulled tramp ship, a vastly more efficient carrier than the sailing ship. Ocean freight rates fell dramatically, and the tonnage of steamships built surpassed that of sailing vessels for the first time. From 25 per cent of the total shipping afloat in 1880, it increased to 92 in 1914. A network of submarine telegraphs, coal depots, and dry docks along the main trading routes completed the revolution in maritime transport. These developments were an essential contribution to the tenfold increase of world trade between 1850 and 1913, since the maritime component of this was around 90 per cent.[27] Now ship owners in London or Hamburg could transmit instructions and receive information from around the world in a matter of hours.

This complex system of transport, chiefly promoted and implemented by British interests, was as vulnerable as it was economically efficient. The daily business of the financial centre of the world, the City of London, depended on the safe, timely delivery of foodstuffs to feed the population and raw materials to keep the factories working. Disruption to this traffic would be catastrophic for the British economy. That is why commerce warfare became a potentially decisive strategy in the industrial era, as the two world wars would later prove. Britain was, of course, an extreme case and particularly vulnerable in this respect, though other countries were affected to different degrees.[28]

Navies grew as instruments of foreign policy in European affairs, too. A clear illustration involves the preliminaries of the Franco-Russian alliance of 1893, which ended French isolation and confronted Germany with the prospect of a two-front war. In the balance of power in Central Europe, it was armies, not navies, that mattered. Yet it was the latter which featured in the most visible political gestures. To signal the alliance between the two countries, a French fleet called at Kronstadt in July 1891. It was happily received by the Russian authorities and public. The tsar visited the fleet and even listened respectfully to the revolutionary hymn the *Marseillaise*. This clear sign of Franco-Russian rapprochement was seen as a provocation in Germany. Two years later, a Russian squadron returned the visit at Toulon, where it was received by President Sadi Carnot and another enthusiastic crowd. After days of celebrations, the Russian admiral and a delegation of the fleet travelled to Paris, where further celebrations took place. The exuberance of these events, the lavish press coverage, and its impact on European public opinion made it one of the big media events of its time. Shortly thereafter, the alliance was officially concluded.[29]

This up-swell of public support seems to have been one of the principal objectives of these stage-managed events. In this respect, it is worth pointing out the modest strength of the Russian squadron: it was made up of only five units. The most powerful was a second-class battleship. It was, in other words, hardly an impressive force in military terms, yet it still effectively symbolised the power of the Russian Empire. What is truly remarkable is the explosion of empathy it triggered between two societies on opposite extremes of the European ideological spectrum: the most conservative and the most progressive. The modern warship was the means of communication between them. This did not go unnoticed by the British defence expert Sir George Sydenham Clarke, who identified navies as 'powerful agents for the interchange of national sentiment'. He observed that:

> Out of the visits of the Russian and French squadrons to each other's ports sprang an alliance which has already borne fruits of importance. The Russian and French people know nothing of each other, and are unlike in most essential respects. The visits of the respective squadrons touched the imagination of the masses as no diplomatic correspondence could have done. It was something which those masses could understand.[30]

The choice of Toulon for the naval gathering was inevitably perceived by Britain and Italy as a threat to their Mediterranean interests. Both Russia and France were also expanding in Asia. In particular, Russian advances in the Pamir and French expansion in Siam seemed to threaten the British position in India. Franco-Russian naval presence in the Mediterranean also posed a serious challenge to the British empire's main line of communication. Although this was not the intended purpose, it triggered one of the war scares to which the British public was so prone and which resulted in the Spencer Programme. The popular writer William

Le Queux took advantage of the situation to publish his fictional bestseller *The Great War in England in 1897* (1894). Typical of the scare literature of the times, it described the invasion of England by a French and Russian army. It was first published in serialised form in the weekly *Answers*, a journal directed to a lay readership. The following year, it was released as a book, prefaced by General Lord Roberts, held then as the foremost military expert in Britain. By 1899, it had gone through sixteen editions; it had received praise from military experts, and was commented on in the French and Italian press.[31]

These interactions between defence affairs and the wider population were not unique to Europe. A similar case occurred in Japan in July 1891, when a Chinese squadron visited the port of Yokohama. The public was impressed by the battleship *Chen Yuen*, recently built in Germany. The Japanese navy simply had nothing that could remotely approach its fighting power. The press featured a debate on defence policy, and Chinese naval superiority was driven home to the government and to the public. Consequently, the Navy Minister tried to have a building programme approved,[32] which although unsuccessful demonstrates the emotive, political power of navies in this case too.

Navalism and the new navies

> Only complete political confusion and naïve optimism can prevent the recognition that the unavoidable efforts at trade expansion by all civilized bourgeois-controlled nations, after a transitional period of seemingly peaceful competition, are clearly approaching the point where *power alone* will decide each nation's share in the economic control of the earth, and hence its people's sphere of activity.
>
> Max Weber, 1898[33]

Weber's argument for a big navy, in support of the German navy law of 1898, reflects the zeitgeist of the 'age of empire'. At the turn of the century, European international relations were focused on overseas issues. Whilst the continent was comparatively quiet, a series of events, including the Sino-Japanese War, the German occupation of Tsingtao, or the American conquest of the Philippines reflected the tensions rising in the Far East.[34] The year 1897 is a convenient vantage point to explore the increasing complexity of the situation. That year, the British government staged a grand fleet review at Spithead to celebrate Queen Victoria's Diamond Jubilee. The naval force gathered for the event consisted of more than 150 state-of-the-art ships. This was achieved without moving a single vessel from overseas deployments, and it was far more than any other navy could put together. Yet, this time, the flaunting of sea power failed to intimidate rivals. Instead, it only whetted their appetite.[35] Expert observers, such as Friedrich Ratzel in his seminal work *Politische Geographie*, were well aware of the erosion of British naval hegemony that was hidden behind such displays.[36] For years, other states had been building up their naval forces. Whilst in 1883 Britain had more battleships than the rest of the world put together, by 1897, despite having doubled the number, it had only two thirds of the total. Brassey's *Naval Annual*, 1897 edition, the British navalist's Bible, openly recognised the significance of emergent sea powers. 'In former years', it observed,

> we used to confine the comparisons . . . to the fleets of France and Russia; but during the past year it has become more and more evident that we must take into consideration the Navies of all the principal Naval Powers. [37]

The major new actors were Germany and, for the first time, two extra-European countries: the United States and Japan. Their naval development can be traced through the actions of three remarkable personalities: Admiral Alfred von Tirpitz, President Theodore Roosevelt, and Admiral Yamamoto Gonnohyoe. In 1897, Kaiser Wilhelm II appointed the two key statesmen who helped him create the German High Seas Fleet: Navy Minister Tirpitz and Secretary of State Bernhard von Bülow. That same year, the German navy intervened in two remote places. It practised gunboat diplomacy with the Haitian government over German commercial interests, and the East Asia Squadron seized the Chinese port of Tsingtao, which became the German colony of Kiaochou. Bülow justified these actions as part of Germany's *Weltpolitik* in his famous 'place in the sun' speech before the Reichstag. All of this happened in the aftermath of a Germanophobic campaign in the British press, in response to the Kruger Telegram and stiff German commercial competition.

Tirpitz was an able politician, unlike his predecessor. He managed to gather support from the middle classes and the industrial bourgeoisie. This enabled him to overcome opposition to increased naval spending from both agrarian Junkers, who supported the Prussian army, and pacifist Social Democrats. Moreover, until 1912 he benefited from the concerns of army command over changes to an institution traditionally composed of Prussian aristocratic officers and peasant soldiers. It feared the political consequences of an increase in military strength. This would mean a large influx of new officers and recruits from urban and industrial backgrounds, exposed to Socialist ideas. As a result, the army budget was frozen until the eve of World War One, thus liberating funds for the navy.

One of Tirpitz's main instruments was an extremely efficient propaganda service, the *Nachrichtenbureau*. It used the most modern, sophisticated techniques to target the different sections of German society. These included pamphlets, journals, a naval annual, and film. It organised naval reviews and launching ceremonies, and set up a navy league that by 1914 counted over one million members, by far the largest and most successful in any country.[38] Tirpitz himself contacted prominent personalities who could support his project, including shipping magnates Albert Ballin, manager of the transatlantic *Hamburg-Amerika* line, and Adolf Woermann, owner of steamer lines to West and East Africa. In this way, the old Hanseatic cities of Hamburg, Bremen, and Lübeck came to supply officers and seamen from their large seafaring communities. Tirpitz also enlisted the help of the academic elites. Known as *Flottenprofessoren*, this group included some of the most brilliant contemporary minds.[39] Hans Delbrück, Otto Hintze,

Theodor Mommsen, Gustav Schmoller, and Max Weber, to cite only some of the best known, wrote the most intellectually elaborate navalist literature, which has largely been ignored by Anglo-Saxon historiography.

This propaganda effort transformed the navy into an effective nation-building instrument, which in turn generated its own support. It was perceived as a genuinely German institution, as opposed to the army. This was, of course, immensely popular, but it was seen as essentially Prussian. It was represented at the Prussian diet, whilst the navy, as a truly national institution, was represented at the Reichstag, by a proper secretary of state, and its budget was voted by the whole nation. The navy also took recruits from all German states and officers, chiefly from the middle classes. If the navy failed in its broader purpose of keeping Germany's communications with the Atlantic open, Tirpitz was nonetheless immensely successful from an institutional point of view. By 1914, the German navy was second only to the British, and this was achieved in a state without a maritime tradition.

Although the motivations behind Imperial Germany's pursuit of a large navy have been the matter of much speculation in Anglo-Saxon historiography, in many ways it was a natural policy to adopt. Michael Epkenhans gives three reasons. First, since he was a child, Wilhelm II had been an admirer of British sea power and had lately become a devout follower of Mahan's theories. Second, it was essential to protect Germany's increasing overseas commerce and interests, as Max Weber pointed out. Finally, the navy provided a nation-building tool, which supported domestic industry, appealed to the middle classes, and helped to stave off the proletarian threat.[40] Certainly, Germany's booming economy had become highly dependent on overseas markets, both for manufacturing and capital exports and for imports of foodstuffs and raw materials. Direct commercial competition with Britain, and the location of the main German ports, Hamburg and Bremen, on the south coast of the North Sea, meant that only the English Channel could provide easy access to the Atlantic. Free circulation through it was a vital interest for the German economy. This meant that Germany could not afford to depend on British goodwill. Even the Anglophile Mahan conceded this.[41]

This does not rule out prestige as a motivation. A big navy was certainly essential to achieve world-power status. The claim that this was an unnecessary indulgence and something which Germany, in particular, could ill afford was simply a rhetorical device used by potential enemies that was targeted at popular audiences. Indeed this idea of a German 'luxury fleet' has since been taken up by some historians, although, as Sir Michael Howard observed, the German need for a big navy was perfectly obvious to expert contemporary opinion.[42] Sir Eyre Crowe, a high-ranking British official, observed in 1907 that, regardless of whether her foreign policy was aggressive or not, 'Germany would clearly be wise to build as powerful a navy as she can afford'.[43] Captain Darrieus of the French navy, a well-known naval strategist, was of the same opinion.[44] A solid, objective, geopolitical reason, therefore, existed, which dovetailed naturally with the pursuit of prestige.

The second personality of note was Theodore Roosevelt, appointed Assistant Secretary of the US Navy in 1897. Although technically only deputy to the secretary, his strong personality and drive played a major role in the preparation of the navy for the war against Spain. When he became president, his two greatest projects were the building of a battle fleet and, to facilitate its deployment in response to changing global circumstances, an interoceanic canal in Panama. In his first annual message, Roosevelt proclaimed that

> the work of upbuilding the Navy must be steadily continued. No one point of our policy, foreign or domestic, is more important than this to the honor and material welfare, and above all to the peace, of our nation in the future.[45]

He achieved his objective with the invaluable help of two fellow navalists: his close friend Henry Cabot Lodge, the Republican senator for Massachusetts, and Captain Alfred T. Mahan, USN.[46] Through his influence and enthusiasm, Roosevelt converted navalism into a genuine mass movement in the United States. Indeed, he created what was arguably its greatest manifestation: the cruise of the Great White Fleet (1907–1909). Made up of sixteen battleships, this fleet sailed around the world specifically to show that the United States had become a world power.[47]

This was achieved at the turn of the century by first asserting US supremacy in the Western Hemisphere, converting the Caribbean into an American lake, and declaring an open-door policy in China. These policies required sea power. During the Venezuelan Crisis of 1902, President Roosevelt sent a fleet to warn off an intervention by British, German, and Italian naval forces.[48] The following year, Colombia became the target of US imperialism. The new state of Panama, created through US intervention, provided the favourable conditions to build the interoceanic canal. When Japan emerged as a powerful rival after victory in the Russo-Japanese War, Roosevelt sent the Great White Fleet into the Pacific Ocean. This was a far cry from the four cruisers sent to Europe back in 1889. That year, the US Navy, which still had no battleships, sent its most modern ships to show that its old wooden ships equipped with obsolete muzzle-loaders were being replaced by state-of-the-art steel ships with modern guns.

The third key personality in major fleet-building was Admiral Yamamoto, of the Japanese navy. He was Tirpitz's less well-known counterpart in Japan, but he faced similar challenges and achieved comparable results. Victory in the war with China, which elevated Japan to a major regional player, provoked the intervention of France, Germany, and Russia to limit her gains. Japan felt this as a severe humiliation. It had outfought China, both on land and at sea, but it was not powerful enough to confront the three European powers. The response was to build a large navy to prevent further Western interference. As a result, the parliament voted an 1897 naval budget that for the first time surpassed the army's. It included a large shipbuilding programme as ambitious as the German First Navy Law. Yamamoto was the man behind the programme. Soon after, as Navy Minister (1898–1906), he developed the Japanese navy into a first-class force and continued to compete successfully with the army for financial resources.[49]

These were the most noteworthy examples, but far from the only ones. Any state not interested in, or incapable of pursuing, this game would be seen as a second-rate or declining power. *Weltpolitik* became an indispensable element of great-power status, though the Sino-Japanese (1894–1895), Spanish–American (1898), and Russo-Japanese wars (1904–1905) were only the most spectacular episodes. Naval forces were frequently involved in other ways around the globe, and gunboats saw more active service than larger units. Sometimes their mere symbolic value could cause major international incidents. A classic example is the case of the German gunboat *Panther*. The appearance of this small ship, equipped with just a few guns, before the port of Agadir in 1911 triggered the Second Moroccan Crisis.[50]

At times, states sought to flaunt their power simply for reasons of prestige. This is what happened in China in 1900. Foreign intervention to suppress the Boxer Rebellion makes a good case study of the increased number of European players in overseas affairs. An international force of more than thirty warships gathered off Taku, the port nearest to Peking. Besides the usual Russian, British, and French ships, newcomers, such as German, Japanese, American, and Italian vessels, were also present. Even the Austro-Hungarian Empire, which had no colonies, sent a squadron of four units. The German contribution, however, was the largest. The murder of the German plenipotentiary in Peking had so outraged the Kaiser that he chose to send an additional force. The expedition included four battleships and 20,000 men. The *Hamburg-Amerika* and *Norddeutscher Lloyd* shipping lines, by then the largest in the world, duly provided eighteen large steamers for troop transport. A further thirty-nine carried materiel, victuals, and horses. This was an impressive show of long-distance power-projection capability, hitherto reserved to Britain. The German shipbuilding and shipping industry, an indispensable element of sea power, had become second only to Britain and had actually overtaken her in the largest, most technically advanced steamships. Yet this display of new capabilities, based on a personal decision of the Kaiser, was the last thing that the statesmen most closely associated with the creation of the German navy, Tirpitz and von Bülow, wished to see. Their policies were aimed at keeping German naval development as inconspicuous as possible, so as not to raise concerns in Britain.[51]

There is a certain inevitability about the effect on British naval policy as well. Already, in 1901, Britain conceded that it could no longer maintain the two-power standard.[52] The Boer War dealt a heavy blow to her prestige, morale, and state finances. The ongoing naval race with France and Russia, the development of the German navy, and the emergence of two extra-European great powers all led to a revision of commitments. Thus, Britain began its retreat from America and recognised de facto US hegemony.

The following year, circumstances finally forced Britain to conclude a formal alliance, the first in many years, with Japan. In some respects, Japanese naval forces were being used, therefore, to contain Russian imperialism in the Far East. In 1904, Britain also entered the *entente cordiale* with France, shortly after transformed into the Triple Entente when Russia joined. Accordingly, when Admiral

Fisher was appointed First Sea Lord (professional head of the navy) in 1904, he introduced necessary reforms. More than 150 vessels policing the empire were decommissioned, and the released resources were concentrated on the North Sea. By 1914, even the Mediterranean Fleet, one of the major symbols of the British Empire, had been dismantled. Britain's world position had dramatically changed: its ability for unilateral action was greatly diminished and the long-held two-power standard was reduced to one.

Despite the decline in Britain's global position, its geopolitical position vis-à-vis Germany gave her ample superiority. German access to the ocean could be controlled from new bases at Harwich, Rosyth, and Scapa Flow, but anti-German propaganda conveniently ignored this and appealed for a more dramatic response. By concentrating on mere ship numbers, navalists generated more public support for the ongoing naval race. During the 1909 scare, the British government had to cede to the popular slogan: 'We want eight [battleships] and we won't wait'.[53] To the Chancellor of the Exchequer, David Lloyd George, these demands looked preposterous. They ran counter to the policies of the Liberals, who had come to power on a programme of social reform and reduced military expenditure.[54] Such was the broader political appeal of the navy and its essential value as an instrument of state power.

Strategy and politics

After 1870, the expansion of mass armies placed a heavy burden on defence budgets, and the distribution of resources between armies and navies was a major issue. The United States and Great Britain were the exceptions. Neither was directly exposed to invasion. Both countries could comfortably do away with large, extremely costly armies. Instead, they could concentrate their resources on their navies. Britain's easy access to the Atlantic and control over approaches to the North Sea put Germany in an unfavourable strategic situation. The Russian case was even worse, though its economy was less dependent on foreign markets. As we have seen, Russia's fragmented coastline and difficult access to the ocean severely handicapped its efforts to create a unified, powerful navy. These essential factors determined the structure, size, and function of navies as much as contingent causes did.

They also determined the nature of naval arms races. The Anglo-French (1884–1904) and Anglo-German (1905–1912) races, for example, were asymmetric. French and German commitments to their respective navies were limited because the main threat to their security was invasion across their land borders. France focused its defence on the north-east frontier; Germany had to deal with the threat of a two-front war against both France and Russia. British naval policy did not have this constraint.

The resurgence of protectionism and colonial expansion in turn revived the mercantilist trinity of production, commerce, and colonies. The causes of colonial competition in the seventeenth and eighteenth centuries again became a significant feature of European politics. Mahan's influential book *The Influence of*

Sea Power upon History (1890) reflected these concerns. At the same time, with increased literacy and enfranchisement, governments now had to seek a wider consensus. The naval scare of 1884 in Britain and the celebrations at Kronstadt (1891) and Toulon (1893) are good examples of popular involvement. Statesmen could count on the help of naval officers who had suffered with poor career prospects for years. In 1878, for example, Captain Phillip H. Colomb of the British navy complained that a liberal democracy would never support a big navy in the absence of an imminent threat. The government and parliament, he despaired, would only sufficiently fund a force to police the seas.[55] Of course, parsimony meant more officers on half pay and fewer opportunities for promotion. It has already been mentioned that the future Admiral Fisher helped create the 1884 scare. Similar cases in other navies abounded. After the Franco-Prussian War, the French naval budget was reduced. Due to his extreme political and professional views, Admiral Aube, the principal exponent of the *Jeune École*, was passed over for promotion. Yet his ideas appealed to radical republicans, who liked the idea of a low-cost navy, which would not interfere with the build-up of the army. It also appealed to young naval officers, as great numbers of small boats provided abundant command jobs for them. Mahan's argument for the development of the US Navy in the 1890s also had a significant corporatist component. He shared Colomb's concerns about the effect of mass politics on naval policy:

> Whether a democratic government will have the foresight, the keen sensitiveness to national position and credit, the willingness to insure its prosperity by adequate outpouring of money in times of peace, all of which are necessary for military preparation, is yet an open question. Popular governments are not generally favorable to military expenditure.[56]

Until late in the century, the sheer extent of naval hegemony obviated the British need for strategic theorising. Arguably, strategy, like economy, is less pressing when the available means are unlimited. For most of the nineteenth century, virtually unlimited resources, both industrial and financial, relative to potential enemies, and the unconditional support of British society sustained this dominance with little effort. It was occasionally asserted in various ways. One of them was the construction of huge, extremely expensive ships, which rivals could not afford to build, in response to real or perceived challenges. The paddlewheel frigate *Terrible* (1845) was commissioned during the build-up of the French steam navy. The ironclad *Warrior* (1860) was the direct answer to the first French ironclad, *Gloire* (1858). The cruiser *Powerful* (1895) was designed to hunt Russian commerce-raiding cruisers. The most famous was the *Dreadnought* (1906), built to demonstrate that, although the all-big-gun ship was not a British idea, only Britain had the financial and industrial resources to build such a ship in a short time. With the exception of the *Dreadnought*, however, these vessels generally turned out to be white elephants. Besides quickly becoming obsolete, they were so expensive and inefficient that even the British navy could not deploy them in meaningful numbers. Although they were impressive and powerful statements of superiority, the three five-year programmes discussed above constituted more effective responses, since they resulted in real increases in military power, as well as also reminding rivals of Britain's immense resources.

French naval policy, on the other hand, was subject to significant restrictions. The first was due to the army's position as the mainstay of the Republic. It constituted the core defensive capability against Germany, the instrument of an eventual *revanche*, and the country's main asset as a great power. After the Franco-Prussian War, the navy's main function was to act as an auxiliary to the army in any European war. Its primary duty was to ensure the safe passage of the XIX army corps from Algeria to Southern France and of green replacement troops in the opposite direction, as part of the general mobilisation plan. For parties at both extremes of the political spectrum, monarchists and radical republicans alike, expenditure on the navy for any other purpose felt like a diversion of precious resources. The country, they argued, could not afford a continued naval presence overseas, nor join in the ongoing competition for empire. Moderate republicans, however, did not agree.

In the 1880s, two prominent French statesmen, Leon Gambetta and Jules Ferry, strove to consolidate the republican system through policies of prestige and the opening of new markets for French manufactures. Ferry, an advocate of colonial expansion, wanted to maintain a blue-water navy, to uphold France's status as a maritime power, second only to Britain, which invariably meant involvement in the colonial race.[57] The Sino-French War, discussed above, is an example of this policy. For two decades, the argument between a high-seas fleet for sea control and power projection on one hand and a sea-denial force for coastal defence and commerce warfare on the other, the public dimension of this debate, and the high turnover of ministers destabilised French naval policy. These difficulties were compounded by the need to confront two different enemies: the Triple Alliance and Britain. The existing force sufficed to confront the former. To directly tackle the latter lay beyond France's capabilities. The *Jeune École*, as the materiel school came to be known in the 1880s, proposed a strategy of attrition. Radical republican naval officers advocated this low-cost solution.[58]

In case of war with Britain, an alternative force of coast-defence ships, torpedo boats, and cruisers would be able to defend the country's coasts and attack British trade. There was nothing new in the concept: the *guerre de course* had been the strategy of the weak for centuries and had shown its value recently in the American Civil War. Now, technological developments enabled a more comprehensive, effective approach to asymmetric warfare, with previously unknown types of warships and weapons. Industrialisation, the international division of labour, and the consequent dependence of Britain on imported foodstuffs and raw materials seemed to make this strategy a potentially decisive one. Ruthless attacks on shipping would not only cause severe disruption of commerce and panic, but also starve the population. A high degree of industrialisation and overdependence on commercial networks, which had made Britain wealthy, also made her vulnerable.

Another group of officers argued for a strategy of annihilation. This meant a traditional, balanced force, with the battleship as the core unit. The main objective of the fleet would be to destroy the enemy in a climactic battle and thus achieve command of the sea. This line of thought was based on the lessons of history, especially the great maritime wars in the age of sail. Known as the historical school, its main exponents were Admiral Jurien de La Gravière (1812–1892) and Alfred T. Mahan (1840–1914). The timing of the release of the latter's *The Influence of Sea Power upon History* in 1890 explains its enthusiastic reception. It was a reaction to the anti-imperialist materiel school, and it appealed to statesmen that opposed heavy expenditure in naval armaments. Mahan skilfully synthesised existing French literature on the subject. One of his most famous assertions, for example, that regardless of technological innovations the principles of strategy were immutable, had been set forth shortly before by Édouard Chevalier, a well-known author who wrote in a similar context of technical uncertainty.[59] Up to then, La Gravière's *Guerres maritimes sous la République et l'Empire* (1847) had been the great naval bestseller of the century. Yet before the 1880s, few states were interested, or capable, of overseas expansion. By 1890 this had changed. European overseas expansion, the spread of industrialisation, and the rise of navalism were in full swing. Literature on imperialism proliferated and had a large readership. The works of Paul Leroy-Beaulieu and John Seeley enjoyed phenomenal success.[60] Mahan's book followed in their wake; it was a good synthesis that blended naval history with theories of imperialism. It was as much a work of political science as an historical essay, and it appealed to a wider public than La Gravière's or List's works. Mahan's book was published as part of a campaign orchestrated by navalist groups and by the US Navy to transform it from a cruiser into a battleship force.[61] By 1890, the United States had finished its imperial expansion in North America and become a great power with a dynamic, industrialised economy, immense natural resources, and the potential to create large armed forces. If this project materialised, it would change the balance of power in the Western Hemisphere and alter the character of relations between Europe and America. No wonder Mahan's ideas were received with interest. His ideas were widely diffused internationally between 1894 and 1896, when the leading European naval journal, the *Revue Maritime et Coloniale*, published by the French ministry of the navy, released his book in serialised form. Translation into other languages soon followed.

The development of powerful artillery and submarine weapons over the previous two decades had called into question the role of the battleship, very few of which were built in this period as a result. Mahan, however, reassured naval officers and navalists. Here, now, was a theory for a blue-water navy which vindicated the battleship as its centrepiece, and it justified big navies. Governments and public opinion could be persuaded that it was worthwhile to invest in large fleets for prestige and overseas expansion. Mahan's ideas were hardly new, but his book was a skilful synthesis of French naval thought appearing at a particularly opportune moment. It was the intellectual basis for Tirpitz's, Yamamoto's, and Roosevelt's narratives. Yet the implementation of Mahanian theories was far from straightforward. Big navies must compete with armies for resources. Except for the special cases of the United States and Great Britain, this would be the subject of intense political debate, as the French case shows.

After the Franco-Prussian War, the officer corps of the French navy was divided. Reduced personnel needs made entry to the *École Navale* very selective. Only graduates from secondary school, then still an elitist institution, were accepted. Promotion depended on the verdict of a committee made up of aristocratic, conservative officers, coming mostly from the General Staff or the Mediterranean fleet. They generally favoured those who had served under their orders. Officers serving overseas, on the other hand, had fewer chances.[62] Aube belonged to this latter group, and his well-known heretical views did not endear him to the dominant elite. Yet he had the sympathies of young officers and left-wing parties.

Aube was appointed Navy Minister in January 1886. Due to the instability of French politics, he stayed in office only one and a half years, but he had time to translate his ideas into policy. He stopped work on the four battleships then under construction, ordered additional torpedo boats, and planned the building of fourteen commerce-raiding cruisers.[63] These contentious measures left the navy divided. Over the following two decades, French naval policy oscillated between the two strategic theories, according to the incumbent minister. The debate was conducted in public and merged into the political squabbles between conservatives and republicans.[64] Advocates of battleships came to be seen as conservative, monarchists, and imperialists; radical republicans championed torpedo boats and were anti-imperialists. Sectarianism was carried to such an extreme that some navy ministers avoided the construction of battleships for fear of being branded anti-republican.[65] The result of these erratic policies was that by 1904, when the *entente cordiale* was concluded, the French battle fleet was hopelessly outclassed, consisting of a motley collection of vessels, very much like the British ironclad fleet of the 1860s. A navy that throughout the nineteenth century had been second only to the British one was overtaken by the US, German, and Japanese navies.[66]

Relative French decline, however, does not alter the fact that continental states could be successful at creating large navies. This happened not only to Germany, the obvious example, but also to Russia and Austria-Hungary, who built considerable naval forces, including dreadnought battleships, on the eve of World War One. Their cases shared the characteristic features of German navalism: the combination of a powerful head of state particularly interested in sea power, as the three emperors were; navy ministers who stayed in office for sufficiently long periods to implement their policies; and, a bourgeois nationalism that supported naval development.[67]

Naval development on the eve of World War One

> Navalism, naval militarism, is the twin brother of militarism on land and bears all its repulsive and virulent features. It is at present, to a still higher degree than militarism on land, not only the consequence but also the cause of international dangers, of the danger of a world war.
>
> Karl Liebknecht, *Militarismus und Antimilitarismus* (1907)[68]

In an apparently paradoxical way, heavy spending on navies went on unabated despite the rising tensions in Europe after the Russo-Japanese War and the consequent great land armaments race. In addition to armies, navies now also had to compete with social welfare demands, notably in Britain and Germany. It is no wonder that Socialists, from the moderate August Bebel to the radical Karl Liebknecht, were against anything that seemed unnecessary. Although battleships were no defence against invasion, naval budgets of the 1905–1914 period increased at the same rate as army budgets did; that is, they doubled. In some cases, such as those of Austria-Hungary and Italy, the increase was even higher.[69] By the beginning of 1914, even France, which was struggling to match German military power, had no less than ten dreadnoughts under construction. But as soon as the war began, work on half of them was suspended to concentrate the available resources on land armaments.

The remarkable increase featured in Table 6.2 shows only the quantitative picture. When qualitative factors are considered as well, a truly impressive picture emerges. The introduction of the dreadnought-type battleship meant a quantum leap in unit size and cost. By 1914, both had doubled. These 'castles of steel', as Winston Churchill called them, constituted the largest, costliest, most complex pieces of military equipment hitherto ever made. The most technically demanding component was the main armament. The heavy guns, mountings, and other elements of the revolving turrets required the most advanced heavy engineering plant and skills and took longer than the hull, engines, or armour to build. Indeed, it was the supply of adequate heavy artillery that set the building schedule of these ships. The Italian navy, for example, needed forty-eight heavy guns for four dreadnoughts ordered in 1913. However, the domestic industry was capable of delivering only eighteen in time. The rest had to be contracted from British firms.[71] Increase in size also meant additional costs in infrastructure, such as the extension of dry docks, basins, and canals. The German government was forced to widen the Kiel Canal, essential for the strategic mobility of the German fleet between the Baltic and North seas. Enlargement works started in 1907, only

Table 6.2 Dreadnought construction, 1906–1914. Hulls laid down[70]

	1906	1907	1908	1909	1910	1911	1912	1913	1914	TOTAL
Britain	5	4	1	6	6	5	7	6	2	42
Germany	nil	4	5	3	3	5	3	2	2	27
France	1*	2*	3*	nil	2	2	3	4	1	18
Russia	nil	nil	nil	4	nil	3	nil	4	nil	11
A-H	nil	2*	nil	1*	2	nil	2	nil	nil	7
Italy	nil	nil	nil	1	3	nil	nil	2	1	7
USA	1	2	1	2	2	2	2	1	1	14
Japan	1*	nil	nil	2	nil	2	3	1	nil	9
TOTAL	8	14	10	19	18	19	20	20	7	135

* Pre-dreadnought battleship

twelve years after inauguration; they took no less than seven years and exceeded the original construction cost.

Admiral Fisher took the decision to introduce this new type of ship. HMS *Dreadnought* was laid down in October 1905 and built in the record time of one year, less than half the usual time for a ship of its size. Its main features were an all-big-gun armament with ten heavy guns, as compared to four on existing battleships. It was also fast, the first large warship fitted with steam turbines. In short, it made all existing battleships obsolete. Here was an impressive display of industrial and technological prowess, which delighted British navalists. The downside was a greatly increased unit cost. Presence overseas was drastically reduced to concentrate naval resources single-mindedly on the North Sea. Fisher was aware of the controversy the ship would cause, and, as usual, he appealed to public opinion. He took advantage of the launching ceremony to make his case through the press. He had brochures prepared, with detailed information for journalists, worthy of the German navy's *Nachrichtenbureau*. Nevertheless, the move towards larger, more expensive ships initially met with strong opposition from expert opinion.[72] Even Mahan, who placed the battleship at the centre of his theory of sea power, argued against such big, costly vessels.[73] Yet the other countries had no alternative but to follow, and now they had the means and the political will to do it. Indeed, by 1913 Germany and the United States had actually overtaken Britain in industrial output, and there was no reason to think that they could not eventually build navies that were just as big.

Secondary powers also joined in the dreadnought mania. In the heyday of nationalism, the enormous costs involved seemed tolerable in light of the gains in political leverage, status, and nation-building potential that the possession of just one or two of these leviathans offered. This widespread extension of navalism constituted a destabilising factor in contemporary international relations. Since they lacked the resources to build them domestically, secondary powers generally resorted to foreign shipyards and finance. Huge costs, long building times (two to three years), fluid international relations, and weak finances made some reconsider their policies. Once jingoist sentiment had cooled down or a diplomatic solution had been reached, the folly of such expenditures became obvious.[74] The solution was to sell the ships, often in an advanced state of construction. Battleships that usually took two-and-a-half years to build became available for delivery in months. In these circumstances, the change in ownership of one such unit was enough to alter the naval balance of power, not only among the smaller, but also among the great powers. On the eve of World War One, First Lord of the Admiralty Winston Churchill was concerned that 'besides the Great Powers, there are many small states who are buying great ships of war and whose vessels may be purchased, by some diplomatic combination, or by duress, and be brought into the line against us'.[75] By the beginning of 1914, there were six ships under construction in these circumstances: two for Argentina in American shipyards; and two for Chile, one for Brazil, and one for Turkey in British yards.

Despite their concerns, by August 1914 the British had achieved a clear-cut superiority in the North Sea.[76] The Anglo-German naval race had actually ended two years before, when the German army reasserted its priority in the defence budget. Nevertheless, the naval balance in the Mediterranean was precarious, since the British Mediterranean Fleet had been disbanded. France had to meet the Italian and Austro-Hungarian navies with an obsolete fleet and little foreign help. Though nominally allies within the Triple Alliance, Italy and Austria-Hungary were actually engaged in an armaments race of their own for control of the Adriatic. Turkey, for its part, was rearming against Greece to challenge the results of the Balkan Wars and against Russia to prevent a *coup de main* on Constantinople. In this context, the Clausewitzian term 'war by algebra' attained its literal sense. The French statesman Gabriel Hanotaux observed that the calculations of European diplomacy were based on ships that were not yet afloat and guns that could not yet shoot.[77] The case of the Brazilian *Rio de Janeiro* is illustrative.

This ship had three different owners in less than one year. With her powerful battery of fourteen heavy guns, her mere existence and anticipated completion significantly affected the explosive situation caused by the outcome of the Balkan Wars and the naval balance of power in the Mediterranean. Although the spark that started World War One flared up in Sarajevo, the focus of concern was the Aegean Sea. Both Greece and Turkey were disappointed with the peace settlement, and the latter was determined to recover the lost islands as soon as possible, at any cost.[78] The acquisition of the *Rio de Janeiro*, scheduled for completion in August 1914, would give Turkey the needed superiority over the Greek navy. The other powers were concerned, however, that the renewal of hostilities could spread into a wider conflict.

In 1910, the Brazilian government first ordered the battleship from the Armstrong shipyard of Newcastle. Construction started the following year, but by September 1913 the Brazilian government had run into financial difficulties and chose to sell the ship. She immediately attracted the attention of both Turkey and Greece. Italy also briefly considered buying the ship, since its industry could not compete with that of France, a potential enemy until 1915. Turkey had already had one dreadnought under construction in Britain, the *Reshadieh*, but its completion was not scheduled until the second half of 1914. Greece had ordered a battleship from a German yard, aptly called *Salamis*, but it would not be ready until the spring of 1915. The Greek government also tried to purchase the *Rio*, both to deny it to its enemy and to balance the *Reshadieh*. Since the cost of the *Rio* was equivalent to approximately one quarter of its annual income, the Greek government negotiated a loan in France. France herself was interested in Greece acquiring the ship to prevent the Italians from buying it. Finally, after complex negotiations among Brazilian, Greek, Turkish, Italian, and Armstrong representatives, Turkey acquired the ship in December 1913. Only eight months later, the three-year construction was finished and the ship was ready. The Greek reaction was immediate.

After an unsuccessful attempt to buy one of the two Chilean ships under construction, the Greek government ordered another dreadnought from France. British shipyards could produce a better, cheaper product in less time. Yet the ship was to be paid through a loan floated in France, and one of the conditions was that it had to be built by French industry. Still, the Turkish ships would be ready long before the French and German ships could be delivered. In July 1914, Greece took the desperate measure of acquiring two obsolete pre-dreadnought battleships from the US Navy. Although these were inferior vessels, the Greeks counted on their superior personnel, which had yielded decisive results in the Balkan Wars.[79] There was yet another party concerned about the Turkish build-up, however.

The imminent delivery of the two Turkish dreadnoughts also alarmed Russia. This would suddenly cancel her naval superiority in the Black Sea and thus wreck Russian plans to capture Constantinople. International treaties forbade the transit of large warships through the Dardanelles, and the four Russian dreadnoughts under construction in the Black Sea yards would not be ready before the second half of 1915. The freedom that British firms enjoyed to export armaments often upset British foreign policy. In this case, by training and arming its archenemy, it undermined Russia's position in the region. Russian Prime Minister Sazonov protested twice, in May and again in July 1914. By the end of that month the ships were ready for delivery, and the Turkish crews had arrived in the United Kingdom. Sazonov finally sent urgent instructions to his ambassador in London. He explained to him that it was 'a matter of the highest degree of importance that Turkey not receive the two Dreadnoughts'; he should 'make the English government aware of the overriding importance of this question for us, and impress upon them energetically that these ships must be retained in England'.[80]

Fortunately for Russia, the ships never left Britain. As soon as the war broke out, the British government requisitioned them for good reasons of its own, together with the almost-completed Chilean *Almirante Latorre*. Her sister ship was still at an early stage of construction. This was done as much to prevent the ships from falling into the hands of potential enemies as to reinforce the British fleet with three fine units. Public opinion in Turkey was outraged. The ships were the most visible elements of Turkey's rearmament to prevent another humiliating defeat. To pay for the last instalments, the government resorted to public subscription, thus involving large sectors of Turkish society. Donations were collected from special boxes set up in schools, hospitals, mosques, coffeehouses, and railway stations. The government had even planned a naval exhibition to celebrate the arrival of the ships.[81] The resulting disappointment created anti-British sentiment and popular support for entering the war on the side of the Central Powers.

Nevertheless, a new twist of fate went some way to compensate for Turkish frustration. The German government had set up the *Mittelmeerdivision* in 1912 to monitor events during the Balkan Wars. This was made up of two of the most modern units in the German navy: the battle-cruiser *Goeben* and the light cruiser *Breslau*. The outbreak of the war caught them in hostile waters, patrolled by British and French forces. Their attack on Algerian ports, followed by a successful escape to Constantinople, and their subsequent acquisition by Turkey together make up one of the most spectacular episodes of the war. The immediate consequences were momentous, as well. The addition of a single battle-cruiser, worth twice the annual Turkish naval budget, suddenly overturned the balance of power in the

Black Sea. The five obsolete battleships of the Russian fleet were no match for the battle-cruiser. The *Goeben* not only prevented a Russian attack on Constantinople, but also restricted the Russian army's strategic mobility on the coast of the Black Sea. In this way, the fate of single ships thus reveals the capabilities, both real and perceived, of these 'castles of steel'. Their huge cost and immense power, in a similar way to nuclear weapons during the Cold War, transcended purely military considerations.

Conclusions

Not long after Mahan published his seminal work, Halford Mackinder expressed a completely different point of view. Recognising the growing importance of the large, land-based giants, Russia and the United States, he predicted the relative decline of the importance of maritime power.[82] Yet by the end of the nineteenth century there was little sign of any such decline. The diffusion of sea power and popular politics had led to an increase of public interest in naval and colonial affairs. Navies were seen as essential instruments of competitive imperial expansion and as status symbols, not only by the ruling elites, but also by the public. Navalism duly emerged as a significant factor in domestic politics, and the popular appeal of big ships was cleverly exploited by statesmen and other interest groups. It was largely responsible for the huge expenditure in naval construction on the eve of World War One.

In many ways, Britain's growth as a naval power and the huge expansion of maritime trade was a double-edged sword. On one hand, it led to a profitable global network of coaling stations, dry docks, and submarine telegraph stations, together with efficient steam merchant ships, which served the world's markets with all kinds of commodities. However, this extremely complex system, directed chiefly from the City of London, turned out to be vulnerable as well as profitable. Britain and indeed Germany, in particular, had become dangerously dependent on exports and imports from overseas. This would become apparent during the First World War, when Germany suffered desperately after becoming cut off from Atlantic routes. For Britain, the immense effort to keep supplies flowing and to maintain the blockade of Germany would seriously limit overall military capability and lead to the need for American help to avoid defeat. In some respects, Britain had become a victim of its own success. Despite its continued pre-eminence, its position as the world's naval giant, unassailable at the beginning of the nineteenth century, had been steadily undermined by the very popularity of navies it had done so much to provoke and by the enthusiastic adoption of naval power in different ways by the other powers. With the outbreak of the Great War, the dangers of this relative decline would soon become all too real.

Notes

1 E.J. Hobsbawm, *The Age of Empire 1875–1914* (London: Phoenix Press, 2000), p.324.
2 Michael Howard, *War in European History* (Oxford: Oxford University Press, 1976), p.124. See also George W. Baer, *One Hundred Years of Sea Power: the U.S. Navy, 1890–1990* (Stanford: Stanford University Press, 1994), p.33.

3 The literature on naval races is rich. Of the works mentioned, see: Michaels Epkenhans, 'Was a Peaceful Outcome Thinkable? The Naval Race before 1914', in Holger Afflerbach and David Stevenson (eds), *An Improbable War: the Outbreak of World War I and European Political Culture before 1914* (New York: Berghahn Books, 2007), pp.113–29; Mariano Gabriele and Giuliano Friz, *La politica navale italiana dal 1885 al 1915* (Rome: Ufficio Storico della Marina Militare, 1982); Jean Martinant de Preneuf, 'Du Rival méprisé à l'adversaire préféré: l'Italie dans la stratégie navale française de 1870 à 1899', *Revue Historique des Armées*, 250 (2008), pp.34–52; N.A.M. Rodger, 'Anglo-German Naval Rivalry, 1860–1914', in Michael Epkenhans, Jörg Hillmann, and Frank Nägler (eds), *Jutland: World War I's Greatest Naval Battle* (Lexington: University Press of Kentucky, 2015), pp.7–23; Theodore Ropp, *The Development of a Modern Navy: French Naval Policy, 1871–1904* (Annapolis: Naval Institute Press, 1987); Jan Rüger, *The Great Naval Game: Britain and Germany in the Age of Empire* (Cambridge: Cambridge University Press, 2007); Lawrence Sondhaus, *The Naval Policy of Austria-Hungary, 1867–1918: Navalism, Industrial Development, and the Politics of Dualism* (West Lafayette: Purdue University Press, 1994).

4 Brian Bond, *War and Society in Europe, 1870–1970* (London: Fontana, 1984), pp.32–38; David French, 'The Nation in Arms II: the Nineteenth Century', in Charles Townshend (ed.), *The Oxford History of Modern War* (Oxford: Oxford University Press, 2000), pp.79–82.

5 Jean Doise and Maurice Vaisse, *Diplomatie et outil militaire 1871–1969* (Paris: Imprimerie Nationale, 1987), pp.29, 72.

6 N.A.M. Rodger, 'The Dark Ages of the Admiralty, 1869–1885', *Mariner's Mirror*, 61 (1975–1976); Harold Sprout and Margaret Sprout, *The Rise of American Naval Power, 1776–1918* (Annapolis: Naval Institute Press, 1980), p.175.

7 For the technical difficulties involved see Bernard Brodie, *Sea Power in the Machine Age* (New York: Greenwood Press, 1969); William Hovgaard, *Modern History of Warships* (London Conway Maritime Press, 1971). For a good, well-illustrated, albeit Anglo-centric, summary see David K. Brown, 'The Era of Uncertainty 1863–1878', in Robert Gardiner and Andrew Lambert (eds), *Steam, Steel and Shellfire: the Steam Warship 1815–1905* (London: Conway Maritime Press, 1992), pp.75–94.

8 Lawrence Sondhaus, *Naval Warfare, 1815–1914* (London: Routledge, 2001), pp.108–59.

9 Paul Dislere, *La Marine cuirassée* (Paris: Gauthier-Villars, 1873), pp.208–29; Roger Chesneau and Eugene Kolesnik (eds), *Conway's All the World's Fighting Ships, 1860–1905* (London: Conway Maritime Press, 1979), p.340.

10 Compiled from Chesneau and Kolesnik (eds), *Conway's All the World's Fighting Ships 1860–1905*; Randal Gray (ed.), *Conway's All the World's Warships, 1906–1921* (London: Conway Maritime Press, 1985).

11 John L. Rawlinson, *China's Struggle for Naval Development, 1839–1895* (Cambridge: Harvard University Press, 1967), pp.109–28; Ropp, *The Development of a Modern Navy: French Naval Policy, 1871–1904*, pp.148–50.

12 *Revue des Deux Mondes*, 14 September 1884, pp.466–67.

13 Arne Perras, *Carl Peters and German Imperialism, 1856–1918: a Political Biography* (Oxford: Clarendon Press, 2004), pp.102–03; Lawrence Sondhaus, *Preparing for Weltpolitik: German Sea Power before the Tirpitz Era* (Annapolis: Naval Institute Press, 1997), pp.154–55.

14 Franco Micali Baratelli, *La Marina militare italiana nella vita nazionale, 1860–1914* (Milano: Mursia, 1983), pp.222–24.

15 Rolf Hobson, 'Prussia, Germany and Maritime Law from Armed Neutrality to Unlimited Submarine Warfare, 1780–1917', in Rolf Hobson and Tom Kristiansen (eds), *Navies in Northern Waters 1721–2000* (London: Frank Cass, 2004), p.108; William L. Langer, *European Alliances and Alignments, 1871–1890* (New York: A.A. Knopf, 1931), pp.281–318.

16 Paul Robiquet, *Discours et opinions de Jules Ferry*, vol. 5 (Paris: Armand Colin, 1897), p.218.
17 John Beeler, *British Naval Policy in the Gladstone-Disraeli Era, 1866–1880* (Stanford: Stanford University Press, 1997), pp.265–68.
18 W.T. Stead, 'What is the Truth about the Navy?', *Pall Mall Gazette*, 15 September 1884, 1.
19 John Beeler, 'In the Shadow of Briggs: a New Perspective on British Naval Administration and W.T. Stead's 1884 "Truth about the Navy" Campaign', *International Journal of Naval History*, 1, 1 (2002).
20 Arthur J. Marder, *The Anatomy of British Sea Power: a History of British Naval Policy in the Pre-Dreadnought Era, 1880–1905* (London: Frank Cass, 1972), pp.121–23.
21 Jon T. Sumida, *In Defence of Naval Supremacy: Finance, Technology and British Naval Policy, 1889–1914* (Boston: Unwin Hyman, 1989), pp.13–18.
22 William H. McNeill, 'The Industrialization of War', *Review of International Studies*, 8, 3 (1982), pp.207–10. Gladstone's quotation from Martin Daunton, '"The Greatest and Richest Sacrifice Ever Made on the Altar of Militarism": The Finance of Naval Expansion, c.1890–1914', in Robert Blyth, Andrew Lambert, and Jan Rüger (eds), *The Dreadnought and the Edwardian Age* (Aldershot: Ashgate, 2011), p.31.
23 Cord Eberspächer, 'Arming the Beiyang Navy. Sino-German Naval Cooperation 1879–1895', *International Journal of Naval History*, 8, 1 (2009).
24 Ropp, *The Development of a Modern Navy*, pp.216–26.
25 Jonathan A. Grant, *Rulers, Guns, and Money: the Global Arms Trade in the Age of Imperialism* (Cambridge: Harvard University Press, 2007), pp.11–12.
26 Robert W. Love, *History of the U.S. Navy*, vol. 1 (Harrisburg: Stackpole Books, 1992), pp.349–58.
27 André Reussner and L. Nicholas, *La Puissance navale dans l'historire, vol. 2, 1815–1914* (Paris: Editions Maritimes et Coloniales, 1961), p.140; Daniel Headrick, *The Tentacles of Progress: Technology Transfer in the Age of Imperialism, 1850–1940* (New York: Oxford University Press, 1988), p.23.
28 Charles E. Fayle, *Seaborne Trade, vol. 1, The Cruiser Period* (London: John Murray, 1920), pp.28–29; Avner Offer, *The First World War: an Agrarian Interpretation* (Oxford: Clarendon Press, 1989), pp.81, 83, 88.
29 William L. Langer, *The Franco-Russian Alliance, 1890–1894* (Cambridge: Harvard University Press, 1929), pp.42, 45–46, 48–49,184–87, 335–36.
30 George S. Clarke, *Russia's Sea-Power: Past and Present, or the Rise of the Russian Navy* (London: John Murray, 1898), pp.132–33.
31 I.F. Clarke, *Voices Prophesing War* (London: Oxford University Press, 1966), pp.65–66; Cecil D. Eby, *The Road to Armageddon: the Martial Spirit in English Popular Literature, 1870–1914* (Durham: Duke University Press, 1988), p.26.
32 J. Charles Schenking, *Making Waves: Politics, Propaganda, and the Emergence of the Imperial Japanese Navy, 1868–1922* (Stanford: Stanford University Press, 2005), pp.55–57.
33 Max Weber, 'Die Ergebnisse der Flottenumfrage' (the results of the opinion poll on the fleet), *Münchener Allgemeine Zeitung*, 13 January 1898, quoted in Wolfang Mommsen, *Max Weber and German Politics, 1890–1920* (Chicago: University of Chicago Press, 1984), p.77.
34 William Mulligan, *The Origins of the First World War* (Cambridge: Cambridge University Press, 2010), pp.38–49; A.J.P. Taylor, *The Struggle for Mastery in Europe, 1848–1918* (Oxford: Oxford University Press, 1971), pp.346–402.
35 Paul M. Kennedy, *The Rise and Fall of British Naval Mastery* (London: Penguin, 2017), pp.205–10.
36 Friedrich Ratzel, *Politische Geographie* (Munich/Leipzig: Oldenbourg, 1897), p.106.
37 *The Naval Annual*, 1897, 56.
38 Wilhelm Deist, *Flottenpolitik und Flottenpropaganda: das Nachrichtenbureau des Reichsmarineamtes, 1897–1914* (Stuttgart: Deutsche Verlags-Anstalt, 1976);

Jan Rüger, *The Great Naval Game: Britain and Germany in the Age of Empire* (Cambridge: Cambridge University Press, 2007).

39 Wolfgang Marienfeld, *Wissenschaft und Schlachtflottenbau in Deutschland, 1897–1906* (Berlin: E.S. Mittler & Sohn, 1957).

40 Michael Epkenhans, 'Was a Peaceful Outcome Thinkable? The Naval Race before 1914', in Afflerbach and Stevenson (eds), *An Improbable War: the Outbreak of World War I and European Political Culture before 1914*, p.117.

41 Alfred T. Mahan, *Retrospect & Prospect: Studies in International Relations, Naval and Political* (Boston: Little, Brown, and Co., 1902), pp.165–67; and, 'Sea Power and the Present War', *The Academy*, 12 September 1914, p.294.

42 Michael Howard, 'The Edwardian Arms Race', in Michael Howard (ed.), *The Lessons of History* (New Haven: Yale University Press, 1991), pp.87–88.

43 Eyre A. Crowe, 'Memorandum on the Present State of British Relations with France and Germany, 1 Jan. 1907', in G.P. Gooch and Harold Temperley (eds), *British Documents on the Origins of the War* (London: HMSO, 1928), p.417.

44 Gabriel Darrieus, *War on the Sea: Strategy and Tactics* (Annapolis: Naval Institute Press, 1908), pp.315–16.

45 Theodore Roosevelt, 'First Annual Message', 3 December 1901. Published online by Gerhard Peters and John T. Woolley, *The American Presidency Project*. www.presidency. ucsb.edu/ws/?pid=29542. Accessed 11 December 2014.

46 Serge Ricard, 'The Roosevelt Corollary', *Presidential Studies Quarterly*, 36, 1 (2006), p.21.

47 Henry J. Hendrix, *Theodore Roosevelt's Naval Diplomacy: the U.S. Navy and the Birth of the American Century* (Annapolis: Naval Institute Press, 2009), pp.155–76; Carl C. Hodge, 'The Global Strategist: the Navy as the Nation's Big Stick', in Serge Ricard (ed.), *A Companion to Theodore Roosevelt* (Chichester: Wiley-Blackwell, 2011), pp.257–73.

48 Hendrix, *Theodore Roosevelt's Naval Diplomacy*, pp.25–53; Walter Russell Mead, *Special Providence: American Foreign Policy and How it Changed the World* (New York: Routledge, 2002), pp.3–4.

49 Schenking, *Making Waves*, pp.84–90.

50 Jean-Claude Allain, *Agadir 1911. Une crise impérialiste en Europe pour la conquête du Maroc* (Paris: Publications de la Sorbonne, 1976).

51 Admiralstab der Marine, *Die Kaiserliche Marine whärend der Wirren in China 1900–1901* (Berlin: Mittler und Sohn, 1903), pp.234–35; Patrick J. Kelly, *Tirpitz and the Imperial German Navy* (Bloomington: Indiana University Press, 2011), pp.232–33.

52 John Gooch, 'The Weary Titan: Strategy and Policy in Great Britain, 1890–1918', in Williamson Murray, MacGregor Knox, and Alvin Bernstein (eds), *The Making of Strategy: Rulers, States, and War* (Cambridge: Cambridge University Press, 1994), p.289.

53 Arthur J. Marder, *From the Dreadnought to Scapa Flow, vol. 1, the Road to War, 1904–1914* (Barnsley: Seaforth, 2013), pp.151–185.

54 David Lloyd George, *War Memoirs*, vol. 1 (London: Odhams Press, 1938), p.5.

55 Bernard Semmel, *Liberalism and Naval Strategy: Ideology, Interest, and Sea Power during Pax Britannica* (London: Allen & Unwin, 1986), p.125.

56 Quoted in Jon T. Sumida, *Inventing Grand Strategy and Teaching Command: the Classic Works of Alfred Thayer Mahan Reconsidered* (Washington: Woodrow Wilson Center Press, 1997), p.85; Alfred T. Mahan, *The Influence of Sea Power upon History 1660–1783* (Boston: Little, Brown, and Co., 1890), p.67.

57 Robiquet, *Discours et opinions*, pp.82, 215.

58 See Martin Motte, *Une Éducation géostratégique. La pensée navale française de la Jeune École à 1914* (Paris: Economica, 2004); Arne Roksund, *The Jeune École: the Strategy of the Weak* (Leiden: Brill, 2007); Ropp, *The Development of a Modern Navy*.

59 Édouard Chevalier, *Histoire de la marine française pendant la guerre de l'indépendance américaine* (Paris: Hachette, 1877), p.5.

60 Paul Leroy-Beaulieu, *De la Colonisation chez les peuples modernes* (Paris: Guillaumin et Cie., 1874); J.R. Seeley, *The Expansion of England* (London: Macmillan and Co., 1883).

61 Mark Russell Shulman, *Navalism and the Emergence of American Sea Power, 1882–1893* (Annapolis: Naval Institute Press, 1995).

62 Motte, *Une Éducation géostratégique*, pp.199–200.

63 Ropp, *The Development of a Modern Navy*, p.171.

64 Etienne Taillemite, 'L'Opinion française et la Jeune École', in *Marine et technique au XIXe siècle* (Paris: Service Historique de la Marine, 1988), pp.477–93.

65 Jean-Louis de Lanessan, *Le Bilan de notre marine* (Paris: Félix Alcan, 1909), p.48.

66 For the interaction of naval policy and domestic politics in Germany and Japan see Kelly, *Tirpitz and the Imperial German Navy*; and, Schenking, *Making Waves*.

67 Rolf Hobson, *Imperialism at Sea: Naval Strategic Thought, the Ideology of Sea Power and the Tirpitz Plan, 1875–1914* (Leiden: Brill, 2002), p.324.

68 Quoted in Dirk Bönker, *Militarism in a Global Age: Naval Ambitions in Germany and the United States before World War I* (Ithaca: Cornell University Press, 2012), p.1.

69 David Stevenson, *Armaments and the Coming of War: Europe, 1904–1914* (Oxford: Clarendon Press, 1996), pp.7–8.

70 Compiled from Randal Gray (ed.), *Conway's all the World's Warships, 1906–1921* (London: Conway Maritime Press, 1985).

71 Stevenson, *Armaments and the Coming of War*, p.34.

72 Rüger, *The Great Naval Game: Britain and Germany in the Age of Empire*, pp.79–81; Nicholas A. Lambert, *Sir John Fisher's Naval Revolution* (Columbia: University of South Carolina Press, 1999), pp.135–42.

73 Alfred T. Mahan, 'Reflections, Historic and Other, Suggested by the Battle of the Japan Sea', *Naval Institute Proceedings*, 32 (1906), p.452.

74 Seward W. Livermore, 'Battleship Diplomacy in South America, 1905–1925', *Journal of Modern History*, 16, 1 (1944), pp.45–46.

75 Quoted in Paul G. Halpern, *The Mediterranean Naval Situation 1908–1912* (Cambridge: Harvard University Press, 1971), pp.342–43.

76 At the beginning of the war the British had twenty-two dreadnoughts plus nine battle-cruisers in service, against fifteen plus five for the Germans. The British had, as well, thirteen dreadnoughts and one battle-cruiser under construction, against five and three German respectively. Paul G. Halpern, *A Naval History of World War I* (London: UCL Press, 1994), p.7.

77 Gabriel Hanotaux, *La Guerre des Balkans et l'Europe 1912–1913* (Paris: Plon-Nourrit et Cie., 1914), pp.87–88.

78 Aksakal, Mustafa. *The Ottoman Road to War in 1914: the Ottoman Empire and the First World War* (Cambridge: Cambridge University Press, 2008), pp.42–56.

79 Halpern, *The Mediterranean Naval Situation 1908–1912*, pp.339–54.

80 Sean McMeekin, *The Russian Origins of the First World War* (Cambridge: Belknap Press, 2011), pp.34–40, 103.

81 Stanford J. Shaw and Ezel K. Shaw, *History of the Ottoman Empire and Modern Turkey*, vol. 2 (Cambridge: Cambridge University Press, 1977), pp.11, 309.

82 Paul M. Kennedy, 'Mahan versus Mackinder. Two Interpretations of British Sea Power', *Militärgeschichtliche Mitteilungen*, 2 (1974); H.J. Mackinder, 'The Geographical Pivot of History', *The Geographical Journal*, 23, 4 (1904).

7 World War One

Blockade, neutrality, and the submarine

Carlos Alfaro Zaforteza

World War One challenged many assumptions about the conduct of war, and the lessons it provided were easily as profound for war at sea as for war on land. The length, scale, and manner of the first total war of the industrial era began to apply a brake to the enthusiasm for battle fleets that had been accelerating since the 1880s. Early hopes for a successful, rapid offensive operation and a climactic, decisive confrontation to end the war were dashed for naval staffs and their military colleagues alike. Like the land offensives on the Western Front that came to a standstill, rival navies found their movements similarly constrained. This, too, was partly the effect of the introduction of new industrial weapons, but the character of the war at sea was shaped more than anything by unprecedented logistical pressures in what quickly became a long attritional war. The over-riding need was to keep armies supplied and manned, as well as populations fed, and factories supplied with raw materials. As a result, battle fleets were kept ready but inactive in their bases, and the essential but dull, tedious duty of blockade and trade protection was mostly taken up by a mix of various small, obsolete warships, armed merchantmen, and purpose-built antisubmarine escort ships.

The battleship could do little to stop German armies, for example, whereas the submarine could certainly deal a fatal blow to Britain's vulnerable economy. Indeed, the Entente war effort was focused on the Western Front and thus depended on the flow of American supplies across the Atlantic. The battle to ensure safe passage on one side, and sink as many ships as possible on the other, dominated the entire war at sea. As a consequence, the construction of large ships was quickly set aside in favour of merchant shipping and escort ships and submarines respectively. In the end, the great fleets of extremely specialised battleships that had been designed exclusively to engage each other in battle, and into which so much money and so many hopes had been invested, lacked flexibility and spent most of the war at anchor.

The conduct of war at sea was also affected by the wide diffusion of the influence of European navies and of the globalisation of naval warfare since the nineteenth century, the best illustration of which is the transformation of Japan and its rise as a military power. Of course, this rise included the rapid development of the Imperial Japanese Navy (IJN), which was directly modelled on its British counterpart.[1] The IJN continued to grow in the war, and it played a role picking up German colonies and establishing the Western Pacific as Japan's sphere of influence. Significantly, too, Japan became the first Asian power to produce its own armaments. It was only the global influence of the United States, however, that had a really decisive impact on the war, and this was precisely because it could tip the balance in this crucial attritional struggle at sea over resources between the Central Powers and the Allies. Ostensibly neutral at the outset, the United States always favoured the Entente and was its main supplier of capital, foodstuffs, raw materials, and manufactured products. Its entry into the war along with its immense resources which effectively assured Allied victory was the direct result of the German unrestricted submarine campaign of 1917. In the experience of World War One, therefore, we see both the enduring value of navies and the adaptation of the force structures of the belligerents to the unprecedented circumstances of large-scale industrial, or 'total', war of the twentieth century. The independent use of navies, which so preoccupied the attention of theorists such as Mahan and Aube, who were also naval officers, did not turn out as expected. In other words, the conduct of naval warfare involved a more traditional, integrated use of navies, as auxiliaries to armies or as diplomatic assets.

Blockade and counter blockade

Immediately upon the outbreak of war, Britain implemented the blockade of Germany, its traditional strategy. However, this was done in a hitherto unknown way. Blockades could no longer be conducted by deploying ships on enemy coasts. Owing to improvements in coast-defence technology, this had become too dangerous. Instead, war zones were declared, and ships inside those areas would be searched. The North Sea was easily fenced in by guarding the approaches to the Channel and the passages between Scotland, the Shetlands, and the Scandinavian Peninsula.[2] In this way, the area was sealed off to German traffic, depriving the country of raw materials and essential foodstuffs. The objective was to strangle Germany's economy and starve her population. Since this was a breach of international law, especially the terms of the Declaration of London of 1909, it provided Germany with the moral justification to retaliate with unrestricted submarine warfare in what was, in a sense, a blockade of British trade of its own.

Since British naval superiority would not allow the effective use of surface ships by the Germans, submarines would have to do the job. When surfaced, however, they too were vulnerable to gunfire or ramming from merchant ships which were frequently equipped with small guns. To be effective, therefore, U-boats had to attack submerged and without warning, a mode of attack that had already been proposed by the theorists of the *Jeune École* in the 1880s.[3] There could be no question in these circumstances, however, of ascertaining a ship's flag or the existence of contraband goods on board, let alone of sending a prize crew or taking care of the ship's personnel as international law prescribed. This might sound unremarkable to a modern audience, after a century of conspicuous violence inflicted on civilians, but in 1914 an attack of this sort was considered an atrocity. Nevertheless, in February 1915, the German government started its first unrestricted submarine campaign. It declared the waters around the British Isles a war zone and said that any ship found in the area, whether of belligerent or neutral flag, would be considered a legitimate target and might be sunk without warning.[4] Suddenly, the submarine had become a powerful weapon against enemy shipping, and no effective countermeasures were in place.

At the turn of the century, the submarine was still an unproven, experimental weapon deemed fit only for coastal defence. Only a quick series of technological breakthroughs made its development into an ocean-going offensive weapon possible. This is a good example of the amazing speed of technological development during this second industrial revolution. The first modern submarine, the French *Narval*, introduced the double-hull design and entered service in 1900.[5] Only five years later, the French navy fitted a submarine with diesel engines for the first time, giving it the range needed to operate beyond coastal waters. These two innovations provided the standard model for all navies for half a century until the introduction of nuclear-powered submarines. In 1904, a German engineer, Hermann Anschütz, invented the gyrocompass, which enabled reliable submerged navigation, though it was not fitted to a submarine until 1910. Finally, in 1905, the introduction of the air heater, together with the recently-introduced gyroscope, made the torpedo an effective, reliable weapon.[6] Now a ship could fire a torpedo at longer distances with better chances of hitting a moving target. The development of the submarine, in particular, however, had been so fast that few strategists had foreseen its value as an instrument of commerce warfare. It was down to a writer of fiction, Sir Arthur Conan Doyle, to anticipate its impact in a remarkably prescient story published in July 1914.[7] To the general public, the submarine as an effective weapon of war had been virtually unknown, and its use came as a complete shock.

These innovations were all still in the process of adoption when the war broke out. The German navy, a late comer to submarine development, had its first unit delivered in 1906, and its first diesel boat entered service as late as July 1913, only one year before the war. When the conflict did break out, it had only ten submarines of this new type, although it soon led in submarine technology.[8] For the Entente powers, shipping, the main target of submarines, was the key to maintaining the war effort, and there was simply never enough of it. In December 1916, shortly before the start of the main unrestricted submarine campaign conducted by the Germans, David Lloyd George described merchant shipping as 'the jugular vein, which, if severed, would destroy the life of the nation' in his first speech in Parliament as prime minister.[9] Although not a formal part of navies themselves, it was an essential element of sea power, and its defence shaped the wartime naval policy of the Allies.

New construction was just one of three ways to try to meet the demand for shipping. The others were the maintenance and repair of existing tonnage and the building of escort ships, which also consumed considerable shipyard resources.

These policies naturally competed, however, with land armaments for the supply of resources, which included steel, marine engineering plants, and skilled labour. Thus to integrate merchant ship construction efficiently into the general war effort, the Allies placed their respective shipbuilding industries under direct state control. The British government set up the Ministry of Shipping in 1916, and the US government created the Emergency Fleet Corporation in 1917.[10]

Shipping was in demand for a number of reasons. First, it was needed as an auxiliary to naval and military operations. Warships were insufficient in number for the blockade and control of shipping to neutral ports, as well as for action against the enemy. Armed merchant ships, therefore, were used as auxiliary cruisers, to escort convoys and search for enemy surface raiders. The *Lusitania*, for example, famously sunk by a German U-boat in 1915, and other fast liners were built to mount deck guns in a national emergency and to act as merchant cruisers. The supply of coal and oil to various naval bases, likewise, absorbed considerable tonnage. Merchant steamers were also used to transport troops and supplies across the British Empire. The expeditions to the Dardanelles and Palestine, or the rescue of the retreating Serbian army (as many as 155,000 men) from Albanian ports, for example, temporarily diverted a considerable amount of tonnage from the main theatre of war. Yet the most demanding task was keeping the mobilised economies of the Entente countries working. This meant a steady provision of foodstuffs to feed the population and raw materials to keep up industrial production. Of course, the bulk of this came across the Atlantic.

British and German dependence on a world-wide network of trade is well known, but other countries also depended on imports. In the case of France, the area overrun by the German armies in the initial stages of the war contained no less than 58 per cent of the country's steel production, 49 per cent of its coal, and 83 per cent of the iron ore.[11] To offset this loss, the French armaments industry, the largest of the Entente powers, relied on imports. Italy's entry into the war placed a further burden on Entente logistics; 80 per cent of her coal needs and 70 per cent of other materials needed for her war effort had to be imported. She had to be supplied with abundant foodstuffs, as well, since agricultural production broke down when a large number of peasants were drafted into the army. As a result, the Gibraltar–Genoa route was one of the busiest, although most of these supplies originated in the United States.[12]

Of course, this traffic also required an enormous number of escort vessels, whose construction imposed further pressure on the maritime industries of the Entente. The existing type whose main duty was to escort fleets was the destroyer, but it was an expensive, high-technology ship. Although a building programme for the US Navy eventually yielded a total of 273 units, there was never enough of them. In 1917, at the height of the crisis, the Japanese navy sent some squadrons to the Mediterranean, and the French navy ordered twelve units from Japanese shipyards. British, American, and French building capacity was stretched to the limit, and French dockyards were busy producing materiel for the army. Requisitioned merchant ships were not enough to complement destroyers either. The solution was small, cheap, purpose-built escorts that could be mass-produced in large numbers, and would not further strain the supply of steel or skilled labour. British shipyards delivered 285 units based on the hull of fishing trawlers, built to three basic designs. American ship-yards completed a series of 441 small submarine chasers, including 100 for the French navy, to a single standard design. These vessels were specifically designed to be built of wood by small shipyards, which were otherwise incapable of con-tributing to the war effort. Only thirty-two metres in length and equipped with a small gun and a depth charge thrower, they were too small to be really effective beyond coastal waters.[13] But given the crude state of antisubmarine warfare, a large number of small vessels covering critical choke points, such as certain chan-nels and the entrances to the main ports, effectively jeopardised the operations of German submarines. Once they were forced to remain submerged at periscope depth in this way, their mobility and ability to spot convenient targets were severely restricted. Quantity, therefore, was a very welcome substitute to quality in the fight against the submarine, a pillar of German strategy.

Once the initial German advance in France had been stopped, it was clear that this would not be a short war. So General Falkenhayn, the German chief of staff, devised a strategy of attrition that was made up of two elements. One was successive offensives to bleed the French army white; the other was the sub-marine campaign to undermine its logistics. Although Tirpitz now supported unrestricted submarine warfare, the Kaiser and Chancellor Bethmann-Hollweg chose to suspend it for political reasons. To them, the fear of antagonising the United States and bringing her into the war outweighed the prospect of any increased efficiency of the submarine campaign.[14] For some time, therefore, Germany conducted submarine war but subject to limitations. These restric-tions, of a political, rather than a military nature, frustrated Tirpitz to the extent that he chose to resign in March 1916.[15]

The United States, neutrality, and freedom of the seas

The clash of neutral with belligerent rights in maritime war has always been a major source of trouble in international relations. That is why, although the United States did not become a belligerent until 1917, it was never really a neu-tral power.[16] From the very outbreak of the war, its virtually unlimited resources played a deciding role. For this reason, it is easy to overlook the fact that tensions over the British blockade and neutral rights initially made for a complex Anglo-American relationship.[17] A brief look at those tensions helps explain the issues involved and the mind-set of the main actors. US public opinion had by no means been entirely sympathetic to the Entente cause, and it was subjected to the propa-ganda efforts of both sides. Indeed, initially, the British blockade caused as much ill feeling as the German one. True, the Anglo-Saxon community had pro-British and French sympathies, yet the central European, Irish, and Jewish communities tended to be pro-German.[18] Moreover, American farmers of all stripes pro-tested against the British seizure of foodstuffs and cotton. They demanded their government uphold its neutral rights against this threat to their interests. Furthermore, the dearth of shipping caused by the demands of the war caused a serious disruption of American exports. The US merchant marine was disproportionately small, while British and most neutral shipping was busy carrying supplies to the belligerents. In an attempt to alleviate the problem, the US government planned to purchase 350 German merchant ships interned in its ports. Britain, however, could not afford to lose control over transatlantic shipping in this way. Always wishing to protect their maritime pre-eminence and the leverage this gave them in international relations, the British protested and intervened to stop this acquisition. The British government threatened not to recognise the transfer to US registration, and British warships even stopped some reflagged oilers of the Standard Oil Company. In the end, the Anglophile President Wilson yielded to British pressure and, thus, avoided a major diplomatic crisis with London.[19]

For many in the United States, however, this was further proof that Prussian militarism and British 'navalism' were equivalent evils. This belief, together with Wilson's idiosyncratic ways, produced inconsistencies in the conduct of US foreign policy. Freedom of the seas was an elementary principle of US foreign policy, later enshrined as the second of Wilson's famous fourteen points, and was incompatible with a disregard for constant British violations of international law. Indeed, Wilson himself believed that British 'absolute control of the seas' was as abhorrent as German militarism and felt that it needed to be balanced.[20] The idea was similar to what the German elites thought about the matter. As the historian Friedrich Meinecke observed at the time:

> Universal maritime supremacy is only another form of universal monarchy, which cannot be tolerated and must, sooner or later, fail. England is fighting against the spirit of modern development . . . Her significance as a world nation and a world civilization, which we recognize, will not suffer if the balance of power, which she has tried in the past to restrict artificially within the limits of Europe, is extended to include the oceans and the world beyond. Only then will every nation have the free breathing space it requires.[21]

In one of the most famous incidents of the war, in May 1915 the British transatlantic liner *Lusitania*, en route from New York to Liverpool, was sunk without warning by a German submarine off the Irish coast with heavy loss of life, including 124 Americans. This certainly shifted American public opinion against the Germans, but it did not end the debate altogether. To feed the sense of outrage, the fact that the *Lusitania* had been carrying a cargo of ammunition and military stores, which technically made it a legitimate target, was being conveniently overlooked, and so advocates of neutrality and pro-German groups began to lose the propaganda war.[22] Nevertheless, despite the widespread shock, and the strongly worded protest from the US government, there were still elements within government and among the population who favoured neutrality and who criticised Wilson's brazen concessions to British policy and the flow of supplies to the Entente powers.

The publication soon thereafter of the first English translation of Hugo Grotius's celebrated essay *Mare Liberum*, three centuries after its original appearance, with a preface by prominent jurist James Scott Brown, was part of the propaganda struggle.[23] Its appearance clearly demonstrated the dim view that American and German elites shared of Britain's so-called 'maritime rights'. From the British side, just two weeks after the *Lusitania* tragedy, the British naval historian and strategist Julian Corbett wrote an article in the *New York Times*. His objective was to celebrate the benign character of British naval supremacy and to demonstrate just how the United States benefited from it. Yet despite capitalising on the public mood, still reeling from the recent heavy loss of life, Corbett undermined his case by relying, in a way that was not usual for him, on old clichés that could only really appeal to British nationalist opinion. The tone was, in fact, quite dismissive and condescending toward the Germans. After defending the British attack on Copenhagen in 1807, one of the most contentious actions of the wars of the French Revolution and Empire, he extolled the benefits of *Pax Britannica* throughout the nineteenth century. In particular, he stressed how for decades British sea power had been the only effective support of the Monroe Doctrine, how Britain had adopted a benevolent attitude during the Spanish-American War, and how it had supported the policy of the Open Door in China.[24]

Ongoing Anglo-American tensions were further exacerbated by subsequent British actions, such as the brutal suppression of the Irish Easter rebellion, the commercial blacklisting of eighty-five American firms for doing business with Germany, and the extension of the contraband inventory, all of which further alienated American opinion. Many believed that these measures were, in fact, part of a plan to prevent the United States from becoming a trading competitor after the war. Even Wilson was irritated, taking advantage of these concerns to bolster his own popular support. The 'preparedness' movement gained momentum, and this affected the mood of his constituency in an election year. When he wrote to his confidant and de facto secretary of state Colonel House, 'let us build a navy bigger than [Britain's], and do what we please', he knew that this was the most effective way to capitalise on domestic hostility to Britain and to pressure her to respect US interests. More menacingly, the Naval Act of 1916 included ten battleships and six battle-cruisers, each individually more powerful than anything the British had. Backed by American economic and industrial might, it would provide the United States with a navy that would be 'second to none' and go beyond simply deterring Britain. It would ensure that US interests would be respected after the war, regardless of which side emerged as the victor, and end British naval hegemony.[25]

The role of battle fleets

The anticipated decisive battle at sea, one aimed at destroying the enemy fleet in the spirit of the iconic battles of Trafalgar or Tsushima, never occurred. It was only natural, after all, that the German and Austro-Hungarian fleets would not want to square up against a superior force. Indeed, Kaiser Wilhelm II, on the advice of his chancellor, Bethmann-Holweg, specifically ordered his fleet not to engage the enemy. For the German government, its greatest value would not be in action, but as a diplomatic asset once hostilities were brought to a swift conclusion elsewhere.[26] The British and French fleets, too, were constrained, denied free, safe movement by submarines and mines. The British navy initially experienced several losses due to an incorrect assessment of the new threat. On 22 September 1914, U-9 sank three armoured cruisers in the North Sea. The material loss was not too serious, as the cruisers were obsolete. However, it was a blow to the reputation of the navy. The loss of 1,500 lives could not be kept secret. One month later, the brand-new battleship *Audacious* was sunk by a mine off Northern Ireland, in waters that had been deemed safe. Although there was no loss of life, this was a state-of-the-art dreadnought battleship, a core element of the Grand Fleet, whose loss would certainly be felt, and which would affect domestic morale, providing a corresponding propaganda coup for Germany. Unfortunately for Britain, the sinking had been witnessed by American passengers on a nearby liner and was soon recounted in the US press.[27]

The French navy had a similar experience in the Adriatic Sea, where it had overwhelming superiority. After covering the transport of troops to and from Algeria, and before Italy entered the war, the French Mediterranean Fleet was in charge of gaining command of the sea in the Adriatic. The Austro-Hungarian Navy was inferior and would not come out to do battle, but it was actively engaged in 'sea denial'. In December 1914, an Austro-Hungarian submarine torpedoed the dreadnought *Jean Bart*. The ship was not sunk, but it was badly damaged. The French commander, Admiral Boué de Lapeyrère, chose to withdraw his battleships from the Adriatic. France simply could not afford to risk losing a modern battleship in such 'secondary' duties as blockade or bringing supplies to the Montenegrin Army. Thereafter, only obsolete armoured cruisers, similar to the three British ones mentioned above, patrolled that sea, and one of these met the same fate. In February 1915, the *Leon Gambetta* was torpedoed and sunk with heavy loss of life. This led to another decision by Boué de Lapeyrère: now only light forces would sail north of the Straits of Otranto.[28] These experiences in the North Sea and Adriatic show, on one hand, the irrelevance of battle fleets in this type of war and, on the other, the great efforts to keep them out of harm's way until they could prove their value, either in decisive battle or as powerful statements when peace negotiations came.

There were, in fact, only two major fleet actions in the war, none of which yielded the expected results. The first of these was the Entente attack on the Dardanelles on 18 March 1915, which was expected to force the Straits and reach Constantinople. First Lord of the Admiralty Churchill assumed that this would take Turkey out of the war, provide a route to help Russia, and secure access to Russian grain supplies through the port of Odessa.[29] However, the entrance was well defended with coastal batteries and minefields. The attack was repelled with heavy losses; three old battleships, two British and one French, were sunk and others heavily damaged, including the British battle-cruiser *Inflexible*. The attackers suffered further losses when three old battleships providing fire support to troops fighting on the Gallipoli Peninsula were sunk by torpedoes. The material loss was not serious, as pre-dreadnought battleships were considered expendable. Yet the flagship, the dreadnought *Queen Elizabeth*, along with the *Inflexible*, were quickly recalled to the North Sea as soon as Admiral Fisher, commander-in-chief of the navy, learned of the imminent arrival of German submarines in the area. Secretary of War Lord Kitchener, on the other hand, objected to the departure of the *Queen Elizabeth*, arguing that it would have a negative effect on the morale of the army.[30] This serves to demonstrate just how much value was attributed to dreadnoughts, the strategic weapons of the period, and the need to protect them and to concentrate them in the North Sea. Ironically, it also illustrates just how much wartime service was actually conducted by old, obsolete ships unfit for fleet duties, though effective in their newly assigned roles.

It was a fleet encounter in the North Sea that was expected to be the crucial contest. The dreadnought battleships there were waiting for the decisive battle that never quite materialised, however. When the opportunity did come, it ended in frustration for both sides. The Battle of Jutland of 1916 was essentially a stand-off between the British and German fleets during which a lot of damage was inflicted, but in which neither fleet was destroyed.[31] A lot has been written on this battle. Yet whatever else can be said about it, including the fear in Britain that Admiral Jellicoe could potentially 'lose the war in an afternoon' or about the strategic advantage that Britain retained with its control of German sea lanes unbroken, one of the most significant aspects of the battle is what it reveals about entrenched assumptions about the value and configuration of fleets and of the battleship at their heart. In the end, the battle itself changed nothing. Worse, inflated expectations meant that it had actually been something of a moral defeat for Britain. Naval officers and the general public alike were utterly disappointed when the Grand Fleet failed to inflict a crushing defeat on its German counterpart. The German fleet not only escaped destruction but inflicted considerable damage on its exulted enemy. What is more, to dodge torpedoes Admiral Jellicoe had ordered the Grand Fleet to turn away from the enemy, which ran counter to British tradition and offended lay opinion. The German fleet, for its part, could claim that it showed superior leadership and tactical acumen.

Expectations in Britain were not reasonable, however. A second Trafalgar could not take place between such qualitatively similar opponents. The dramatic, clear-cut victory that Nelson had achieved over the Franco-Spanish fleet in 1805 was possible only because of the poor condition of the French and Spanish ships, the lack of experienced crews, and their low morale. It was not just Trafalgar that people had in mind, however. A hundred years later, Admiral Togo set a still higher standard for navies in battle. Japanese victory at the Battle of Tsushima in 1905, just over a decade before Jutland, had been even more decisive, though, again, the Russian fleet had been in notoriously poor condition. At Jutland, in contrast, the Grand Fleet merely enjoyed quantitative superiority, and this had been achieved only by concentrating all of Britain's capital ships in the North Sea.

Still, the British public demanded an explanation as to why British superiority, thirty-seven capital ships against twenty-one, and 362 guns against

244, mostly of smaller calibre, had not resulted in annihilation of the enemy. The soul-searching process soon degenerated into an acrimonious debate which lasted for the whole interwar period.[32] David Hannay, a journalist and naval historian, expressed the embarrassment of the government and the feelings generated by the indecisive result:

> Was this negative result, this mere demonstration that the German fleet could not win a stricken field, and, therefore, could not raise the blockade, nor cut the transport of troops and supplies, nor drive the British Navy off the North Sea, all the country had a right to expect? . . . [A]ll at once, a public carefully prepared to expect only unqualified triumph was compelled to learn that . . . the British fleet had suffered heavy loss; that the German fleet was not destroyed, but that our own naval authorities could only affirm, with no convincing appearance of confidence, that the enemy had suffered about as much loss as he had inflicted. Disappointment was but the natural product of the non-fulfilment of high expectations.[33]

Despite the acrimony of the debate, no one would mention Tsushima, the recent model that everybody had in mind. British pride prevented open recognition that they had done worse than the Japanese. At a time when racial discrimination played such a large part in the formation of national identity and in international affairs, this would be one humiliation too far.

If battle fleets had very limited impact on the course of the war, their very idleness gave them a certain political volatility. By 1917, those that had been most inactive, that is to say the German, Russian, and Austro-Hungarian battle fleets, had become significant sources of unrest. The long, quiet periods suffered by crews, combined with deteriorating material conditions and a growing political awareness among the men, caused rising tensions with officers with very serious consequences. In the case of the German navy, for example, as soon as its leaders learned of the imminent surrender they attempted one last, suicidal sortie to save the honour of the corps. The crews got wind of their intentions and mutinied. To defuse the situation, Admiral Scheer, commander of the High Seas Fleet, dispersed the ships, sending them to different ports, yet this only served to disperse the rebellious movement more widely.

The Russian Baltic Fleet was gripped by more virulent convulsions. In March 1917, as part of the wider revolutionary uprising, mutinies broke out in the naval bases of Helsingfors (modern Helsinki) and Kronstadt. Unlike in Germany, however, there was bloodshed, and many officers were murdered. In October of the same year, the radicalised personnel of the naval establishment at Kronstadt were among the staunchest supporters of the Bolshevik coup and played a prominent role in the assault on the Winter Palace. The guns of the cruiser *Aurora*, which had sailed up the River Neva, gave the signal for the attack. The ship's material and moral contribution to this epoch-making event made her an icon of the revolution and during World War Two a target for the attentions of the Luftwaffe, which hoped to destroy it precisely for the cultural value it had. Fortunately, the *Aurora* survived and today exists as a museum ship at St Petersburg and as a testimony to the prominent role that the Russian Navy played in the Soviet Revolution.[34] In a strange way, then, it could be said that the actions of the British and Germans had indeed destroyed the fleets of their enemies, just not in the way expected. They had not been destroyed by artillery fire but from the rebellion and revolution within that resulted from the pressures under which they had been put.

The 1917–1918 crisis and US belligerency

Three momentous events that changed the course of the war occurred in 1917: the German declaration of unrestricted submarine warfare, the United States' declaration of war, and the collapse of Russia. The second was a direct cause of the first. The third ended Germany's two-front war and enabled the concentration of its military power on the Western Front. It also ended the Allied commitment to the Arctic convoys, thus liberating considerable shipping tonnage for the main theatre of operations at a critical moment. When Hindenburg replaced Falkenhayn as chief of the German general staff in 1916, he also advocated unrestricted submarine warfare as an indispensable complement to the attrition strategy on the Western Front. As the British blockade was becoming more effective, only in this way, he believed, could the war be shortened and defeat averted. In July 1916, the British government revoked the Declaration of London (1909), which limited its options, and asserted again its 'maritime rights' in full.[35] Pressure on the Netherlands and the Scandinavian countries led to a reduction of their food exports to Germany. The problem was compounded with the failed harvest of 1916. During the following winter, the German population felt the effects of food deprivation. Consequently, it was easy to mobilise public opinion against Britain, which was seen as the villain, guilty of starving the German people.[36]

Chancellor Bethmann-Holweg still opposed unrestricted submarine warfare, knowing that it would likely lead to war with the United States, but he had public opinion and the military leadership against him now, including such influential figures as Hindenburg, his deputy Ludendorff, and the new chief of naval staff, Admiral Holtzendorff. Holtzendorff saw a window of opportunity in the failed harvest of 1916 to press his views. Under present conditions, submarines were becoming less efficient as more merchantmen were being equipped with guns. Indeed, in the last months under restricted conditions, three quarters of the ships that were sunk had been hit with conventional gunfire from surfaced German submarines. The process involved identifying the target vessel as a belligerent and making sure the crew abandoned the ship before sinking it, a dangerous and time-consuming task. In a memorandum presented to Hindenburg in December 1916, Holtzendorff argued that without restrictions his submarines could sink 600,000 tons of shipping per month, approximately twice as much as under the present conditions. The increased risk would deter a high proportion of neutral tonnage from working for the Entente. In five months, the available shipping to supply Britain would be reduced by 40 per cent, forcing her to sue for peace.[37] True, this could well trigger the American entry into the war, but its army was minuscule by European standards. The United States had the resources to create a mass army and the shipping to move it and provide its logistics 3,000 miles across the Atlantic, but this would take more than a year. By then, it would be too late; Germany would have won the war. The decision, therefore, was taken in January 1917. The opinion of the military leaders prevailed against the moderate opinion of Wilhelm II and his chancellor; the unrestricted campaign started on 1 February.

At this point, Germany had a total of 105 U-boats in service. To make up for losses and to step up the campaign, however, this number had to be increased. To be able to achieve this, the navy had to free shipbuilding resources. This was done by stopping the construction of two battleships and five battle-cruisers. Tirpitz, the father of the German fleet, had resigned some months before, but even he sanctioned this measure, since he had come around to the idea that submarine warfare was decisive. The medium-sized type UB-III type (the forerunner of the famous VII-C type of World War Two) is the most representative of this period. It was a balanced design that responded to conflicting requirements, with sufficient range and seaworthiness to operate around the British Isles and the Mediterranean. It also carried ten torpedoes and a gun with 140 rounds of ammunition. The gun was essential, since the number of torpedoes was limited. At the same time, the UB-III had a moderate size and cost and, therefore, did not need a large crew or great amounts of steel, so it could be built quickly and in numbers. Out of a total of 201 planned, however, only ninety-five were completed before the end of the war. Shortages of steel, skilled labour, and key components, as well as the general conditions of a strained war economy, precluded the completion of the programme. Yet, given that these constraints were more acute than those faced by the Entente, and far more than in the US, this still represents an impressive industrial achievement.[38]

This increase in efficiency of the U-boats was countered by the United States' entry into the war. This meant that the Allies now enjoyed a comfortable superiority, though it was not immediately evident and it took time to materialise. The American shipbuilding and shipping industries were small relative to the country's economy. In 1914, it had the largest economy in the world, but the United Kingdom came first in terms of shipping, with 44.4 per cent of the world's total; then came Germany, with 11.9 per cent. Although the United States was the third greatest ocean carrier, it had a paltry 4.9 per cent.[39] The shipbuilding industry was also small and specialised in coasting and naval vessels. As a consequence, only a small proportion of the country's foreign trade was carried by US-flagged ships.

When Admiral Sims, USN, met Admiral Jellicoe, the British First Lord of the Admiralty, in April 1917 to co-ordinate efforts, he found a dismal picture. The official position was that the Allies were confident of winning the war. Yet, despite the acquisitions mentioned above in the preceding chapter and the completion of five super-dreadnoughts of the *Queen Elizabeth* class, the British were uneasy about their margin of superiority over the German fleet. They tried to buy two Japanese battle-cruisers or have them loaned, but the Japanese government declined the request. As soon as the United States entered the war they requested, and got, a squadron of battleships to reinforce the Grand Fleet. This represented a considerable diplomatic effort, since it forced the US government to abandon the principle of concentration of the fleet and send a detachment abroad.[40] It was the lack of shipping, however, that was the most important issue. The figures that Jellicoe produced, which were kept secret from the public, showed that unless the rate at which merchant shipping was being sunk was reduced, British surrender was only a matter of months away. The president of the Board of Trade had already told the cabinet at the end of 1916 that at the present rate of sinking the supply of the British Isles would soon collapse.[41]

During the first year of unrestricted warfare, German U-boats sank 3.5 million tons of British shipping, as compared with 1.5 million for 1916. Moreover, by January 1918, 1.5 million tons of damaged shipping, either by accident or enemy action, were under repair. This naturally further absorbed shipyard resources and slowed down the completion of new construction.[42] French and Italian construction was negligible. The British shipbuilding industry was simply unable make up for these losses. In 1916, it completed only 539,000 tons, and with state management this figure approximately doubled for 1917. Overall, however, German submarines were quite simply sinking many more ships than British shipyards could build.

The solution to the problem was to maximise the efficiency of existing tonnage, provide adequate defence, and build as much as possible. To achieve this, governments regulated non-essential imports and sought alternative ways to deliver certain commodities. In January 1918, the British government introduced food rationing and used the French railway system as an alternative to supply coal to Italy. Neutral shipping, initially frightened off by the declaration of unrestricted warfare, was pressured in various ways to work again for the Entente.

More significantly, the introduction of the convoy system and the commissioning of escorts in vast numbers drastically reduced shipping losses. Convoys had previously been greatly resisted by both the Admiralty and ship owners. The navy overestimated the number of ships needed, which, it was feared, would deplete the Grand Fleet of its much-needed destroyers, thus curtailing its operational capability. For ship owners, the time lost in gathering the ships, the slow speed of a convoy, and the waiting time to unload the cargo resulted in an unacceptable loss of efficiency. Ports were designed to handle cargo at a certain rate. Under normal circumstances, ships arrived in a steady stream and were duly unloaded. To do the same with a full convoy in a reasonable period required a reorganisation of the whole port management system.[43] Yet the radical reduction of losses more than justified the effort.

When ships sailed independently, U-boat commanders around the British Isles or in the Mediterranean did not have to search for targets. They were simply presented with an endless procession of ships that covered the surface of the ocean, with no escort in sight. Once the convoy system was implemented, however, ships sailed in concentrated formations. In the immensity of the ocean, a large convoy was little more visible than a single ship. Usually, one or two obsolete warships, of which there were plenty, were sufficient to ward off a possible surface raider until the convoy approached the British Isles, where most German submarines operated. There, it would meet with a destroyer force that escorted it through the submarine-infested coastal waters.[44]

Escorts had to be provided in large numbers, both for direct escort work and for independent patrols. Destroyers were expensive, relatively scarce ships, and a high proportion of them were used for fleet duties. The American and Japanese navies provided some of the additional units needed, but these still had to be complemented with low-cost units which provided the large numbers required. These included diverse types of ships, from the above-mentioned submarine chasers and fishing trawlers to thousands of requisitioned yachts, fishing boats, and small merchant steamers. They were far from devastating submarine-killers, but their continued presence in certain areas distracted the U-boats' attention and compelled them to take evasive action. The result was that they could not concentrate on their objective. Moreover, although U-boats were most effective when on the surface, where they were more mobile and could use their gun, even the small guns of these makeshift escorts represented a threat to them. Again, it was a case of quantity counting more than quality.

Just as Britain and Germany had done, as soon as the United States entered the war it changed its naval policy. It stopped construction of battleships and concentrated on destroyers and other minor vessels. To address the need for merchant shipping, the government decided to commandeer the controversial interned German ships lying in US ports and all ships above 2,500 tons being built in private shipyards. The other measure was to create shipyards *ex novo*, designed to mass-produce standard models. Given the financial might of the US government and the private sector management expertise, it was comparatively straightforward to mobilise the abundant human and material assets of the country. The creation of the Hog Island yard near Philadelphia is a representative example. It was the largest shipyard in the world, with fifty slipways, 215 buildings, eighty miles of track, and 30,000 workers. The keel of the first ship was laid in February 1918, and when it completed the last in January 1921 it had built a total of 122 ships, 110 of which were built to a single, standard model. This technique would be repeated on a larger scale during World War Two. As a result, the US merchant marine rose from 2.75 million tons in April 1917 to 9.5 million by September 1918.[45] By mid-1918, the Allies were at last building more shipping than the Germans could sink.

No increase in tonnage, however, was ever sufficient. The logistics of an American army of two million men deployed in Europe required no less than four million tons of shipping. The safe transport of troops was an especially sensitive issue, because of the strong impact heavy loss of life at sea could have on public opinion and morale. To minimise the threat from submarines, it was carried out in fast steamers. Some of the great German transatlantic passenger ships, interned in US ports, along with British ones, were used in this way. Because of their high speed, they were virtually immune to U-boat attack, and

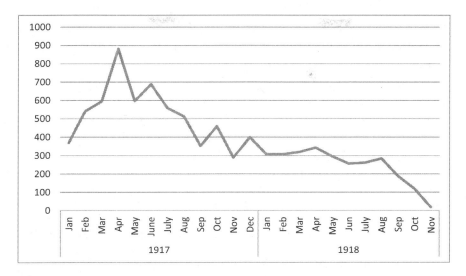

Figure 7.1 Shipping tonnage sunk by U-boats (x 1,000 tons)[46]

not a single ship was lost in this duty. Thus, between January and October 1918, the fast steamers transported 1.8 million soldiers across the Atlantic. In this sense, it is no exaggeration to say that the steam bridge over the Atlantic had won the war.[47]

Conclusions

In a protracted conflict such as World War One, in which initial offensive operations degenerated into a strategic stalemate, it is not surprising that logistics and resources should have become the difference between victory and defeat and that the war at sea should have been characterised by blockade and counter blockade. Since most supplies and men had to be transported by sea and, of course, the colossal resources of the United States which determined the course of the war lay across the Atlantic, navies and sea power provided the necessary conditions for maintaining the war effort. For many people, however, the conduct of the war challenged some particularly cherished assumptions. Merchant shipping, which for centuries had been an important element of sea power, assumed a more prominent role than ever, to the point that attacking or defending it became the main purpose of belligerent navies. The German response was the most strident and momentous. Attrition on the Western Front and the submarine war at sea became the two pillars of their strategy. Thus it was that the submarine, and not the battleship, came to play the leading role in the war at sea.

The status of the battleship and its function as the embodiment not just of naval power but of the health and vitality, indeed the very survival prospects, of a nation had not received the confirmation that had been expected. In this respect, World War One sits at the end of a long history of European navies, the acceleration toward the end of which had been marked by the emotional impact of the sheer size and power of battle fleets, by the popular embrace of navies, and by a corresponding political investment in them. Change came slowly, however. World War One was not the end of the battleship. It remained an important element of diplomatic posturing, the focus of elaborate interwar arms limitation negotiations, and among the most prominent and menacing features of the general rearmament leading up to the fighting in World War Two, when it would be the accelerated pace of technological change and the intensity of global combat that landed the telling blow.

There is another perspective, however, which the history of European navies affords, one which looks beyond the life-cycle of the status of the battleship. This presents World War One as an opening act of sorts and affirms the enduring value of sea power more generally. Considered alongside World War Two and the Cold War, this was, in fact, the first of three great conflicts of the twentieth century in all of which, at sea, submarines and shipping were the key to victory or defeat. Although the Cold War did not erupt into open hostilities, it nevertheless betrayed the same patterns and the same priorities as the other two. The main duty of Western navies then was antisubmarine warfare, to fight the huge Soviet underwater fleet that had been designed to prevent US reinforcements from reaching Europe in the event of open war. In this environment of large-scale conflicts between economic giants, in which the over-riding priority was control of resources, Mahan's ideas can seem a slightly awkward fit. Whereas the continental thinking of Théophile Aube and others who were faced with the prospect of asymmetric warfare had long recognised the defining purpose of navies in guaranteeing or attacking the flow of resources, external factors in the twentieth century associated with escalation affected the conduct of war, largely transcending any canonical strategic thought. Be that as it may, navies continue to be indispensable to any military power today, and they reflect the lessons that emerged out of World War One and the simple fact that war at sea is essentially all about controlling resources.

Notes

1   J. Charles Schenking, *Making Waves: Politics, Propaganda and the Emergence of the Imperial Japanese Navy, 1868–1922* (Stanford: Stanford University Press, 2005); David C. Evans and Mark R. Peattie, *Kaigun: Strategy, Tactics and Technology in the Imperial Japanese Navy, 1887–1941* (Annapolis: Navy Institute Press, 1997).
2   Arthur J. Marder, *From the Dreadnought to Scapa Flow: The Royal Navy in the Fisher Era, 1904–1919*, vol. 2 (London: Oxford University Press, 1961–1970), pp.3–4.
3   Arne Roksund, *The Jeune École: The Strategy of the Weak* (Leiden: Brill, 2007), p.25.
4   Paul G. Halpern, '"Handelskrieg mit U-Booten": the German Submarine Offensive in World War I', in Bruce A. Elleman and S.C.M. Paine (eds), *Commerce Raiding: Historical Case Studies, 1755–2009* (Newport: Naval War College Press, 2013), p.139.
5   William Hovgaard, *Modern History of Warships* (London: Conway Maritime Press, 1971), pp.289–90; Theodore Ropp, *The Development of a Modern Navy: French Naval Policy, 1871–1904* (Annapolis: Naval Institute Press, 1987), pp.51, 347.

6 Edwyn Gray, *The Devil's Device: the Story of Robert Whitehead, Inventor of the Torpedo* (London: Seeley Service, 1975), pp.83, 155–60.

7 Jan S. Breemer, *Defeating the U-boat: Inventing Antisubmarine Warfare* (Newport: Naval War College Press, 2010), pp.11–12; Duncan Redford, *The Submarine: a Cultural History from the Great War to Nuclear Combat* (London: I.B. Tauris, 2010), pp.95–96.

8 Bernard Brodie, *Sea Power in the Machine Age* (New York: Greenwood Press, 1969), pp.295–99; Breemer, *Defeating the U-boat*, pp.13–16.

9 Elizabeth Greenhalgh, *Victory through Coalition: Britain and France during the First World War* (Cambridge: Cambridge University Press, 2005), p.104.

10 Gerd Hardach, *The First World War, 1914–1918* (Berkeley: University of California Press, 1977), p.47; W.C. Mattox, *Building the Emergency Fleet* (Cleveland: Penton Publishing, 1920), p.2.

11 David Stevenson, *1914–1918: the History of the First World War* (London: Penguin Books, 2004), pp.31, 229.

12 Keith Neilson, 'Reinforcements and Supplies from Overseas: British Strategic Sealift in the First World War", in Greg Kennedy (ed.), *The Merchant Marine in Inernational Affairs, 1850–1950* (London: Frank Cass, 2000), pp.34, 41–44, 47; Brian R. Sullivan, 'The Strategy of the Decisive Weight: Italy, 1882–1922', in Williamson Murray, MacGregor Knox, and Alvin Bernstein (eds), *The Making of Strategy: Rulers, States and War* (Cambridge: Cambridge University Press, 1994), pp. 42, 45, 340.

13 Jean Labayle Couhat, *French Warships of World War I* (London: Ian Allan, 1974); Frederick J. Dittmar and J.J. Colledge, *British Warships, 1914–1919* (London: Ian Allan, 1972); Paul G. Halpern, *A Naval History of World War I* (London: UCL Press, 1994), pp.398–99; Paul H. Silverstone, *U.S. Warships of World War I* (London: Ian Allan, 1970).

14 Holger H. Herwig, 'Strategic Uncertainties of a Nation-state: Prussia-Germany, 1871–1918', in Murray, Knox and Bernstein (eds), *The Making of Strategy: Rulers, States, and War*, pp.268–69.

15 Halpern, A Naval History of World War I, pp.291–309.

16 John W. Coogan, 'Wilsonian Diplomacy in War and Peace', in Gordon Martel (ed.), *American Foreign Relations Reconsidered, 1890–1993* (London: Routledge, 1994), p.79; Russell Freure, 'When Memory and Reality Clash: the First World War and the Myth of American Neutrality', *Northern Mariner*, 22, 2 (2012), pp.141–63.

17 Kevin J. O'Keefe, *A Thousand Deadlines: The New York City Press and American Neutrality, 1914/17* (The Hague: Martinus Nijhoff, 1972), pp.46–50.

18 Arthur S. Link, *Wilson: the Struggle for Neutrality, 1914–1915* (Princeton: Princeton University Press, 1960), pp.20–25.

19 Nicholas A. Lambert, *Planning Armageddon: British Economic Warfare and the First World War* (Cambridge: Harvard University Press, 2012), pp.250–54; Jan Martin Lemnitzer, 'Woodrow Wilson's Neutrality, the Freedom of the Seas, and the Myth of the "Civil War Precedents"', *Diplomacy & Statecraft*, 27, 4 (2016), pp. 23, 26–7; Douglas C. Peifer, *Choosing War: Presidential Decisions in the Maine, Lusitania and Panay Incidents* (New York: Oxford University Press, 2016), pp.91–117.

20 Gideon Rose, *How Wars End: Why We Always Fight the Last Battle* (New York: Simon & Schuster, 2011), p.30.

21 Quoted in Matthew Stibbe, *German Anglophobia and the Great War, 1914–1918* (Cambridge: Cambridge University Press, 2001), pp.62–64.

22 Frank Trommler, 'The *Lusitania* Effect: America's Mobilization against Germany in World War I', *German Studies Review*, 32, 2 (2009), pp.241–66.

23 Hugo Grotius, *The Freedom of the Seas* (New York: Oxford University Press, 1916).

24 Julian S. Corbett, 'The Bugbear of British Navalism', *New York Times*, 25 May 1915.

25 George W. Baer, *One Hundred Years of Sea Power: the U.S. Navy, 1890–1990* (Stanford: Stanford University Press, 1994), pp.59–63; George C. Herring, *From*

Colony to Superpower: U.S. Foreign Relations since 1776 (New York: Oxford University Press, 2008), pp.404–6.

26 John C.G. Röhl, *Wilhelm II: into the Abyss of War and Exile, 1900–1941* (Cambridge: Cambridge University Press, 2014), p.1150.

27 James Goldrick, *Before Jutland: the Naval War in Northern European Waters, August 1914–February 1915* (Annapolis: Naval Institute Press, 2015), pp.156–60.

28 G. Clerc-Rampal, *La Marine française pendant la Grande guerre (août 1914–novembre 1918)* (Paris: Larousse, 1919), pp.169–70.

29 Christopher M. Bell, *Churchill and the Dardenelles* (Oxford: Oxford University Press, 2017).

30 Halpern, *A Naval History of World War I*, p.117.

31 John Brooks, *The Battle of Jutland* (Cambridge: Cambridge University Press, 2016).

32 Eric Grove, 'The Memory of the Battle of Jutland in Britain', in Michael Epkenhans, Jörg Hillmann, and Frank Nägler (eds), *Jutland: World War I's Greatest Naval Battle* (Lexington: University Press of Kentucky, 2015), pp.297–306.

33 David Hannay, 'The Battle of Jutland', *Edinburgh Review*, 233, 475 (1921), pp.31–32.

34 Israel Getzler, *Kronstadt 1917–1921: the Fate of a Soviet Democracy* (Cambridge: Cambridge University Press, 1983), p.153ff; Daniel Horn (ed.), *The Private War of Seaman Stumpf: the Unique Diaries of a Young German in the Great War* (London: Leslie Frewin, 1969); Lawrence Sondhaus, *The Great War at Sea: a Naval History of the First World War* (Cambridge: Cambridge University Press, 2014), pp.39–48, 278–90, 303–8.

35 Nicholas Tracy, *Attack on Maritime Trade* (London: Macmillan, 1991), pp.100–06.

36 Sondhaus, *The Great War at Sea*, pp.246–47.

37 Dirk Steffen, 'The Holtzendorff Memorandum of 22 December 1916 and Germany's Declaration of Unrestricted U-Boat Warfare', *Journal of Military History*, 68, 1 (2004), pp.215–24.

38 Halpern, *A Naval History of World War I*, pp.338–40.

39 Spencer C. Tucker (ed.), *World War I: the Definitive Encyclopedia and Document Collection*, 5 vols (Santa Barbara: ABC-CLIO, 2014), s.v. Merchant Shipping.

40 Marder, *From the Dreadnought to Scapa Flow*, vol.4, pp. 43–44; William N. Still, *Crisis at Sea: the US Navy in European Waters in World War I* (Gainesville: University Press of Florida, 2006), p.411.

41 C.E. Fayle, *Seaborne Trade* (New York: Longmans, Green & Co., 1924), p.74; David Lloyd George, *War Memoirs*, vol. 1 (London: Odhams Press Limited, 1938), pp.670–71.

42 Marder, *From the Dreadnought to Scapa Flow*, vol. 5, p.77.

43 Sondhaus, *The Great War at Sea*, p.255.

44 Breemer, *Defeating the U-boat*, passim.

45 John G.B. Hutchins, 'History and Development of Shipbuilding 1776–1944', in F.G. Fassett (ed.), *The Shipbuilding Business in the United States of America* (New York: Society of Naval Architects and Marine Engineers, 1948), p.53; David Stevenson, *With Our Backs to the Wall: Victory and Defeat in 1918* (London: Allen Lane, 2011), pp.338–39.

46 Compiled from Stevenson, *With Our Backs to the Wall*, p.312.

47 Benedict Crowell and Robert F. Wilson, *The Road to France: the Transportation of Troops and Military Supplies 1917–1918*, 2 vols (New Haven: Yale University Press, 1921); Stevenson, *With Our Backs to the Wall*, p.345.

8 1919–1939

A time of fractured peace

Malcolm Murfett

Despite the horrors of the 1914–18 campaigns, the 'war to end all wars' didn't live up to its popular epithet. A time of fractured peace descended after Armistice Day as the victorious Allies set about administering a draconian punishment to the Central Powers of Germany, Austria-Hungary, Bulgaria, and Turkey for supposedly starting the war that they ended up finally losing. In the wake of the conferences held at Versailles, St Germain, Trianon, Neuilly, and Sèvres, together with the continuing fall-out from the Russian Revolution of 1917, the European world was distinctly – some might say ruthlessly – changed. Many of those empires that had once dominated the continent and beyond were no more. While the British, French, and Dutch survived the conflagration, seriously weakened though they were, the Italians, in particular, felt as if they had lost even though they had won. There was, therefore, much unrest, lost pride and aggravated talk of the *dolschstosslegende* (the stab-in-the-back myth) and *vittoria mutilate* (mutilated victory), as the various powers came to terms with what was being offered to them in the so-called peace conferences.[1]

All countries lose in war, some obviously more than others, but after the Great War both the US and Japan appeared to have bucked the trend by becoming stronger than before. Neither had suffered to anything like the same economic extent as their fellow allies had done and both were intent on increasing their military reach by building up their naval strength appreciably in the years to come. It wasn't an idle boast of the Americans to build a navy second to none.[2] They had the financial and industrial resources and the political will and resolve to do it. Equally, the Japanese felt suitably empowered by further victories in war after their defeat of China (1894–95), the Russians (1904–05), the annexation of Korea (1910), and the capturing of the German territories in China and its island chains in the Pacific (1914). They too had every intention of building up the Imperial Japanese Navy to be the regional hegemon in the Western Pacific.[3]

Quite where this left the British was a moot question. It was a genuine matter of concern to the Admiralty, who saw its unrivalled lead in naval strength being undermined by its erstwhile allies on either side of the Pacific Ocean. Although it could justifiably lay claim to having the most powerful and well-balanced fleet in the world in 1918, the Royal Navy also had a lot of old clutter that had long passed its sell-by date and needed to be quietly junked. These antiquated vessels still counted as active ships, but would be quite useless if they were forced into combat with modern warships. Therefore, if their allies were really serious about building substantially larger navies than they possessed hitherto, the fabled 'two-power standard' that the British had relied upon for much of the 19th century would be no more. It was simply impossible for the British to do more than keep pace at best with one but definitely not both of these naval powers when it came to new construction.[4]

If the British had problems when it came to facing up to the future, the post-Armistice period was going to be similarly testing for the other European nations too. What were the victorious continental allies going to do about their navies in the light of what had happened in the war and the desperate need for infrastructural reconstruction and rehabilitation in the years ahead? What money there was available to the governments in London, Paris, and Rome would only go so far. It was, as always, a case of priorities. Allied insistence on punitive reparations for the Central Powers reflected therefore not just the popular desire for revanche; it was also a psychological ploy, a useful means of keeping Germany et al. weak and ineffective, as well as being a suitable vehicle for the reimbursement of war damages. While France was the most intransigent of the Allies in this respect, Clemenceau was not far ahead of Lloyd George, who could turn his populist hand to anything at a moment's notice.[5]

While the idealist in Woodrow Wilson saw hope in the most important of his Fourteen Points – the League of Nations – to ameliorate discord and maintain peace, the isolationist US Congress manifestly did not. It was not alone in its scepticism. Wilson's European partners were unlikely to be as convinced of its merits if the US wasn't going to be a part of this world assembly of nations. Again, the French led the way in their resistance to the concept of collective security that was supposed to regulate matters between future adversaries, believing it to be impractical at best and unrealistic at worst. It wasn't a case of ignoble cynicism on the part of the prescient French, but more a shrewd sense of what they saw as the limits of multilateralism when it came to tackling emotive issues of national sovereignty or divisive pride between states. No one in Western Europe doubted that the US was by now the leading economic and industrial power in the world. If the US wasn't going to assume the leading role in the League of Nations, who on earth was?[6]

As the peace conferences exacted their destructive toll on the defeated nations, the victory of the Bolshevik forces in the Russian Civil War complicated matters for the Allies by bringing a troubling element of uncertainty to bear. It's fair to say that in the capitals of Western Europe the consolidation of Lenin on the scene was extremely unwelcome and deeply regrettable. What would communism mean for those nations that were driven by capitalism and called themselves democratic? Who knew? Communism was a work in progress and few, if any, in the West had a clue as to what questions it might pose in the future. Poland didn't wait to see the answer to that question and went to war with Soviet Russia and Soviet Ukraine in February 1919 while the peacemakers were gathered at Versailles to begin thrashing out the boundaries of the new Europe.[7]

While their leading statesmen were caught up with peace-making on a grand scale, the real issue for the naval authorities of the victorious powers was to learn the lessons of the Great War at sea. These were striking to say the least. What had been confidently expected hitherto, namely that the war at sea would be ultimately decided by the capital ship fleets of the leading naval powers, had proved to be considerably wide of the mark. A grand set-piece battle had not determined the fate of the war and far more damage to the enemy had been caused by submersibles than the largest and most powerful surface craft. It was palpably clear from the 1914–18 campaigns that both battleships and battle-cruisers had had a very mixed war. Let down by equipment failures and inadequate technology, these warships had been made even more vulnerable by deficiencies in training and the dangerous practices adopted by their officers and crews. To undermine the predictive element still further, the weaker enemy forces had preferred to remain as fleets-in-being rather than sail to the sound of the guns and accept their ritual destruction at the hands of a superior enemy. Although blockading the enemy coastline had worked to some extent, it hadn't proved to be quite as decisive as many had expected. Much the same could be said of naval gunnery, especially in long-distance engagements. Spotting an enemy fleet was not the same as hitting it when battle was joined and evasive action was being taken by those under attack. To compound matters still further, shells had proved to be nothing like as reliable as previously anticipated, so even if a moving target was hit, the destructive quality of the shell remained in doubt until the moment of impact. Frustration, therefore, was much in evidence among those who had been aboard ship and who had survived the war years.[8]

If Mahanian orthodoxy had not won out at sea, what had? Until the early months of 1917 the emphatic answer to that question was the U-boat. It had been the instrumental factor in the German *guerre de course* that had threatened to bring the British to their knees. After blithely ignoring its merits for the first two and a half years of the war, the Admiralty belatedly woke up to the fact that convoy needed to be employed to counter the grave threat to its trade being posed by the previously underestimated submersible arm of the Kaiserliche Marine. It was not before time, as its merchant shipping was being decimated by unrestricted submarine warfare. Once a system of convoy was finally established and independent sailings became the exception rather than the norm, the toll on Allied shipping fell precipitously. Aided by improvements in antisubmarine warfare, the destroyer escorts began to wrest the initiative from the U-boats. As convoy losses fell to below 1% in 1918 and supplies of war material ended up on the dockside rather than at the bottom of the ocean, the tide of the war at sea turned decisively in favour of the Allies.[9]

As for the vanquished, whether the lessons learnt from the war could be put to positive use or not in the future was entirely contingent upon the victors who would decide their fate at the peace conferences of 1919–20. Punitive terms were bound to be exacted and the peacemakers didn't disappoint in this regard. Once-proud blue water navies were reduced in status to little more than localised self-defence forces under the peace treaties. It was a fate that the Reichsmarine (the successor to the Kaiserliche Marine) refused to contemplate. Planned secretly in advance, the scuttling of the German Hochseeflotte (High Seas Fleet) took place at its internment base of Scapa Flow on 21 June 1919. It took the Royal Navy by surprise, as much had in recent years.[10]

Looking ahead, the leading European naval powers had reason to wonder at the future impact of the aeroplane, the service potentiality of both radio and radar, and the shadowy world of ciphers and signals intelligence. Initially, however, the accent was on restoring their naval strength before addressing the longer-term implications of the 1914–18 war and the challenges that these would bring in their wake. Of all the European powers in the immediate post-war period, France and its Marine Nationale was decidedly in the worst shape. Judged by its numerical size it was still the fourth largest navy in the world, but numbers are not everything and in this case they hid the fact that its aging capital ship fleet was ponderous and in vital need of replacement. This, alas, was not all, as much needed to be done to revitalise its other classes of warship too. While the Marine Nationale languished with inferior vessels and outmoded thinking, its southern neighbours the Italians were alive to new possibilities. Their Regia Marina, constrained though it was by financial restrictions, had nonetheless used its money well to build new battleships and design flotilla craft that could comfortably put the French in the shade by the early years of the new decade.[11]

Military planning for the years of peace was always likely to be influenced, if not dominated, by the actions of others. A determination by the American and Japanese to build much larger fleets naturally had national security implications for those nations who had overseas empires to protect. This was also bound to have a knock-on effect among the rest of the European naval powers as they couldn't be seen to be doing nothing in the face of competitive rearmament. This movement looked unstoppable until it was arrested by President Harding's surprising invitation to the leading naval powers to come to Washington in November 1921 to discuss its antithesis – disarmament.[12]

If the delegates to this conference thought it was going to be something of a well-intentioned opportunity for amicable discussion and numerous photo opportunities, they were very much mistaken. Secretary of State Charles Evans Hughes pulled the rug from under the feet of the other delegates with an opening speech that did far more than welcome them to the US capital. He had done his homework on the likely new arms race and had concluded that the answer going forward was not more competitive shipbuilding with its massive economic cost and volatile nationalistic fervour, but a substantial and consolidated programme of naval disarmament. Already alarmed by his opening rhetoric, the members of his audience then found themselves subject to his detailed proposals that bore decisively upon their own navies. Although the word 'coup' is arguably over-used these days, this resembled one back then! From that opening salvo onwards the foreign delegations sought to limit the damage that Hughes proposed to inflict upon them. Over the course of the next three months the powers argued the toss between themselves but knew that ultimately the leading financial, economic, and industrial power in the world held all the winning cards in its hands.

Making the best of the deal became the motif for the British, Japanese, French, and Italians. Of the four of them only the Italians emerged with more satisfaction than regret. According to the Five-Power Naval Limitation Agreement which established the capital ship ratio of 5:5:3:1.75 (525,000 tons for the Royal Navy and US Navy; 315,000 tons for the Japanese navy; 175,000 tons for the Marine Nationale and Regia Marina) the Italians were treated similarly to the French at the bottom end of the ratio charts.[13] This demeaning comparability infuriated the latter, who complained loudly and found ratifying the treaty in 1923 one of their most unsavoury and embarrassing tasks. Although treated better than the French, the Japanese were far from ecstatic about the negotiations in Washington. While they were confirmed as the world's third naval power, they were not given the 10:7 ratio that their nationalists sought but had to make do with the lesser 5:3 standard vis-à-vis the Royal Navy and the US Navy – an outcome which their right-wing figures deeply resented. Nonetheless, they parlayed their opposition into securing a prohibition against the building of first-class naval bases in the Pacific any closer to Japanese shores than Pearl Harbor and Singapore for the Americans and the British. This effectively provided the Japanese navy with a degree of monopoly control over the Western Pacific. It was not the stipulation that the British favoured since Singapore to Tokyo/Yokohama was roughly the same distance as from Southampton to New York (3772 nautical miles [nm] to 3632 nm) and it ensured that existing bases such as Hong Kong (or Midway for the Americans) couldn't be substantially improved to enable them to service a first-class fleet if one was needed in these waters in future.[14]

American opposition to the Anglo-Japanese Alliance and their desire to see it abrogated in favour of a more general regional treaty was another price which the old allies had to pay for the implementation of the Washington system. This was not necessarily an unwelcome development to many of the more rigorous elements within the Japanese navy who didn't wish to be circumscribed by moderate consensual agreements with foreign powers, but it represented a considerable downturn in fortune for the British, who could no longer rely upon their Japanese ally to cover for them in the Far East. Viscount Jellicoe had already predicted that the potential enemy that the Royal Navy would have to guard against was the Japanese navy. Even if Jellicoe was being unduly alarmist, it was difficult for those in Whitehall not to see the future in a good deal bleaker light than when the Anglo-Japanese Alliance had been in existence.[15]

While the victors grappled with the new reality of the Washington treaty system and its acceptance of widespread disarmament together with a ten-year 'naval holiday' for capital ship construction, the one naval power from the original Triple Entente that wasn't accounted for in their discussions was Russia. After the tumultuous events of 1917–20 it had become an international pariah – despised and rejected by those who once fought with it against the Central Powers. If not actively feared, Bolshevik Russia was regarded with a disturbing sense of unease by the capitalist countries of the West. It was a rogue elephant in the room and few of the leading powers knew what to do about ushering it from their midst. Moreover, they hadn't a clue as to what Lenin and his cohorts might do about their navy. Western intelligence had revealed little or nothing on this score. In this case ignorance was not bliss. Wishful thinking had to make up for hard facts. Time would tell, but in the interim the West recognised that Soviet Russia would not be bound by its ideological enemies and that anything was possible. In an attempt to put as much economic pressure on the communist leadership in Moscow and Petrograd as they could, the West sought to cut Russia off from the international system of trade. It was also deliberately discriminated against when it came to membership of the League of Nations. Already bereft of the US, the League began life shorn of Russia as well as the Central Powers.[16]

If the admiralties of the world still believed that the battleship was the queen on the chessboard – and most, if not all of them, emphatically did – the other pieces in the game excited growing interest too. None more so than the aircraft carrier. No other vessel changed so much between the wars, emerging from an embryonic form to rival and then surpass that of the figurative queen herself. As the potentialities of the aeroplane rose in the post-war years beyond reconnaissance to embrace both attack and defence duties, the thrust to make the aircraft carrier more formidable gained pace. While the new capital ship would transform the future navies of the world, further significant design and operational improvement also came to the humble submarine – the vessel that had provided a greater impact on the war at sea than its more distinguished naval brethren. Despite suffering massively from the U-boat in the recent past, the British were initially reluctant to embrace the merits of the submersible, seeing it as a rather unworthy and devious craft in the hands of unsporting foes. Fortunately, this peculiar old-world amateurism did not last long in the face of a competitive rejection of these views by the other leading naval powers, particularly the French, who had little difficulty in seeing its impressive virtues in waging a destructive war on trade. Evidently, therefore, the infernal submarine was here to stay and the British couldn't wish it away. As such, the need to improve anti-submarine warfare ought to have been a major consideration for all the powers who had suffered at its hands in the war, but in the face of perennial budgetary restraint vital developmental measures needed to detect and destroy the submarine were largely ignored. It would be a costly mistake that would come back to haunt those powers who missed the opportunity to improve their ability to strike at the unseen predator.[17]

In the political and economic chaos that accompanied the early years of peace, the Fascist breakthrough in Italy was astonishing. Benito Mussolini, who had been decisively rejected by the Milanese in 1919, triumphed spectacularly two years later on exactly the same political platform. Thereafter, the pressure on the government exerted by the Fascists was unrelenting. Seizure of Italian cities and threats to 'March on Rome' added further complications to the internecine chaos and personal agendas that bedevilled relations among the political elite. It all led to the elevation to the premiership of the unsmiling Mussolini in October 1922. Italy had turned its back on its allies and assumed its own course. Whatever that might be was anyone's guess. At worst, it offered an unedifying prospect to the rest of Western Europe and made the French even more wary of their mercurial southern neighbour than before, if that were possible. For their part, the British had been generally too dismissive of the 'wild man from the north' and still believed that his days would be numbered. They were, of course, but nonetheless amounted to far more than the British Foreign Office had ever imagined. Pride in being Italian might take many forms, but one obvious way it could be generated was through the building up of its military status as a Mediterranean power of substance. This would be a challenging statement of intent to the French and to the British as well, who relied upon uninterrupted passage through the Mediterranean for both commercial and naval purposes. If the Italians built up their Regia Marina as a living symbol of their confidence and regional presence, what would this mean for the Mediterranean fleets of the British and the French? It didn't need a towering intellect to predict that whatever moves the Italians might make, the others would have to cover.[18]

One way of making its presence felt in the Mediterranean was for the Regia Marina to build up those classes of warship that the Washington Conference hadn't specifically regulated, in particular cruisers, flotilla vessels, and submarines. Cruisers could be employed in a wide-ranging capacity, from acting as long-range scouting vessels to commerce-raiding activities. They could fulfil both an offensive and defensive role and be a vital complement to a well-balanced fleet. Naval architects began designing fast 10,000-ton cruisers with 203mm (7.99 inches) guns even before Mussolini had seized power. Speed was a particular fascination for the Italians when it came to these and other auxiliary classes of warship and they were to become noted for their expertise in this area. Their designs were often innovative and sleek but not always as seaworthy as their less exuberant rivals. Part of the problem was that they tried to do too much, and some effectiveness was lost as a result.[19]

Nonetheless, the fact that the Regia Marina was very much in business under the Fascists was sufficient incentive for the French not to neglect their own Marine Nationale. This was unlikely given their rather low opinion of the world beyond their own borders. Appalled by American domination of the Washington Conference and suspecting British perfidy behind the scenes, the French – who were unquestionably the biggest losers in the discussions held in the US capital in 1921–22 – were determined to do as much as they could to repair the damage wrought by international diplomacy to their pride and dignity as a leading naval power. It would take time to do so. Heavy cruisers were a three-year project in themselves, but a start had to be made and the necessity was timely given the problems that were being spawned by the peace treaties.[20]

By the end of 1922 the political merry-go-round had seen five French and six Italian prime ministers and seven German chancellors come and go since the end of the Great War. Lloyd George, the British war leader, had also fallen in October 1922. Continuity was not in vogue and neither was a desire for reconciliation and rapprochement, as could be seen by the French and Belgian occupation of the Ruhr in January 1923 in direct retaliation for the Germans not paying their war debts (in this latest case the non-provision of more than 100,000 telegraph poles). It was a move intended to extract economic supplies at source, but it failed miserably to do this and led to fierce German resistance and hyperinflation, which ruined the Mark as a unit of currency and in doing so vastly complicated the whole concept of reparations going forward.[21] Anglo-French relations, already toxic, now plumbed new depths of alienation. Political instability became the norm. Governments came and went on both sides of the border amid grave financial privation and extremist threats to the Weimar Republic. This air of endemic crisis seeped into 1924 before the American-inspired Dawes Plan brought some much-needed economic sense to bear. International relations had left much to be desired since the end of the war but at last the British, French, and German politicians got the message that diplomacy was not always a zero-sum game. Credit for this must largely be given to the complex and contradictory nationalist figure of Gustav Stresemann, but he was not alone in helping to reshape Western European relations in the middle years of the 1920s. Aristide Briand and Austen Chamberlain, the other Nobel Peace Prize laureates, were also key figures in setting the tone for the forging of the Locarno treaties of 1 December 1925. These returned the continent to some sense of normality and offered up a new positive spirit of mutual rapprochement to replace that of retribution and revenge. In this new environment talk was of the fulfilment of real peace and harmony rather than crisis and enmity. It was not entirely the win-win situation that it seemed to offer up, but the fact that there wasn't an 'Eastern' Locarno was blithely ignored by all those wishing to turn the page on the wearisome events of the previous seven years.[22]

A sense of guarded optimism prevailed for a time. A seemingly chastened and cooperative Germany entered the League of Nations in 1926 and the leading powers of Europe began to look beyond governing solely in the short term, perhaps for the first time since the Armistice. Not all was peace and light, however, but life rarely is. Fascism and communism were neither retreating from the fray nor alarmed by the contempt of their ideological opponents. Their nuisance value was currently limited by their domestic circumstances, but what might happen with them in the years ahead and what manner of tests they might pose for the other powers remained obscure. American isolationism was also a burden, even though some chinks in their shield of non-commitment were discernible and offered a small ray of hope for their capitalist friends across the Atlantic.

Despite the elegant success that tripartite statesmanship had yielded, the naval authorities in both Britain and France weren't carried away with it. They were only too conscious of their responsibilities to defend their empire overseas if the need arose. Sea lines of communication needed to be preserved at all cost and for that both the Royal Navy and the Marine Nationale lost little time in building new 10,000-ton eight-inch gun cruisers (known colloquially as treaty cruisers) for their blue water fleets. For service in the Mediterranean, however, the French much preferred a class of light, fast *contre-torpilleurs* (destroyers) armed with a mix of powerful guns and torpedoes. By 1926 there were twelve on order – the first six of which (the Jaguar class) – were nearing completion. It excited a predictable Italian response given that the Jaguars were intended to deal with any threat the Regia Marina might pose to French colonial interests in North Africa.

By building twelve significantly faster and only marginally less powerful *esploratori leggeri* (light scouts) of the Navigatori class, the Italians were essentially countering the French move. As with all new construction, however, it would merely lead to more competitive development in the coming years.[23]

Before the next escalation occurred, the League of Nations, building on the success of the Locarno treaties, attempted to get into the act with the establishment of the Preparatory Commission for a General Disarmament Conference. Its stated purpose was to invite both League members and non-members, such as the US and Russia, to come together to discuss the groundwork needed for a future disarmament conference. Unfortunately, the three sessions that took place in Geneva between May 1926 and May 1927 didn't achieve this goal at all but instead underlined the disharmony that existed between the leading continental and island powers on the thorny question of future arms limitation. Frustrated by this impasse, US president Calvin Coolidge sought a way forward in February 1927 by inviting the leading Washington treaty powers to come to Geneva to expedite naval matters, but both the French and the Italians for a range of motives declined to come. This proved to be an inauspicious sign of things to come. Beginning on 20 June 1927, the tripartite naval conference between the Americans, British, and Japanese might have been better than nothing, but it quickly exposed the differences between them on future cruiser strength, which had become such a touchstone for their naval constituencies. As a result, tempers frayed, intransigence took over, and no meeting of minds became possible on total tonnage levels, parity, or ratios. A yawning gulf opened up between the three delegations (aided and abetted by interference from their governments) and without any prospect of compromise the conference came to an acrimonious end on 4 August. Anglo-American relations were now at their worst point since the end of the war and the Japanese were less accommodating than they had been in 1921–22. It was not a comforting picture.[24]

Winston Churchill, the Chancellor of the Exchequer in Stanley Baldwin's Conservative government in London, was much less worried about the latter than the former. He thought the Japanese threat to British interests in the Far East and most notably to the Malayan peninsular and the island of Singapore was overblown. In his opinion, if relations with Washington could be much improved – he was much less exercised about the number of cruisers than his beloved Admiralty was – the future could be addressed with much greater confidence. He demonstrated this view by initiating the move passed in July 1928 to make the 'ten-year no-war rule' a rolling directive for departmental estimates planning purposes.[25] Less than six weeks later Churchill's confidence in the avoidance of war was echoed by the signing in Paris on 27 August 1928 of the Kellogg–Briand Pact in which the original fifteen signatories (the five Washington treaty powers together with Australia, Belgium, Canada, Czechoslovakia, Germany, India, the Irish Free State, New Zealand, Poland, and South Africa) officially agreed to renounce war as an instrument of national policy. It was a feel-good agreement that ultimately over sixty sovereign nations agreed to sign and respect. In reality, its importance lay in what it sought to do (outlawing war) than what it actually did (which was precious little). If this seems unduly cynical, it's worth remembering that only two years would pass after the pact had come into existence (24 July 1929) before the Japanese blatantly ignored its provisions to strike at the Chinese in Manchuria (19 September 1931).[26]

By the time the Kellogg–Briand Pact officially came into existence, Baldwin's Conservative government had fallen and Ramsay MacDonald, the Labour Party leader, had become prime minister for the second time. MacDonald was essentially a pacifist. He loathed war and the arms race and had shown his opposition to the building of a first-class naval base at Singapore during his previous brief foray as a minority government leader in the opening months of 1924. He would have no qualms in reasserting his disdain for the 'Singapore Strategy' once he returned to 10 Downing Street. He was also anxious to meet the new US president, Herbert Hoover, and begin the process of improving the dire state of Anglo-American relations. He saw disarmament as a key feature in being able to do just that, and in his October visit to Hoover's retreat at Rapidan Camp in Virginia he convinced his Republican host that better days lay ahead. Buoyed by their discussions and supported by Hoover's approval, MacDonald felt emboldened to issue invitations to the Washington treaty powers to reconvene in London in January 1930 to discuss new naval provisions for the next few years.[27]

MacDonald's confidence in the future was as endearing as it was fleeting. Stresemann's untimely death on 3 October 1929 cast a pall over Franco-German relations and the calamitous Wall Street Crash (24–29 October) brought on the Great Depression with grievous politico-economic effects that swept the globe – humbling administrations, undermining confidence in capitalism and democracy, and giving sustenance to nationalist and extremist forces. MacDonald may have hoped for a time of peace and calm but he wasn't going to get it.[28]

In the wake of these two awful shocks to the system, MacDonald was even more determined than ever to ensure that the London Naval Conference would put the frustrations of Geneva behind it and become a resounding success. He paved the way to accomplishing this objective by engaging directly with the leading statesmen of the treaty powers. He considered it essential that everyone was on the same page when it came to setting out what the discussions were designed to achieve. While Hoover appreciated MacDonald's desire to be accommodating, sensing the US Navy would become a distinct beneficiary of this tendency, the same couldn't be said for Georges Leygues, the French Minister of Marine, whose brief didn't run to seeing the Marine Nationale come off worst vis-à-vis its own Armée de Terre let alone the navies of the other leading powers. French opposition to anything other than its own best interests was reinforced by its jaundiced view of what had transpired at Washington in 1921–22. This was not an unreasonable stance to adopt at the outset of 1930 as the world – and particularly the European continent – suddenly looked a good deal less secure than it had only a couple of years before. From a naval perspective, the French were conscious of their need to defend their empire (18,109 nm of coastline and 33,850 nm of sea lines of communication), support their overseas trade (66% of total imports) and be prepared for emergencies in several oceans simultaneously. This wouldn't be achieved from mere parity with the Italians and they had no wish to see the capital ship ratio of 5:5:3 extended to other auxiliary classes of warship. Instead the French wanted a 'global limitation' formula in which the leading naval powers would each be given an overall tonnage allocation which they could then use on those classes of warship that best suited their defence obligations. Again, their proposal was not without merit, but it wouldn't cut any ice with their Anglo-American treaty partners, who wished to save money by placing a straitjacket on the other naval powers.[29]

Despite all of MacDonald's preparatory work, the London Naval Conference was not going to be an easy diplomatic triumph to bring off. Even so, it began positively by extending the capital ship naval-building holiday much favoured by the Royal Navy and US Navy until 31 December 1936. It also confirmed that the French and the Italians could proceed with replacing their old dreadnoughts with two battleships of 35,000 tons at a time of their own choosing. They had foregone the opportunity in 1927 and 1929 but were disinclined to wait much longer before addressing this old question. Essentially the treaty powers were required to scrap their older vessels to ensure that their capital ship fleets would reflect the long-term parity levels set out previously at Washington, namely fifteen for the Royal Navy and US Navy, nine for the Japanese navy, and five each for the Marine Nationale and the Regia Marina.[30]

On the question of aircraft carriers the definition was modified to reflect recent construction practices, particularly those of the Japanese, who had built *Ryuho* under the previous tonnage limit of 10,000 tons. From now onwards, the carrier would be "any surface vessel of war, whatever its displacement, designed for the specific and exclusive purpose of carrying aircraft, and so constructed that aircraft can be launched therefrom and landed thereon."[31] Just as for capital ships, the tonnage levels for carriers set out at Washington were retained at London (135,000 tons for the Royal Navy and US Navy, 81,000 tons for the Japanese navy, and 60,000 tons for the Marine Nationale and Regia Marina). In addition, no light carriers of less than 10,000 tons where the maximum gun calibre permitted was 155mm (6.1 inches) were to be built by any of the powers for the duration of the treaty, while those that exceeded that tonnage level would remain subject to a limit of between eight to ten guns of 203mm (8 inches).[32]

Success in this area spilled over into others as well. Part II of the treaty established agreement on a maximum displacement figure of 2,000 tons for future submarines and stipulated that the maximum gun calibre they could carry must not exceed 130mm (5.1inches). Even so, there were some existing submarines that exceeded both the displacement figure and gun calibre limits agreed upon and so a compromise solution was found that enabled each contracting power to retain or build up to three submarines not exceeding 2,800 tons and carry guns that were not to exceed 155mm. A further exception was made for the big French submarine *Surcouf* (2,880 tons and with guns of 203mm), which had been launched in 1929, but her completion was made contingent on the basis that two others of the same class wouldn't be built.

Those submarines that weighed in at under 2,000 tons but with gun calibres exceeding 130mm could also be retained as long as they had been built by the cut-off date of 30 April 1930.[33]

So far so good, but the real test would be if all five delegations could agree on the rules surrounding cruisers (surface warships exceeding 1,850 tons and/ or those equipped with at least one gun above 130mm) and destroyers (all those surface vessels that would not exceed 1,850 tons or carry guns above 130mm). Notwithstanding the haggling that went on over these classes of warship, the real issue lay not between the British and the Americans on this occasion (though they didn't see eye-to-eye on the value of light- and heavy-gunned cruisers), but with the French and the Italians, who were ill disposed to accept any agreement that undermined their existing complement of ships. In the end, the Mediterranean powers refused to adopt Part III of the treaty, which was only signed by the representatives of the Royal Navy, US Navy, and Japanese navy. It provided for two categories of cruisers – those with guns exceeding 155mm and those carry-ing guns below that figure. Although the heavy-gun cruiser (much beloved by the US Navy) could not exceed 10,000 tons, the light-gun cruiser (preferred by the Royal Navy) could be from 1,850 tons up to but not exceeding 10,000 tons. Looking ahead, the powers agreed that the number of heavy-gun cruisers must not exceed eighteen for the US Navy (180,000 tons), fifteen for the Royal Navy (146,800 tons), and twelve for the Japanese navy (108,400 tons). This unequal allocation meant that the British and the Japanese were to be given additional tonnage in the light-gun cruiser category to compensate for their shortfall in heavy cruisers (192,200 tons for the Royal Navy, 143,500 tons for the US Navy, and 100,450 tons for the Japanese navy). In designing this formula, the Anglo-American delegations finally accepted the desire of the Japanese for a 10:7 parity on both light cruisers and destroyers rather than the 10:6 one which had prevailed at Washington nearly a decade before. Agreement was also reached between the three powers on what became known as 'flying deck cruisers', but enthusiasm for this hybrid vessel had cooled perceptibly in Washington even before the new treaty expired in 1936.[34]

While destroyers were not as avowedly contentious an item of business as cruisers, and tended to be seen by both the British and the Americans as expend-able fleet torpedo boats, the fact remained that many would need to be replaced in the coming years as they reached the age where they would become increas-ingly inefficient and before they sank into a state of obsolescence. Two types of destroyer were allowed: a 'leader' or large destroyer of 1,850 tons, of which there could be 16%; and a 'standard' destroyer that couldn't exceed 1,500 tons. In terms of total destroyer strength, the Royal Navy and US Navy were to be allocated 150,000 tons and the Japanese navy 105,500 tons. Of the three leading powers, the Japanese felt somewhat thwarted by these regulations but not suf-ficiently to withhold their signature from Part III of the treaty.[35]

Although the Anglo-American delegations would have preferred to outlaw the submarine, this was never going to happen given the degree to which the French, in particular, and the Italians to a lesser extent had built up their submersible fleet in the 1920s. It was clear that the French and the Japanese saw the submarine as a 'force multiplier' and one which could help to redress the balance of disadvantage in which they had been placed vis-à-vis the Anglo-American capital ship fleets by the original Washington treaty. In these years Italian submarine building tended to be essentially reactive and driven by the principle of trying to cover whatever the French were doing in this area. Not surprisingly, the Regia Marina didn't succeed in keeping up with the Marine Nationale since the latter sought to build the submarine arm up to 90,000 tons to service its global needs. Supported by the government, the Marine Nationale had used the post-Washington period to move resolutely towards that figure and consequently had substantially more ocean-going fleet submarines and coastal patrol vessels on its books in 1930 than either of its cross-channel or Mediterranean rivals. Alone on the issue of banning the submarine, therefore, the Anglo-American delegations adopted a steely pragmatism towards the subject. They would get the best deal they could. This meant that unrestricted submarine warfare would be outlawed once more, but they would have to give way on the existence of the vessel itself. As a result, the Royal Navy, US Navy, and Japanese navy were each allowed to build up their submarine fleet to a total of 52,700 tons with the latter being allowed to lay down 19,200 tons of replacement submarine tonnage by 31 December 1936.[36]

As a rider to Part III of the treaty, national security considerations could be invoked by any of the three signatory powers to build in excess of the levels agreed upon if the French and the Italians decided to embark on significant new construction in these classes of warship.[37]

Of all the signatories of the London Treaty on 22 April 1930, the Americans were undoubtedly the most satisfied. They had saved money, reconfirmed their status vis-à-vis the other naval powers, and kept a tight rein on the Japanese. None of the rest were wildly enthusiastic about what had taken place in London, including the British, who felt that their cruiser strength was appreciably lower than it ought to be (40 as opposed to 70). Japanese aggravation about further injustices at the hands of the Western nations and concern about the relative age of its fleet (rather exaggerated) ensured that much inflamed rhetoric would be spilled before the treaty was ratified by the Japanese Diet in October 1930. French and Italian sentiment was shown by their failure to ratify those parts of the treaty that they had already signed. Notwithstanding these objections, it's difficult not to feel that there was an air of "the lady doth protest too much" about much of this criticism and a playing by some of the naval authorities to the nationalist political gallery.[38]

Despite their reservations about some aspects of the London Naval Treaty, the British still had many reasons for quiet satisfaction when it came to their maritime situation. They retained by far the greatest mercantile fleet in the world (20,438,444 tons in comparison to 11,388,000 tons for the US or 29.4% to 16.4%), and one that was a good deal younger than its American equivalent. As Greg Kennedy pointed out over twenty years ago, the British also had a chain of naval bases and stations that circled the globe – all of which were connected with the most advanced cable and radio networks – providing an unrivalled infrastructure for commercial and military exploitation. In addition, the Royal Navy's stock of auxiliary vessels (605,934 tons) could be drawn upon to support the logistical requirements of the fleet in any number of ways, from laying and sweeping mines to providing fuel, ammunition, and water. So while it had been forced to give up its historic two-power naval standard, the Royal Navy could continue to believe (and with good reason) that it was still *primus inter pares* and would be for some years to come.[39]

If the major naval powers were hoping for a period of studied calm after the turbulence of the previous year, they were to be sadly disabused of this notion. Quiescence would not be a prominent feature of the 1930s. Economic disruption and malaise would take its place as financial indebtedness, rising inflation, and increasing unemployment spread and intensified around the world in the wake of the Wall Street Crash and the onset of the Great Depression. Money was in short supply, loans were called in but couldn't be repaid, restructured war debts became no more than illusionary promises, and the service ministries were left in no doubt at all as to the urgent need to cut programmes and expenses.

There is much truth in the suggestion that political extremism thrives in conditions of economic penury. Moderate parties or governments that appear not to have the answers to the great questions of the day are abandoned by those who seek a stronger message. Hitler's rise to power in Germany is a classic example of this tendency. In the May 1928 federal elections, the Nazis won only 2.6% (810,000 votes) of the popular vote and were the smallest party in the Reichstag (twelve seats). When the country went to the polls again in September 1930, Hitler's message, though essentially the same as it had been at the previous election, now generated 18.3% of the popular vote and won the Nazis 107 parliamentary seats (second largest). By July 1932 he had eclipsed even these figures with 37.3% of the popular vote (over thirteen million) and 230 seats in the Reichstag – by far the largest party in that chamber.[40]

As chaos descended on Europe with the collapse of the Austrian Creditanstalt in May 1931, the days of Taishō democracy in Japan were also numbered. While economic disarray was a feature of Japanese life even before the stock market crash of October 1929, the real impetus for radical change may have come from a general sense of dissatisfaction that the Occidental countries were not giving Japan its due in international affairs. Nationalism is a very sensitive issue at the best of times and slights real or imagined in international relations are liable to stir up those on the right of the political and military spectrum and make them extremely unhappy both with the foreign perpetrators of the act and their domestic opponents who failed to do anything about it. Unfortunately, neither the Washington nor London conversations had won over even the moderate corps of the Japanese navy let alone its right-wing protagonists, who seethed with anger about many of the provisions of what to them were distinctly unequal treaties, and looked to a time when they could be swept aside. When the military crisis broke in September 1931, however, it didn't come from the ranks of the Japanese navy but from dissident members of the Imperial Japanese Army, who were determined to steal a march on even the young Showa emperor Hirohito and his government by initiating a crisis in Manchuria that could lead to a full-scale invasion.[41]

What the Mukden incident demonstrated above all was that restraint can easily be abandoned if national interests are invoked to justify assertive action. By staging a small explosion on the tracks of the South Manchurian Railway, the Kwantung Army achieved its purpose and the League of Nations was confronted by its first huge crisis and one which, alas, it was powerless to do much about. During the 1920s there had been few international crises that had involved any of the great powers. This would not be the case in the new decade. When the League needed leadership, it was singularly lacking. It wasn't that the other powers didn't care about what was happening to China, but the main focus of their attention was much closer to home. In London Ramsay MacDonald's Labour government had collapsed as a direct result of the financial crisis and a coalition government had been formed to succeed it in August 1931. MacDonald remained prime minister but was weakened by what had taken place. In Paris the economic crisis hadn't yet struck the French government as severely as it had with its neighbours, but its disenchantment with collective security remained, whoever was in the Élysée Palace.[42]

Shortly after Lord Lytton had been appointed by the Council of the League to conduct his ill-fated inquiry into the Manchurian crisis, the World Disarmament Conference welcomed its delegates, including those from the US and the Soviet Union, to Geneva on 2 February 1932. Acting under the presidency of the former Labour cabinet minister Arthur Henderson, the disarmament conference began its tortuous deliberations only days after the Japanese had begun bombing the city of Shanghai. It was not the kind of augury the delegates needed, even if it did help to reinforce the message that world peace was much needed. Whatever hopes for disarmament there may have been at the outset were dashed repeatedly hitherto. Initiatives from Tardieu, Hoover, Simon, and Herriot came and went without gaining support across the board from all the leading powers. To make matters worse, by the time the findings of the Lytton Commission were issued on 2 October 1932, the Japanese had already recognized the state of Manchukuo they had initially proclaimed in February 1932 and were evidently not in the mood to yield what they had now secured by force. As such, it's difficult not to see this latest demarche in the Far East as a crucial watershed in the fortunes of both the League and the disarmament conference. It was the beginning of the end for both, even though they would lurch on for some time to come.[43]

A Japanese withdrawal from the League on 24 February 1933 in response to criticism of it in the Lytton Commission Report confirmed that all was not well among the great powers. Militarism with its expansionist tendencies was back. This ominous message had already been delivered with the rise of Hitler to the post of German Chancellor on 30 January 1933. Disarmament began to look passé and supine. In other words, not the sort of qualities that a state determined to assert itself should adopt.

As France staggered from one government to the next – it had twelve from 1932–34 – any coherence in foreign policy making became a casualty of the political system. Radical left-wing concern about German revanchism clashed with right-wing sentiment that favoured strong government and had similar enemies (communists, democrats, Jews, and socialists) to those that the Nazis opposed so vehemently.[44]

Fascist Italy had survived the financial meltdown after the Wall Street Crash better than most and this did much to burnish the megalomania of Mussolini. His advocacy of the Four-Power Pact (July 1933) to resolve European problems looked like an excuse to improve his international image with the British, French, and Germans and deal a blow to the much-reviled League at the same time. It was both.[45]

Mussolini's emergence as an international statesman coincided with a strategic retreat on the world stage made by the new Roosevelt administration in the US. Any hope that the Americans might lead the free world out of the mire was quickly snuffed out by their peculiar volte-face over the World Economic Conference in London during the summer of 1933. A retreat from a limited internationalism to a position of isolationism was not what the rest of the Western democracies needed from the Americans at this time, but that is what they received.[46]

Another blow quickly followed with the announcement of the German withdrawal from both the League and the World Disarmament Conference on 14 October 1933. In doing so the Germans left the other powers in no doubt whatsoever that they considered themselves no longer bound by the diktat of Versailles and its restrictions on their armed forces. They meant what they said. It was the death knell for disarmament.[47]

This left the other European powers little choice but to review their own foreign and defence policies: the French sought to breathe new life into the Little Entente they had established in the 1920s with the successor states of the Austro-Hungarian Empire (Czechoslovakia, Poland, Romania, and Yugoslavia) and take refuge in the Maginot Line if the Entente didn't prove effective; the British had already officially interred the 'ten-year no-war rule' in March 1933, but could hardly embark on massive rearmament given the economic mess they were in; the Italians, though delighted that Germany had turned its back on democracy and keen on furthering their links with the Nazi state, were nonetheless still wary of the latent threat of an Austrian *Anschluss* being formed to create a *Gross Deutschland*; the Soviets reached out to the US, France, and their neighbouring states (Poland, Romania, and the Baltic States) as well as the Czechs in a bid to mend their diplomatic fences and in doing so ironically became a member of the League when it was stumbling towards its eventual denouement.[48]

Against a background of increasing international bellicosity and its own futility, the World Disarmament Conference adjourned in May 1934 without making the world any safer for those who wished to live in peace. Following hard on the heels of this predictable setback came unsettling news of a wave of murderous purges in Germany at the end of June and a coup attempt in Vienna brought on by the assassination of Chancellor Engelbert Dollfuss at the hands of Austrian

Nazis on 25 July.[49] Mussolini, who had upstaged his fellow dictator Hitler in Venice in June without fully understanding the linguistic nuance of their subsequent talks, felt betrayed by the murder of his Austrian protégé and reacted by sending four troop divisions to the Brenner Pass in a show of steely defiance. Taken aback by Mussolini's agitated response and the failure of the coup, Hitler did his best to make the peace with Il Duce. Although thwarted in this area for the time being, Hitler soon had cause to celebrate as he succeeded the dead Paul von Hindenburg as German president on 2 August 1934.[50]

Violence was not confined to Central Europe, alas, as the French Foreign Minister Louis Barthou and King Alexander I of Yugoslavia discovered to their cost as they were assassinated on their drive through the streets of Marseilles on 9 October 1934. This double tragedy was followed by the promotion of the unscrupulous Pierre Laval to the Quai d'Orsay. Seen from close-up or afar, Europe looked in a convulsive state with the democracies in some disarray and the authoritarian states calling the tune.[51]

Under these circumstances the building of any capital ships was bound to cause a stir. After foregoing the opportunity of building two battleships in the 1920s, the Marine Nationale laid down the *Dunkerque* (26,500 tons) in December 1932 and her sister ship *Strasbourg* in November 1934, but Mussolini and the Fascist Grand Council were not to be denied and the Regia Marina was allowed to lay down two much larger battleships of its own, *Littorio* (40,724 tons) and *Vittorio Veneto* in October 1934. This declaration of intent could be interpreted as a direct challenge to the other powers and prompted both the Germans and the French to respond by laying down further battleships of their own, namely *Scharnhorst* and *Gneisenau* (both 34,841 tons) in the early summer of 1935 and *Richelieu* (35,000 tons) and *Jean Bart* (35,000 tons) in the autumn of 1935 and the winter of 1936 respectively.[52]

In the UK the national government led by an increasingly frail prime minister wrestled with a deteriorating situation in both Europe and the Far East without much clue as to what it should do for the best. Ominous news from the Far East on 30 December 1934 indicating that the Japanese would no longer adhere to the terms of the Washington Naval Treaty left the Admiralty in a quandary. For instance, if the Japanese navy was going to expand beyond the 5:5:3 capital ship ratio, the 'Singapore Strategy' might need to be overhauled and given more substance than it had at this time.[53]

Further pause for thought came when the population of the Saar voted overwhelmingly for a return to German sovereignty in January 1935 and when Göring and Hitler acknowledged on 9 and 16 March respectively that German rearmament was a fact of life and henceforth they wouldn't be bound by the clauses of the Versailles treaty. It looked unmistakeably as though the proverbial writing was on the wall. And yet on the very same day that the Führer announced the resumption of German conscription and his intention to build an army of twelve corps and thirty-six divisions, he offered the British an enticing prospect that had swirled around for several months. In a private discussion with Sir Eric Phipps, the British ambassador, he declared that he was prepared to build the

Reichsmarine (shortly to be renamed the Kriegsmarine) up to a level not exceeding 35% of the Royal Navy. Whatever the Foreign Office thought of this proposal (Sir John Simon sensed it would infuriate the French and lead to an unlimited arms race), Sir Bolton Eyres Monsell, the First Lord of the Admiralty, had no doubt as to its value.[54]

Pulled hither and thither by competing possibilities with the Treasury loth to sanction a significant rearmament programme, the British looked for a way out of their dilemma. MacDonald and Simon tried to find it at a conference with the French and the Italians at Stresa on the shores of Lake Maggiore in April 1935, but the ensuing discussions led to no great breakthrough on what to do about Germany and were more show than anything else. Pious talk about the inviolability of existing agreements seemed curiously out of place in this new era and were soon put into perspective by the secret talks in London that led to the announcement of the Anglo-German Naval Agreement on 18 June 1935. Predictably, the French, who had announced the forging of a Soviet treaty in the previous month, were not impressed by the idea that the Kriegsmarine would become more powerful than ever and achieve full parity in submarines with their own Marine Nationale. Their objections, though posted late, were simply ignored by the Baldwin-led government that had taken over from that of the ailing MacDonald on 7 June. This didn't say much for either the newly formed Stresa Front or for the prime minister's aptitude in foreign policy. His disinterest in this area was profound, and he willingly yielded greater control to Sir Samuel Hoare, his newly appointed foreign secretary, than was perhaps advisable.[55]

By the time the Admiralty had laid down its first purpose-built carrier (*Ark Royal*) in September 1935, the Italians were on the point of waging war against Abyssinia (Ethiopia). It soon became obvious to one and all that Mussolini had embarked upon a war of aggression (3 October) against another League member and that sanctions would have to be mandatorily applied under the terms of the League's Covenant. What kind of sanctions – effective or ineffective, trade or military – was the issue, and the League members, led by Laval and Hoare, ducked the challenge. Whatever one thinks of Anglo-French diplomacy in these years, what followed over the course of the next two months was as shameful as it was pragmatic. Avoidance of war was key, as was trying to keep Italy onside with its Stresa partners, but sacrificing another country's territorial sovereignty on the basis that 'might was right' was simply unacceptable. British and French public opinion castigated the deal when its terms were leaked to the press and both authors of the notorious Hoare–Laval Pact were obliged to resign their ministerial posts in December and January respectively.[56]

As the reverberations from Mussolini's colonial war with Abyssinia continued, the leading naval powers returned to London to begin another round of disarmament talks. These lasted from 9 December to 25 March 1936 and made useful progress in the area of qualitative limitation, even though the Japanese withdrawal on 15 January suggested that in the Far East at least the days of quantitative disarmament had passed. As Norman Gibbs sagely observed: "The London Naval Treaty of 1936 was an attempt to hold back a tide which had already turned."[57] Even before the naval delegates had returned home, the latest blow to the Locarno Treaty was delivered on 7 March with the German reoccupation of the Rhineland. Unfortunately, the tepid Anglo-French diplomatic response to the fait accompli underscored the fact that robust action to thwart Hitler's plans was not on the agenda. War was the last thing on the minds of the politicians and their military experts at this stage. Self-interest had prevailed and another step on the road to appeasement had been taken.[58]

If Hitler's gamble could be rationalized on the grounds that it was merely reoccupying German territory, the question of what to do about Mussolini and his colonial war in the Horn of Africa was a delicate matter. This couldn't be explained away as a return to the status quo ante. An oil embargo could easily become a *casus belli* for the Fascist dictator and might lead to him leaving the League and attacking the Sudan. His unreliability was marked; he was capable of saying or doing anything if the mood suited him. He would not be denied his victory in Abyssinia, so provoking him and creating a crisis in the Mediterranean seemed like a bad idea to those in the corridors of power in London and Paris.[59]

These were changing with significant effect. In May the left-wing Popular Front triumphed in the French elections on a platform of 'Bread, Peace, and Liberty' and formed a government under Léon Blum. Within weeks it was faced by a fresh crisis in the Mediterranean. This time Mussolini was not immediately or directly involved, but that would soon change as General Franco's mutinous rebellion against the Spanish Republic in mid-July drew his support like a moth to a flame. If Franco was victorious and Spain was drawn into a fascist orbit it might pose serious geo-strategic complications for the British at the western end of the Mediterranean, threatening the passage of their mercantile trade as well as exposing their important naval base at Gibraltar to an existential threat. It was not much better for the French, who could not be blasé about what was going on just across the Pyrenees. Blum found himself in a huge dilemma. While he wished to support the Spanish government, he knew that any kind of intervention in the Civil War would almost certainly lead to a political crisis in a deeply divided France. This realisation provided the impetus for the promotion by his government of a non-intervention committee (August 1936) to keep the other powers from interfering in the course of the Civil War. It singularly failed to achieve this end, but the diplomatic charade lurched on regardless. Working through his son-in-law Galeazzo Ciano, his new foreign minister, Mussolini played a double game, seeking to hide his involvement in the Civil War through diplomatic posturing and yet reaching out to Germany in the hope of persuading it to form a Rome–Berlin axis. Mussolini needed little encouragement from Hitler to see the Mediterranean as his *mare nostrum* and entertain wild thoughts of attacking the British Mediterranean Fleet at Malta and sweeping it to defeat in a war lasting no more than seven weeks. While the journalistic hacks in Italy spoke glowingly of lightning war tactics that could defeat any foe, the senior officers of the Regia Marina were disinclined to try these out.[60]

Quite what form that axis would take when it was announced on 1 November was far from clear to the other democratic chancelleries of Europe. It was unlikely to be virtuous, but just how sinister it would be was a matter of lively debate. This much could also be said of the announcement by Germany and Japan on 25 November of the forging of the Anti-Comintern Pact between them. While it symbolised their mutual hatred of communism, the decisive question was whether this new Euro-Asiatic ideological axis was going to have profound implications in other spheres as well? Looking at what Roosevelt eventually would describe as the "three bandit nations", Anthony Eden, the British foreign secretary, had little difficulty in identifying Italy as the weakest of them and the one to disattach from the other two if at all possible. His hope in playing the Italian card was encouraged by the Fascist leader, whom he described as having the "mentality of a gangster".[61] Master of the double game, Mussolini offered up the enticing prospect of an understanding on the Mediterranean with the very power that he disdained as being long past its prime. Under these forlorn circumstances of mutual distrust, the so-called 'Gentlemen's Agreement' confirming "the freedom of entry into, exit from, and transit through, the Mediterranean" of 2 January 1937 was born.[62] It was seen as something better than nothing, but whether its terms would be respected was another matter altogether. Judging from the hopelessly compromised and easily circumvented Non-Intervention Committee patrol scheme, the signs were not propitious.

As the Italian military contribution to the Nationalist cause increased in the early months of 1937, the easy victory for Franco's forces that had been anticipated in Rome turned out to be nothing like the procession it was meant to be. A Republican victory at Guadalajara in March and their bombing of the Nationalist port of Palma de Mallorca and the Italian cruiser *Barletta* on 24 May infuriated Il Duce, while the bombing of the German pocket battleship *Deutschland* near Ibiza on 29 May prompted Hitler to order a massive retaliatory bombardment, which was delivered on the undefended port of Almeria in southern Spain at dawn on 31 May by the German heavy cruiser *Admiral Scheer* and four destroyers. Italian unwillingness to let matters rest was demonstrated as the summer drew on by their submarine attacks on all mercantile shipping engaged in trading with the Republican forces. In August 1937 twenty-six vessels (totalling roughly 200,000 deadweight tons) belonging to neutral states were sunk in this new war on trade.[63]

This scale of destruction prompted Yvon Delbos, the French foreign minister, to call for a naval conference to put a stop to this piratical behaviour. Meeting at Nyon in Switzerland from 10–14 September, the nine powers present (with Germany and Italy being significant absentees) agreed upon a formula which allowed their warships the right to attack and sink any unidentified submarines in those areas where mercantile shipping had been attacked. For once the agreement held and was enforced. It led to a suspension of submarine attacks that lasted for the rest of the year and which only resumed in January 1938 once the beefed-up naval patrol scheme had been relaxed as a result of its recent success! Thereafter, threats of retaliatory action by the British and the French were sufficient to restore order with the submersibles, but Franco's surface fleet and his air force continued to strike at those vessels trading with the enemy. They didn't always have it their own way, however, as the heavy cruiser *Baleares* found out when she was torpedoed and sunk by the Republican destroyer *Lepanto* at the Battle of Cape Palos off Cartagena in the early hours of 6 March.[64]

Although the attention of the European naval powers was largely devoted to action in the Mediterranean in 1937–38, those with empires overseas, such as the British, Dutch, and French, were acutely aware that the Japanese invasion of China following the Marco Polo Bridge incident of 7 July 1937 might have profound implications for the defence of their territories in both the Far East and Southeast Asia. If the Japanese army was able to subjugate the Chinese, would the Japanese Imperial General Headquarters stop there or be encouraged to embrace the legendary drive to the south (*nanshin-ron*). If it did, the future would suddenly look very bleak for Hong Kong, French Indochina, Malaya, Singapore, and the Dutch East Indies. Under these circumstances war could scarcely be avoided, but could any of the European states afford to contest such a war and win it? After all, in purely naval terms the Japanese navy would exercise monopoly power in these waters. Eden thought the answer lay in joint action with the US Navy in the Far East, and devoted the latter half of 1937 and most of January 1938 to trying to achieve this condominium of power. Despite encouraging sounds from Roosevelt, the prospect of mounting a naval demonstration in force in Far Eastern waters proved to be just as elusive as Prime Minister Neville Chamberlain suspected it would.[65]

If the democracies wouldn't stand up to the dictatorships, the only answer appeared to lie in appeasing them in the hope of maintaining peace. Once the *Anschluss* with Austria was proclaimed on 12 March, Hitler was in his element. Eden had gone; Blum having gone once would go again; Mussolini, now adorned with the title First Marshal of the Empire, was as supportive as he was unreliable. As the summer drew on and Hitler began to give vent to his avowed policy of *lebensraum*, the Western Powers found themselves being pushed towards making a stand on the question of Czechoslovakia. They did so without enthusiasm. Italy had already left the League and joined the Anti-Comintern Pact in December 1937, underscoring and yet undermining the Committee of Imperial Defence's description of it as neither a reliable friend nor a probable enemy (February 1937) when it did so. Nonetheless, Chamberlain and his chiefs of staff (COS) put what hopes they had in maintaining peace in the Anglo-Italian agreement of April 1938. This was meant to take Italy out of a future war equation and hopefully place it in a mediatory capacity with its axis partner in Berlin. It was a gamble not least because Mussolini, the double dealer par excellence, regarded the Czechs as inferior Slavs whose artificial state should be removed from the map of Europe. Encouraging Hitler with visions of military support for what he regarded as a good cause, he still accepted with his customary egotism Chamberlain's eleventh-hour appeal for him to be an arbitrator in the Czech crisis. Referring to the British as suffering from a menopausal disorder, he saw himself as the honest broker at the Munich conference in late September 1938 and revelled in the adulation that came his way as the peacemaker of Europe.[66]

This unaccustomed role was soon ditched in favour of aggressive intent against a string of adversaries including the Albanians, French, and Swiss. On 30 November, a parliamentary demonstration was staged in Rome when the Italian deputies rose to their feet and lustily demanded the annexation of Nice, Corsica, and Tunis. This had the opposite effect of what it was intended to achieve. Instead of being paralytic in fear of their southern neighbour, the French promptly ignored the provocation and focussed instead on the need for rearmament. Chamberlain and his malleable foreign secretary Lord Halifax doughtily pursued the spectre of better relations with the Italians and went to Rome in January 1939 with this in mind, but their talks with Mussolini failed comprehensively to lure the new Bismarckian figure away from his Nazi compact.[67]

Failure on this score was worsened by intelligence reports received in London later in the month that Germany was preparing to wage war on Holland. This galvanized the COS to complete their European Appreciation (February 1939) dealing with the nightmare scenario of war on several fronts. It also led to the holding of further Anglo-French staff talks and the issuing of guarantees of assistance to Poland (March 1939), Greece, and Romania (April 1939), once the rump of the Czechoslovakian state left intact after the Munich settlement had been acquired by Germany through the foulest diplomatic means on 15 March 1939. Conscious that a villainous campaign of intimidatory diplomacy had been mounted against President Hacha, Chamberlain was forced to admit two days later in Birmingham that his appeasement policy had come to nought. It may have bought the democracies a few extra months of peace, but it had also given their likely enemies the same preparation time too. Franco's victories in Barcelona and Madrid in January and March had effectively ended the Spanish Civil War in favour of the Nationalists; Mussolini's wholly unnecessary and cynical war on Albania in April and his signing of the Pact of Steel with Hitler on 22 May demonstrated where his loyalties lay, and those were aligned to war rather than peace.[68]

Erich Raeder, C-in-C of the Kriegsmarine, understood that *lebensraum* would not always go uncontested and this likelihood had been the impetus for the devising of the *Z-Plan* in 1938–39 for dealing with Germany's main adversaries at sea. In essence, the rearmament programme envisaged the Kriegsmarine becoming a massively powerful force exceeding at least one million tons of surface warships spearheaded by between seventeen and twenty-nine capital ships, including at least four aircraft carriers and accompanied by a full retinue of cruisers and destroyers as well as a submarine fleet of 249 vessels. This would naturally take many years to construct before it could be wielded in battle. Raeder hoped to buy time to build at least part of this new fleet before going to war (1944), but his Führer's public abandonment of the Anglo-German Naval Agreement and the Non-Aggression Pact with Poland (28 April) left the German Naval High Command (Oberkommando der Marine [OKM]) in little doubt as to the imminence of war. As such, the *Z-Plan* was consigned to history and instead the OKM scrambled to get ready for what would happen once Hitler sent his forces into Poland.[69]

On the other side of the military divide, the British and French governments found themselves in a quandary about what to do with the elephant in the room – the

Soviet Union. Could a peace front be established with Stalin's regime in Moscow? Did it represent the last chance of saving the world from hurtling towards the brink of war? Would Hitler think twice about crossing the Polish border if he thought the Red Army would contest such an incursion? Unfortunately, Chamberlain and Édouard Daladier, the two leaders who had returned from the Munich conference in September 1938 having bought peace at great cost to the Czechs, looked at the USSR option from two radically different perspectives. Chamberlain abhorred communism and agreed with his military experts that as a result of the military purges that had taken place in the USSR, the Red Army was of doubtful military value beyond its own borders. Daladier, on the other hand, agreed with his foreign minister Georges Bonnet that a military alliance with the Soviet Union was vital. Unfortunately, negotiations between the three powers to try and effect some form of agreement between them were laboured and took over three months before a joint military mission was sent to Moscow and began discussions with Marshal Voroshilov on 12 August. Led by General Doumenc and Vice-Admiral Drax, the talks with Marshal Voroshilov soon became deadlocked on what form the Eastern Front would take in the event of a military alliance being signed between the three governments. Voroshilov's penetrating questions, which cut to the heart of the matter, were left unanswered by the time the talks were broken off on 21 August. Two days later the very thing that the French had feared all along, the Nazi–Soviet Pact, was signed by Ribbentrop and Molotov in Moscow. Such a non-aggression treaty gave both signatories what they wanted (at least for the time being), cleared the way for war, and left the Western democracies as well as the Italians and the Japanese in a bit of a bind.[70]

Appeasement was at an end; there would no new Munich; Poland wouldn't be sacrificed as Czechoslovakia had been the year before. If war came it would be because Hitler wanted it. This left Mussolini with very few options that he liked. He couldn't be the hero any more. Despite all his rabid bluster and indecisiveness, he finally opted for a position of non-belligerence if war came. As for the Japanese, their visceral hatred of communism – deepened still further by their defeat at Nomonhan – left them disenchanted with the sudden demise of the Anti-Comintern Pact.[71]

Anger about being let down by their allies and partners felt by the authoritarian powers contrasted with the relief of the democracies that the prolonged spectre of a three-front war involving Germany, Italy, and Japan had somehow magically dissolved within a matter of days.

Notes

1　Boris Barth, *Dolchstoßlegenden und politische Desintegration: Das Trauma der deutschen Niederlage im Ersten Weltkrieg 1914–1933* (Düsseldorf: Droste, 2003), pp.167, 340f; Martin Clark, *Modern Italy, 1871 to the Present* (Milton Park: Routledge, 2014), pp.244–46.
2　Michael D. Besch, *A Navy Second to None: the History of U.S. Naval Training in World War I* (Westport: Greenwood Press, 2002).
3　David C. Evans and Mark R. Peattie, *Kaigun: Strategy, Tactics, and Technology in the Imperial Japanese Navy, 1887–1941* (Annapolis: Naval Institute Press, 1997).

4   John Jordan, *Warships After Washington: the Development of the Five Major Fleets 1922–1930* (Annapolis: Naval Institute Press, 2011), pp.xii–24.

5   Alan Sharp, *The Versailles Settlement: Peacemaking After the First World War, 1919–1923* (Basingstoke: Palgrave, 2008; 2nd edition).

6   John Milton Cooper, *Breaking the Heart of the World: Woodrow Wilson and the Fight for the League of Nations* (Cambridge: Cambridge University Press, 2001).

7   Ronald Grigor Suny, *The Soviet Experiment: Russia, the USSR, and the Successor States* (Oxford: OUP, 2010; 2nd edition), pp.56–106.

8   Paul Halpern, *A Naval History of World War I* (Annapolis: Naval Institute Press, 2012); Malcolm Murfett, *Naval Warfare 1919–1945: an Operational History of the Volatile War at Sea* (Milton Park: Routledge, 2013; 2nd edition), pp.1–3.

9   Eberhard Roessler, *Die Unterseeboote der Kaiserlichen Marine* (Bonn: Bernard & Graefe, 1997); Joachim Schroeder, *Die U-Boote des Kaisers* (Bonn: Bernard & Graefe, 2002); Richard Compton-Hall, *Submarines at War 1914–18* (Penzance: Periscope Publishing Ltd, 2004).

10 Dan Van der Vat, *The Grand Scuttle: the Sinking of the German fleet at Scapa Flow in 1919* (Edinburgh: Birlinn, 2007).

11 Jordan, *Warships After Washington*, pp.16–24, 39–44.

12 Malcolm H. Murfett, 'Look Back in Anger: the Western Powers and the Washington Conference of 1921–1922', in B.J.C. McKercher (ed.), *Arms Limitation and Disarmament: Restraints on War, 1899–1939* (Westport: Praeger, 1992), pp.83–103.

13 Although the 5:5:3:1.75 capital ship ratio was what Hughes originally wanted, the actual tonnage figures ended up as being 525,000 for the Royal Navy and US Navy, 315,000 for the Japanese navy, and 175,000 for the Marine Nationale and Regia Marina. This meant that the ratio for the latter two navies effectively became 1:66.

14 Jordan, *Warships After Washington*, pp.48–73, 310–16.

15 Malcolm H. Murfett, 'Reflections on an Enduring Theme: the "Singapore Strategy" at Sixty', in Brian Farrell and Sandy Hunter (eds.), *Sixty Years On: the Fall of Singapore Revisited* (Singapore: Eastern Universities Press, 2002), pp.3–28.

16 While Austria and Bulgaria became members in 1920, Hungary in 1922, Germany in 1926, and Turkey in 1932, the Soviet Union remained excluded from the organisation until 1934.

17 Jordan, *Warships after Washington*, pp.153–93, 217–61.

18 Denis Mack Smith, *Mussolini: a Biography* (New York: Alfred A. Knopf, 1982), pp.35–68.

19 Oscar Parkes (ed.), *Jane's Fighting Ships 1931* (London: Sampson Low Marston & Co, 1931), p.vi; Murfett, *Naval Warfare*, p.11; Jordan, *Warships After Washington*, pp.108–10, 112, 116–18, 125–26, 128–29, 131–32, 134, 141–46, 149, 151–52.

20 Jordan, *Warships after Washington*, pp.108–09, 112–17, 119–20, 125–26, 128–32, 134–35, 138–43, 146–49, 151–52.

21 Sally Marks, 'The Myths of Reparations', *Central European History*, 11, 3 (1978), pp.231–55.

22 Hans W. Gatzke, *Stresemann and the Rearmament of Germany* (New York: W.W. Norton & Co., 1969); Jon Jacobson, *Locarno Diplomacy: Germany and the West 1925–1929* (Princeton: Princeton University Press, 1972); Eberhard Kolb, *Gustav Stresemann* (Munich: C.H. Beck, 2003).

23 Jordan, *Warships after Washington*, pp.194–216.

24 Richard W. Fanning, 'The Coolidge Conference of 1927: Disarmament in Disarray', in B.J.C. McKercher (ed.), *Arms Limitation and Disarmament*, pp.105–27.

25 Christopher M. Bell, 'Winston Churchill and the Ten Year Rule', *Journal of Military History*, 74, 4 (2010), pp.1097–1128; N.H. Gibbs, *Grand Strategy. Vol. I: Rearmament Policy* (London: HMSO, 1976), pp.69–89.

26 Sally Marks, *The Illusion of Peace: International Relations in Europe, 1918–1933* (Basingstoke: Palgrave, 2003); Zara Steiner, *The Lights that Failed: European International History, 1919–1933* (Oxford: Oxford University Press, 2005); Antony

Best, Jussi M. Hanhimäki, Joseph A. Maiolo, and Kirsten E. Schulze, *International History of the Twentieth Century* (London: Routledge, 2004), pp.48–54.

27 David Marquand, *Ramsay MacDonald* (London: Jonathan Cape, 1977).

28 Marks, *The Illusion of Peace*, pp.83–160; Steiner, *The Lights that Failed*, pp.565–706, 755–816.

29 Jordan, *Warships after Washington*, pp.286–309, 317–24; Gregory C. Kennedy, 'The 1930 London Naval Conference and Anglo-American Maritime Strength, 1927–1930', in B.J.C. McKercher (ed.), *Arms Limitation and Disarmament*, pp.149–71.

30 Ibid.

31 Jordan, *Warships after Washington*, p.318.

32 Ibid., pp.311, 318.

33 Ibid., pp.299–300.

34 Ibid., pp.301–06.

35 Ibid., pp.303–06, 321–23.

36 Ibid., pp.306–09.

37 Ibid., p.323.

38 Ibid., pp.308–09.

39 Kennedy, 'The London Naval Conference', pp.157–61.

40 Mary Fulbrook, *History of Germany 1918-2008: The Divided Nation* (Oxford: Wiley-Blackwell, 2009: 3rd edition), pp.38–55.

41 Best et al., *International History*, pp.62–63, 65–68.

42 Piers Brendon, *The Dark Valley: a Panorama of the 1930s* (New York: Vintage Books, 2003).

43 B.J.C. McKercher, 'Of Horns and Teeth: The Preparatory Commission and the World Disarmament Conference, 1926–1934', in B.J.C. McKercher (ed.), *Arms Limitation and Disarmament*, pp.173–201.

44 Alfred Cobban, *A History of Modern France. Vol. 3: France of the Republics 1871–1962* (London: Penguin Books, 1977), pp.137–48.

45 Mack Smith, *Mussolini*, p.182.

46 Robert Dallek, *Franklin D. Roosevelt and American Foreign Policy, 1932–1945* (Oxford: Oxford University Press, 1995), pp.23–97.

47 McKercher, 'Of Horns and Teeth', p.190.

48 Zara Steiner, *The Triumph of the Dark: European International History 1933–1939* (Oxford: Oxford University Press, 2011), pp.9–99.

49 Ibid., pp.75–76; Ian Kershaw, *Hitler, 1889-1936: Hubris* (New York: W.W. Norton, 2000), pp.522–23.

50 Mack Smith, *Mussolini*, pp.181–87.

51 Cobban, *A History of Modern France*, pp.163–64.

52 Joseph A. Maiolo, *Cry Havoc: the Arms Race and the Second World War, 1931–1941* (London: John Murray, 2010); Murfett, *Naval Warfare*, pp.12, 19.

53 Malcolm H. Murfett, 'Living in the Past: A Critical Re-examination of the Singapore Naval Strategy, 1918–41', *War and Society*, 11, 1 (1993), pp.73–103; Christopher M. Bell, *The Royal Navy, Seapower and Strategy Between the Wars* (Basingstoke: Macmillan, 2000), pp.59–98; Andrew Boyd, *The Royal Navy in Eastern Waters: Linchpin of Victory 1935–1942* (Barnsley: Seaforth, 2017).

54 Joseph A. Maiolo, 'The Admiralty and the Anglo-German Naval Agreement of 18 June 1935', *Diplomacy and Statecraft*, 10, 1 (1999), pp.87–126; Gibbs, *Grand Strategy*, pp.133–85.

55 Maiolo, 'The Admiralty and the Anglo-German Naval Agreement', pp.87–126.

56 Mack Smith, *Mussolini*, pp.188–203; Gibbs, *Grand Strategy*, pp.187–226.

57 Gibbs, *Grand Strategy*, pp.332; Meredith W. Berg, 'Protecting National Interests by Treaty: the Second London Naval Conference, 1934–1936', in B.J.C. McKercher (ed.), *Arms Limitation and Disarmament*, pp.203–27.

58 Gibbs, *Grand Strategy*, pp.227–72; Gerhard Weinberg, *Hitler's Foreign Policy 1933–1939: The Road to World War II* (New York: Enigma Books, 2010), pp.163–205.
59 Best et al., *International History*, pp.166–69; Cobban, *A History of Modern France*, pp.146–57, 163–69.
60 Mack Smith, *Mussolini*, pp.206–12.
61 Ibid., p.210.
62 Gibbs, *Grand Strategy*, p.383.
63 Antony Beevor, *The Battle for Spain: the Spanish Civil War 1936–1939* (London: Weidenfeld & Nicolson 2006), pp.289–90; Hugh Thomas, *The Spanish Civil War* (New York: Modern Library Paperbacks, 2001), pp.663–67.
64 Murfett, *Naval Warfare*, pp.25–26.
65 Malcolm Murfett, *Fool-Proof Relations: the Search for Anglo-American Naval Cooperation during the Chamberlain Years 1937–1940* (Singapore: Singapore University Press, 1984), pp.41–161.
66 Mack Smith, *Mussolini*, pp.223–27; Gibbs, *Grand Strategy*, pp.380–93.
67 Mack Smith, *Mussolini*, pp.225–27.
68 Murfett, *Fool-Proof Relations*, pp.187–268.
69 Keith W. Bird, *Erich Raeder: Admiral of the Third Reich* (Annapolis: Naval Institute Press, 2006); Robert Gardiner (ed.), *Conway's All the World's Fighting Ships 1922–1946* (London: Conway Maritime Press, 1980); Vincent P. O'Hara, *The German Fleet at War, 1939–1945* (Annapolis: Naval Institute Press, 2011).
70 Gibbs, *Grand Strategy*, pp.719–65.
71 Stuart D. Goldman, *Nomonhan 1939: the Red Army's Victory That Shaped World War II* (Annapolis: Naval Institute Press, 2012); Mack Smith, *Mussolini*, pp.231–37.

9 European navies and the war at sea, 1939–1942

Malcolm Murfett

A far more confined naval war to that which many in London and Paris had feared might take place broke out in response to Germany's blitzkrieg attack on Poland on 1 September. Instead of the worst-case scenario of a global war on several fronts involving the Italians, Japanese, Soviets, and Spanish, the Royal Navy and the Marine Nationale were initially confronted by a Kriegsmarine that was still several years away from performing at optimum capacity. If that was any cause for quiet satisfaction, the moment was fleeting. Within hours of the British and French declaration of war on Germany on 3 September, the German U-boat *U30* had torpedoed and sunk the British passenger liner SS *Athenia* in the Western Approaches to the North Atlantic with the loss of at least 112 passengers and crew.[1]

U-30 was one of ten ocean-going Type VIIA U-boats that was located in a grid system fashioned by the German Seekriegsleitung (Naval War Staff) in the North Atlantic at the outset of war. Kapitän Zur See und Führer der U-boote Karl Dönitz had another six Type VIIBs in the Atlantic grid, five early Type IX models in Spanish waters, and seventeen of his smaller Type II boats and one of his experimental Type 1A vessels in the North Sea. In terms of a submersible fleet it didn't look much of an immediate threat, but, as Correlli Barnett indicated more than two decades ago, numbers are not always everything, and so it proved.[2] A German fleet of surface warships that included four battleships – two fast (*Scharnhorst* and *Gneisenau*) and two long past their sell-by date (*Schlesien* and *Schleswig-Holstein*), three pocket battleships (*Deutschland, Admiral Graf Spee*, and *Admiral Scheer*), two heavy cruisers (*Blücher* and *Admiral Hipper*), five light cruisers, and seventeen destroyers was not the stuff of Großadmiral Raeder's Z-Plan dreams, but the vessels would still be made use of selectively in the war against trade, using the element of surprise to overwhelm any unsuspecting and overmatched mercantile craft belonging to the enemy. Two of the pocket battleships were already in position waiting for action when the Polish border was breached: *Admiral Graf Spee* was deployed off the Brazilian coast of Pernambuco and *Deutschland* in the area south of Greenland.[3]

Opposing the Kriegsmarine was the Home Fleet based at Scapa Flow in the Orkney Islands, consisting of three R-class battleships of World War One vintage (*Ramillies, Royal Oak*, and *Royal Sovereign*), two Nelson-class battleships launched in 1925 (*Nelson* and *Rodney*), the newly commissioned aircraft carrier *Ark Royal* with a mix of twenty-six Fairey Swordfish and twenty-four Blackburn Skuas, two battle-cruisers (*Hood* and *Repulse*), the heavy cruiser *Norfolk*, fourteen light cruisers, the A.A. (anti-aircraft) cruiser *Calcutta*, seventeen destroyers, and twenty-one submarines. Its other carrier, *Furious* (36 aircraft), had been extensively refitted and would remain on training duties until early October, while the old World War One battle-cruiser *Renown* (the sister ship of *Repulse)* was recommissioned in late August and pressed into patrolling duties in the North Sea shortly thereafter. Four hundred and forty-five nautical miles to the south and operating off the Lincolnshire port of Grimsby, the Humber Force contained two light cruisers and eight J-class destroyers; while the Channel Force was based at Portland in Dorset, containing two carriers (the rebuilt *Courageous* and the smaller *Hermes*), the remaining two R-class battleships (*Resolution* and *Revenge*), a couple of light cruisers and the A.A. cruiser *Cairo*, along with nine A-class destroyers. Rounding out the Home Fleet were another fifty destroyers which were dispersed along the coast from Milford Haven in Pembrokeshire to Dover.[4]

Although the French were committed to deploying the bulk of their Marine Nationale in the Mediterranean just in case the Regia Marina belatedly entered the picture, they would still be able to provide some material support for the Royal Navy in the Bay of Biscay and in the Western Approaches. Based at Brest on the coast of Brittany under the command of Admiral Gensoul, the Force de Raid consisted of the modern battleships *Dunkerque* and *Strasbourg*, along with the only French carrier, *Béarn*, the seaplane tender *Commandante Teste*, three light cruisers, and eight super-destroyers. Two pre-World War One dreadnoughts (*Courbet* and *Paris*) also featured at Brest, but both were initially deemed too old for active duty and were only used for training purposes. Their status would change with the German attack on France and the Low Countries on 10 May. Brest was also home to four super-destroyers (almost light cruisers), twelve regular fleet destroyers, a dozen submarines, and a number of assorted other light craft. Further up the coast and 10 km from the Belgian border, Dunkirk (Dunkerque) was the seat of the French command centre for naval operations in both the English Channel and the North Sea. Four submarines were based there, along with a whole slew of light surface vessels from sloops and torpedo boats to sub-chasers and a mine-layer. In addition, three naval air squadrons provided reconnaissance duties along the coastline and out to sea.[5]

While the British and the French naval hierarchy were grateful that their worst strategic nightmare had been avoided and war wouldn't be extended to the Mediterranean or the Pacific at least at the outset, the Poles were not in such exalted company. At 0448 hours on 1 September the pre-World War One battleship *Schleswig-Holstein*, supposedly on a goodwill visit to Danzig and lying at anchor in the harbour, suddenly opened fire on the military transit depot on the Westerplatte and disembarked a mix of SS troops and marines numbering 1,725 to invade the peninsula. It was expected to be a very routine affair since the German troops were attacking an unimposing facility defended by a small mixed force of regular and reservist soldiers only a fraction of their size. Instead of being easily mopped up, however, the 209 defenders performed heroically amidst saturation bombing and artillery assaults and held out for a week before finally surrendering. Their resistance to overwhelming force was both heartening and inspirational. Elsewhere, the German blitzkrieg offensive made swifter progress. Unfortunately, the rather decrepit Polish Naval Air Squadron was bombed out of existence on the first day of the campaign and the main focal point of Poland's naval forces (a small destroyer and submarine flotilla) was simply not strong enough on its own to thwart the German offensive. Knowing this in advance, the Polish Navy sought to live another day by activating Operation *Pekin*. Three of their four destroyers (*Burza*, *Blyskawica*, and *Grom*) made their escape to England on 30 August before the first salvoes of war rang out, while the sole remaining destroyer (*Wicher*) protected a mine-layer as it sowed mines in the Gulf of Danzig. Its five submarines did their best to avoid being trapped in the Baltic and made as much of a nuisance of themselves as they could by mining the route to the East Prussian ports in the hope of causing as much damage to German shipping as possible. All survived the first couple of weeks of the war, but once the Soviets had entered the picture on 17 September three of them sought internment in neutral Swedish waters, while the remaining two (*Wilk* and *Orzel*) escaped detection and destruction and made it across the North Sea to Rosyth on 20 September and 14 October respectively.[6]

Although a heightened state of alert was present wherever units of the Marine Nationale and Royal Navy were clustered around the globe, the overwhelming focus of attention in the early months of the war lay in the seas off Northwestern Europe. What the destruction of the *Athenia* had shown conclusively was the potentiality of the German U-boat fleet to be a real threat again and that a cardinal mistake of World War One – the failure to employ convoys for the first two and a half years of the naval war – wouldn't be repeated on this occasion. Protection of mercantile shipping was essential since vitally important war supplies needed to get safely through contested waters to home ports. Therefore, a convoy system for passage across the North Atlantic from east to west was established on 7 September and in the opposite direction from American to British ports a week later. Refinements to distinguish between fast and slow convoys would be made in due course. These arrangements worked well and forced the U-boats to concentrate much of their attention on gaps in the system or in those areas where convoys were not in place and independent sailings continued. Dönitz was convinced that given sufficient vessels, his U-boat fleet could severely punish the Allies and that the war on trade could be won even against convoy-protected shipping.[7] From the outset, therefore, the aim of the Kriegsmarine was to sink more vessels than the numbers of new vessels emerging from Allied shipyards. If this mismatch between sunken and replacement vessels could be continued on a sustained monthly basis for as long as possible, Raeder and his senior officers trusted that victory would eventually be theirs.

This assumption might well have been proved valid if the Allied powers had not been reinforced by the addition of the US in December 1941. Back in 1939, however, the overall picture was far more blurred. Existing US neutrality legislation complicated matters considerably and would need to be carefully managed in the months to come to circumvent the regulations without running afoul of them. This was made a whole lot easier because President Roosevelt was clearly sympathetic to the Allied cause. In the end, a 'cash and carry' provision was built into the 1939 Neutrality Act to enable the Allies to buy their war supplies directly from the Americans on a cash basis and then convoy them back across the Atlantic in their own ships. It stretched the legal concept of neutrality to the borders of non-belligerency and yet was absolutely vital for an island nation such as the UK which was dependent upon overseas trade for its long-term survival.[8]

Within three weeks of the war beginning, even the modest U-boat fleet that Dönitz possessed at the outset of hostilities had demonstrated its potential for causing havoc when the carrier *Courageous* was sunk by *U29* while out on anti-submarine operations off the southwest coast of Ireland on 17 September. Only three days prior to this loss another carrier (*Ark Royal*) out on similar hunting duties had survived a torpedo attack by *U39* off the west coast of Scotland. Both of these incidents showed what the Allies were up against in trying to detect and destroy these underwater predators.[9] Regrettably, anti-submarine warfare (ASW) techniques had not improved markedly in the inter-war period as financial stringency had meant that research and development on ASDIC had not been encouraged. Economising in this way given what harm the U-boat had done in World War One was very short-sighted of the Admiralty and as a direct result of this lack of time, attention, and funding, ASW left an awful lot more to be desired in 1939 than ought to have been the case. ASDIC was far from being the finished article. It was only really effective in calm, fairly shallow seas. Even then its range was limited and blind-spot problems persisted once the surface warship equipped with ASDIC drew close to its intended victim. In anything more turbulent with heavy swells, under-surface currents, and multi-layered opacity, it became largely inoperable.[10]

If ASW was problematic, so too were the severe technical issues related to torpedoes that confronted even the best and most daring of the U-boat commanders. They could manoeuvre their vessel into the perfect position to sink or at least damage an intended victim and find to their utter frustration that the ship would survive as a result of any number of torpedo faults, from running too deeply or off target to prematurely exploding or failing to explode upon impact. Günther Prien, who achieved instant fame by penetrating the main fleet base defences at Scapa Flow on 15 October to torpedo and sink the battleship *Royal Oak*, was one of many who would lend his voice to the growing chorus of criticism about the malfunctioning German torpedoes. He complained that it was like having to fight with a dummy rifle.[11] Dönitz empathised with his U-boat aces. He never stopped complaining about the flawed nature of the G7a compressed air torpedoes and the later G7e electric torpedoes until their faults were finally addressed in 1942.[12] It was perhaps just as well for the Allies that the Germans were battling technical difficulties because it doesn't take much imagination to wonder at the degree of chaos that would have been caused had the torpedoes been as efficient as the Japanese models.[13]

Both surface warships and U-boats needed help in finding their intended victims in the vastness of the oceans. It was recognized by both sides in the war that signals intelligence (SIGINT) held the real key to unlocking the mysteries of what moves the enemy was planning in advance. Therefore, if the codes and ciphers of their enemies could be broken on a regular basis, invaluable information would become available to the side which had secured this priceless advantage. If the highly confidential information obtained from SIGINT was correctly analysed it could be used to counter the plans of an adversary and enable a naval power to turn defence into attack. Breaking the ultra-complex, machine-driven German Enigma code, for instance, was an extraordinary achievement by Allied cryptanalysts. Some codes defied the best mathematical brains for weeks and months at a time, but eventually through the brilliant work of these very gifted and often highly idiosyncratic individuals at Bletchley Park, the astonishing jumble of letters and numbers that was intercepted constantly throughout the day and night could be decrypted and ultimately turned into understandable messages or orders.[14]

A critical element of this cipher war was ensuring that if a code had been broken it should never be revealed or compromised in any way. As it was, the codes were frequently changed and made still more complex, but if the Germans had come to learn that their codes were not secure, the benefits of securing this vital information (ULTRA) would be immediately imperilled or lost altogether.[15] Both sides played this high-stakes game. Unfortunately, in the early years of the war the British naval cipher was easier to unravel than any variant of Enigma. This meant that the German equivalent of the British GC&CS (Government Code and Cipher School), the Beobachtungs-Dienst (B-Dienst), could furnish the German Naval High Command (Oberkommando der Marine, or OKM) and Dönitz with fairly detailed instructions as to the routes that would be taken by some convoys or those mercantile ships that were being allowed to steam independently from one location to another. Armed with this information, Dönitz and his staff were able to deploy a number of U-boats (commonly described as a wolf pack) along the route to strike at their victims in a coordinated series of attacks (*Rudeltaktik*) which were designed to confuse and overcome even well-defended convoys let alone those vessels that weren't blessed with these advantages.[16]

Despite its torpedo shortcomings, the U-boat remained the vessel of choice in conducting the war on trade. It was relatively cheap and quick to build and appeared to offer the Kriegsmarine a better return on its investment than might be offered by any individual unit of the surface fleet. Consequently, within a month of the beginning of war a host of the more formidable warships from Raeder's *Z-Plan* had been cancelled, with fifty-five ocean-going U-boats and sixteen smaller coastal submarines (Type IID) being ordered to replace them. A month later, the German shipbuilding firms received another boost with the ordering of another sixty large U-boats destined for work in the North Atlantic.[17]

Raeder acknowledged that time had not been on his side when it came to new construction, but still felt that his beloved surface fleet could be used profitably to take the fight to the enemy. Battleships of any description and heavy cruisers could do an awful lot of damage to the Allied cause if they fell upon their prey. Winston Churchill, who had returned to the Admiralty at the outset of war, shared that opinion and devoted unremitting efforts to try and eliminate the threat posed by them whenever they emerged from their home bases on a raiding mission. Churchill would assemble large task forces for the purpose of hunting and destroying them and they would conduct vast sweeps of the seas in which the warships had last been seen. Often the predators would conduct hit-and-run missions and escape back from whence they came. This was doubly frustrating for the Allies because it tied up vast resources and the end product – the destruction of the armed raider – was rarely achieved. Sometimes, however, the ends justified the means, and this was the case with the long-term pursuit of the pocket battle-ship *Admiral Graf Spee* from October to December 1939.[18]

This sole warship, in the hands of her daring and imaginative captain, Hans Langsdorff, proved to be an elusive quarry and was responsible for a vast Allied dragnet consisting of five carriers, four battleships, a battle-cruiser, twenty cruisers, nine destroyers, a sloop, and a submarine that combed the Indian Ocean and the South Atlantic looking for the German raider. Langsdorff revelled in his risky exploits, always staying ahead of his pursuers by setting enterprising plans and making high-speed passages that confounded them and left them bereft. His orders were not to risk destruction by seeking battle with any of the hunting groups, but Langsdorff's deeply felt self-confidence in his own ship-handling skills and his underestimation of the opponents ranged against him was such that he was always prepared to ignore those instructions. In the end, hubris was his Achilles heel and this failing more than anything else brought an end to his epic journey at 2200 hours on 17 December in the waters off Montevideo. Langsdorff scuttled his ship and committed suicide two days later. When informed of his death, Hitler was unmoved. Heroes swiftly became zeroes if they didn't perform to the Führer's satisfaction.[19]

By the time the *Admiral Graf Spee* had been blown apart by her own explosive charges, the Phoney War that had briefly settled over the Baltic once Poland had been defeated had already evaporated with the cynical attack on Finland by the Soviet Union on 30 November. At sea the Winter War was a spasmodic and relatively low-key affair since the Finnish Navy was only a small coastal defence force and couldn't be expected to survive for long if pitched against the much more formidable Red Banner Baltic Fleet. Nonetheless, the harsh wintry conditions did much to neutralise the Soviet naval threat as a very thick sheet of ice covered the Baltic in December 1939, ensuring that only icebreakers could move around with any degree of freedom for weeks thereafter. Even on land the Red Army didn't have its own way as the resolute and doughty Finns used the harsh conditions and their intimate knowledge of the terrain to conduct guerrilla operations against them. By avoiding set-piece battles, striking hard, and melting away across the snow and ice, they survived much longer than expected before the effects of a naval blockade and sheer numbers on land prevailed and a peace settlement was drawn up by the victorious Soviets in March 1940.[20]

While one side of the Nazi–Soviet Pact was finding the going rough in Scandinavia, the Germans were doing far better at sea in taking the fight to their Allied opponents. Using the opportunity brought about by the *Graf Spee*'s exploits and the absence of major naval units which were chasing after her, the OKM had used a variety of vessels to conduct minelaying operations in the North Sea, causing the destruction of twenty-two mercantile ships (37,075 tons) in December alone. Given that another twenty vessels (34,948 tons) had fallen victim to U-boats in British coastal waters in the same month, the statistical returns were suggestive that the Kriegsmarine was getting the job done at the Allies' expense.[21]

While there was obvious room for satisfaction in the OKM and Seekriegsleitung as the year closed, the Allies could also take some comfort from both the positive outcome of the Battle of the River Plate and the quite exceptional convoy statistics it had secured in its operations from September to December 1939 in the North Atlantic, the Mediterranean, and along the West African coast with loss rates of only 0.70%, 0.63%, and 0.66% respectively.[22]

1940

It didn't take long for this sort of naval equilibrium to disappear. Within the first six weeks of the new year a patrol group of sixteen U-boats had accounted for the destroyer *Exmouth* and nineteen merchant vessels in the North Sea alone (67,831 tons) for the loss of *U15*, while six U-boats operating independently had claimed twenty-four more victims (92,800 tons) in the North Atlantic for the loss of two of their number. Admittedly, the vast majority of these merchant vessels were small freighters, but their loss along with their cargo couldn't be written off as a matter of little consequence. At this stage, there were still too many gaps in the convoy system for comfort – not least in home waters, where too many vessels were forced to sail independently – and Dönitz's U-boats exploited these weaknesses with unalloyed relish. Although bad enough, things could have got much worse for the Allies if the Luftwaffe had sown its stock of 22,000 magnetic mines in British coastal waters. As it was, some aerial minelaying was conducted in the Humber, Thames, and Tyne river estuaries, but much more could have been done and presumably to far greater effect had Hermann Göring been more supportive of the policy.[23]

Ironically, a bombing error by his beloved Luftwaffe in the previous November had left two magnetic mines on the mud flats at Shoeburyness in the Thames estuary. These proved to be of inestimable value to the Allies after they had been recovered and defused by explosive experts. Once their hidden mysteries had been discovered, countermeasures could be taken to render them ineffective. As a direct result of this simple bombing error, a degaussing system was developed that had the effect of wiping magnetism from a ship's hull, allowing those vessels that had been electrically-treated in this way to pass over this type of mine without causing an explosion. Contact mines – more the stock in trade of the U-boat minelayers – were a different proposition and needed to be swept from those channels in which they were laid. For this purpose, minesweepers were a vital component of any navy that had coastal waters to protect or trade routes to safeguard.[24]

Although the new year had begun promisingly for Raeder's Kriegsmarine, not everything the Germans touched in 1940 turned to gold. Some of their operational sorties went badly awry, as was the case with two of their Type 1934 destroyers, *Leberecht Maass* and *Max Schultz*, who succumbed to a combination of 'friendly fire' from Heinkel He-111 aircraft and British mines on 22 February. By the same token, the Allies weren't always on the receiving end of things either.[25] A few days before the German destroyer losses in the North Sea, a startling coup had been carried out by Captain Philip Vian in his destroyer *Cossack* against the prison ship and tanker *Altmark*, which had gone aground in the neutral waters of Jøssingfjorden along the southwest coast of Norway. By forcefully boarding the supply ship with bayonets and cutlasses at the ready in order to release the 303 prisoners being held in her hold, Vian and his crew were in breach of both international law and Norwegian neutrality. Churchill approved of his buccaneering methods despite the enraged and predictable furore from Scandinavian quarters that accompanied this dashing exploit.[26] Notwithstanding its piratical elements, the *Altmark* incident had far greater significance than the 'feel good' factor it engendered in British circles, because it led to a reassessment of Norway's future role in the war by both the Allies and the Germans.

Both sides realised what was at stake. Essentially it came down to deciding whether Norway could be trusted to be neutral and even-handed between the belligerents. This was not an idle question since 40% of Germany's iron ore supplies came from Sweden and during the winter months when the Gulf of Bothnia was frozen over these vital mineral ores were transported by rail across Norwegian territory to the northern port of Narvik and then shipped down the west coast to Germany. As the Allies wavered on whether they should mine Norwegian waters to disrupt or prevent the ferrying of these supplies and the likely military ramifications of doing so, the Germans were less preoccupied by the constitutional niceties of neutrality and opted to invade both Denmark and Norway on 8–9 April so as to pre-empt whatever the enemy was planning to do in these northern latitudes. From the outset, therefore, the Germans always seemed a step ahead of the Allies when it came to the Norwegian campaign.[27]

A combination of elementary Admiralty errors, mistaken assumptions, and poor leadership meant that the Home Fleet, bereft of the carrier *Furious*, wasn't deployed to prevent the German invasion from taking place. When it did react, units of the Royal Navy performed heroically and in two spirited battles on 10 and 13 April at Narvik ten modern German fleet destroyers were destroyed – a loss that the Kriegsmarine could ill afford and one that helped to undermine its future efforts in the English Channel. Thereafter, the British faltered badly. An ill-starred combined-arms invasion of Norway which followed in mid-April failed miserably and had to be abandoned at the end of the month in the face of an unremitting bombing assault on its positions by the Luftwaffe. Leaving the best to last, over 10,000 troops were somehow evacuated from the ports of Andalsnes, Molde, and Namsos under a blitz of bombing over the course of four days (30 April to 3 May) for the loss of only two destroyers and a sloop. It was a remarkable feat by the Royal Navy and one that was destined to be repeated on a much larger scale in late May and June at Dunkirk.[28]

Following their overall success in Norway, the Germans launched the next stage of their conquest of continental Europe with a blitzkrieg attack on France and the Low Countries on 10 May. Uncomfortable in the role as war leader and paying the price for the Norwegian debacle, Neville Chamberlain lost the premiership to Churchill on the same day. Judged on his hapless performance over Norway, Churchill was distinctly fortunate to have been promoted; but he had other gifts to offer that eluded the only viable alternative, Lord Halifax, and so the First Lord exchanged the Admiralty for Downing Street and became minister of defence in addition to being prime minister.

He soon had a major crisis on his hands as the British Expeditionary Force, which had been ferried across the Channel once war had begun in September 1939, became trapped by the advancing German forces in a narrow salient between the ports of Boulogne and Ostende with no possibility of escape except by sea. In a case of 'cometh the hour, cometh the man', Vice-Admiral Sir Bertram Ramsay, in charge at Dover, was appointed to oversee the evacuation process in what would be a race against both time and overwhelming force. It's difficult to imagine anyone who could have performed better in this role than him. He was a superb logistician, a planner of great insight and awareness, a leader by example, and someone who was prepared to delegate authority to others. He led and others willingly followed. Whatever his sterling qualities, the odds against Operation *Dynamo* succeeding were very long indeed. If this depressed him, he didn't show it. In the end, as a result of a quite staggering series of fortuitous circumstances and much heroism, 338,226 members of the Allied armed forces were taken off the beaches and quayside at Dunkirk over the course of eight days (27 May to 4 June) by an armada of craft of all shapes and sizes and brought back safely to English shores.[29] As a feat, it was little short of miraculous and those with faith had little doubt about God's hand in their own deliverance.

Wars are not won by evacuations, no matter how brilliantly staged they might be. Churchill needed no convincing of this doleful fact, particularly in the light of the weaponry and war supplies that had been left behind on French soil and which would now be acquired by the Germans. Moreover, as one evacuation came to an end another began. A final curtain needed to be drawn down on the disappointing Norwegian episode. This involved bringing home 24,500 Allied troops from the Allied base at Harstad in the Lofoten Islands (Operation *Alphabet*). It was hoped that by raiding Narvik both by air and sea the Allies would dupe the Germans into believing that they were determined to keep a foothold in Norway when the intention was quite the opposite. This high-stakes game unravelled immediately because on exactly the same day that *Alphabet* began (4 June) Admiral Wilhelm Marschall left Kiel in his flagship *Gneisenau*, accompanied by her sister battleship *Scharnhorst*, the heavy cruiser *Admiral Hipper*, and four destroyers, seeking to wreak as much damage as possible to the Allied cause at Harstad (Operation *Juno*). As Marschall's forces drew closer to Norwegian waters they learned from SIGINT sources that an Allied evacuation was underway. Raiding Harstad now took on a subordinate role to intercepting the two troop and supply convoys that had left the Lofoten Islands for Scapa Flow on 7 June. If Marschall succeeded in finding these troopships pandemonium was almost guaranteed with massive loss of life.[30]

He never found them. Instead his 80cm *Seetakt* radar discovered the rebuilt carrier *Glorious*, accompanied by the destroyers *Acasta* and *Ardent*, steaming south at seventeen knots in the middle of a Saturday afternoon, blissfully unaware of what was in store for them. Commanded by the temperamental Guy D'Oyly-Hughes and maintaining no aerial reconnaissance or even a lookout in the crow's nest to make up for the absence of radar, the Allied task force soon found itself caught up in a battle for survival that it hadn't expected. Although D'Oyly-Hughes continued to perform ineptly until a shell from the *Gneisenau* killed him less than half an hour after hostilities began, his destroyer escorts put up a valiant fight before succumbing to overwhelming force. Such was their feistiness that *Scharnhorst* emerged from her duel with them damaged by their shelling (two of her guns had been put out of commission), and a huge hole had been carved in her starboard side as a result of a torpedo hit from *Acasta*. Faced with a battleship that had taken on 2,500 tons of saltwater and was listing five degrees, Marschall was left with little alternative but to return to Trondheim so that *Scharnhorst* could be patched up before limping back to Kiel for major repairs. By the time *Gneisenau* and *Admiral Hipper* resumed their quest for the troop convoys on 10 June, the vulnerable quarry had safely left Norwegian waters. Therefore, as a direct result of the gritty performance of these two hopelessly overmatched destroyers, the lives of thousands of Allied servicemen were spared. Unfortunately, 1,515 men from *Glorious* and her task force were not accorded that same good fortune.[31]

As Marschall resumed his vain chase for the troopships, the Italians finally entered the war on the side of their Axis partner. In an address to the graduating class of the University of Virginia, President Roosevelt responded to this cynical attack by stating: "On this tenth day of June 1940, the hand that held the dagger has struck it into the back of its neighbor".[32] It was hardly a surprising development since Mussolini had been threatening to stab his French neighbour from the time of the German invasion a month before. He had waited to declare war until a French defeat was virtually guaranteed so that he could claim some of the spoils of victory without too much cost. Characteristically, when it came to discussing military intervention he exaggerated wildly and changed his mind constantly. Military strategy oscillated from one extreme to the next, leaving his commanders bereft of well-coordinated plans or ideas as to what they might be expected to achieve once war was declared. Whatever he might propose on land, he was utterly dismissive of the British and favoured an offensive strategy at sea in which the Regia Marina would be required to expel the Royal Navy in short order from the Mediterranean, Aegean, and Red Sea. That would be much easier said than done given that only two of its six battleships were operational (the other four were being refitted). Nonetheless, it still had seven heavy cruisers, fourteen light cruisers, sixty-one destroyers, 144 torpedo boats, and 117 submarines to achieve Mussolini's purposes of making the Mediterranean into Italy's *mare nostrum*.[33]

A start on this project could have been made with an invasion of the British island of Malta, lying only 50 nm off the southern tip of Sicily. Its geo-strategic importance was obvious to anyone with a map of the Mediterranean since it commanded a virtual midpoint position between the other British naval bases in Gibraltar (990 nm to the west) and Alexandria (820 nm to the east). Acutely vulnerable, Malta looked almost certain to be overrun in the early days of a Mediterranean war and yet inexplicably Mussolini didn't launch the invasion that the Allies were expecting and which they were probably incapable of resisting.[34] It was one of Il Duce's major strategic mistakes and would figure prominently in the list of crass military errors he made during the war. Once again, what might have been thought inevitable didn't take place. By the time Mussolini woke up to the fact that Malta was a thorn in his side, the British had done much to make its extraction far more painful than it would have been in June 1940.

Italy's entry into the war vastly complicated the strategic picture for the Allies because if properly directed the Regia Marina and the Regia Aeronautica possessed the means to make the Mediterranean a fiercely contested waterway at the very least and pose a significant challenge to the Allied position in North Africa. If the Axis partners could persuade Franco to enter the picture as well, Gibraltar was almost certain to be lost and with it any sort of control the rocky fortress exercised over the Straits at the western entrance to the Mediterranean.[35]

Visions of this nature were already dark enough without the swift loss of France, but that was exactly what happened with the armistice signed at Compiègne on 22 June. Apart from swiftly orchestrating another series of evacuations in order to bring back 191,870 Allied troops from nine French ports scattered along the Channel and Biscay coastlines, Churchill and his chiefs of staff (COS) were left pondering about what to do about the warships of the Marina Nationale once France withdrew from the war on 25 June. One thing was certain: the British were determined that the Kriegsmarine must not inherit them or be in a position to use them against the Royal Navy. This was the genesis of the highly contentious Operation *Catapult* and its stark ultimatum that Vice-Admiral Sir James Somerville was appointed to deliver to Admiral Marcel Gensoul, the commanding officer of the French naval forces drawn up at the Algerian base of Mers-el-Kébir. Gensoul must either comply with the British ultimatum of 3 July or face the almost certain destruction of his fleet at the hands of Somerville's warships (Force H). Somerville was not happy with his orders to open fire on his former ally if the ultimatum was rejected (which it was) and his execution of these orders subsequently left a great deal to be desired. In the triple bombardment that was unleashed on the French warships in the harbour by Force H, one battleship was blown up (*Bretagne*) and two others were badly damaged and beached (*Dunkerque* and *Provence*), the destroyer *Mogador* lost her stern, and the aircraft depot ship *Commandante Teste* was set on fire. Remarkably, the modern battleship *Strasbourg* and five large destroyers survived intact, escaping undetected from the chaos and making it across the Mediterranean to the naval base of Toulon. *Catapult* was bound to cause deep resentment amongst those running the collaborationist Vichy French authorities. It didn't disappoint. Relations with London were instantly broken off. Other challenging Anglo-French naval exchanges took place at Alexandria (diplomatically solved), Dakar (explosively dealt with), and in several British ports where French warships were peremptorily seized (Operation *Grasp*).[36]

Only a day after the modern French battleship *Richelieu* had been torpedoed in Dakar (8 July), Admiral Sir Andrew Browne Cunningham's Mediterranean Fleet was fortunate to escape from a 105-minute duel with a qualitatively superior Italian fleet under Admiral Inigo Campioni that had intercepted it off the southeast coast of Calabria (Battle of Punta Stilo). If the Italians had used the intelligence they had received about Cunningham's planned sortie more decisively, the impact upon British naval policy in the Mediterranean could have been exceptionally severe. As it was, Cunningham managed fortuitously to engineer an escape from the trap that had been set for him. It served as a warning to him not to underestimate the Regia Marina. In the right hands and with less involvement from Mussolini, it could be a formidable opponent in its own waters. Strikingly, neither of those conditions prevailed in the coming months as the Regia Marina failed to make the most of its opportunities either in clashes with Cunningham's Mediterranean Fleet on 19 July (Cape Spada, Crete), the next day in the Gulf of Bombah (off Tobruk) and at Cape Teulada (Sardinia) on 27 November, or in being able to prevent reinforcement convoys steaming through the heart of the Mediterranean to Alexandria (Operation *Hats*) in late August or those coming through the Red Sea and the Suez Canal in September. A real lack of coordination between the services and Mussolini's habitual interference – though important defects – were not the only reason for this catalogue of failure. Some of the responsibility must fall upon Admiral Domenico Cavagnari directing the naval staff (Supermarina) and upon Campioni as fleet commander. They were too cautious; more concerned with preserving their fleet rather than risking it in a bold move that could go wrong; overawed by the threat of alienating Il Duce, who could turn against them at a moment's notice; and imbued with greater respect for the Royal Navy than they might care to reveal.[37]

If the Italian military didn't live up to the boasting of Mussolini, the Kriegsmarine more than made up for it in other theatres. U-boat crews, aided by good SIGINT and now benefitting operationally from their bases in the Norwegian fjords and along the French coast, improved on their *Rudeltaktik* and began to make major inroads into British mercantile traffic from June onwards. It became a 'happy time' for them as they became a real scourge for the Admiralty to deal with even when convoys were well defended, as SC.7 and HX.79 discovered to their cost from 17–20 October. Despite the bonus of SIGINT when it could be broken, the means of detecting and destroying the U-boat remained frustratingly hit and miss. Improvements in centimetric radar, direction finding, range estimation, and aerial spotting procedures were needed to discover exactly where they were and better mortars were required to finish off the job more effectively than depth-charging in hope and ramming when it was possible to do so. At least eighteen months would pass before this wish list could be assembled. Meanwhile, the U-boats would hold the upper hand. Dönitz sensed that a great opportunity was being missed. He needed more craft to prey on this traffic and believed the more he had the greater their impact would be. He was almost certainly right and his enemies were unlikely to dispute his reasoning.[38]

While the Germans were making great strides in one area, Göring's Luftwaffe attempted in late summer and early autumn to wrest aerial control over the Channel from the RAF in what became known as the Battle of Britain. They failed (barely) in their attempt and this had an immediate knock-on effect in postponing and ultimately cancelling Hitler's plan of invading the UK (*Fall Seelöwe*). Once again, the margins between success and failure were small. One doesn't need to be a fan of counter-factualism to think what might have happened had the Luftwaffe prevailed.[39]

As it was, success in the skies over Britain and more evidence of Roosevelt's support for the democratic cause in the transfer of fifty over-age destroyers for the use of several British bases in the Bahamas, Bermuda, the Caribbean, and Newfoundland in early September contrasted with two distinct failures for the Allies in West African waters later in the same month. Not only did Force H fail to stop three light cruisers and three large destroyers belonging to the Vichy French from imperiously steaming through the Straits of Gibraltar and making their unmolested way down the coast to Dakar in Senegal (11–15 September), the joint operation (*Menace*) between the British and Free French forces of Brigadier-General Charles de Gaulle against the same port ended in abject futility (23–25 September).[40]

A somewhat halting invasion of Egypt in September and an embarrassing military rebuff in Greece in early November suggested that the Italian military contribution to the Axis was problematic at the very least. Dönitz had already come to the same conclusion. He regarded the Italian submarine contingent he had inherited as being pampered and ineffective, and deployed them in areas where they wouldn't get in the way of his own U-boat crews. Admiral Campioni's surface fleet – bolstered by having all six of its battleships finally operational – ought to have been made of sterner stuff, but it too seemed to lack vitality and purpose. Things soon got much worse for the Regia Marina and those associated with it. A daring night raid on Taranto harbour by two waves of Swordfish aircraft from the carrier *Illustrious* on 11–12 November (Operation *Judgement*) succeeded in damaging 50% of the Italian capital ship fleet and infuriated Mussolini, whose lack of respect for carriers was well known.[41] After Taranto both Cavagnari and Campioni were on borrowed time and it was scarcely surprising that they were replaced within a month by Admiral Arturo Riccardi and Admiral Angelo Iachino respectively. Would the Regia Marina become more effective under their direction? It was a moot question since Cunningham's Mediterranean Fleet was still very much in the ascendant as the year ended with aerial attacks on Rhodes, a bombardment of Valona, and supply convoys and reinforcements brought into Malta.[42]

1941

At this stage in the war there were already significant entries in the debit and credit columns of both the Kriegsmarine and the Royal Navy as well as the Marine Nationale. Those within the Regia Marina were less sanguine about its performance in the first six months of the war and were determined to do something about it. Unfortunately, when they laid their plans to arrest this decline in its fortunes in late March an unmitigated disaster occurred.

Before the anti-climax of Matapan was reached, however, some satisfaction could be gained from the fact that German Ju-87 dive bombers had caught up with the carrier *Illustrious* west of Malta on 10 January and again in Valetta harbour over the next few days, causing sufficient damage to put her out of action for the rest of the year. Taranto had been partly repaid.[43] More was supposed to follow and that was the impetus for Operation *Gaudo* in late March – a proposed attack on two lightly defended Allied convoys (AG.9 and GA.9) going in opposite directions between the ports of Alexandria and Piraeus. On this occasion, the planning was fine, the objective was realistic, but the vital necessity of secrecy was lost through Italian mistakes and Allied SIGINT breakthroughs. When alerted to what was afoot, Cunningham embraced the opportunity to take action and set up his own plan to catch Iachino's fleet unawares south of Crete. He succeeded. From lunchtime on 28 March, when the first carrier raid took place on his fleet, Iachino sensed that *Gaudo*'s potential glory days were gone. By mid-afternoon, when his flagship *Vittorio Veneto* was torpedoed, the main issue was no longer laying down a marker against Allied shipping but simply getting his fleet home safely without further damage. He may have succeeded had it not been for the last carrier plane (Albacore 5A) which made an attack on his fleet at dusk and succeeded in torpedoing and totally immobilizing the heavy cruiser *Pola*. After leaving the stricken ship to her own devices, Iachino thought better of his decision and thirty-two minutes later sent back the other two Zara-class heavy cruisers with a squadron of four destroyers to tow *Pola* to safety. It was a noble gesture but the wrong one to have made. As Admiral Carlo Cattaneo, the divisional commander, reached *Pola* so did Cunningham's Force A (the carrier *Formidable*, three battleships, and nine destroyers) and at point blank range its radar-controlled guns swiftly pummelled all three of the Italian heavy cruisers and two of the destroyers into oblivion. Iachino might also have perished had it not been for a sloppily-worded order from Cunningham that Vice-Admiral Sir Henry Pridham-Wippell erroneously assumed was meant for Force B (four light cruisers and four destroyers), resulting in him calling off the chase for the damaged

Vittorio Veneto. Iachino survived, unlike Cattaneo and the 2,302 officers and men of the Regia Marina who were lost off Cape Matapan.[44]

Mussolini brazenly reacted to the disaster by describing it as a stunning Italian success. Others since have been much less charitable, most notably the journalist Gianni Rocca, who called it nothing less than a naval Caporetto.[45] Iachino somehow remained at the helm, but his good fortune didn't extend to much else that the Regia Marina did under his command. Within days, for example, his ships were on the receiving end of more punishment from the British in the Red Sea and along the coast of Eritrea, where they lost the port of Massawa and a host of naval and mercantile vessels (151,760 tons) into the bargain. It seemed to sum up the entire Italian military effort at this time – embarrassed by the Greeks and forced back into Albania and overwhelmingly reliant upon Rommel and his Afrika Korps in Libya.[46]

By the time the Germans came to the aid of Italy in Yugoslavia and Greece in early April, Bulgaria, Hungary, and Romania had all joined the Axis. Concerned that unless something was done to shore up the Greeks the Aegean might fall to superior force and vastly complicate the strategic situation in the Eastern Mediterranean, Churchill had prevailed upon his COS to send 58,000 troops from North Africa to reinforce the Allied position in Greece. Cunningham was unimpressed by his premier's momentous decision. After all, his Mediterranean Fleet would have to oversee this risky logistical operation (*Lustre*) and suffer the consequences.[47] Within weeks of landing, these same troops had to be evacuated (Operation *Demon*) from the coastal area between Athens and Korinth and on the island of Peloponnesus over a fiercely contested six-day period from 24 April. Again, the evacuation was brilliantly staged – this time under the command of Pridham-Wippell – and only lost four transports and two destroyers in the process.[48]

As all this was going on to the south and east of them, the boats of the Kriegsmarine were reaping their rewards in the Battle of the Atlantic. Steep U-boat successes continued apace and Raeder's beloved heavy surface ships sent out as armed raiders also got into the act and showed what damage they could do to the Allied cause unless checked in some way. Hard though Admiral Tovey and the Home Fleet tried to apprehend these warships, they seemed to bear a charmed life by evading the formidable naval dragnet that was out searching for them. On the same day that Cunningham registered his emphatic victory off Cape Matapan, a ray of hope at last shone through for his former second-in-command with the news that the *Gneisenau* and the *Scharnhorst* had sought shelter in the harbour at Brest. It looked like Admiral Lütjens had made a cardinal error at the end of a highly successful campaign of mercantile attrition (*Fall Berlin*). Hemmed in by Tovey's ships waiting offshore and battered from the air, the 'two sisters' looked as though their days would be numbered and they would never emerge to haunt the Admiralty again. This was an exercise in wishful thinking, as the 'Channel Dash' would prove in February 1942 (*Fall Cerberus*).[49]

A more sustained level of success fell to the Allies in the realm of intelligence windfalls planned by Harry Hinsley and his signals analysts at Bletchley Park and executed flawlessly by units of Tovey's Home Fleet in March, May, and June respectively. Better still a priceless naval Enigma machine was recovered on 9 May from the battered *U110*, the U-boat captained by Fritz-Julius Lemp, whose *U30* had sunk the SS *Athenia* at the start of the war. Lemp, controversial to the last, perished in the waters off Greenland. He was not alone. Two of Dönitz's U-boat aces (Prien and Schepke) had also been lost in action in March and the 'Tonnage King', Otto Kretschmer, had been captured. Nostalgia has little place in warfare and Dönitz couldn't afford to dwell on his losses. Instead he could point to the fact that in May alone his U-boats had sunk more than half a million tons of enemy shipping (ninety-two ships).[50]

Success and failure continued to dog both sides in the naval war. Raeder's desire to use his surface fleet to decimate convoys (*Fall Rheinübung*) led to the spectacular destruction of the British battle-cruiser *Hood* on 24 May and the *Bismarck*, the second largest battleship ever built for the Kriegsmarine, only three days later.[51] Mixed news of this nature in one theatre contrasted with the deterioration in the British position in the Eastern Mediterranean, where the German invasion of Crete was emphatically decisive (20–27 May) and led to yet another evacuation of 17,000 Allied troops from the small fishing village of Cora Sfaxion (Sphakia) on the southern coast of the island. Cunningham's fleet was battered by the Luftwaffe, who flew hundreds of sorties against it and left him only two battleships (*Valiant* was slightly damaged), three cruisers (two of which were damaged), and seventeen destroyers to confront the Regia Marina, the Marine Nationale, and any U-boats the Kriegsmarine might send to the Levant or the Eastern Mediterranean to stir the pot. No matter how bereft it might be, the Mediterranean Fleet continued to show up and perform sterling work, whether in support of Allied land forces in Syria or in keeping Malta supplied through the reinforcement activities of Force H based at Gibraltar.[52]

By mid-summer the naval war had taken on a far more complex dimension. Although the Americans were not formally in the war as a belligerent power, it was obvious to one and all that they were no longer neutral. Roosevelt had no doubts on this score. He clearly meant what he had said in a radio broadcast of 29 December 1940 about the US becoming the 'arsenal of democracy' and had demonstrated this with his fervent support for the Lend-Lease Act (11 March 1941), which ensured that henceforth the vital task of supplying the Allies no longer relied upon the latter having the cash and vessels to make the trade. As the US Navy widened its patrol of the North Atlantic, arranged a deal with the Danes to assume a de facto protectorate over Greenland, and seized sixty-five ships belonging to foreign powers that had been detained or laid up in American ports and transferred them to Allied control, the growing involvement of the US in the everyday business of fighting the war at sea was marked.[53]

Hitler's decision to jettison the Nazi–Soviet Pact and to invade the Soviet Union, which he had had to put on hold because of the Balkan and Greek problems bequeathed to him by his Axis partner Mussolini, finally came to fruition on 22 June with *Fall Barbarossa*. Suddenly, the war at sea for his Kriegsmarine took on four new fronts spread across Europe and Asia as the Soviet Baltic, Black Sea,

Northern, and Pacific fleets turned from being pragmatic accomplices to deadly enemies overnight. Of the four locations, the Baltic was bound to be fiercely contested and both sides took immediate steps to construct formidable mine barrages upon which they hoped the other would founder. Although the Soviet navy was dominant in the Black Sea at the outset of hostilities, this would be challenged once the Ukraine fell to the Germans and when the Danube could be used to ship all kinds of vessels to the Romanian coast.[54]

As a naval force, the Soviet navy was a mixture of the obsolescent and the modern. It had been critically underfunded during the 1920s, but had enjoyed a metamorphosis in the 1930s as Stalin became convinced that the USSR should build a huge navy able to hold its own against all-comers wherever they might appear as a threat in the future. In a sense, it was a Soviet *Z-Plan*. In order to get to that position, he ordered the immediate construction of a number of massive shipyards (some built with slave labour) across the Soviet Union. Like Raeder, however, he needed years to get his big-fleet navy ready, but with the abrupt ending of the Nazi–Soviet Pact he wasn't granted that time. By mid-August 1941 the deteriorating situation in the Ukraine meant that the Soviet naval base at Nikolayev on the Bug River had to be abandoned and all the warships that were under construction at the Andre Marti Shipyard, including the 45,000-ton battleship *Sovetskaya Ukraina*, had to be blown up to prevent them falling into German hands. A similar situation happened at the Kommunar 61 North shipyard, where the 35,240-ton battle-cruiser *Sevastopol*, the 11,300-ton cruiser *Sverdlov*, and four destroyers all had to be destroyed for fear that they would be completed by the Germans and then used against them in future.[55]

It didn't take Stalin long to appeal to Churchill for the opening of a second front in either the northern regions of Norway or in France so as to draw off substantial forces from the German assault on the Soviet Union. While broadly sympathetic to Stalin's plight, the British premier had little difficulty in ruling out such a bizarre possibility at this stage and settled for supplying the Red Army with war supplies from the Icelandic port of Hvalfjordur to Murmansk and Archangel on the White Sea. In September, another convoy route was opened from Scapa Flow to Archangel. While these supplies bolstered the Soviet forces in the Arctic, they were of no material assistance to the thousands of troops that were in retreat before the Axis forces in the Ukraine. Mass evacuations to the Crimea some 168 nm away were resorted to as the Black Sea port of Odessa fell after a two-month siege to the Germans and their Romanian allies in October. Soviet proficiency in these withdrawals was no less impressive than those staged by the Mediterranean Fleet. In one night alone, for example, 35,000 troops were evacuated to Sevastopol (15–16 October) with the loss of only one transport.[56]

Retreat was the order of the day for the Red Banner Fleet in the Baltic too. German progress through the Baltic States had been rapid and evacuations initially from the Gulf of Riga (Latvia) to Tallinn (Estonia) and then onto Kronstadt in the Gulf of Finland took place even before the end of August. Extreme pressure from the Luftwaffe together with the difficulty of negotiating the *Juminda* mine barrage combined to take a savage toll of these rescue missions. Forty-one vessels (including nineteen transports) were either sunk or run aground and seven other craft including the flotilla leader *Minsk* were badly damaged. Throughout the autumn the Baltic Fleet provided artillery support for the embattled Red Army onshore and continued to take supplies to the dwindling number of Soviet outposts in Finland. Its only respite came as winter returned to these northern latitudes, imposing its usual harsh conditions upon all the combatants.[57]

In the Mediterranean, the Axis wasn't making the kind of progress that Hitler thought it ought to be. Despite Mussolini's bombastic utterances, Tobruk remained in Allied hands and was being regularly supplied at night by destroyers from the Mediterranean Fleet. Since its fall would assist Rommel and his Afrika Korps in obtaining more supplies and put pressure on the 8th Army, Hitler offered to send twenty U-boats (six had arrived by early October) to disrupt these supply missions. Hitler also fretted about Malta's continued existence, but Mussolini's pride was such that he refused the Führer's offer to put Field Marshal Kesselring in charge of a sustained attack on the island.[58]

What Mussolini didn't know was that the cryptanalysts at Bletchley Park had managed to figure out how the Hagelin C38m encryption machine worked. This breakthrough had allowed them to crack the Italian naval cipher for the first time in June 1941. It meant that Cunningham could be supplied with ULTRA signals traffic on the activities of the Regia Marina, such as the timing and routes being used by its troopships and supply vessels to Tripoli. This harvest of information proved to be put to very good use by Captain 'Shrimp' Simpson's submarines and Captain Bill Agnew's Force K (two light cruisers and two destroyers) operating out of Malta in the late autumn. Agnew surpassed himself in destroying the *Beta* supply convoy in the early hours of 9 November. In forty-two minutes, he sank all seven supply ships (39,787 tons) and their cargoes of fuel, ammunition, and 389 vehicles, along with a fleet destroyer, while damaging two more in the process. No wonder he was immediately conferred the CB as a reward for his post-midnight exploits.[59]

SIGINT proved invaluable in other ways too. Cunningham was able to route his own convoys through the Mediterranean with a little more optimism than would have otherwise been the case. This was true of Operation *Halberd*, which evaded units of the Regia Marina and steamed from Gibraltar to Malta in late September with nine transports (81,000 tons of equipment) for the island garrison. Nonetheless, while sterling successes such as supporting Tobruk and relieving Cyprus were achieved by his fleet, Cunningham didn't need reminding that the Mediterranean could not be taken for granted. A forceful reminder of this came in the torpedoing of the carrier *Ark Royal* by *U81* on 13 November and the sinking of the battleship *Barham* by *U331* on 25 November. These successes convinced the Kriegsmarine to send another eighteen U-boats to the Mediterranean in December.[60]

Although the Americans were proving an ever more reliable 'unofficial' partner in the Atlantic after the Churchill–Roosevelt meeting at Argentia Bay (9–12 August), the situation in the Far East looked far darker. Japan appeared to be on the move in Southeast Asia. Its seizure of Camranh Bay on 24 July and the airfields in the southern provinces of Vietnam shortly thereafter stung the US into action by freezing all Japanese assets in its possession and imposing an oil embargo on Prince Konoye's government in Tokyo. Since the US supplied 80% of Japan's oil supplies, the embargo would profoundly affect its ability to complete its southern advance (*nanshin-ron*). Any hope for Japanese moderation appeared to fall away with the resignation of Konoye and the appointment of General Hideki Tojo as prime minister in the middle of October. Faced with a very uncertain future in the Far East, the Admiralty chose a variant of the Drax–Backhouse 'flying squadron' principle of March 1939 to finally implement its 'Singapore Strategy'. Unfortunately, Force G got off on the wrong foot entirely when *Indomitable*, its sole carrier, went aground in the Caribbean on 3 November and never joined up with the rest of the squadron in Singapore. It was not a propitious start and things would only get worse for acting-Admiral Sir Tom Phillips and what was left of Force G within a few days of their arrival in Singapore on 2 December.[61]

1941–1942

President Roosevelt referred to 7 December 1941 as a day of infamy. By attacking the US Navy's Pacific base at Pearl Harbor in Hawaii, the Japanese violently changed the course of World War Two and brought together an extraordinary Grand Alliance of ideological enemies (the British Commonwealth, Soviet Union, and US) to do battle with the Axis forces. Hitler and Mussolini's imprudent decision to declare war on the US in the wake of the Pearl Harbor attack widened the war still further and set the seal on what was to come.[62]

Churchill's palpable sense of relief that the US was finally an active belligerent in the war contrasted markedly with his later bewilderment that the extensive British and Dutch empires in the Far East could fall with such astonishing speed to the marauding Japanese military juggernaut over the course of the next few weeks. An emphatic start to that process began on 10 December when the Mahanian doctrine of naval strategy that had held sway for half a century was ruthlessly swept away in exactly two hours and seven minutes as first the battle-cruiser HMS *Repulse* and subsequently the modern battleship HMS *Prince of Wales* were overwhelmed and sunk by the medium bombers of the Japanese navy's 22nd Naval Air Flotilla. Their sinking brought an end to the primacy of the capital ship and ushered in the aircraft carrier as the new queen on the chessboard.[63] Notwithstanding its unique qualities, the carrier was not alone in being able to dominate the game. Even the smallest submersibles could wreak disproportionate damage upon those who got in their way as the three Italian Maiali submersible chariots proved conclusively in the early hours of 18–19 December when sinking Cunningham's battleships *Queen Elizabeth* and *Valiant* and damaging the destroyer *Jervis* in Alexandria harbour.[64]

A new year that began on an inauspicious note for what was left of the Mediterranean Fleet proceeded to get much worse for the Allies in the weeks to come as the Japanese navy demonstrated its mastery of amphibious operations by bringing thousands of infantry troops to seize a swathe of islands and territories strung out across the Asia-Pacific. By the end of April 1942, the Japanese had rolled up the old colonial empires as Hong Kong, Malaya, Singapore, and the Dutch East Indies fell like shattered hulks under a wrecking ball. Having secured the sources of oil that was always the intention of the southern advance, the Japanese now stood poised to consolidate their hold over their newly acquired empire.[65]

As the Americans started to come to terms with the shocking attack on Pearl Harbor and the subsequent fall of Guam and Wake Island, and the invasion of the Philippines, the Germans brought the war to their eastern shores in January with the concerted U-boat campaign *Fall Paukenschlag* (*Case Drumbeat*). Dönitz's low-stakes gamble (only five U-boats were committed at the outset) paid off handsomely. Over the next six months three distinct waves of Type IX U-boats feasted on the non-convoyed traffic that plied the waters between Cape Hatteras and Newfoundland, sinking 220–230 vessels – mostly tankers and freighters (approximately 1.25 million tons) – and torpedoing another twenty-nine (in excess of 200,000 tons). It was another 'happy time' for Dönitz's handpicked crews. Further notable successes were achieved by their compatriots in Caribbean waters (particularly off Trinidad) and in pockets of the Gulf of Mexico where independent sailings were still allowed. As this maritime slaughter was going on in their own waters, the Americans inexplicably looked the other way. Why they did so is deeply puzzling. Convoy's merits ought to have been obvious to Admiral Ernest J. King and his senior US Navy officials in Washington, but instead of promptly regulating maritime traffic and implementing convoy as they should have done, several months went by without any coordinated system being introduced. It was a crass and costly mistake that was only rectified in mid-May.[66]

Hitler sought to add to the Allied gloom of these early months of 1942 by using Raeder's surface fleet to attack the Arctic supply convoys to the Soviet Union. This was the impetus behind the break-out of the 'two sisters', *Gneisenau* and *Scharnhorst*, and the heavy cruiser *Prinz Eugen* from Brest harbour on 11 February (*Fall Cerberus*). It was a daring enterprise and one that was expected to expose them to great risk as they steamed through the English Channel, the Straits of Dover, and the North Sea in order to get back to their bases on the Jade and the Elbe. Embarrassingly for the Allies, who were suffering from one of their intelligence blackouts, it was executed almost flawlessly with far more trouble being caused by random mines than anything orchestrated by the British armed forces. Relieved though he was to get his heavy ships back, Raeder saw their return as a mixed blessing since their escape meant that the ships of the Royal Navy were finally released from their vigil off the Atlantic coast of France and could be put to good use elsewhere. Admiral Sir Dudley Pound could grasp at the few straws that were on offer after what became known as the 'Channel Dash', but worryingly it had exposed real weaknesses in inter-service coordination, and underlined the critical importance of possessing SIGINT. Without it, the Admiralty could be challenged and found desperately wanting.[67] It would be again in July with its notorious handling of the PQ.17 convoy to Murmansk.

Fortified by Roosevelt's adoption of the 'Europe First' strategic principle and reliant upon Chester Nimitz's fleet to grapple with the Japanese in the Pacific, the Royal Navy concentrated most of its attention west of Suez, where the bulk of its forces were. While it had accumulated an Eastern Fleet of three carriers and five battleships within weeks of the fall of Singapore, Vice-Admiral Nagumo's raid on its Ceylonese base over Easter had exposed its qualitative weaknesses (obsolescence being the worst feature); sunk a light carrier, two heavy cruisers, an auxiliary cruiser, two destroyers, and a corvette from it; and forced its new C-in-C, Sir James Somerville, to ruefully withdraw the rest of it across the Indian Ocean from Colombo to the much safer environs of Kilindini harbour in Mombasa.[68]

Over 3,000 nm to the northwest of Kenya, Cunningham's Mediterranean Fleet had lost its cutting edge. For the time being, therefore, Iachino and the Regia Marina had a fine opportunity to assert themselves throughout the Mediterranean. Once again, however, their record was mixed. They performed admirably in supplying Rommel with war material for his Afrika Korps, but whenever Iachino seemed poised to take the fight to the enemy forces at sea something always happened to bring the operation to a premature close. In this way both battles of Sirte (December 1941 and March 1942), which ought to have been won decisively by the Italians if they had been more adventurous and self-confident, wound up by being drawn or inconclusive affairs.[69] Moreover, they still couldn't prevent the Allies from replenishing Malta or running convoys through enemy waters with annoying regularity. In essence, Iachino was a solid performer but not a dashing cavalier. Il Duce cast a long shadow over his senior military officers. Who could afford to gamble with him hovering in the background? Iachino had survived one Matapan, but he didn't need reminding that he was unlikely to survive another.

Out in the North Atlantic the first in a series of significant improvements in U-boat detection began to be made with the introduction of the 10cm Type 271 radar set and High-Frequency/Direction-Finding radios, but as long as a gaping 1,200-mile mid-Atlantic 'air gap' persisted where aerial surveillance and support was lacking the U-boats could safely congregate in wolf packs and lie in wait for their next victim. A fleet of Very Long Range aircraft such as Liberators and Fortresses were needed to plug this gap, but limited numbers of these aircraft and urgent calls upon their services from other domains meant that more than a year would pass before this Atlantic vulnerability would be addressed. Meanwhile, Dönitz – who rarely stood still for long – began to develop the Type 14 U-boat supply tanker (known as the *Milchkuh*) in order to keep the U-boat fleet on station for longer operational periods and cut down on transit times when they were out of action.[70]

After sixteen US carrier-based B25B medium bombers had brought the war home to an incredulous Japanese public by staging the Doolittle Raid on Tokyo, Yokohama, Kobe, and Nagoya on 18 April, Admiral Yamamoto's determination to get his own back on the impertinent Americans and cause them grief grew markedly.[71] Planning for the Midway adventure went into overdrive, but as was usual with Japanese war planning the simple was eschewed in favour of the complicated. Buoyed up by the exploits of Nagumo and Vice-Admiral Ozawa in the Indian Ocean and the mistaken belief that the US only had one carrier in the area, the Japanese decided to intensify their hold on the Southwest Pacific by conducting a multi-pronged attack on Port Moresby and the southern Solomon chain of islands. Useful though a dominant presence in the Coral Sea would be, Operation *Mo* wasn't an essential pre-requisite for launching the Midway operation (*MI*). Like most superfluous undertakings, it could have been deferred until the time was right. Instead, the carrier battle that was staged in the Coral Sea on 8–9 May (the first naval engagement fought exclusively by aircraft without any ship-to-ship interaction) was to have detrimental material and psychological effects on the ability of the Japanese navy to perform at its peak at Midway in June.[72]

If the Coral Sea represented a slowing of the Japanese momentum in the war, Midway became a dramatic watershed in their fortunes. After five months of colossal achievement, the loss of four carriers in a single day (4–5 June) brought this triumphant wave of victories to a bitter close. Midway was a profound shock to the system. Yamamoto's plans to deal a telling blow to the US carrier fleet had ended up in severely wounding his own. Thereafter the air of menacing invincibility that had grown up in the wake of the attack on Pearl Harbor was dispelled. It didn't mean the Japanese navy and army were condemned to overall defeat, but it proved the US Navy was a fearsome opponent and should not be underestimated in future as it had been in the recent past.[73]

A sobering defeat for the Japanese in the Central Pacific was somewhat compensated for by victories for their Axis partners in North Africa, where the fortress of Tobruk belatedly fell to the Afrika Korps on 20 June, and in the Crimea, where despite courageous seamanship by Vice-Admiral Oktyabrskiy and his Black Sea Fleet the naval base at Sevastopol finally succumbed to Erich von Manstein's 11th Army at the end of the month. More success came its way early in July with the dismantling of Arctic convoy PQ.17 on its way from Reykjavik to the White Sea with cargo worth an estimated $700 million. Unable to rely upon SIGINT to assist his decision making, Admiral Pound assumed the worst, namely that Raeder's heavy ships had sortied from their Norwegian fjords and were about to fall upon the convoy. Fearing wholesale destruction of the entire convoy, Pound panicked, withdrew its escort vessels and ordered the convoy to scatter. It was a horrendous mistake for the first sea lord to have made and showed a deep lack of confidence in the principle of convoy. In the days that followed, U-boats and aircraft savaged what was left of PQ.17. Raeder's heavy ships – the bête noire of both Pound and Churchill – were not involved. As it was, 210 aircraft, 430 Sherman tanks, and 3,350 vehicles, along with material supplies for 50,000 troops, ended up on the seabed rather than on the docks of Archangel. PQ.17 was an Allied nightmare. Admiralty officials had feared that something like this would eventually happen if the Germans really got their act together in the Arctic Circle.

Now they had and the results were punishing. PQ.17 lost more ships than any other convoy of the entire war. It was not confidence-inspiring, to say the least. It was hardly surprising that Soviet disenchantment with a perceived lack of steely purpose on the part of the British – never far removed from the scene – hove again into sight in the aftermath of this troubled mission.[74]

Another largely self-inflicted blow for the Allies came with the calamitous decision to test the Channel defences of the enemy by orchestrating a 24-hour amphibious raid on Dieppe in mid-August using 6,000 troops (mostly Canadian) and a tank brigade. Operation *Jubilee*, recklessly promoted by Admiral Mountbatten and rashly supported by Churchill, was an unqualified disaster costing the lives of 1,179 Allied troops and consigning another 2,190 to life behind bars as POWs. Although it's easy to criticize, *Jubilee*'s only positive contribution lay in the discovery that much greater use had to be made of radar in combined operations and that wishful thinking was no substitute for meticulous planning when it came to any future cross-Channel invasion.[75]

More Axis success came in the Caucasus, where a massive amphibious operation (*Fall Blücher*) brought the 46th Infantry Division to secure the Taman Peninsula in early September. As the German and Romanian net closed in on the Soviet 47th Army, Rear-Admiral Sergei Gorshkov at the head of the Azov Flotilla came to the aid of the Red Army by engineering a three-day evacuation which took it to the embattled naval base of Novorossisk. Already woefully overcrowded and lacking adequate resources, the Soviet city promptly fell to the German V Army Corps. In the chaos that ensued yet another evacuation had to be hastily undertaken to spirit these troops to the next defence line at Gelendzhik, further south on the Black Sea coast.[76]

If the dominant Allied message of the summer of 1942 was one of doom and gloom – the mauling of Operation *Pedestal* to Malta in August, for example, being virtually as bad as that inflicted upon PQ.17 in the previous month – the late autumn began to conjure up a sense of cautious optimism, inspired in part by the fact that American industrial production had geared up to the point that it was redefining the war on trade by building new ships faster than Dönitz's U-boat crews could destroy the existing stock of maritime vessels. Real progress had also been made in the methods of detecting and destroying U-boats. Magnetic anomaly detection equipment and sono-buoys had become far more reliable than earlier prototypes and with the arrival of the Hedgehog, Retrobomb, and Fido mortars, bombs, and acoustic torpedoes respectively began to come into their own against the submersible. Even so there was no room for complacency, as the fate of convoy ON.127 (where the escort group's radar capability was lost entirely and eight ships, including the destroyer *Ottawa*, were sunk and four tankers were torpedoed), PQ.18's misfortunes (shown in its attrition rate of 28%), and the *Laconia* tragedy (made far worse by base errors of judgement) demonstrated graphically in September alone.[77]

In the South Pacific, the fiercely contested battle for control of Henderson Airfield on Guadalcanal showed no signs of slackening as both sides strove to consolidate their hold on what had become a strategically vital chain of Solomon

Islands. As the US and Japanese navies traded blows off Cape Esperance and the Santa Cruz Islands, landed troop reinforcements, bombarded enemy positions, and tried to disrupt their supply missions, the tantalising gap between victory and defeat remained narrow.[78]

Elsewhere, the battle for supremacy between the Allied and Axis forces showed signs of becoming more decisive once Montgomery's 8th Army had defeated Rommel's Panzerarmee Afrika at El Alamein in early November. However, in order to exploit this crushing victory and enable it to become a springboard for further Mediterranean campaigns in the future, the Allies would need to secure Tunisia. Unfortunately, that was not a prime objective of the simultane-ous tri-pronged attack on Morocco and Algeria that they mounted with over 96,000 (largely American) troops on 8 November. This hotly disputed inva-sion (Operation *Torch*) was designed primarily to clear the Vichy French out of North Africa and to destroy their warships. Although the amphibious phase of the operation went largely according to plan, it had been inadvertently assisted by the lamentable performance of Dönitz's sixty-five U-boats in failing to disrupt the invasion in any meaningful way. A combination of aging boats, equipment failures, and the scale of attritional damage to sixteen of his ocean-going fleet left the admiral and the OKM in little doubt as to the scale of the problem they faced in future without substantial improvements being made to their capacity to wage war.[79]

While the Italians belatedly began to run troop and supply convoys to Bizerta, a port Mussolini ought to have secured at the outset of the war to support his hold on Libya, the Germans responded to the *Torch* offensive by occupying Vichy France (*Fall Anton*) and making plans to take over the naval base of Toulon and secure the warships of the Marine Nationale for use by the Axis subsequently (*Fall Lila*). These controversial plans were thwarted by Admiral Jean de Laborde as C-in-C of Forces de Haute Mer. He was not alone in taking a very dim view of how the collaboration with the Nazis had ended and secret plans were laid to ensure that the fleet wouldn't fall into German, let alone Italian, hands. In the early hours of 27 November, the day that the 7th Panzer Division was supposed to seize the port and take over the fleet, Laborde defiantly issued orders for his increasingly disaffected officers and men to scuttle the fleet. In this way three bat-tleships, seven cruisers, fifteen destroyers, thirteen torpedo boats, six sloops, and twelve submarines amongst other auxiliary ships were either blown up or sunk by their crews. Hitler, whose contempt for expensive surface fleets had risen since the war began, was far more blasé about the loss of these vessels than a frustrated and angry De Gaulle was. His Free French naval forces could have done with being supplemented by more than the few desultory submarines that stole away from Toulon to join him.[80]

Vichy France was no more and change was coming to the Caucasus too. After yielding ground to the Axis for the past sixteen months, the Soviet forces had begun to build a formidable redoubt at Tuapse, a port lying to the north of Sochi on east coast of the Black Sea, and by the end of the year a squadron of warships under Vice-Admiral Vladimirskiy had begun a series of sorties along the Bulgarian, Romanian, and Crimean coastlines and had even appeared off the Bosporus as well. Although little more than showing-the-flag exercises, they demonstrated that the Axis no longer held the upper hand in the region.[81] This would be confirmed by the surrender of the German 6th Army at Stalingrad on 31 January.

Glimpsing a real turning of the tide on the Eastern Front, Stalin was in no mood to compromise and demanded more rather than less help from his Allied partners. He was profoundly unimpressed by the *Torch* offensive and refused to see it as the second front which he had been calling for since Hitler had torn up the Nazi–Soviet Pact in June 1941. Moreover, he had also been angered by the British decision to suspend the Arctic convoys in the wake of the PQ.17 and .18 disasters, and had insisted on thirteen freighters sailing independently from Reykjavik to Murmansk and Archangel on 29 October, bringing much-needed supplies to his Red Army troops. Another sorry mess occurred with 46% of the ships being sunk, but Stalin was undeterred by this scale of loss. For him the 54% that got through was the crucial figure. Churchill understood the Soviet dictator's position and supported the resumption of the Arctic convoys in the winter months on the grounds that the almost perpetual darkness in these northern latitudes meant that the German forces would be hard pressed to operate as effectively as they had during summertime, when it remained light nearly 24 hours a day.[82]

After the successful convoy runs of QP.15 and JW.51A, the next in line, JW.51B, left the Scottish port of Loch Ewe bound for Murmansk on 22 December. Raeder saw this as an ideal opportunity for his surface fleet to strike as resounding a blow against the Allies as the U-boats and Luftwaffe had dealt to such great effect in July and September. It would be a timely reminder to Hitler that the heavier units of the Kriegsmarine had a future beside that of Dönitz's U-boat fleet. *Fall Regenbogen* brought two heavy cruisers (*Admiral Hipper* and *Lützow*) and six destroyers to bear upon JW.51B on New Year's Eve, but thanks to a combination of poor weather, outstanding ship-handling skills on the part of the Allied destroyer captains, and a peculiar listlessness that seemed to engulf both Vizeadmiral Oskar Kummetz and Kapitän zur See Rudolf Stange, the convoy reached port largely unscathed in the early days of the new year. By degrees both embarrassing and infuriating, the Battle of Barents Sea did much to undermine Raeder's position and confirm Hitler's contempt for a surface fleet that seemed incapable of performing at an optimum level even when the odds were stacked in its favour.[83]

Notes

1　Jürgen Rohwer, *Chronology of the War at Sea 1939–1945: the Naval History of World War Two* (London: Chatham Publishing, 2005), pp.1–4; Peter Padfield, *War Beneath the Sea: Submarine Conflict during World War II* (New York: John Wiley, 1996), pp.1–7.
2　Correlli Barnett, *Engage the Enemy More Closely: the Royal Navy in the Second World War* (London: W.W. Norton, 1991), pp.61–64.

3 Malcolm Murfett, *Naval Warfare 1919–1945: an Operational History of the Volatile War at Sea* (Milton Park: Routledge, 2013), p.34.

4 Ibid., p.33; James P. Levy, *The Royal Navy's Home Fleet in World War II* (Basingstoke: Palgrave, 2003), pp.19–34.

5 Paul Auphan and Jacques Mordal, *The French Navy in World War II* (Westport: Greenwood Press, 1976), pp.21–24, 389–90.

6 Murfett, *Naval Warfare*, pp.49, 62n.2; Michael Alfred Peszke, *Poland's Navy 1918–1945* (New York: Hippocrene Books, 1999).

7 Support for this belief can be seen in the statistics of the first three years of the war, where his U-boat fleet managed to sink 1,904 Allied or neutral ships (totalling 9,235,113 gross registered tons).

8 Robert Dallek, *Franklin Roosevelt and American Foreign Policy, 1932–1945* (Oxford: Oxford University Press, 1995), pp. 200–32; Justus D. Doenecke, *Storm on the Horizon: the Challenge to American Intervention, 1939–1941* (Lanham: Rowman & Littlefield, 2000), pp.51, 59–68, 119–20.

9 Clay Blair Jr., *Hitler's U-boat War. Vol. I: the Hunters 1939–1942* (New York: Random House, 1996), pp.87–91; Barnett, *Engage the Enemy*, pp.69–70.

10 Terry Hughes and John Costello, *The Battle of the Atlantic* (New York: Dial Press/John Wade, 1977), pp.31–34; Padfield, *War Beneath the Sea*, pp.23–24.

11 Hughes and Costello, *Battle of the Atlantic*, p.67.

12 Murfett, *Naval Warfare*, pp.77, 286n.44, 462.

13 Ibid., pp.151, 282, 466, 502 n.32.

14 A vast amount has been written on both Enigma and Bletchley Park in recent years. Useful starting points are John Ferris, 'The Road to Bletchley Park: the British Experience with Signals Intelligence, 1892–1945', *Intelligence and National Security*, 17, 1 (Spring 2002), pp.55–84; Hugh Sebag-Montefiore, *Enigma: the Battle for the Code* (London: Phoenix, 2001); Michael Smith, *Station X: the Codebreakers of Bletchley Park* (London: Channel 4 Books, 1998).

15 Stephen Budiansky, *Battle of Wits: the Complete Story of Codebreaking in World War II* (New York: The Free Press, 2000).

16 Jak P. Mallmann Showell, *German Naval Codebreakers* (Annapolis: Naval Institute Press, 2003).

17 Murfett, *Naval Warfare*, pp.53–54.

18 Eric Grove, *Price of Disobedience: the Battle of the River Plate Reconsidered* (Stroud: Sutton, 2000).

19 Murfett, *Naval Warfare*, pp.54–61, 485–86.

20 H.M. Tillotson, *Finland at Peace and War, 1918–1993* (Norwich: Michael Russell, 1993), pp.121–75; Carl Van Dyke, *The Soviet Invasion of Finland, 1939–40* (London: Frank Cass, 1997).

21 Rohwer, *Chronology of the War at Sea*, pp.10–12.

22 Murfett, *Naval Warfare*, pp.61, 530.

23 V.E. Tarrant, *The U-boat Offensive 1914–1945* (London: Arms and Armour, 1989), pp.81–96; John Terraine, *Business in Great Waters: the U-boat Wars, 1916–1945* (London: Leo Cooper, 1989), pp.255–74.

24 Hughes and Costello, *Battle of the Atlantic*, p.50; Rohwer, *Chronology of the War at Sea*, p.13.

25 Paul Kemp, *Friend or Foe: Friendly Fire at Sea, 1939–1945* (London: Leo Cooper, 1995), pp.40–46.

26 Richard Wiggan, *Hunt the Altmark* (London: Robert Hale, 1982), pp.118–55; Stephen Howarth, 'Admiral of the Fleet Sir Philip Vian', in Stephen Howarth (ed.), *Men of War* (New York: St. Martin's Press, 1993), pp.491–505.

27 Adam Claasen, 'Germany's Expeditionary Operation: the Invasion of Norway, 1940', in Peter Dennis and Jeffrey Grey (eds), *Battles Near and Far: a Century of Operational*

Deployment (Canberra: Army History Unit, 2005), pp.141–62; Vincent O'Hara, *The German Fleet at War, 1939–1945* (Annapolis: Naval Institute Press, 2004), pp.15–59.

28 Murfett, *Naval Warfare*, pp.69–77.

29 W.J.R. Gardner (ed.), *The Evacuation from Dunkirk: Operation Dynamo* (London: Frank Cass, 2000); Barnett, *Engage the Enemy*, pp.140–67.

30 Murfett, *Naval Warfare*, pp.77–80.

31 Geirr H. Haarr, *The Battle for Norway: April–June 1940* (Barnsley: Seaforth, 2010); Levy, *The Royal Navy's Home Fleet in World War II*, pp.50–67. Marschall's woes continued as he swiftly lost the support of Hitler and Raeder along with his role as Flottenchef to Vizeadmiral Günther Lütjens. Within days of his dismissal, his former flagship *Gneisenau* was torpedoed in the bows by the submarine *Clyde* on 20 June and put out of action for several months. She too had to return to Kiel for major repairs (25–27 July).

32 Dallek, *Franklin Roosevelt and American Foreign Policy*, p.228.

33 Robert Mallet, *The Italian Navy and Fascist Expansionism, 1935–1940* (London: Frank Cass, 1998), pp.174–85; James J. Sadkovich, *The Italian Navy in World War II* (Westport: Greenwood Press, 1994), pp.1–55.

34 Denis Mack Smith, *Mussolini: a Biography* (London: Alfred A. Knopf, 1982), pp.246–56, 270–71, 275; Malcolm Murfett, 'Casting Doubt on the Inevitability Syndrome', in Malcolm Murfett (ed.), *Imponderable but not Inevitable: Warfare in the 20th Century* (Santa Barbara: Praeger/ABC Clio, 2010), pp.4–8.

35 Paul Preston, *The Politics of Revenge: Fascism and the Military in Twentieth-Century Spain* (London: Routledge, 1995), pp.51–84; Murfett, 'Casting Doubt on the Inevitability Syndrome', pp.1–4.

36 Auphan and Mordal, *The French Navy in World War II*, pp.122–39; David Brown, *Road to Oran: Anglo-French Naval Relations, September 1939–July 1940* (London: Frank Cass, 2004); George E. Melton, *From Versailles to Mers-el-Kébir: the Promise of Anglo-French Naval Cooperation, 1919–40* (Annapolis: Naval Institute Press, 2015), pp.167–207.

37 Murfett, *Naval Warfare*, p.86.

38 Ibid., p.87; Blair Jr., *Hitler's U-boat War: the Hunters*, pp.166–217.

39 Murfett, *Naval Warfare*, p.89.

40 Patrick Abbazia, *Mr. Roosevelt's Navy: the Private War of the U.S. Atlantic Fleet, 1939–1942* (Annapolis: Naval Institute Press, 1975), pp.91–107; Barnett, *Engage the Enemy*, pp.183–238.

41 David Hamer, *Bombers Versus Battleships* (Annapolis: Naval Institute Press, 1998), pp.67–75; David Wragg, *Swordfish: the Story of the Taranto Raid* (London: Weidenfeld & Nicolson, 2003). *Littorio* and *Caio Duilio* took several months to repair and *Conte di Cavour* never returned to operational status.

42 Michael Simpson (ed.), *The Cunningham Papers. Vol. I: the Mediterranean Fleet, 1939–1942* (Aldershot: Ashgate, 1999), pp.212–16.

43 Jack Greene and Alessandro Massignani, *The Naval War in the Mediterranean, 1940–1943* (London: Chatham Publishing, 1998), pp.133–35; David Wragg, *Carrier Combat* (Stroud: Sutton Publishing, 1997), pp.40–44.

44 Murfett, *Naval Warfare*, pp.103–7; Vincent P. O'Hara, *Struggle for the Middle Sea: the Great Navies at War in the Mediterranean Theater, 1940–1945* (Annapolis: Naval Institute Press, 2009), pp.91–98.

45 Mack Smith, *Mussolini*, p.265; Murfett, *Naval Warfare*, p.105.

46 Marc Antonio Bragadin, *The Italian Navy in World War II* (Annapolis: Naval Institute Press, 1957), pp.73–77; Rohwer, *Chronology of the War at Sea*, pp.66–67.

47 Cunningham lost twenty-five ships (115,026 tons) in the month-long operation. He imagined it could have been a lot worse. Simpson (ed.), *The Cunningham Papers, Vol. 1*, pp.233–37.

48 Ibid., pp.243–44, 370–97, 399, 424; G. Hermon Gill, *Royal Australian Navy 1939–1942* (Sydney: Collins, 1985), pp.317–35.

49 Richard Garrett, *Scharnhorst and Gneisenau: the Elusive Sisters* (Newton Abbot: David & Charles, 1978), pp.58–85; Murfett, 'Casting Doubt on the Inevitability Syndrome', pp.8–11.

50 Murfett, *Naval Warfare*, pp.108–11.

51 David J. Bercuson and Holger H. Herwig, *Bismarck: the Story Behind the Destruction of the Pride of Hitler's Navy* (London: Pimlico, 2003); Graham Rhys-Jones, *The Loss of the Bismarck: an Avoidable Disaster* (Annapolis: Naval Institute Press, 1999).

52 Callum MacDonald, *The Lost Battle: Crete 1941* (London: Macmillan, 1993); Simpson (ed.), *The Cunningham Papers, Vol. I*, pp.244–50, 313, 332, 351, 356, 367, 369–70, 390, 405–06, 449–51, 454, 458, 460, 470, 475, 478–80, 487.

53 Murfett, *Naval Warfare*, pp.117–18; Thomas A. Bailey and Paul B. Ryan, *Hitler vs Roosevelt: the Undeclared Naval War* (New York: Free Press, 1999).

54 V.I. Achkasov and N.B. Pavlovich, *Soviet Naval Operations in the Great Patriotic War, 1941–45* (Annapolis: Naval Institute Press, 1981), pp.24–28, 45–46, 48–51; Friedrich Ruge, *The Soviets as Naval Opponents, 1941–1945* (Cambridge: Patrick Stephens, 1979), pp.11–24, 63–77, 135–48.

55 Milan L. Hauner, 'Stalin's Big-Fleet Program', *Naval War College Review*, 57, 2 (Spring 2004), pp.87–120; Jürgen Rohwer and Mikhail S. Monokov, *Stalin's Ocean-going Fleet: Soviet Naval Strategy and Shipbuilding Programmes, 1935–1953* (London: Frank Cass, 2001).

56 Murfett, *Naval Warfare*, pp.121, 242; Richard Woodman, *The Arctic Convoys, 1941–1945* (London: John Murray, 1994).

57 Achkasov and Pavlovich, *Soviet Naval Operations*, pp.24–25, 56–76; Rohwer, *Chronology of the War at Sea*, pp. 84–88, 91–96, 100, 102, 104–05, 108, 111–12, 114–16, 118–20.

58 Mack Smith, *Mussolini*, pp.270–71.

59 O'Hara, *Struggle for the Middle Sea*, pp.143–47; Greene and Massignani, *The Naval War in the Mediterranean*, pp.174–91.

60 Greene and Massignani, *The Naval War in the Mediterranean*, pp.193, 196–97.

61 Murfett, *Naval Warfare*, pp.120–21, 125–26.

62 Ibid., pp.136–38; John Prados, *Combined Fleet Decoded: the Secret History of American Intelligence and the Japanese Navy in World War II* (New York: Random House, 1995), pp.118–97; H.P. Willmott, with Haruo Tohmatsu and W. Spencer Johnson, *Pearl Harbor* (London: Cassell, 2001).

63 Martin Middlebrook and P. Mahoney, *The Sinking of the Prince of Wales and the Repulse: the End of the Battleship Era* (Barnsley: Leo Cooper, 2004); Murfett, *Naval Warfare*, pp.135–36, 138–40.

64 Simpson (ed.), *The Cunningham Papers, Vol. I*, pp.458–62, 551–59.

65 Murfett, *Naval Warfare*, pp.146–53, 160–64.

66 Blair Jr., *Hitler's U-boat War: Hunters*, pp.431–700; Michael Gannon, *Operation Drumbeat: the Dramatic Story of Germany's First U-boat Attacks along the American Coast in World War II* (New York: Harper Perennial, 1991).

67 Murfett, 'Casting Doubt on the Inevitability Syndrome', pp.8–11.

68 Hamer, *Bombers versus Battleships*, pp.150–64.

69 Murfett, *Naval Warfare*, pp.143–44, 157–60.

70 Marc Milner, *Battle of the Atlantic* (Stroud: Tempus, 2003), pp.93–95; Kathleen Broome Williams, *Secret Weapon: U.S. High Frequency Direction Finding in the Battle of the Atlantic* (Annapolis: Naval Institute Press, 1996).

71 Carroll V. Glines, *The Doolittle Raid: America's Daring First Strike against Japan* (West Chester: Schiffer Military History, 1991).

72 H.P. Willmott, *The Barrier and the Javelin: Japanese and Allied Pacific Strategies, February to June 1942* (Annapolis: Naval Institute Press, 1983), pp.203–87; Murfett, *Naval Warfare*, pp.176–83.

73 Jonathan Parshall and Anthony Tully, *Shattered Sword: the Untold Story of the Battle of Midway* (Washington: Potomac Books, 2005); Murfett, *Naval Warfare*, pp.183–96.

74 Seventeen freighters, four steamers, two tankers, and a rescue ship (142,695 tons) and 120 seamen perished in this troubled mission. Murfett, *Naval Warfare*, pp.196–201; Theodore Taylor, *Battle in the Arctic Seas: the Story of Convoy PQ17* (New York: Thomas Crowell, 1976).

75 Robin Neillands, *The Dieppe Raid: the Story of the Disastrous 1942 Expedition* (London: Aurum Press, 2006); Brian L. Villa, *Unauthorized Action: Mountbatten and the Dieppe Raid* (Toronto: Oxford University Pres, 1989).

76 Achkasov and Pavlovich, *Soviet Naval Operations*, pp.156–61, 188; Ruge, *The Soviets as Naval Opponents*, pp.81–86.

77 Murfett, *Naval Warfare*, pp.223–29.

78 Ibid., pp.230–34; Eric Hammel, *Guadalcanal: the Carrier Battles* (New York: Crown Publishers, 1987), pp.283–331.

79 Murfett, *Naval Warfare*, pp.234–38; Norman Gelb, *Desperate Venture: the Story of Operation Torch, the Allied Invasion of North Africa* (New York: W.W. Morrow, 1992); R.T. Thomas, *Britain and Vichy: the Dilemma of Anglo-French Relations, 1940–42* (London: Macmillan, 1979), pp.138–82.

80 Auphan and Mordal, *The French Navy in World War II*, pp.238–77.

81 Achkasov and Pavlovich, *Soviet Naval Operations*, pp.266–69; Ruge, *The Soviets as Naval Opponents*, pp.87–89, 93–94.

82 Woodman, *Arctic Convoys*, pp.296–309; B.B. Schofield, *The Arctic Convoys* (London: Macdonald & Janes, 1977), pp.79–80.

83 Woodman, *Arctic Convoys*, pp.311–30; Schofield, *The Arctic Convoys*, pp.82–94.

10 Redemption, 1943–1945

Malcolm Murfett

1943

A sense of optimism in Allied circles greeted the new year. Positive things were happening in several theatres across many time zones. A Rubicon of sorts had been crossed; wholesale retreats had been stopped; the sharpness of their opponents had been blunted; efforts to grasp the initiative from their enemies seemed more rather than less likely. Much remained to be done before victory could be won, but it was still a time for the Allies to savour after enduring a torrid time for much of the recent past. Metaphors can be overdone but there did seem some light at the end of a dark tunnel.

In essence, 1943 became a transitional year for those fighting the war at sea. Dönitz had already recognized the signs of change that had begun to appear in the Battle of the Atlantic in late 1942 as the Allies made practical improvements to their anti-submarine warfare procedures and placed the old submariner Admiral Sir Max Horton as C-in-C Western Approaches Command with direct responsibility for dealing with the U-boat menace. This was an inspired appointment. Horton was decisive and sensed what was needed. As I have said elsewhere, this was a classic method of employing a poacher turned gamekeeper to wrest back the initiative from the craft he knew only too well.[1] In the new year this upward trend in Allied fortunes continued as radical improvements in the methods of detection and destruction of U-boats were achieved once the Leigh Light (a powerful 24-inch searchlight fitted to the turret) and ASV Mark III microwave radar sets became standard issue for new squadrons of Wellington bomber aircraft and Hedgehogs (contact-fused bombs), Fido acoustic homing torpedoes, and armour-piercing rockets were added to the existing array of depth-charging, ramming, and gunfire options used by surface vessels to combat the submersible. Aircraft fitted with magnetic anomaly detection (MAD) and destroyer escorts equipped with 'Huff-Duff' (High-Frequency/Direction-Finding radio) sets were also locating the U-boat wolf packs with greater frequency and largely neutralizing them by steering convoys around them and/or inflicting punishing attacks upon them. Once the mid-Atlantic air gap was effectively closed later in the year with the provision of more Very Long Range aircraft operating from an extended range of bases, such as the islands of Fayal and Terceira in the Azores, and the U-boat tankers (*milchkühe*) were being systematically destroyed by Allied escort and support groups, Dönitz became painfully aware that he needed something more than his existing fleet of operational U-boats to break the back of his enemy.[2]

Meanwhile, in the Mediterranean and North African theatre the balance of advantage had finally swung back to the Allies. While admittedly in retreat, the task facing Rommel's Afrika Korps was to use its fall-back position in Tunisia to delay the closing of the Allied military pincer around it for as long as possible. As a result, a series of Italian supply convoys ran the perilous Allied naval gauntlet to Tripoli until the city finally fell to the 8th Army on 23 January.[3] Thereafter a host of destroyers, torpedo boats, and corvettes (forty-eight in number) began an alternative shuttle service to Tunis and Bizerte bringing in troop reinforcements and war supplies while taking off the wounded and POWs to the island of Marettimo (west of Sicily). Supplied but still beleaguered, the Afrika Korps did exactly what was expected of it and kept the Allies at bay for another two months after Rommel had flown out of Sfax on 9 March.[4]

It was a sobering time for the Axis forces. Defeat for them in North Africa followed that of the German capitulation at Stalingrad and the Japanese decision to withdraw from Guadalcanal. Although not attributable to these specific reverses as such, dramatic change swept through the top rungs of the Axis naval establishment in the early months of the year. Raeder paid the price for his surface fleet's inability to perform in a convincingly destructive manner by being replaced as C-in-C of the Kriegsmarine by Dönitz at the end of January; Iachino suffered a similar fate in early April when he was succeeded at the head of the Regia Marina by Admiral Carlo Bergamini; and Yamamoto was killed when his aircraft was shot down by US fighter planes over Bougainville in the Solomons on 18 April.[5]

Ironically, the unsatisfactory 'fleet-in-being' status of the surface fleet that had led to Raeder being hounded into early retirement was retained by his successor. Dönitz sensed that if the officers and crew were paid off and the warships were consigned to the breaker's yard – as Hitler and he had originally intended – it would give the Allies a tremendous psychological boost, reducing their level of angst and leaving them free to concentrate their attention upon dealing with his fleet of U-boats. Therefore, the same old policy of employing the heavy warships to attack the Arctic convoys or threaten a break-out into the North Atlantic would be retained for the foreseeable future. Shortly after the *Scharnhorst* joined the modern battleship *Tirpitz* and the heavy cruiser *Lützow* in Altenfjorden in northern Norway in late March, the Allies countered this redeployment by suspending the Arctic supply convoys during the spring and summer months.[6]

Even before the Axis forces had been cleared out of North Africa, Allied aircraft had begun bombing Italian naval bases in Sardinia and Sicily. It didn't take a strategic genius to guess what would happen next. Pantelleria (60 km off the eastern coast of Tunisia and 100 km south-west of Sicily), an island fortress that had posed potential danger for the Mediterranean Fleet in the past, would need to be overcome before any amphibious invasion of Sicily could take place. Starting in mid-May and intensifying at the end of the month, the island, which Mussolini had believed to be impregnable, became the object of naval shelling from a variety of Allied light cruisers and destroyers. In early June, a massive series of air raids dropped a total of 6,200 bombs on Pantelleria before the 1st British Division went ashore during the night of 10–11 June and swiftly persuaded Rear-Admiral Gino Pavesi, C-in-C of the Italian garrison on the island, to surrender a few hours later.[7]

Pantelleria's fall came shortly after Dönitz suspended his wolf pack attacks on the Atlantic convoys in late May because of their growing futility. His frustration with the overall situation was marked. He knew that his old U-boats built in the late 1930s and early 1940s could still wreak havoc where convoy wasn't in place and sometimes even when it was (as had been seen with their deadly attacks on SC.121, SC.122, and HX.229 in March), but these old workhorses needed replacement by a far more effective new generation of faster, quieter, more powerful, and highly sophisticated models if the Kriegsmarine was to succeed in the war at sea. While he waited in vain for Professor Hellmuth Walter's radical plans for a hydrogen-peroxide powered U-boat to come into effect and the naval construction firm of Bröking and Schürer to build a modified diesel-powered craft that could attain a 19-knot submersible speed and enable it to remain submerged for up to 60 hours consecutively, Dönitz had little option but to put up with what he had at his disposal.[8]

Innovative as he was, Dönitz was confronted by those like Sir John Slessor, the C-in-C of Coastal Command, who was a match for him when it came to tactical awareness. Dönitz hoped that his specially reinforced flak U-boats would be able to hold their own against enemy aircraft, but whatever initial successes there were soon petered out as Slessor modified his tactics and brought more aircraft to bear when combing vital search areas such as the Bay of Biscay used by U-boats both going to and returning from their naval bases dotted along the west coast of France. Group sailings were soon discouraged even though flak U-boats needed to concentrate their fire on aircraft to stand a greater chance of downing them and individual vessels were not allowed to leave their bases unless they were equipped with the new '*Hagenuk*' search receiver, which gave their commanders warning about the enemy's use of 10cm radar.[9]

As the Allies relentlessly pursued Dönitz's U-boats inshore and on the high seas, they were also gearing up for the invasion of Sicily (Operation *Husky*), which was launched on 10 July with seventeen convoys (612 ships) bringing 160,000 troops, 600 tanks, 1,800 guns, and 14,000 vehicles ashore on beaches from Licata in the south-west to Siracusa in the south-east of the island. Admiral Cunningham, restored to the Mediterranean as C-in-C Naval Forces, had assembled over 3,000 vessels of all types to provide the logistical support for the largest Allied amphibious operation of the war thus far. Heavy seas and foul weather combined to make the landings more of an ordeal than had been hoped for, but it also lulled the Italian defenders into thinking that the invasion wouldn't take place in such challenging conditions. It wasn't the first time and it wouldn't be the last that defenders made that critical mistake in WWII. Although motor torpedo boats (MTBs) on both sides duelled with one another and the Luftwaffe and the Regis Aeronautica Italiana sank a destroyer, a minesweeper, and eight transports (54,306 tons), neither Dönitz's U-boats nor Bergamini's submarines performed with anything like the lethality that had been anticipated beforehand and both were reduced to the peripheral role of bystanders.[10]

It took thirty-eight days for the US 7th Army under General Patton and the British 8th Army under Montgomery to capture Sicily. In the days leading up to the fall of the final obstacle – the north-eastern city of Messina on 17 August – Kapitän zur See Gustav Freiherr von Liebenstein showed what the navy could do under pressure by arranging the successful evacuation of more than 100,000 Axis troops and a whole slew of tanks, vehicles, guns, ammunition, fuel, and supplies across the three-mile straits to the Italian mainland of Reggio Calabria (*Fall Lehrgang*). It would not be the last time he would be called upon to use his skills to evacuate marooned troops and equipment in Italy.[11]

Long before Sicily fell, a stupefied and ailing Mussolini had been relieved of his post by King Vittorio Emanuele on 25 July; Marshal Pietro Badoglio being appointed as prime minister in his place. Anxious to exploit this stunning development, the Allies sought to apply maximum pressure on Badoglio in the hope of persuading him to withdraw from the war. As General Eisenhower and his staff were finalizing their plans for the invasion of southern Italy, they were also made aware of peace feelers emanating from Badoglio's representatives in Lisbon. It would take a further three weeks of secret negotiations between the two sides before Eisenhower was able to announce on 8 September that Italy had surrendered.[12]

Anticipating that German troops would flood into northern Italy to ensure that Italy wouldn't become the springboard into central Europe that Churchill desired, the Allies planned to seize as much of the southern mainland as possible while they still could. Operation *Baytown* began the process by taking the 8th Army across the Straits of Messina in a host of landing craft to launch an attack on the province of Reggio Calabria on 3 September. Such was the lack of resistance in the toe of Italy that *Baytown* quickly took on the moniker of the 'Messina Straits Regatta'. It looked for a while as if the hastily improvised attack on the provincial heel of Italy (Apulia) and the seizure of its major naval base of Taranto (Operation *Slapstick*) would also pass off without incident until the minelayer *Abdiel*, regularly used as a fast transport by the Mediterranean Fleet, struck a couple of recently-laid German mines on 10 September and sank in three minutes with heavy casualties.[13]

A day before the Allies launched their attack on Salerno (Operation *Avalanche*) on 9 September, the Germans used eleven Dornier 217 aircraft equipped with FX 1400 wireless-controlled bombs to sink Bergamini's flagship *Roma* and two destroyers, and badly damage the bow of the battleship *Italia* (formerly named *Littorio*). Ruthless though the German action was, the motive was essentially no different from that employed by the British against the Marine Nationale at Mers-el-Kébir in July 1940. Namely, ships that had previously been on their side in the war were not to be used by the enemy against them in the future. Hitler's wish was not to be granted as the remnants of the Regia Marina made their way to Malta over the next few days to join the Mediterranean Fleet. Before they did so,

German troops had taken over their former Axis partner's bases in the Tyrrhenian and Ligurian Seas.[14]

If landing in the toe and heel of Italy had been relatively straightforward, Allied progress thereafter had been slowed by the number of obstacles that had to be cleared by their engineers as they moved up the leg of Italy towards the knee around Salerno and the province of Catania. Although he couldn't prevent further Allied landings south of the Sele River and north of Salerno, Feldmarschall Kesselring, in overall charge of the German forces in the south, ensured that his 10th Army would do everything in its power to stop the Allies from consolidating their beachheads and moving northwards towards Naples roughly 70 km away. For several days, the success of the amphibious invasion hung in the balance before reinforcements were brought in from Tripoli and an ever-increasing naval bombardment of General Veitinghoff's forces tipped the balance in favour of the Allies. It had been a close call and without their warships' gunfire and logistical support – aided by resolute carrier aircraft sorties against the Luftwaffe and strong anti-aircraft defences to keep their warship losses to a bare minimum – the likelihood is that the Allies would have suffered a costly defeat. As it was, however, the shattered city of Naples lay open before them and Lieutenant Mark Clark's forces entered it on 1 October.[15]

Despite suffering several crushing defeats at the hands of the Soviet Red Army in the summer of 1943, the Germans became experts at regrouping and fighting rearguard actions against their adversaries. Massive evacuations, such as *Fall Brunhild* and *Fall Wiking* from the Kuban bridgehead, organized brilliantly by Kapitän zur See Friedrich Grattenauer, almost defied belief given the scale of the enterprise, but even the smaller withdrawals from Sardinia and Corsica were executed almost flawlessly by von Liebenstein, a past master of the art, under the most intense pressure from hostile forces. Although the capacity for improvisation is often thought to be high on the list of virtues demanded of a naval commander, particularly in battle conditions, it's not as vital a component in evacuation exercises. In these often-tumultuous affairs one can't afford to make it up as one goes along. Foresight and logical planning of a highly detailed kind are crucial to the success of the enterprise.[16]

In the Arctic, a period of relative quiescence was about to come to an end with the onset of winter and the anticipated resumption of the convoys to the Soviet ports on the White Sea. Before they were restored, however, Churchill wanted to have another crack at Dönitz's heavy ships (*Tirpitz, Scharnhorst*, and *Lützow*) that were lying in wait for them in the Norwegian fjords. On this occasion, he pinned his hopes on six midget submarines (X-craft) whose task was to manoeuvre their way stealthily into the fjords where the warships were located and release their side cargoes of 3,500 tons of Amatex high explosives underneath the two battleships and heavy cruiser and blow them out of existence. Unfortunately, the X-craft had all kinds of technical and navigational problems (faulty periscopes, gyro compasses, depth handling, and buoyancy issues) that were never satisfactorily resolved before Operation *Source* was launched on 22 September. Three of the six X-craft failed to reach their objective, but the other three found the *Tirpitz*, laid their explosive charges, and caused serious but not catastrophic damage to the battleship. *Tirpitz* survived but was put out of action for six months. Following this attack *Lützow* was immediately ordered back to her home port of Gotenhafen (Gdynia) on the Baltic, evading the Fleet Air Arm as she did so. Churchill's wish had been partly fulfilled; he had broken up the trio of heavy ships, but not permanently. Their survival would continue to frustrate him for months to come.[17]

Italy's defection, though expected, infuriated Hitler and caused him strategic problems in the Aegean and Eastern Mediterranean, where the fates of Greece and Turkey were far from settled. Although Mussolini had been rescued from his isolated Apennine skiing resort by a German commando unit on 12 September and given a face-saving semblance of power as the head of a new fascist republic based at Salò on the shores of Lake Garda in the northern province of Brescia, he was incapable of providing the answer to the strategic puzzle that confronted the Führer. Determined to ensure that the Allies wouldn't secure these prizes, Hitler saw the Aegean as an 'Iron Ring' which would not be yielded. Churchill couldn't persuade the Americans to see it in the same way and as a result Allied policy in the region became half-hearted at best. It was never going to be enough to thwart Hitler's systematic plans for the region as the Germans took over Rhodes and Kos in September and seized the rest of the Dodecanese Islands from light Allied forces in November.[18]

Although German amphibious and mining operations in the Adriatic and their gritty performance in successfully blockading the Eltigen beachhead in the eastern Crimea showed that they were still a naval force to be reckoned with, they couldn't reclaim their former dominance in the Atlantic. Part of the reason came from the fact that B-Dienst could no longer read the new British Naval Cypher No. 5, whereas the Allied cryptanalysts from Bletchley Park were becoming far more successful in reading German signals traffic. This allowed the Admiralty to vector in aircraft to deal with those U-boats that had been identified in this way. Another contributory factor was that the U-boats were far too communicative with one another. Instead of maintaining radio silence, the air waves were full of messages from one boat to another. This dialogue provided a real boon to their enemies, who now had the means to fix their position from the interchange of these signals.[19]

As the Allies found that their stodgy progress in Italy was not the springboard to further success that they had hoped it would be, the need for what Stalin regarded as a proper second front took on ever greater significance. Despite the promises made to him in the past, it would take several more months before sufficient forces had been built up to launch a major cross-Channel invasion. In the interim and as a means of appeasing the Soviet dictator, the Arctic convoys were resumed on 1 November. Admiral Sir Bruce Fraser, the C-in-C Home Fleet, sensed that with *Tirpitz* under repair and *Lützow* safely elsewhere, he might have the chance to tackle *Scharnhorst* if she could be lured out of her Norwegian fjord to prey on one of the convoys. Dönitz duly obliged by sending out the battleship along with a group of five destroyers on Christmas Day with a ringing declaration

to Konteradmiral Erich Bey, the commander of the battle group, to do something for the Wehrmacht by sinking as many cargo ships belonging to convoys
JW.55B and RA.55A as possible (*Fall Ostfront*). Bey, a somewhat jaundiced vet-
eran of the Narvik campaign, was not enamoured with the orders he had been
given or the foul weather (gale force 8) and a heaving sea that battered his ships
from the outset. Denied aerial reconnaissance by the wretched conditions, Bey
made things infinitely worse for himself by deploying his destroyers too far ahead
of him to maintain visual contact with one another and then compounded matters by turning west-northwest away without informing them. *Scharnhorst* was
now alone and would be for her final hours.[20]

Fraser, steaming from the Icelandic port of Akureyri in the battleship *Duke of
York*, accompanied by the light cruiser *Jamaica* and four destroyers, only received
confirmation in the early hours of Boxing Day that *Scharnhorst* had sailed the even-
ing before. He broke radio silence to order convoy RA.55A (twenty-two empty
ships) far to the north and out of harm's way and instructed convoy JW.55B (nineteen loaded cargo ships) to reverse course for more than three hours to ensure she
wouldn't sail into the danger zone too soon. He also urged Vice-Admiral Burnett's
cruiser squadron (Force 1) coming from Murmansk (shortly to be reinforced with
four destroyers that had been formerly attached to RA.55A) to rendezvous with
JW.55B at dawn on Boxing Day in order to give it extra protection.[21]

Once radar on the heavy cruiser *Norfolk* picked up the battleship at a range of
30 km at 0834 hours on 26 December, the hunt was on. Less than an hour later
Norfolk opened fire with her 203mm guns and hit *Scharnhorst* twice, crucially
knocking out her top FuMO27 radar as she did so. Although *Scharnhorst* used
her speed of 30 knots to escape, Burnett accurately sensed that she would return
to attack the convoy again later the same day. As such, Force I now shadowed
JW.55B and waited for the battleship to reappear. Bey didn't disappoint Burnett.
After looping around the convoy to hit it from the opposite side, *Scharnhorst* was
picked up at 22 km distance by the Type 273 radar on the light cruiser *Sheffield*
at 1210 hours. Nine minutes later, in poor conditions, all three of Burnett's
cruisers opened fire on *Scharnhorst*. In reply *Norfolk* was hit twice and *Sheffield*
near-missed before Bey suddenly withdrew to the south at speed. It looked as if
his intention was to return home to his Norwegian base. What he didn't know
and what his defunct radar couldn't tell him was that he was retiring straight into
the path of Fraser's Force 2. *Scharnhorst* discovered this at 1647 hours when star
shells illuminated her presence before the *Duke of York* began shelling the battleship shortly thereafter. Hit repeatedly, *Scharnhorst* wheeled away and appeared
to have escaped from the trap she had fallen into, but a final shell from the *Duke
of York* appears to have struck the boiler room on the starboard side of the vessel and ruptured a steam pipe. As a result, *Scharnhorst* lost two thirds of her top
speed, which brought her back into play at 1850 hours for Fraser's destroyers to
try and torpedo her. This proved to be beyond most of them except for HMS
Savage, which hit her with three of her eight torpedoes and fatally slowed her,
allowing Fraser and Burnett's warships to smash her into oblivion with a mixture
of shells and torpedoes. By 1948 hours *Scharnhorst* was no more.[22]

Although Churchill was delighted with the news of *Scharnhorst*'s destruction, the day-long pursuit of the battleship had revealed that even with the advantages of radar, ULTRA intelligence, overwhelming force, and better decision-making on its side, the Home Fleet had still been very fortunate to succeed in sinking its quarry. *Scharnhorst* had always been known as a lucky ship, but when she needed it most that most intangible and fickle asset had finally deserted her.[23]

1944

Dönitz began the new year worse off than he had been twelve months before. Apart from the fact that his U-boat fleet was smaller (160 as opposed to the 212 he had relied upon in January 1943) and far more vulnerable than it had been hitherto (twenty were lost in the North Atlantic alone in the first two months of the year), his surface warships were scattered and materially weaker than the 'fleet-in-being' he had taken over from Raeder on 30 January 1943.[24] As he had never placed much faith in the Italians or their Regia Marina, their defection in the previous autumn had not troubled him greatly. Strangely enough, his optimism and resourcefulness were undimmed by these setbacks since he firmly believed that the new generation of U-boats would hold the key to future German success at sea and that the existing fleet when fitted with the new *Schnorchel* breathing tube would make his U-boats more difficult to spot from the air since they would remain submerged for longer. He was wrong on both points but only time would prove it conclusively.[25]

As head of the Royal Navy, Cunningham ought to have been more satisfied with his lot, but with the inexhaustible Churchill to handle on a daily basis, wariness became the order of the day. Having suffered in the past from his Hellenic adventures, the first sea lord was far from convinced that the prime minister's latest strategic ploy – the attack on Anzio and Nettuno (Operation *Shingle*) – would befuddle Kesselring and convince him to weaken the Gustav defensive line around Monte Cassino and make it easier for the Allied troops to march on Rome. ABC (as Cunningham was widely known) was proved correct because even though the 380 vessels assigned to the initial landing on 22 January did their job magnificently – despite the presence of mines and the strafing attentions of the Luftwaffe – it would take four months before the troops and their reinforcements could break out of their constricted beachhead and join the other Allied armies on their slog up the Apennine mountain ridge towards the capital city, which only fell on 4 June. During that time eight cruisers and several destroyers were deployed to bring in supplies by sea from Naples. Although Dönitz hoped to disrupt the Anzio supply train, the presence of a squadron of US Catalina flying boats equipped with MAD kept his pack of U-boats under control, proving yet again that the cutting edge they had once possessed had been temporarily blunted.[26]

In the Baltic theatre the Soviets, having been on the defensive for more than two years, began to assert themselves in mid-January. After a durable two-month supply effort from their Baltic Fleet that had brought 44,000 troops, over 200 tanks, 600 guns, 2,400 vehicles, and 6,000 horses to bear, the 2nd Assault Army was finally in a position to take the initiative. Aided by an opening week in which 24,000 shells were fired at the German front lines by the battleships *Petropavlovsk* and *Oktyabrskaya Revolyutsiya*, the cruisers *Kirov*, *Maksim Gorkiy*, and *Tallin*, eight destroyers, and four gunboats, the Red Army troops were able to raise the siege of Leningrad. Nonetheless, success in the eastern part of the Gulf of Finland didn't immediately translate into dominance elsewhere. Instead the Germans and their Finnish partners responded by adding 7,599 new mines and 2,795 barrage protection devices to the narrow waters of the Gulf to make it even more difficult for Soviet submarines to get out into the Baltic.[27]

In the Black Sea and the Caucasus, however, the Soviets had definitely turned a corner in their fight against the Axis forces. Despite Hitler's defiant unwillingness to accept that the Crimea could not be held, the fall of Nikolayev (Mykolayiv) on 28 March and that of Odessa on 10 April ought to have convinced him otherwise. It didn't and instead of arranging for a timely withdrawal of the 17th Army from Sevastopol, he ordered troop reinforcements and the bringing in of 45,000 tons of supplies to the naval base. It would be a costly mistake. As the Germans were pushed back from the Perekop and Kerch peninsulas, another series of evacuations was required to take 10,000 troops to Balaklava and Sevastopol in a fleet of naval ferry barges. This merely compounded a growing problem as nothing could be done to arrest the progress of the Red Army as it opened its drive across the southern Crimea. Hitler belatedly saw sense and gave permission on 8 May for a withdrawal of troops from Sevastopol. Better late than never, the evacuation took off 130,000 by sea but lost thirty ships and 8,100 troops in doing so, while another 21,000 others were airlifted out of the city. This still left 78,000 troops behind to face an uncertain future as a conquered foe of the Red Army.[28]

By the early summer the naval war was showing unmistakeable signs of a growing ascendancy for the Allies in most of the regions of Europe. Apart from the Arctic, North Atlantic, and North Sea, where the U-boats were being hunted almost into extinction, the western and central parts of the Mediterranean were already firmly in Allied hands, even if the Aegean remained under German control, and the Adriatic was still up for grabs. In the English Channel, where the Germans used their MTBs and small auxiliary craft to mine the sea lanes and attack shipping to aggravating effect, the systematic build-up of Allied supplies and forces for the forthcoming invasion of France (Operation *Overlord*) was proceeding apace. Both sides knew what was coming, but the Germans could neither discover where the main landing site would be nor when the invasion would be launched. It was one of the most remarkable and best-kept secrets of all time.[29] It was also a superbly planned and logistically sound amphibious operation – the largest of its kind ever assembled. General Eisenhower, the Supreme Allied Commander, was convinced that the execution of the naval aspect of this cross-Channel invasion (Operation *Neptune*) could be safely left in the hands of the uniquely talented Bertram Ramsay. Plucking him from the Admiralty Retired List, the Supreme Headquarters Allied Expeditionary Force appointed Ramsay as the Allied Naval Commander for the invasion. Ramsay needed no second bidding and set about preparing his first set of detailed plans for *Neptune* even before he had returned to the Active Duty List of the Royal Navy. In Ramsay, the Allies had found the key to their future amphibious success. His team was outstanding and he led them magnificently.[30]

D-Day (6 June) began when the Germans least expected it and along the Normandy beaches that Hitler had feared might be used but which Rommel, whom he had appointed to organize the defence of northern France, had rejected as likely landing spots in favour the area around the Pas-de-Calais. Ramsay's vast armada of vessels that had been gathering at ports from the Bristol Channel to the Thames Estuary for weeks past, and estimated at roughly 7,000, would be pressed into service over the course of the next three months. On the first day alone 2,775 assorted landing craft brought 132,715 troops ashore on the five beach sectors that had been selected to receive them (designated *Utah*, *Omaha*, *Gold*, *Juno*, and *Sword*) across 41 km of the Baie de la Seine. This fleet was supported by an impressive covering defence force that included seven battleships, twenty-four cruisers, two monitors, 135 destroyers, fourteen destroyer escorts, sixty-eight corvettes, sixteen frigates, twenty-four trawlers, and a host of other smaller vessels that conducted supply runs from larger ships offshore to the beachhead.[31]

Ramsay's brief was not only to ensure that the initial troops were landed in the correct sector but to provide them with massive reinforcements, sufficient supplies and military stores thereafter. For this purpose, he selected Rear-Admiral William Tennant, his deputy from the *Dynamo* operation at Dunkirk, to organize the supply chain. Tennant's appointment was another real coup for the success of *Neptune*. He took responsibility for the building of two artificial Mulberry Harbours (large concrete caissons) that could be towed across the Channel and then erected (sunk into the seabed) offshore to provide ships with a sheltered anchorage. Although 'Mulberry A' was improperly erected and foundered in raging seas off the *Omaha* sector from 18–22 June, the other one, 'Mulberry B', did all that was expected of it if not more off *Gold* and according to ABC's later estimate helped to increase the landing of supplies by as much as 15%.[32]

Landing in poor weather and heavy seas would always be tricky and so it proved, especially on the beach sectors assigned to the Americans (*Utah* and *Omaha*), where the swollen tide did its worst to disrupt the Allied navigation plans and the reinforced German defences shelled the landing craft, killing in excess of 2,500 troops and wounding many others. Although the sea conditions weren't as rough further to the east where the British and Canadian troops landed, the toll on the troops as they came ashore on *Gold*, *Juno*, and *Sword* pushed the total number of fatalities on all five beaches to more than 4,400 and those injured to probably more than 5,000.[33]

A host of countermeasures were resorted to by Dönitz in the days after the initial landings took place, but the thirty-six U-boats and flotillas of MTBs, torpedo boats, and motorised minesweepers employed for this task didn't do enough harm to wreck the *Neptune* supply chain. Although the Kriegsmarine was found wanting in resisting the invasion, the coastal batteries at Cherbourg and Querqueville consistently out-performed them and kept the Allies at bay for as long as possible. Cherbourg, much needed as a forward supply base, only fell on 27 June. It would take a further two months for the old Atlantic port to be fully operational again. Meanwhile, denied these dockyard and quayside facilities, the Allies had to continue using the system that Ramsay and his team at Southwick House near Portsmouth had devised from the outset. By 2 July the Allies had landed 929,000 troops, 177,000 vehicles, and 586,000 tons of supplies from the largest troop transports, landing craft, Liberty ships, and small coastal craft. This huge military wave might be arrested on occasion by stout defence but it was unlikely to be thrown back into the sea. Germany's defeat was now all but certain even if the timing of it remained unclear.[34]

June was a bad month for the Axis. A huge victory for the US in the Battle of the Philippine Sea on 19–20 June (which could have been even deadlier had their force's commander, Admiral Raymond Spruance, been a little less conservative), and the utterly devastating eclipse of the Japanese carrier aircraft in what was called 'the Great Marianas Turkey Shoot', left the Japanese navy in acute disarray and the thousands of Japanese troops spread throughout the Pacific islands as essentially hostages to fortune. They would fight on relentlessly and at great cost to themselves and to others, but ultimate victory in the war was now beyond them.[35]

In the Baltic, the Finns were beginning to wrestle with the same problem. Their participation in the so-called Continuation War against the Soviet Union was beginning to go badly. A major Red Army land offensive in June caught the Finns by surprise, forced them to yield territory, and left them short of military supplies. At the same time, enemy penetration of the mine barrages in the Gulf of Finland meant that their offshore islands of Narvi and Koivisto could now be seized by the Soviets using fast torpedo cutters backed up by artillery bombardment from heavier units such as the battleship *Oktyabrskaya Revolyutsiya*. It would not be long before the idea of negotiating a ceasefire began to take hold and by 19 September an armistice had been arranged with the USSR.[36]

Their German partners were also suffering in the Tyrrhenian Sea and along the Ligurian coast of Italy. Senegalese riflemen of the French 9th Colonial Division secured the island of Elba on 17 June by using shallow-draught vessels to ease past the German mine barrages that had been set up around the island, and a couple of Anglo-Italian chariot raids into the naval base of La Spezia shortly thereafter led to the blowing up of the two heavy cruisers *Bolzano* (on 21 June) and *Gorizia* (five days later) – the former being already under repair and the latter the only surviving member of the Zara class that had perished at Matapan in 1941.[37]

Although Kesselring ensured that progress on land in northern Italy would be frustratingly slow for the Allied armies, the truth was that this had become a subsidiary theatre of operations (much as Stalin had imagined it would be); the main action lay elsewhere in northern France. No matter how good the Gothic Line north of Florence was, it was merely delaying, not defining, the war in Europe. In order to do something to arrest the German decline in the north-west of the continent, the Kriegsmarine tried various methods of interdicting the Allied supply train in the English Channel. Whatever it chose – U-boats, MTBs, or submersibles, such as Marder, Neger, and Biber craft from the Kleinkampfverband (K-Verband – small battle units), Allied countermeasures ensured that the results were fairly dismal and far too costly to be continued indefinitely.[38]

By mid-to-late summer the net was drawing in on the Germans from all directions. After consolidating their bridgehead in Normandy, the Allies broke through the German lines on the Cotentin Peninsula at the end of July and cut off the Atlantic ports of Brest, Lorient, and St Nazaire by 13 August – the day on which the city of Nantes fell on the Loire. Faced with an endless series of evacuations, German defence forces began scuttling their tankers, freighters, and other merchant ships in these harbours. In Nantes, they also blew up eight warships, and at Bordeaux three U-boats and a destroyer weren't spared either.[39]

In the south of France Operation *Dragoon* set about establishing a second land front at four sites along the Riviera coastline (15 August) and did so at minimal material cost to the Allied cause. This highlighted the bankruptcy of the Kriegsmarine at this time. Only eight vessels of the 881 assault craft and 1,370 other smaller craft that were used in this operation were lost (seven by mines and one by a glider bomb). Within three days more than 86,000 troops had been landed (the number would swell to over 324,000 by 25 September) and by the end of the month they had captured Cannes, Marseilles, and Toulon.[40]

By the time the Allied armies from the *Neptune/Overlord* and *Dragoon* operations met at Burgundy on 11 September, Paris had already fallen (25 August), and Lyons and Brussels had been liberated (3 September), as had Antwerp and Ghent (4–5 September). Le Havre, which had stoically resisted while others had thrown in the towel, was not spared. Its defences were pummelled by the battleship *Warspite* and the monitor *Erebus* on 10 September, and the RAF dropped 807 tons of bombs on it the next day before the port city was finally surrendered to the Allies (12 September). Although German forces in Calais and Dunkirk held out longer, they were surrounded by vastly superior forces and had no chance of lifting the siege on them. As such, it would only be a matter of time before they too would have to admit defeat.[41]

Much further to the east, Soviet troops had pushed the Wehrmacht back to the banks of the River Vistula and waited patiently (many would say cynically) to benefit from the Warsaw Uprising, which took a savage toll on both the Polish resistance movement as well as the German forces in the city. One thousand kilometres to the south-east, in the Black Sea the Soviets carried all before them. A massive air raid on Romania's major naval base of Constanza on 20 August wrought considerable damage on Axis shipping in the port and contributed to growing dissatisfaction with the pro-German military dictatorship of Marshal Ion Antonescu, which fell victim to a coup three days later. It was replaced by a regime led by Constantin Sanatescu that brought the war with the Allies to an end and prepared the way for the Romanians to switch sides in the conflict. Before the armistice was signed on 12 September, the Germans had quit the Balkan scene, sailing the best of their ferry barges up the Danube, sinking those craft that couldn't be brought to safety at Constanza on 24 August, and scuttling the rest of their vessels – some 200 or so in number – off Varna on 29–30 August. Their last three U-boats continued operations against the Soviet Black Sea Fleet until they ran out of fuel and were scuttled off the Turkish port of Eregli on 11 September.[42]

Beaten in the Black Sea, pushed out of the Mediterranean, and threatened in the Adriatic, the Germans were in considerable disarray in the autumn of 1944. It was no better in the Baltic theatre either. Finland's withdrawal from the war in early September, coupled with Soviet progress in Estonia and Latvia, left the Germans with few realistic options other than to add new mine barrages to these already congested waters in a bid to keep the Red Banner Baltic Fleet at bay for as long as possible. They also used their heavy cruisers *Lützow* and *Prinz Eugen* to shell the Soviet positions along the Latvian and Lithuanian coastline, but it was never more than an inconvenience and definitely not enough to arrest the Red Army's momentum. Ultimately, the German High Command became painfully aware that there was little they could do other than to evacuate as many of their forces from one location to another as circumstances allowed.[43]

Hitler's 'Iron Ring' in the Aegean took a little longer to dismantle, but there too German resistance was being whittled away by the close attentions of Admiral John Mansfield's recently formed British Aegean Force. Again, it was only a matter of time before a staged withdrawal from the region was set in motion. A couple of days after the German forces quit Piraeus (12 October), Athens fell. Salonika, home to those German vessels that had evaded the Allied dragnet and the mines that littered these waters, lasted until 31 October before the Germans finally withdrew, scuttling their last seven warships as they did so.[44]

Withdrawal and evacuation was also the name of the game in the Arctic too. After a long struggle for supremacy along the Polar coast and the Barents Sea in which the naval base of Kirkenes in the northern Norwegian region of Finnmark played a prominent role, convoying German supplies to their forces along the Northern Front, the XIX Mountain Corps were eventually pulled back from the Murmansk front, leaving the Soviet 14th Army to take their place. When the Soviet 131st Rifle Corps entered Kirkenes on 26 October the Germans had left in a series of evacuation convoys, taking 40,000 tons of supplies with them. A whole range of submarines, torpedo cutters, and MTBs from Admiral Arseni Golovko's Northern Fleet tried to catch and destroy these convoys but largely failed in their quest. This didn't stop them from claiming a scale of destruction that far exceeded the twenty vessels that were sunk – only eight of which they were responsible for – but truth is often a casualty of war and where it's not deliberate wishful-thinking often takes its place.[45]

While the Germans could evacuate troops and supplies as well as any other power, the problem the OKM/OKW (Oberkommando der Wehrmacht, or army high command) faced was which bases were safe enough to handle them. RAF Bomber Command had been bombing Bremerhaven, Emden, Gotenhafen, Hamburg, Kiel, Stettin, and Wilhelmshaven since the start of the year and mining shipping routes in the Baltic, Kattegat, North Sea, and Skagerrak from the time of D-Day onwards. To make matters worse, it now joined forces with carrier aircraft from the Home Fleet to carry out a punishing series of air raids on Norwegian bases, such as Alesund, Bergen, Egersund, and Kristiansand, that the bulk of the German convoy traffic had been using to good effect in the past four years.[46]

Further south, where the North Sea merged with the English Channel, the Allies had adopted such a stranglehold of these waters in the wake of Operation *Neptune* that the Kriegsmarine was virtually absent from them. This didn't stop the K-Verband from trying to disrupt the Allied naval presence off the Belgian coast with a flotilla of explosive motor boats (*Linsen*) during the night of 5–6 October, but their introduction failed spectacularly to achieve its fiery purpose with the only destructive element lying in the loss of thirty-six *Linsen*. An Allied naval build-up continued with an invasion of the Dutch island of Walcheren being the ultimate objective (Operation *Infatuate*). This proved to be an awkward assignment from the outset. Twenty-six landing craft were lost in putting the Commandos ashore on 1 November, and subduing the German 70th Infantry Division would take the Allies over a week of combined-arms operations before the garrison finally surrendered.[47]

Four days after Walcheren surrendered, the last of the modern German battleships, *Tirpitz*, lost her battle with the Allies. She had survived nine previous attempts from both carrier and land-based aircraft to sink her from April onwards and although she was reduced in status to a floating battery after a Tallboy bomb of 5,443 kilos had damaged her grievously on 15 September, Churchill was determined to finish her off even in this capacity. On the morning of 12 November a squadron of long-range Lancaster bombers based in Lossiemouth, Scotland, took off for her final anchorage in Lyngenfjorden near Tromso with that intention in mind (Operation *Catechism*). This time good weather and the absence of a dense smokescreen ensured that nothing obscured the target from the bombers. At least two Tallboy bombs smashed their way through her port side amidships and as many as four may have near-missed her. This was too much even for a Bismarck-class battleship and within eleven minutes *Tirpitz* had rolled over and capsized, settling on the bottom of the fjord at an angle of 135 degrees.[48] It was the end of an era.

1945

By the beginning of 1945 it would have taken a miraculous feat of arms for Germany to have reversed the fortunes of war. Allied dominance was incontestable in most of the major operational theatres. Dönitz may have pinned his hopes on his new classes of U-boat (XXI and XXIII) to perform such a feat, but their promise went largely unfulfilled. Allied methods of detection and destruction had improved exponentially as the war had proceeded and the latest U-boats, stealthier and faster, more durable and manoeuvrable though they were, simply could not compete.

Although the new generation of U-boats still tried to interfere with the Arctic convoys and make life tough for their enemy in British coastal waters, their success in these ventures was sporadic and their losses while engaged in these activities were far higher than they could sustain over the long term. This was especially true of the K-Verband's one-man midget submarine (*Biber*) and one-man human torpedo (*Molch*) vessels in the English Channel. Their losses were so high that Dönitz referred to their pilots as *Opferkämpfer* (sacrificial fighters). A far better record was achieved by the new Type XXVIIB U-boat, but these (*Seehunde*) came on stream six months too late to affect matters. D-Day had passed and so had their opportunity to strike a blow against Operation *Neptune*. It was yet another case of what might have been.[49]

Once the Red Army had opened its three-front drive on East Prussia in mid-January, however, any remaining German illusions of avoiding a comprehensive defeat in the war were swept away. It was now patently clear that the war was lost beyond recall. As such, the role of the Kriegsmarine in the Baltic was one of trying to delay the end for as long as possible so that it could retrieve as many German forces and civilians from the Eastern Front as time and circumstance allowed. Waters had to be mined; enemy positions needed to be shelled by the guns of those heavy surface warships that had somehow avoided destruction; and a wholesale series of withdrawals and evacuations had to be processed from one Baltic port to another, with Pillau and Hela being the main focal points of these operations. It must have been a heart-wrenching experience for everyone involved. Any hopes of victory they had once entertained had been comprehensively dashed, but in facing defeat they still had to exercise their duty to their fellow citizens whether in uniform or not and did so in a most accomplished manner. As a result, over the course of the next four months over two million refugees were evacuated by the Germans from the Pomeranian coast and the ports in the Gulf of Danzig. There were, of course, horrendous losses too, such as the passenger liners and transport ships that were sunk en route, but the overall survival record was a tribute to the remarkable work of Generaladmiral Oskar Kummetz and Konteradmiral Conrad Engelhardt, who were responsible for planning and orchestrating the largest evacuation of its kind that had ever been attempted.[50]

As each month of the new year passed so RAF Bomber Command attacked German cities and industrial infrastructure without restraint. By the end of March German ports and naval bases were undergoing massive bombing attacks and the deluge continued into April with the Luftwaffe powerless to do anything about it. In a series of raids stretching from 30 March to 10 April thousands of bombs caused colossal damage to the docks at Hamburg, Kiel, Bremen, and Wilhelmshaven and the ships caught sheltering there. Apart from destroying the pocket battleship *Admiral Scheer*, the light cruiser *Köln*, thirty-four U-boats, an S-boat, seven minesweepers, and seventeen other vessels, the bombs struck and badly damaged the heavy cruiser *Admiral Hipper* and the light cruiser *Emden*. A few days later the heavy cruiser *Lützow* was near-missed at her berth south of Swinemunde, causing her to run aground in the Kaiserfahrt.[51]

Once Berlin was encircled by Red Army troops on 25 April, the end of the war looked to be fast approaching. Accepting what was by now inevitable, Dönitz and the OKM were determined not to let the Soviets inherit what was left of the Kriegsmarine. In bases along the Baltic, Ligurian, and Adriatic coastlines, therefore, notable warships and less-storied auxiliaries were either blown up or sunk where they lay at anchor. After Hitler's suicide on 30 April this trend accelerated as Dönitz became leader of the nearly vanquished state.[52] Submariners in major German ports from the North Sea to the Baltic destroyed 135 U-boats in the first three days of May. Eighty-three more perished in fourteen other locations a day later. When the British XII Corps occupied Hamburg on 3 May they found the harbour littered with the shattered remains of nineteen floating docks, fifty-nine large and medium ships, and approximately 600 smaller vessels that had been destroyed by one method or another. About sixty U-boats and sundry other vessels based in the Baltic chose to make their way to Norway rather than face a self-inflicted destruction, but the RAF was not so accommodating and over the course of several days of aerial sorties (2–6 May) a host of Beaufighters, Liberators, Mosquitos, and Typhoons managed to bomb and sink seventeen U-boats, eleven steamers, three minesweepers, a gunboat, an MTB, and other smaller craft.[53]

Once Germany had surrendered its forces in Denmark, Holland, and northwest Germany on 4 May, the rest of the naval bases in the Aegean and on the French Atlantic coast surrendered over the course of the following week, Dunkirk being the last to do so on 11 May. Those ships that might have hoped for some kind of asylum in Danish and Norwegian waters did not receive such favourable treatment from their hosts. Instead the Allies were permitted to enter their waters and accept the surrender of all German vessels within them. In this way, the heavy cruiser *Prinz Eugen* and the light cruiser *Nürnberg* surrendered to Captain Herbert Williams at Copenhagen on 9 May and a total of sixty-seven U-boats did the same to other Allied representatives in Norwegian ports over the course of the next week.[54]

Although the European phase of the war was over, the campaign in the Pacific looked as though it could continue for a long time to come. Rolling up the Japanese Empire was not going to be an easy undertaking. It would be hard enough eliminating its armed presence in the islands and territories that it held in early 1945, but it would become infinitely more difficult and far costlier if victory could only be won by invading Japan (Operation *Olympic*). Appreciating this likely scenario, Churchill had met Roosevelt at the OCTAGON Conference in mid-September 1944 and offered him the use of a Royal Navy fleet to help the US Navy in the Pacific.[55] This was the genesis of the British Pacific Fleet (BPF) that was to be formed of four carriers (*Indefatigable, Indomitable, Illustrious*, and *Victorious*), two battleships (*Howe* and *King George V*), seven light cruisers, and three flotillas of destroyers. Another fleet – the British East Indies Fleet (BEIF) – was distinctly older and more modest and assigned to dealing with regional matters in the Bay of Bengal and the Straits of Malacca. Lacking any fleet carriers, the BEIF – consisting of the battleship *Queen Elizabeth* and the battle-cruiser *Renown*, together with a motley assortment of eight cruisers and twenty-four destroyers – could be used for bombarding enemy ports and communication facilities on the Burmese coast and Japanese positions in the Andaman and Nicobar Islands, but it couldn't be expected to cope with Japanese land-based aircraft or deal with those inland oil refineries on the island of Sumatra that were far removed from the coast and beyond the artillery range of its big-gun ships.[56]

Beginning its work in the Pacific as Task Force 57 in late March, the BPF was initially assigned to putting the airfields in the southern Ryukyus out of action and destroying as many Japanese land-based planes as possible before the US invasion fleet went ashore on the island of Okinawa (Operation *Iceberg*) on Easter Sunday (1 April). As anticipated, the invasion of Okinawa proved to be the deadliest test yet for the Allies in the Pacific and one that provided a vivid foretaste of what an invasion of the Japanese mainland would be like. Arduous as the land offensive was, the naval support units were not spared either as they were targeted by waves of kamikaze planes intent on destroying them come what may. A combination of fierce anti-aircraft fire, astute ship-handling, and pilot error helped to keep the potentially lethal kamikaze from causing the deadly toll the Japanese hoped they would. Nonetheless, their unpredictability and the numbers of aircraft devoted to the ten waves of raids (*Kikusui 1* to *10*) that broke over Allied shipping in the 83-day struggle for Okinawa (1 April to 22 June) meant that it was difficult for even the most experienced sailors to become totally blasé about them.[57]

After the fall of Okinawa, the end of operations on the Philippines, major inroads against Japanese forces on the oil-rich island of Borneo, and massive bombing of Japanese cities and their military and industrial installations, Churchill looked forward to a time in the near future when the British might assemble a task force sufficient to recapture Malaya and Singapore (Operation *Zipper*) and by so doing help to repair the damage wrought by their ineffective defence of these colonial territories in 1941–42. Once again, however, his plans for this part of Southeast Asia were overtaken by events beyond his control.[58]

After the atomic bombing of Hiroshima and Nagasaki on 6 and 9 August respectively, and the Soviet declaration of war on his country in between, Emperor Hirohito took to the radio for the first time on 15 August to broadcast Japan's surrender. Although the war was formally over and surrender ceremonies were officially convened over the course of the next three weeks, the British guilelessly invaded Malaya on 9 September. Whatever Churchill and Mountbatten's wistful hopes for *Zipper* may have been, pitching 100,000 troops against a non-existent enemy was nothing more than pure theatre. Lame and unconvincing, the amphibious operation did nothing to persuade the locals, let alone anyone else, that the British were back in Southeast Asia with a vengeance. Unfitting as an epilogue, *Zipper* was a stark and embarrassing contrast to the savage and unremitting naval war that had preceded it.[59]

Notes

1 Malcom Murfett, *Naval Warfare 1919–1945: an Operational History of the Volatile War at Sea* (London: W.W. Norton, 1991), p.240.
2 Ibid., p.265, 275–77; Marc Milner, *Battle of the Atlantic* (Stroud: Tempus, 2003), pp.142–55.
3 Escorting these convoys were a range of vessels from minesweepers and submarines to steamers and sailing vessels.

4 Murfett, *Naval Warfare*, pp.258, 267; Bruce Allen Watson, *Exit Rommel: the Tunisian Campaign 1942–43* (Westport: Praeger, 1999); Alan J. Levine, *The War against Rommel's Supply Lines, 1942–43* (Westport: Praeger, 1999).

5 Murfett, *Naval Warfare*, pp.266, 271, 508n.99.

6 Ibid., pp.266–67.

7 Barbara Brooks Tomblin, *With Utmost Spirit: Allied Naval Operations in the Mediterranean, 1942–1945* (Lexington: University Press of Kentucky, 2004), pp.125–31; Denis Mack Smith, *Mussolini: a Biography* (London: Alfred A. Knopf, 1982), pp.291–92.

8 David Syrett, *The Defeat of the German U-boats: the Battle of the Atlantic* (Columbia: University of South Carolina Press, 1994), pp.96–144; Milner, *Battle of the Atlantic*, pp.157, 163–64, 167, 171–72.

9 Murfett, *Naval Warfare*, pp.275–78.

10 Viscount Cunningham of Hyndhope, *A Sailor's Odyssey: the Autobiography of Admiral of the Fleet Viscount Cunningham of Hyndhope* (London: Hutchinson, 1951), pp.284–99, 534–56; Jack Greene and Alessandro Massignani, *The Naval War in the Mediterranean, 1940–1943* (London: Chatham Publishing, 1998), pp.284-99.

11 Murfett, *Naval Warfare*, pp.278–80; Tomblin, *With Utmost Spirit*, pp.147–94.

12 Mack Smith, *Mussolini*, pp.267–300; James J. Sadkovich, *The Italian Navy in World War II* (Westport: Greenwood Press, 1994), pp.285-350.

13 Murfett, *Naval Warfare*, pp.291–94; Tomblin, *With Utmost Spirit*, pp.241–93.

14 Marc Antonio Bragadin, *The Italian Navy in World War II* (Annapolis: Naval Institute Press, 1957), pp.307–22; Greene and Massignani, *The Naval War in the Mediterranean*, pp.300-09.

15 Des Hickey and Gus Smith, *Operation Avalanche: the Salerno Landings, 1943* (London: Heinemann, 1983), pp.61–282; Murfett, *Naval Warfare*, pp.293–94.

16 Murfett, *Naval Warfare*, pp.295–96.

17 Paul Kemp, *Underwater Warriors* (London: Arms and Armour, 1996), pp.128–57.

18 Murfett, *Naval Warfare*, pp.300–02, 307–09, 318n.8.

19 Terry Hughes and John Costello, *Battle of the Atlantic* (New York: Dial Press/John Wade, 1977), pp.289–93; Milner, *Battle of the Atlantic*, pp.169–76.

20 Richard Humble, *Fraser of North Cape* (London: Routledge & Kegan Paul, 1983), pp.178–224; Vincent O'Hara, *The German Fleet at War, 1939–1945* (Annapolis: Naval Institute Press, 2004), pp.155–65.

21 Richard Woodman, *The Arctic Convoys, 1941–1945* (London: John Murray, 1994), pp.344–75.

22 Only thirty-six sailors survived out of a total complement of 1,968 officers and crew. Murfett, *Naval Warfare*, pp.310–15.

23 A flaw in the *Duke of York*'s main armament meant that only 55.75% of its shells could be propelled in the eighty broadside salvoes it had fired, and torpedo execution on the part of the destroyers remained poor even when the *Scharnhorst* was virtually dead in the water.

24 Clay Blair Jr., *Hitler's U-boat War. Vol. II: the Hunted* (New York: Random House, 1998), pp.478–82.

25 Dan Van der Vat, *The Atlantic Campaign: the Great Struggle at Sea, 1939–1945* (London: Hodder & Stoughton, 1988), pp.346–48, 351, 369, 373–79; Peter Padfield, *War Beneath the Sea: Submarine Conflict during World War II* (New York: John Wiley, 1996), pp.374, 424–31.

26 Eric Linklater, *The Campaign in Italy* (London: HMSO, 1977), pp.184–209; Murfett, *Naval Warfare*, pp.326–27, 353–54.

27 V.I. Achkasov and N.B. Pavlovich, *Soviet Naval Operations in the Great Patriotic War, 1941–45* (Annapolis: Naval Institute Press, 1981), pp.175–77; Friedrich Ruge, *The Soviets as Naval Opponents, 1941–1945* (Cambridge: Patrick Stephens, 1979), pp.38–39.

28 Achkasov and Pavlovich, *Soviet Naval Operations*, pp.283–88; Ruge, *The Soviets as Naval Opponents*, pp.122–34.

29 Malcolm Murfett, 'Casting Doubt on the Inevitability Syndrome', in Malcolm Murfett (ed.), *Imponderable but not Inevitable: Warfare in the 20th Century* (Santa Barbara: Praeger/ABC Clio, 2010), pp.11–18.

30 Robert W. Love, Jr., and John Major, *The Year of D-Day: the 1944 Diary of Admiral Sir Bertram Ramsay* (Hull: University of Hull Press, 1994); Warren Tute, John Costello, and Terry Hughes, *D-Day* (London: Sidgwick & Jackson, 1974), pp.57–65, 71–105.

31 Murfett, *Naval Warfare*, pp.339–40.

32 Tennant also organized the system (*Pluto*) of piping fuel oil across the Channel for storage and use by the troops. Cunningham, *A Sailor's Odyssey*, pp.595–96.

33 Three hundred and four landing vessels were destroyed on D-Day alone. Murfett, *Naval Warfare*, pp.341–46.

34 Robin Neillands, *The Battle of Normandy, 1944* (London: Cassell, 2002), pp.136–54; Jürgen Rohwer, *Chronology of the War at Sea 1939–1945: the Naval History of World War Two* (London: Chatham Publishing, 2005), pp.330–31, 334–35.

35 Prime Minister, Minister for War, and Chief of the Army General Staff Tojo Hideki and Minister of the Navy and Chief of the Navy General Staff Shimada Shigetaro paid the price for this unsatisfactory situation by losing their portfolios in July. Murfett, *Naval Warfare*, pp.346–53.

36 Achkasov and Pavlovich, *Soviet Naval Operations*, pp.247, 250–51; Ruge, *The Soviets as Naval Opponents*, pp.40–42.

37 Murfett, *Naval Warfare*, p.354.

38 Kemp, *Underwater Warriors*, pp.183–200; O'Hara, *German Fleet at War*, pp.220–41.

39 Murfett, *Naval Warfare*, pp.359-60.

40 William B. Breuer, *Operation Dragoon: the Allied Invasion of the South of France* (Shrewsbury: Airlife, 1988).

41 V.E. Tarrant, *The Last Year of the Kriegsmarine: May 1944–May 1945* (London: Arms and Armour, 1995), pp.84–113; Paul Auphan and Jacques Mordal, *The French Navy in World War II* (Westport: Greenwood Press, 1976), pp.341–50.

42 Murfett, *Naval Warfare*, p.369.

43 Ruge, *The Soviets as Naval Opponents*, pp.40–51; Rohwer, *Chronology of the War at Sea*, pp.351–53, 356–57.

44 Lew Lind, *Battle of the Wine Dark Sea: the Aegean Campaign, 1940–45* (Kenthurst: Kangaroo Press, 1994), pp.165–68; Tarrant, *The Last Year of the Kriegsmarine*, pp.117–25.

45 Twelve were destroyed by bomber aircraft. Aubrey Mansergh (ed.), *With the Red Fleet: the War Memoirs of the Late Admiral Arseni G. Golovko* (London: Putnam, 1965), pp.203–24; Rohwer, *Chronology of the War at Sea*, pp.348, 350, 357–58, 364–65, 368.

46 O'Hara, *German Fleet at War*, pp.248–52.

47 Fire support came from the battleship *Warspite* and the monitors *Erebus* and *Roberts*. Tarrant, *The Last Year of the Kriegsmarine*, pp.155–81.

48 David Hamer, *Bombers Versus Battleships* (Annapolis: Naval Institute Press, 1998), pp.292–306; Murfett, *Naval Warfare*, pp.406–08.

49 Kemp, *Underwater Warriors*, pp.202–14; Murfett, *Naval Warfare*, pp.428–30.

50 Achkasov and Pavlovich, *Soviet Naval Operations*, pp.252–54; Ruge, *The Soviets as Naval Opponents*, pp.51–62.

51 Martin Middlebrook and Chris Everitt, *The Bomber Command Diaries: an Operational Reference Book, 1939–1945* (London: Penguin Books, 1990), pp.692–96; Rohwer, *Chronology of the War at Sea*, pp.399, 404–05, 407–10.

52 Mussolini, his Axis partner, had been murdered by communist irregulars at Lake Como only two days before. Mack Smith, *Mussolini*, pp.319–20.

53 Murfett, *Naval Warfare*, pp.435–36.

54 Twenty of these U-boats were given to the Allies as war booty, while the rest were sunk in an area west of the Hebrides in Operation *Deadlight*, lasting from 25 November to 7 January 1946. Fifteen other U-boats that had been performing in the Arctic were transferred to Loch Eriboll on the north coast of Scotland on 19 May and they too were sunk in the same operation. Ibid., pp.437–38.

55 H.P. Willmott, *Grave of a Dozen Schemes: British Naval Planning and the War against Japan* (Annapolis: Naval Institute Press, 1996); John Winton, *The Forgotten Fleet: the British Navy in the Pacific, 1944–1945* (New York: Coward McCann, 1969), pp.

56 Murfett, *Naval Warfare*, pp.404–05, 416n.84, 418–19, 428, 438, 443–44, 446–47, 452, 456n.63.

57 Ibid., pp.439–43; Edwin P. Hoyt, *The Kamikazes* (New York: Arbor House, 1983).

58 Winton, *The Forgotten Fleet*, pp.233–35; David Hobbs, *The British Pacific Fleet: the Royal Navy's Most Powerful Strike Force* (Barnsley: Seaforth, 2011).

59 Murfett, *Naval Warfare*, pp.452–53.

Conclusion

Alan James, Carlos Alfaro Zaforteza,
and Malcolm Murfett

World War Two was the violent, dramatic outcome of centuries of escalation in naval warfare. European navies projected power and applied force on an almost unbelievable scale, yet paradoxically, it seems, the war also marked the end of their perceived value.[1] The abrupt end to the fighting brought disruption to navies and even raised questions about their effectiveness and indeed their very futures. The reliance on strategic bombing, the destructive capacity of the atomic bomb, and the decisive potential of mechanised armies all seemed to spell the end for navies as independent actors in the new strategic environment that would be dominated by the Cold War. Whilst they continued to serve important functions in both peace and war in the Mediterranean, the Middle East, the Far East, and elsewhere (and for the French, British, and Dutch, in particular, navies were important for trying to hold together what remained of their overseas empires), the trend was for European navies to become drawn together under American and NATO direction and to operate more closely with armies and air forces. The end of open war, the fragile post-war economic situation, and the longer-term process of decolonisation had simply made the political case for large, formal navies too difficult to sustain. Indeed, more remarkable even than the sudden change in their configuration or size was this marked decline in their political value and their dwindling influence on status and reputation within the post-war international system. This decline is encapsulated perfectly in the fate of the capital ship, which, since at least the sixteenth century, had had a conspicuous and growing influence on the European powers as a potent symbol of national strength and prestige at sea. When the fighting ended in 1945, battleships lost their primary function, and the cost of maintaining them thereafter was simply prohibitive. No longer the potentially war-winning instruments of power that they were once seen, by some, as being, battleships were also much less effective political expressions of national strength or identity, and their construction came to a sudden and complete stop.[2]

The privileged place of the surface warship had been vulnerable for some time. Submarines clearly posed the most direct, lethal threat, although, as has been demonstrated, improved methods of detecting and destroying them largely eliminated this danger from 1943. A greater challenge, it could be argued, was the political, or strategic, one represented by the rise of air power.[3] The Battle of the

Coral Sea certainly suggests so. Despite being fought entirely at sea, this had been a battle between the air power of rival carrier fleets, without a single ship in sight. Thereafter, other major, game-changing battles such as Midway and the Battle of the Philippine Sea also demonstrated that carrier aircraft were the new capital ships and the decisive factor in winning the day. What this illustrates, more than any comparative technological case or strategic argument about the relative value of air or sea power, however, is one of the main lessons to have come out of the war: the crucial importance of the inter-operability of different services. Navies had always been instruments of amphibious warfare, of course, and had always supported land armies, but the need for co-operation with land and now air forces was emphatically confirmed in the recent fighting. This had an enormous impact on the normative, political value of navies after the war. Indeed, much of the post-war history of navies is shaped by rivalries with other services for political and financial support and even for the maintenance of distinct institutional identities.[4]

In many respects, despite the intensity of the fighting at sea, the experience of the war confirmed that the decline in the political value of large fleets of battleships had already set in. Pre-war German imperialism, for example, had been about *lebensraum*, but it had also had an ambitious naval component in the shape of the Z-plan beloved by Admiral Raeder in 1939, which recalled the earlier Tirpitz plan. It aimed to make the Kriegsmarine into a remarkable show of force that could match the Royal Navy. There was, however, no time to build it, and it never became an integral part of Nazi strategy. The outbreak of the war brought about its immediate abandonment and ever greater reliance on U-boats. For Mussolini and his admirals, too, early hopes for their battleships would be disappointed. Equally, although Stalin had had a Z-plan of his own, of sorts, by the end of the war the Soviet Red Navy had been reduced to just a small handful of antiquated battleships. After the war, existing battleships were not all scrapped, of course, and they continued to be used by all powers which still possessed them. The French navy retained two modern battleships until the late 1960s, whilst the British also kept some for royal tours of the colonies and for other displays of power. Yet there can be no denying the precipitous drop in the use of the battleship and in the political value attached to it and eventually, with the introduction of the all-weather strike aircraft, battleships lost their last remaining potential purpose, which was to hunt down Soviet surface raiders in the North Atlantic in the event of a future major war.

The waning status of navies more generally had actually had quite deep roots that reached well into the upheavals of World War One. Among the many profound changes famously wrought by this conflict was growing concern about economic and social conditions at home which affected the enthusiasm with which government spending by liberal states on conspicuous displays of military might were greeted.[5] Certainly, navies never again achieved the popularity they enjoyed in the decades before 1914. Their fate was sealed over time by a number of conspiring factors. Not least among them were the extraordinary events of World War Two themselves, most spectacularly perhaps the unexpected sinking of the *Prince of Wales* and the *Repulse* by

Japanese bombers in December 1941. Indeed the complexity of the fighting throughout the war, as it has been described in detail above, destroyed any remaining certainties there might have been about the potentially decisive impact of navies. Success or failure in individual clashes at sea seemed to have come down not necessarily to any principles of maritime power or even to raw strength, but to a whole host of such unpredictable and imponderable factors as technical malfunctions or accidents, variable climatic conditions, or simply the courage, pride, mistakes, or even luck of the people involved. Again, the desperation and contingency that is revealed in the simultaneity of events described here is consistent with expectations that had already been changing. Whereas those involved in the Battle of Jutland in 1916, for example, had felt that everything was potentially at stake and that the war could be lost in an afternoon, no one harboured such thoughts in World War Two.

There is something slightly artificial, however, about the prominence of the battleship or the concept of decisiveness as measures of the declining significance or importance of navies. As the Korean War quickly confirmed, conventional war had by no means become obsolete. Nor had naval warfare, in particular, entirely lost its potentially powerful hold over the public imagination. Indeed, this emotive power had been emphatically reconfirmed at the very outset of World War Two, with the sinking of the *Athenia* on 3 September 1939. An outrage that recalled the sinking of the *Lusitania* in the first war, the attack renewed very real fears and immediately established the urgent and desperate need to protect shipping. There would be no equivalent at sea, therefore, to the early Phoney War on land. The Battle of the Atlantic, upon which so much would depend and which lasted for the duration of the war, is all the evidence needed of just how critical sea power was felt to be. For statesmen, too, emotions ran high, and the determined efforts from 1943 to sink the *Tirpitz*, for example, reveal an obsession by Churchill to destroy it for its symbolic value as much as out of the fear he had of German heavy ships. Throughout the war, therefore, navies generated fear and horror just as they built pride and confidence, and in this respect they were a rich source of wartime propaganda that could be used to mobilise public opinion, though in this respect, too, they had to compete with the great innovation of the time, which was air power.

In many ways, the war had been a vindication of sorts for the continental theorists who had long faced the problem of confronting the Royal Navy at sea and who promoted navies as essential instruments of the protection of trade in peacetime and of essential transport of materials and supplies in times of war. Two German intellectuals, in particular, affected domestic public opinion during the war and shaped perceptions of British and American sea power: Carl Schmitt, author of *Land und Meer* (1942), and Karl Haushofer, who wrote *Weltmeere und Weltmächte* (1937). Both stressed the rivalry between land and sea powers and the need to neutralise Anglo-Saxon might through a continental coalition in what was effectively a direct continuation of French theories on Anglo-French rivalry in the eighteenth and nineteenth centuries.[6] In the end, this vindication came from the many different ways in which navies proved their value. Even the defeated German and Japanese navies, for example, performed sterling duties carrying troops or conducting necessary evacuations, as discussed at the outset of this book. The Soviet reliance on the ports of Murmansk and Archangel for keeping the troops on the Eastern Front supplied and fed is as clear an illustration as there could be of just how far from the water the effects of the work of navies could be felt, just as the many Soviet river boats at the Battle of Stalingrad demonstrate the sheer variety of forms that this naval power could take.[7] The Italians proved that a relatively small navy could have a considerable influence,[8] and even the mere presence of a French fleet in Toulon could affect German and British strategy in the Mediterranean. The British attack on the French fleet at Mersel-Kébir on 3 July 1940 and the later scuttling of Vichy ships after the German attack in late November 1942 reveal the seriousness with which French forces were being taken and the need to keep them from falling into the hands of the enemy. Likewise, German surface raiders might not have had a decisive influence on the war, but they could still be a nuisance and affect Allied planning, even if just by lurking in a Norwegian fjord somewhere.

For a neutral power such as Norway, the stakes could be very high indeed. In February 1940, for example, a British destroyer entered their territorial waters to liberate POWs being transported in the *Altmark*, a German tanker-cum-prison ship. The German decision to invade a few weeks later can be linked directly to the resulting lack of faith in Norway's ability to uphold its neutrality. Such threats by stronger powers to precious neutrality at sea is a consistent theme of the history of European navies, and it is linked to the overwhelming priority of all powers to control the distribution of resources in war. In this case, the Germans could not risk losing access to Swedish iron ore to the Allies. Indeed, navies could play no greater role than keeping the seas open, and the immense effort of navies in the Battle of the Atlantic was in certain respects a re-run of World War One in the sense that both wars were long, drawn-out conflicts in which the critical factor in victory was the safe transport of American men, arms, and supplies across the Atlantic. What could be described as Britain's initially slow and potentially disastrous response to the U-boat threat in World War One and the eventual successful organisation of an effective system of convoys only serves to reinforce the point.

The sheer scale and intensity of World War Two determined that success depended, perhaps even more than in the wars of the past, upon relative economic strength and resilience and therefore upon navies and the transportation of resources. The economies of all sides were called upon to perform miracles. In Germany, over the course of the war, over a thousand submarines were commissioned, although what Donitz needed late in the conflict was more of the newer, technologically-advanced submarines that were being developed. Fatally, if there was a reliance in German design and production upon quality and technology, this was undermined by the need for an economy that could support production on a simply massive scale. The new submarines could not be produced at the rate required to make a real difference. In contrast, the rapid construction of liberty ships to outpace the rate at which merchant ships were being were sunk is most emblematic of the relative prospects of the two sides in the war.[9] The destruction of the Japanese mercantile fleet by the United States Navy also demonstrates that, along with naval power, it was shipping that really mattered. It was this that eventually allowed the superior economic strength of the Allies, particularly of the United States, to tell.[10]

Thus, whilst in some respects World War Two marked the culmination, and the passing, of the great fleet actions and drama of the past, making it harder for European powers to exploit the political capital of navies, they nevertheless remained essential aspects of national self-definition and key elements of the expanding global economy and international order of the Cold War. Stalin's vision for the place of the post-war Soviet Union on the world stage certainly required the resurrection of the navy. For the Italians, too, fed in part by their traditional self-perception as the masters of the *mare nostrum*, the renamed *Marina Militare* was crucial to defining their place in the new international system, although this could only be permitted under the umbrella of NATO. This capacity to reinforce national self-perception and political power is a consistent theme running throughout the long history of European navies, and there is a direct parallel between the actions of small and newer states after World War Two and the early years of Reformation Europe four centuries earlier. Then, navies began to give voice to the pretensions of newly rising political outsiders. Impressive wooden warships provided an alternative expression of the martial reputation of Renaissance princes. By announcing and justifying their competition for political status, these navies generated political legitimacy as well as fulfilling their more immediate and obvious role as instruments of war. A similar effect is in evidence with the proliferation of new navies of various sizes after World War Two. India, Indonesia, Thailand, and Singapore, for example, have all needed to build navies, and meeting their security needs in this way is entirely consistent with their political invention as rising regional actors in the twentieth century.

The first meeting in 1958 of what would become the United Nations Convention on the Law of the Sea (UNCLOS) of 1994 came about precisely because of this co-existence of big and small states in the new environment in which navies operated. The aim, with Soviet support, was to protect new, Third World countries in light of the increasing exploitation of fisheries and other natural resources. As a result, territorial waters and exclusive economic zones eventually came to be legally defined. Echoing a familiar pattern, powerful states had wished to use the seas unhindered; the weaker favoured the protection of neutrality and international law, and the navies of these smaller states, along with UNCLOS, became the key to controlling ever more valuable offshore resources and ensuring collective security. Involvement in the convention, therefore, was a way not just of protecting essential national interests in these new international circumstances, but of participating in the current global order. True to form, then, navies demonstrated a flexibility and adaptability that was entirely consistent with their long history.

Thus, the history of navies certainly does not end in 1945.[11] Clearly, their military viability during the Cold War had been guaranteed by nuclear submarines as platforms for ballistic missiles and second-strike forces and, more conventionally, navies proved useful as both sides tried to isolate conflicts and avoid escalating them. The prominence of Cold War navies was not just down to deterrence, therefore, or to preparations for a possible 'hot', nuclear war. It was also preparation for a possible war for control of seaborne trade, supply, and communications, which could, in other words, turn out to be something of a third Battle of the Atlantic, after the experience of the first two world wars.[12] Today, the international order of the twenty-first century is still being shaped to a significant extent by the precarious security of important sea lanes and the need to protect global trade. Aircraft carriers have replaced the battleship as the prestige vessel of navies, and they represent a political investment in that same combination of sheer firepower and powerful statement and diplomatic influence that the battleship once offered as well as representing the pinnacle of flexibility in naval forces. The rising pretensions of India and particularly of China, with its interest in acquiring carriers and the unilateral extension of its territorial waters into the South China Sea, suggest that national navies might once again play a defining role in great power competition. Yet, however it is painted, this picture of a modern world of small, medium, and even large navies as symbols of national prestige and standing, all seizing technological and legal opportunities to defend essential economic interests in peace and war and to compete or to co-exist with a naval hegemon, now in the guise of the United States Navy, is a reflection of a well-established historical pattern of European navies.

Nevertheless, wherever the future trajectory of national navies might take us, it is clear that the great conflagration of World War Two was an important final stage of sorts in a long historical cycle. In its aftermath were only the smouldering remains of an extended process of rising, fluctuating, and falling influence of European navies on great power politics. This process had been stoked over the centuries by the heady, combustible mixture of that natural, emotional response that navies can evoke and of the many other broader changes over time that were influencing the evolution of the conduct of modern war. The touch-paper had been lit in the sixteenth century when European princes seized the opportunity to associate themselves with the impressive display and military potential that navies offered, contributing to the general escalation of early modern warfare. Over the centuries, that flame burned ever brighter as it drew added fuel from, at the same time that it accelerated, the changes in the priorities that defined national self-interest and international status. As navies promoted and protected colonial trade, for example, which helped to pay for, and expand, eighteenth-century warfare, they contributed materially to an emerging consensus that economic might was now also a measure of national success and greatness. It was in the fires of the Napoleonic wars, however, that the link was securely forged between navies and the wealth, prestige, industrial strength, and global reach to which nineteenth-century states and their populations would all aspire. Even smaller powers were caught up in the blaze as they took advantage of the elasticity of the generative political potential of navies, defending national interests by challenging Britain not in a contest for naval mastery but, when opportunities arose, over another politically potent principle: neutrality and freedom of the seas. More popular than ever, and feeding off the flames of nationalism, navies swept into the very heart of the European political imagination and eventually engulfed the global international system.

British pre-eminence in the nineteenth century, therefore, had done nothing to dampen the interest of other powers. On the contrary, it set a new standard of international greatness which was contributing to a fundamental change in the great power system itself. Strategists and historians provided the interpretation of the past and the principles that cemented this position of navies in an age of high imperialism. The determination with which a unified Germany, notably, embraced naval power and imperial ambitions as it emerged as the great militarised power of the time is indicative of a world increasingly shaped by extremely large and powerful states and one, correspondingly, that was attracted to 'navalist' thinking. Equally, of course, European navies provided the direct inspiration and model for the development of both the United States Navy and the Imperial Japanese Navy, as these rising powers also invented themselves on the global stage.[13] Among the many powerful impressions to have emerged from World War One was that this had indeed been an imperial war and that size and resources mattered. The next great war, when it came, would necessarily be one of national survival, and it would require control of as many demographic and material resources as possible.[14] The great fleet reviews and public acclamations of pride in feats of engineering and naval construction of the early twentieth century reveal that it was in this dark hour that navies burned brightest as popular embodiments of the nation and its hopes for survival.

Naturally, the extraordinary firepower and lethal technological sophistication of navies contributed directly to the acceleration of the arms race that led to the outbreak of World War Two. Indeed, over their long history of development, navies had always grown, often spectacularly, and in step with growing military and economic pressures. In this sense, they mirrored the long-term escalation of war and the growth of the state system that waged it. Yet it would be a disservice to see this history as just a linked series of instrumental responses. The sheer majesty of navies, the enormous political and financial investment in them, and their popular appeal, indeed even the extraordinary events of World War Two themselves, all suggest that something rather more was at play. Navies had also had an active, creative role in the international system itself. In the past, more than land armies, they were often the greatest consumers of a nation's technological innovation and its industrial capacity, and even, it could be said, of some of the best of its tactical and strategic thought. By driving demand in such ways, navies also had a structural effect as catalysts of wider change. As navies legitimised, announced, and enforced the authority of states, they affected assumptions about the very nature of status and relative standing internationally and never more than in the desperate, global competition for power, resources, and sheer size that caused the breakdown of the international system and the great wars of the twentieth century.

Notes

1 Paul Kennedy, 'The Influence of Sea Power upon Three Great Global Wars, 1793–1815, 1914–1918, 1939–1945: a Comparative Analysis', in N.A.M. Rodger, J. Ross Dancy, Benjamin Darnell, and Evan Wilson (eds), *Strategy and the Sea: Essays in Honour of John B. Hattendorf* (Woodbridge: Boydell, 2016), pp. 109–37.

2 Stalin represents an important exception. He acquired a couple of old ships and ordered the construction of the battle-cruiser *Stalingrad* in 1949. Work on it stopped after his death in March 1953. Milan L. Hauner, 'Stalin's Big-Fleet Program', *Naval War College Review*, 57, 2 (2004), pp.87–120.

3 Tim Benbow, 'The Capital Ship, the Royal Navy and British Strategy from the Second World War to the 1950s', in Rodger et al. (eds), *Strategy and the Sea*, pp.169–178.

4 George W. Baer, *One Hundred Years of Sea Power: the US Navy, 1890–1990* (Stanford: Stanford University Press, 1994), pp.275–313; Eric Grove, *Vanguard to Trident: British Naval Policy Since the Second World War* (London: Bodley Head, 1987).

5 Joseph A. Maiolo, *Cry Havoc: the Arms Race and the Second World War, 1931–41* (London: John Murray, 2010), pp.105–06; Paul Kennedy, *The Rise and Fall of British Naval Mastery* (London: Penguin Books, 2017), pp.271–72.

6 Dan Diner, 'Knowledge of Expansion on the Geopolitics of Karl Haushofer', *Geopolitics*, 4, 3 (1999), pp.161–88; Joshua Derman, 'Carl Schmitt on Land and Sea', *History of European Ideas*, 37, 2 (2011), pp.181–89.

7 Lester W. Grau, 'River Flotillas in Support of Defensive Ground Operations: the Soviet Experience', *The Journal of Slavic Military Studies*, 29, 1 (2016), pp.73–98.

8 Richard Hammond, 'An Enduring Influence on Imperial Defence and Grand Strategy: British Perceptions of the Italian Navy, 1935–1943', *The International History Review*, 39, 5 (2017), pp.810–35.

9 Frederic C. Lane, *Ships for Victory: a History of Shipbuilding under the U.S. Maritime Commission in World War II* (Baltimore: Johns Hopkins University Press, 2001).

10 Malcolm Murfett, 'The Sinking of Japan', *History Today*, 66, 21 (2016), pp.21–27.

11 The value of the flexibility of sea power remains as strong as ever. Geoffrey Till, *Seapower: a Guide for the Twenty-First Century* (Abingdon: Routledge, 2013).

12 Owen R. Cote, Jr., *The Third Battle: Innovation in the U.S. Navy's Silent Cold War Struggle with Soviet Submarines* (Newport: Naval War College Press, 2012).

13 Alessio Patalano, *Post-War Japan as a Sea Power: Imperial Legacy, Wartime Experience and the Making of a Navy* (London: Bloomsbury, 2016).

14 Robert Boyce and Joseph A. Maiolo (eds), *The Origins of World War Two: the Debate Continues* (Basingstoke: Palgrave, 2003).

Select bibliography

Abbazia, Patrick. *Mr. Roosevelt's Navy: the Private War of the U.S. Atlantic Fleet, 1939–1942*. Annapolis: Naval Institute Press, 1975.

Acerra, Martine, and Jean Meyer. *Marines et révolution*. Rennes: Ouest-France, 1988.

Acerra, Martine, Michel Vergé-Franceschi, José Merino, and Jean Meyer (eds). *Les Marines de guerre européennes, XVIIe-XVIIIe siècles*. Paris: Presses de l'Université de Paris-Sorbonne, 1998.

Acerra, Martine, and André Zysberg. *L'Essor des marines de guerres européennes*. Paris: SEDES, 1997.

Achkasov, V.I., and N.B. Pavlovich. *Soviet Naval Operations in the Great Patriotic War 1941–1945*. Annapolis: Naval Institute Press, 1981.

Adams, Brooks. 'The Seizure of the Laird Rams', *Proceedings, Massachusetts Historical Society*, 45 (1912): 243–333.

Admiralstab der Marine. *Die Kaiserliche Marine whärend der Wirren in China 1900–1901*. Berlin: Mittler und Sohn, 1903.

Aksakal, Mustafa. *The Ottoman Road to War in 1914: the Ottoman Empire and the First World War*. Cambridge: Cambridge University Press, 2008.

Alfaro Zaforteza, Carlos. 'Medium Powers and Ironclad Construction: the Spanish Case, 1861–1868', in Craig C. Felker and Marcus O. Jones (eds), *New Interpretations in Naval History*. Newport: Naval War College Press, 2012.

Alfaro Zaforteza, Carlos. *Sea Power, State and Society in Liberal Spain, 1833–1868*. PhD thesis, King's College London, 2011.

Allain, Jean-Claude. *Agadir 1911. Une Crise impérialiste en Europe pour la conquête du Maroc*. Paris: Pulications de la Sorbonne, 1976.

Ames, Glenn J. 'Colbert's Indian Ocean Strategy of 1664–74: A Reappraisal', *French Historical Studies*, 16, 3 (1990): 536–59.

Ameur, Farid. 'La Guerre de Sécession au large de Cherbourg. La France impériale et l'affaire du *CSS Alabama* (juin 1864)', *Relations Internationales*, 150 (2012): 7–22.

Andersen, Dan H. 'La Politique danoise face aux états barbaresques (1600–1845)', in Gérard Le Bouëdec and François Chappé (eds), *Pouvoirs et littoraux: du XVe au XXe siècle*. Rennes: Presses Universitaires de Rennes, 2000.

Anderson, M.S. *The Ascendancy of Europe: Aspects of European History, 1815–1914*. Harlow: Longman, 1972.

Anderson, R.C. 'Denmark and the First Anglo-Dutch War', *The Mariner's Mirror*, 53, 1 (1967): 55–62.

Anderson, R.C. *Naval Wars in the Baltic, 1522–1850*. London: Francis Edwards, 1969.

Armitage, David. 'The Elizabethan Idea of Empire', *Transactions of the Royal Historical Society*, 14, 1 (2004): 269–77.

Armitage, David (ed.). *Hugo Grotius: the Free Sea*. Indianapolis: Liberty Fund, 2004.

Armstrong, Benjamin F. (ed.). *21st Century Mahan: Sound Military Conclusions for the Modern Era*. Annapolis: Naval Institute Press, 2013.

Augeron, Mikaël. 'De La Cause au parti: Henri De Navarre et la course Protestante (1569–1589)', in Christian Hermann (ed.), *Enjeux Maritimes des conflits Européens, XVIe-XIXe Siècles*. Nantes: Ouest Éditions, 2002.

Auphan, Paul, and Jacques Mordal. *The French Navy in World War II*. Westport: Greenwood Press, 1976.

Avenel, Jean-David. *L'affaire du Rio de la Plata (1838–1852)*. Paris: Economica, 1998.

Backhaus, Jürgen G. *Navies and State Formation: the Schumpeter Hypothesis Revisited and Reflected*. Zurich: Lit Verlag, 2012.

Badem, Candan. *The Ottoman Crimean War (1853–1856)*. Brill: Leiden, 2010.

Baer, George W. *One Hundred Years of Sea Power: the U.S. Navy, 1890–1990*. Stanford: Stanford University Press, 1994.

Bailey, Thomas A., and Paul B. Ryan. *Hitler vs Roosevelt: the Undeclared Naval War*. New York: Free Press, 1999.

Balzac, Honoré de. *Oeuvres Completes, vol. 23*. Paris: Calmann Lévy, 1879.

Bardonnet, A. 'Registre de L'amirauté de Guyenne au siège de La Rochelle (1569–1570)', *Archives historiques de Poitou*, 7 (1878): 191–271.

Barlett, C.J. 'Statecraft, Power and Influence', in C.J. Bartlett (ed.), *Britain Pre-Eminent: Studies in British World Influence in the Nineteenth Century*. London: Macmillan, 1969: 172–93.

Barnett, Correlli. *Engage the Enemy More Closely: the Royal Navy in the Second World War*. London: W.W. Norton, 1991.

Barth, Boris. *Dolchstoßlegenden und politische Desintegration: Das Trauma der deutschen Niederlage im Ersten Weltkrieg 1914–1933*. Düsseldorf: Droste, 2003.

Bartlett, C.J. *Defence and Diplomacy: Britain and the Great Powers 1815–1914*. Manchester: Manchester University Press, 1993.

Bartlett, C.J. *Great Britain and Sea Power: 1815–1853*. Oxford: Clarendon Press, 1963.

Bartlett, Ruhl J. *The Record of American Diplomacy: Documents and Readings in the History of American Foreign Relations*. New York: Alfred A. Knopf, 1954.

Battaglia, Antonello. *Il Risorgimento sul mare: la campagna navale del 1860–1861*. Roma: Edizioni Nuova Cultura, 2012.

Battesti, Michèle. *La Marine de Napoléon III: une politique navale*. 2 vols. Vincennes: Service Historique de la Marine, 1997.

Baugh, Daniel A. *The Global Seven Years War, 1754–1763: Britain and France in a Great Power Contest*. Harlow: Longman, 2011.

Baumber, M. *General-at-Sea: Robert Blake and the Seventeenth-Century Revolution in Naval Warfare*. London: Murray, 1989.

Baxter, James P. *The Introduction of the Ironclad Warship*. Cambridge: Harvard University Press, 1933.

Bayly, C.A. *The Birth of the Modern World, 1780–1914: Global Connections and Comparisons*. Oxford: Blackwell, 2004.

Bayly, C.A. *Imperial Meridian: the British Empire and the World, 1780–1830*. London: Longman, 1989.

Beasley, Edward. *Empire as the Triumph of Theory: Imperialism, Information, and the Colonial Society of 1868*. London: Routledge, 2005.

Beeler, John. *British Naval Policy in the Gladstone–Disraeli Era, 1866–1880*. Stanford: Stanford Universtity Press, 1997.

Beeler, John. 'In the Shadow of Briggs: a New Perspective on British Naval Administration and W.T. Stead's 1884 "Truth about the Navy" Campaign', *International Journal of Naval History*, 1, 1 (2002).

Beevor, Antony. *The Battle for Spain: the Spanish Civil War 1936–1939*. London: Weidenfeld & Nicolson, 2006.

Bell, Christopher M. *Churchill and the Dardenelles*. Oxford: Oxford University Press, 2017.

Bell, Christopher M. 'Contested Waters: the Royal Navy in the Fisher Era', *War in History*, 23, 1 (2016): 115–26.

Bell, Christopher M. *The Royal Navy, Seapower and Strategy between the Wars*. Basingstoke: Macmillan, 2000.

Bell, Christopher M. 'Winston Churchill and the Ten Year Rule', *Journal of Military History*, 74, 4 (2010): 1097–1128.

Bellamy, Martin. *Christian IV and His Navy: a Political and Administrative History of the Danish Navy 1596–1648*. Leiden: Brill, 2006.

Benbow, Tim. *British Naval Aviation: the First 100 Years*. Farnham: Ashgate, 2011.

Benbow, Tim. 'The Capital Ship, the Royal Navy and British Strategy from the Second World War to the 1950s', in N.A.M. Rodger, J. Ross Dancy, Benjamin Darnell, and Evan Wilson (eds), *Strategy and the Sea: Essays in Honour of John B. Hattendorf*. Woodbridge: Boydell, 2016: 169–178.

Benbow, Tim. *Naval Warfare, 1914–1918: from Coronel to the Atlantic and Zeebrugge*. London, Amber Books, 2008.

Bercuson, David J., and Holger H. Herwig. *Bismarck: the Story Behind the Destruction of the Pride of Hitler's Navy*. London: Pimlico, 2003.

Berg, Meredith W. 'Protecting National Interests by Treaty: the Second London Naval Conference, 1934–1936', in B.J.C. McKercher (ed.), *Arms Limitation and Disarmament*. Westport: Praeger, 1992: 203–27.

Berghahn, Volker R. *Der Tirpitz-Plan: Genesis und Verfall einer innenpolitischen Krisenstrategie unter Wilhelm II*. Düsseldorf: Droste Verlag, 1971.

Berghahn, Volker R. *Imperial Germany: Economy, Society, Culture and Politics*. New York: Berghahn Books, 2005.

Besch, Michael D. *A Navy Second to None: the History of U.S. Naval Training in World War I* (Westport: Greenwood Press, 2002).

Best, Antony, Jussi M.Hanhimäki, Joseph A. Maiolo, and Kirsten E. Schulze. *International History of the Twentieth Century*. London: Routledge, 2004.

Best, Geoffrey. *War and Society in Revolutionary Europe, 1770–1870*. Leicester: Leicester University Press, 1982.

Bird, Keith W. *Erich Raeder: Admiral of the Third Reich*. Annapolis: Naval Institute Press, 2006.

Black, Jeremy. 'Anglo-Spanish Naval Relations in the Eighteenth Century', *Mariner's Mirror*, 77, 3 (1991): 235–58.

Black, Jeremy. 'British Foreign Policy in the Eighteenth Century: a Survey', *The Journal of British Studies*, 26, 1 (1987): 26–53.

Black, Jeremy. *The English Press in the Eighteenth Century*. London: Croom Helm, 1987.

Black, Jeremy. *European Warfare, 1660–1815*. New Haven: Yale University Press, 1994.

Black, Jeremy. *A Military Revolution? Military Change and European Society, 1550–1800*. Atlantic Highlands: Humanities Press, 1991.

Black, Jeremy. 'Naval Capability in the Early Modern Period: An Introduction', *Mariner's Mirror*, 97, 2 (2011): 21–31.

Black, Jeremy. *Naval Power: a History of Warfare and the Sea from 1500*. Basingstoke: Palgrave, 2009.

Black, Jeremy. *War in Europe: 1450 to the Present*. London: Bloomsbury, 2016.

Blair, Clay, Jr. *Hitler's U-boat War. Vol. I: the Hunters, 1939–1942*. New York: Random House, 1996.

Blair, Clay, Jr. *Hitler's U-boat War. Vol. II: the Hunted*. New York: Random House, 1998.

Blakemore, Richard. 'The Politics of Piracy in the British Atlantic, c.1640–1649', *International Journal of Maritime History*, 25, 2 (2013): 159–172.

Blakemore, Richard, and James Davey (eds). *The Maritime World of Early Modern Britain*. London: Routledge, 2018.

Blanning, T.C.W. *The Pursuit of Glory: Europe, 1648–1815*. London: Allen Lane, 2007.

Bobbitt, Philip. *The Shield of Achilles: War, Peace, and the Course of History*. New York: Knopf, 2002.

Bond, Brian. *War and Society in Europe, 1870–1970*. London: Fontana, 1984.

Bönker, Dirk. *Militarism in a Global Age: Naval Ambitions in Germany and the United States before World War I*. Ithaca: Cornell University Press, 2012.

Booth, Ken. *Navies and Foreign Policy*. London: Routledge, 2014.

Bosher, J.F. *French Finances 1770–1795: from Business to Bureaucracy*. Cambridge: Cambridge University Press, 1970.

Boudriot, Jean. 'Vaisseaux et frégates sous la Restauration et la Monarchie de Juillet', in *Marine et technique au XIXe siècle*. Paris: Service Historique de la Marine, 1988: 65–83.

Bowen, H.V. 'British Conceptions of Global Empire, 1756–1783', *Journal of Imperial and Commonwealth History*, 26 (1998): 1–27.

Bowen, H.V. and A. González Enciso. *Mobilising Resources for War: Britain and Spain at Work during the Early Modern Period*. Pamplona: Universidad de Navarra, 2006.

Bowen, H.V., et al. 'Forum: The Contractor State, c.1650–1815', *International Journal of Maritime History*, 25, 1 (2013): 239–74.

Boyce, Robert, and Joseph A. Maiolo (eds). *The Origins of World War Two: the Debate Continues*. Basingstoke: Palgrave, 2003.

Boyd, Andrew. *The Royal Navy in Eastern Waters: Linchpin of Victory 1935–1942*. Barnsley: Seaforth, 2017.

Bragadin, Marc Antonio. *The Italian Navy in World War II*. Annapolis: Naval Institute Press, 1957.

Breemer, Jan S. *Defeating the U-boat: Inventing Antisubmarine Warfare*. Newport: Naval War College Press, 2010.

Brendon, Piers. *The Dark Valley: a Panorama of the 1930s*. New York: Vintage Books, 2003.

Brenner, Robert. *Merchants and Revolution: Commercial Change, Political Conflict, and London's Overseas Traders, 1550–1653*. Princeton: Princeton University Press, 1993.

Breuer, William B. *Operation Dragoon: the Allied Invasion of the South of France*. Shrewsbury: Airlife, 1988.

Bridge, F.R., and Roger Bullen. *The Great Powers and the European States System, 1814–1914*. Harlow: Pearson, 2005.

Brière, Jean-François. 'Pêche et politique à Terre-Neuve au XVIIIe Siècle: la France véritable gagnante du Traité d'Utrecht?', *Canadian Historical Review*, 64, 2 (1983): 168–87.

Brodie, Bernard. *Sea Power in the Machine Age*. New York: Greenwood Press, 1969.

Brooks, John. *The Battle of Jutland.* Cambridge: Cambridge University Press, 2016.

Brooks, John. *Dreadnought Gunnery and the Battle of Jutland: the Question of Fire Control.* London: Routledge, 2005.

Brooks Tomblin, Barbara. *With Utmost Spirit: Allied Naval Operations in the Mediterranean, 1942–1945.* Lexington: University Press of Kentucky, 2004.

Broome Williams, Kathleen. *Secret Weapon: U.S. High Frequency Direction Finding in the Battle of the Atlantic.* Annapolis: Naval Institute Press, 1996.

Brown, David A. *Palmerston: A Biography.* New Haven: Yale University Press, 2010.

Brown, David A. 'Palmerston and Anglo-French Relations, 1846–1865', *Diplomacy & Statecraft,* 17 (2006): 675–92.

Brown, David K. 'The Era of Uncertainty, 1863–1878', in Robert Gardiner and Andrew Lambert (eds), *Steam, Steel and Shellfire: the Steam Warship, 1815–1905.* London: Conway Maritime Press, 1992.

Brown, David K. *Road to Oran: Anglo-French Naval Relations, September 1939–July 1940.* London: Frank Cass, 2004.

Bruijn, Jaap R. *The Dutch Navy of the Seventeenth and Eighteenth Centuries.* Columbia: University of South Carolina Press, 1993.

Bruijn, Jaap R. 'States and their Navies from the Late Sixteenth to the End of the Eighteenth Centuries', in Philippe Contamine (ed.), *War and Competition between States.* Oxford: Clarendon Press, 2000.

Buchet, Christian. *The British Navy, Economy and Society in the Seven Years War.* Translated by Anita Higgie and Michael Duffy. Woodbridge: Boydell, 2013.

Buchet, Christian (ed.). *The Sea in History / La Mer dans l'histoire.* 4 vols. Woodbridge: Boydell, 2017.

Buchet, Christian, Jean Meyer, and J.P. Poussou (eds). *La Puissance maritime.* Paris: Presses de l'Université de Paris-Sorbonne, 2004.

Budiansky, Stephen. *Battle of Wits: the Complete Story of Codebreaking in World War II.* New York: The Free Press, 2000.

Bullen, Roger. 'The Great Powers and the Iberian Peninsula, 1815–48', in Alan Sked (ed.), *Europe's Balance of Power, 1815–1848.* Basingstoke: Macmillan, 1979: 54–78.

Callwell, Charles E. *The Effect of Maritime Command on Land Campaigns since Waterloo.* London: William Blackwood and Sons, 1897.

Cannadine, David (ed.). *Trafalgar in History: a Battle and its Afterlife.* Basingstoke: Palgrave, 2006.

Capp, Bernard. *Cromwell's Navy: the Fleet and the English Revolution, 1648–1660.* Oxford: Clarendon Press, 1989.

Cass, Lewis. *An Examination of the Question, Now in Discussion, between the American and British Governments, Concerning the Right of Search.* Paris: n.p., 1842.

Cénat, Jean-Philippe. *Le Roi stratège Louis XIV et la direction de la guerre, 1661–1715.* Rennes: Presses Universitaires de Rennes, 2010.

Chaline, Olivier. 'Franco-British Naval Rivalry and the Crisis of the Monarchy, 1759–1789', in Julian Swann and Joël Félix (eds), *The Crisis of the Absolute Monarchy: France from Old Regime to Revolution.* Oxford: Oxford University Press, 2013: 205–221.

Chaline, Olivier, P. Bonnichon, and C.-P de Vergennes (eds). *Les Marines de la Guerre d'Indépendance Américaine, 1763–1783.* Paris: Presses de l'Université de Paris-Sorbonne, 2013.

Chesneau, Roger, and Eugene Kolesnik (eds). *Conway's All the World's Fighting Ships, 1860–1905.* London: Conway Maritime Press, 1979.

Chet, Guy. *The Ocean is a Wilderness: Atlantic Piracy and the Limits of State Authority, 1688–1856*. Amherst: University of Massachusetts Press, 2014.

Chevalier, Édouard. *Histoire de la marine française pendant la guerre de l'indépendance américaine*. Paris: Hachette, 1877.

Claasen, Adam. 'Germany's Expeditionary Operation: the Invasion of Norway, 1940', in Peter Dennis and Jeffrey Grey (eds.), *Battles Near and Far: a Century of Operational Deployment*. Canberra: Army History Unit, 2005: 141–62.

Clark, Martin. *Modern Italy, 1871 to the Present*. Milton Park: Routledge, 2014.

Clarke, George S. *Russia's Sea-Power: Past and Present, or the Rise of the Russian Navy*. London: John Murray, 1898.

Clarke, I.F. *Voices Prophesing War*. London: Oxford University Press, 1966.

Clemmesen, Michael J., and Marcus Faulkner (eds). *Northern Overtures to War, 1939–1941: From Memel to Barbarossa*. Leiden: Brill, 2013.

Clerc-Rampal, G. *La Marine française pendant la Grande guerre (août 1914-novembre 1918)*. Paris: Larousse, 1919.

Coats, Ann, and Philip MacDougall (eds). *The Naval Mutinies of 1797: Unity and Perseverance*. Woodbridge: Boydell, 2012.

Cobban, Alfred. *A History of Modern France. Vol. 3: France of the Republics, 1871–1962*. London: Penguin Books, 1977.

Cobden, Richard. *The Three Panics: an Historical Episode*. London: Ward & Co., 1862.

Colley, Linda. *Britons: Forging the Nation, 1707–1837*. New Haven: Yale University Press, 1992.

Collis, Robert. *The Petrine Instauration: Religion, Esotericism and Science at the Court of Peter the Great, 1689–1725*. Leiden: Brill, 2012.

Compton-Hall, Richard. *Submarines at War, 1914–18*. Penzance: Periscope, 2004.

Consett, Thomas. *The Present State and Regulations of the Church of Russia. Establish'd by the Late Tsar's Royal Edict. Also in a Second Volume a Collection of Several Tracts Relating to His Fleets, Expedition to Derbent, &C*. London: S. Holt, 1729.

Conway, Stephen. *The British Isles and the War of American Independence*. Oxford: Oxford University Press, 2000.

Conway, Stephen. 'War and National Identity in the Mid-Eighteenth-Century British Isles', *English Historical Review*, 116, 468 (2001): 863–93.

Conway, Stephen. *War, State, and Society in Mid-Eighteenth Century Britain and Ireland*. Oxford: Oxford University Press, 2006.

Coogan, John W. *The End of Neutrality: the United States, Britain, and Maritime Rights, 1899–1915*. Ithaca: Cornell University Press, 1981.

Coogan, John W. 'Wilsonian Diplomacy in War and Peace', in Gordon Martel (ed.), *American Foreign Relations Reconsidered, 1890–1993*. London: Routledge, 1994: 71–79.

Cook, Weston F., Jr. *The Hundred Years' War for Morocco: Gunpowder and the Military Revolution in the Early Modern Muslim World*. Boulder: Westview, 1994.

Cooper, John Milton. *Breaking the Heart of the World: Woodrow Wilson and the Fight for the League of Nations*. Cambridge: Cambridge University Press, 2001.

Corbett, Julian S. 'The Bugbear of British Navalism', *New York Times*, 25 May 1915.

Cormack, William S. *Revolution and Political Conflict in the French Navy, 1789–1794*. Cambridge: Cambridge University Press, 1995.

Cote, Owen R., Jr., *The Third Battle: Innovation in the U.S. Navy's Silent Cold War Struggle with Soviet Submarines*. Newport: Naval War College Press, 2012.

Coutau-Bégarie, Hervé. *La Puissance maritime: Castex et la stratégie navale*. Paris: Fayard, 1985.

Coutau-Bégarie, Hervé (ed.). *L'Évolution de la pensée navale*. 8 vols. Paris: Economica, 2000–2008.

Cracknell, W.H. *United States Navy Monitors of the Civil War*. Windsor: Profile Publications, 1973.

Cras, Jérôme, and Geraud Poumarède. 'Entre Finance et diplomatie: les armements du Commandeur François De Neuchèze pour le secours de Candie', in Daniel Tollett (ed.), *Guerres et paix en Europe Centrale aux époques moderne et contemporaine*. Paris: Presses Universitaires de Paris-Sorbonne, 2003: 507–44.

Crouzet, François. 'The Second Hundred Years War: Some Reflections', *French History*, 10, 4 (1996): 432–50.

Crowe, Eyre A. 'Memorandum on the Present State of British Relations with France and Germany (1 Jan. 1907)', in G.P. Gooch and Harold Temperley (eds), *British Documents on the Origins of the War*. London: HMSO, 1928: 397–420.

Crowell, Benedict, and Robert F. Wilson. *The Road to France: the Transportation of Troops and Military Supplies, 1917–1918*. 2 vols. New Haven: Yale University Press, 1921.

Cunningham of Hyndhope, Viscount. *A Sailor's Odyssey: the Autobiography of Admiral of the Fleet Viscount Cunningham of Hyndhope*. London: Hutchinson, 1951.

Curry, Anne. *The Hundred Years War*. New York: Palgrave, 1993.

Daget, Serge. 'France, Suppression of the Illegal Trade, and England, 1817–1850', in David Eltis and James Walvin (eds), *The Abolition of the Atlantic Slave Trade*. Madison: University of Wisconsin Press, 1981: 193–217.

Dakin, Douglas. 'Lord Cochrane's Greek Steam Fleet', *Mariner's Mirror*, 39 (1953): 211–19.

Dallek, Robert. *Franklin D. Roosevelt and American Foreign Policy, 1932–1945*. Oxford: Oxford University Press, 1995.

Daly, John C.K. *Russian Seapower and 'The Eastern Question', 1827–41*. Annapolis: Naval Institute Press, 1991.

Darnell, Benjamin. 'The Financial Administration of the French Navy during the War of the Spanish Succession'. DPhil thesis, University of Oxford, 2015.

Darnell, Benjamin. 'Reconsidering the *Guerre De Course* under Louis XIV: Naval Policy and Strategic Downsizing in an Era of Fiscal Overextension', in N.A.M. Rodger, J. Ross Dancy, Benjamin Darnell, and Evan Wilson (eds), *Strategy and the Sea: Essays in Honour of John B. Hattendorf*. Woodbridge: Boydell, 2016: 37–48.

Darrieus, Gabriel. *War on the Sea: Strategy and Tactics*. Annapolis: Naval Institute Press, 1908.

Darwin, John. *After Tamerlane: the Global History of Empire*. London: Allen Lane, 2007.

Daunton, Martin. 'The Greatest and Richest Sacrifice Ever Made on the Altar of Militarism: the Finance of Naval Expansion, c.1890–1914', in Robert Blyth, Andrew Lambert, and Jan Rüger (eds), *The Dreadnought and the Edwardian Age*. Aldershot: Ashgate, 2011.

Davey, James. *In Nelson's Wake: the Navy and the Napoleonic Wars*. New Haven: Yale University Press, 2015.

Davey, James. *The Transformation of British Naval Strategy: Seapower and Supply in Northern Europe, 1808–1812*. Woodbridge: Boydell, 2012.

Davies, Brian L. *The Russo-Turkish War, 1768–1774: Catherine II and the Ottoman Empire*. London: Bloomsbury, 2016.

Davies, J.D. 'The Birth of the Imperial Navy? Aspects of English Naval Strategy, c.1650–90', in Michael Duffy (ed.), *Parameters of British Naval Power, 1650–1850*. Exeter: Exeter University Press, 1992.

Davies, J.D. *Gentlemen and Tarpaulins: the Officers and Men of the Restoration Navy*. Oxford: Clarendon Press, 1991.

Davies, J.D. *Kings of the Sea: Charles II, James II, and the Royal Navy*. Barnsley: Seaforth, 2017.

Davies, J.D., Alan James, and Gijs Rommelse (eds). *Ideologies of Western Naval Power*. Aldershot: Ashgate, 2019.

Deist, Wilhelm. *Flottenpolitik und Flottenpropaganda: das Nachrichtenbureau des Reichsmarineamtes 1897–1914*. Stuttgart: Deutsche Verlags-Anstalt, 1976.

De La Escosura, Leandro Prados (ed.). *Exceptionalism and Industrialisation: Britain and Its European Rivals, 1688–1815*. Cambridge: Cambridge University Press, 2004.

Derman, Joshua. 'Carl Schmitt on Land and Sea', *History of European Ideas*, 37, 2 (2011): 181–89.

Dessert, Daniel. 'La Marine royale, une filiale Colbert', in Charles Giry-Delaison and Roger Mettam (eds). *Patronages et clientèlismes, 1550–1750*. London: Institut Français, 1995.

Dessert, Daniel. *La Royale: vaisseaux et marins du Roi-Soleil*. Paris: Fayard, 1996.

Devitt, Jerome. 'The "Navalization" of Ireland: the Royal Navy and Irish Insurrection in the 1840s', *Mariner's Mirror*, 101, 4 (2015): 388–409.

Dewar, Helen. 'Canada or Guadeloupe? French and British Perceptions of Empire, 1760–1763', *Canadian Historical Review*, 91, 4 (2010): 637–60.

Diner, Dan. 'Knowledge of Expansion on the Geopolitics of Karl Haushofer', *Geopolitics*, 4, 3 (1999): 161–88.

Dislère, Paul. *La Marine cuirassée*. Paris: Gauthier-Villars, 1873.

Dittmar, Frederick J., and J.J. Colledge. *British Warships, 1914–1919*. London: Ian Allan, 1972.

Dodwell, Henry. *The Founder of Modern Egypt: a Study of Muhammad Ali*. Cambridge: Cambridge University Press, 1931.

Doe, Helen, and Richard Harding (eds). *Naval Leadership and Management, 1650–1950*. Woodbridge: Boydell, 2012.

Doenecke, Justus D. *Storm on the Horizon: the Challenge to American Intervention, 1939–1941*. Lanham: Rowman & Littlefield, 2000.

Doise, Jean and Maurice Vaisse. *Diplomatie et outil militaire, 1871–1969*. Paris: Imprimerie Nationale, 1987.

Doratioto, Francisco Fernando Monteoliva. 'Poder naval e política externa do Império do Brasil no Rio da Prata (1822–1852)', *Navigator*, 12 (2010): 9–20.

Droz, Jacques. *Histoire diplomatique de 1848 à 1919*. Paris: Dalloz, 1952.

Duffy, Michael (ed.). *Parameters of British Naval Power, 1650–1850*. Exeter: Exeter University Press, 1992.

Duffy, Michael, and Roger Morriss. *The Glorious First of June 1794: a Naval Battle and its Aftermath*. Exeter: University of Exeter Press, 2001.

Dülffer, Jost. *Weimar, Hitler und die Marine. Reichspolitik und Flottenbau 1920–1939*. Düsseldorf: Droste, 1973.

Dull, Jonathan R. *The Age of the Ship of the Line: the British and French Navies, 1650–1815*. Lincoln: University of Nebraska Press, 2009.

Dull, Jonathan R. *The French Navy and American Independence: a Study of Arms and Diplomacy, 1774–1787*. Princeton: Princeton University Press, 1975.

Dull, Jonathan R. *The French Navy and the Seven Years' War*. France Overseas. Lincoln: University of Nebraska Press, 2005.

Dunley, Richard. *The Royal Navy and Underwater Weapons, 1900–1914*. PhD thesis, King's College London, 2014.

Eberspächer, Cord. 'Arming the Beiyang Navy. Sino-German Naval Cooperation 1879–1895', *International Journal of Naval History*, 8, 1 (2009).

Eberspächer, Cord. 'To Arm China: Sino-German Relations in the Military Sphere Prior to the First World War', *Berliner-China Hefte*, 33 (2008): 54–74.

Eby, Cecil D. *The Road to Armageddon: the Martial Spirit in English Popular Literature, 1870–1914*. Durham: Duke University Press, 1988.

Eltis, David. *Economic Growth and the Ending of the Transatlantic Slave Trade*. Oxford: Oxford University Press, 1987.

Epkenhans, Michael. *Die wilhelminische Flottenrüstung, 1908–1914: Weltmachtstreben, industrieller Fortschritt, soziale Integration*. München: Oldenbourg, 1991.

Epkenhans, Michael. 'Was a Peaceful Outcome Thinkable? The Naval Race before 1914', in Holger Afflerbach and David Stevenson (eds), *An Improbable War: the Outbreak of World War I and European Political Culture before 1914*. New York: Berghahn Books, 2007: 113–29.

Epkenhans, Michael, Jörg Hillmann, and Frank Nägler (eds). *Jutland: World War I's Greatest Naval Battle*. Lexington: University Press of Kentucky, 2015.

Evans, David C., and Mark R. Peattie. *Kaigun: Strategy, Tactics and Technology in the Imperial Japanese Navy, 1887–1941*. Annapolis: Navy Institute Press, 1997.

Fahmy, Kahled. 'The Era of Muhammad Ali Pasha, 1805–1848', in M.W. Daly (ed.), *The Cambridge History of Egypt*. Cambridge: Cambridge University Press, 1998: 139–79.

Fanning, Richard W. 'The Coolidge Conference of 1927: Disarmament in Disarray', in B.J.C. McKercher (ed.), *Arms Limitation and Disarmament: Restraints on War, 1899–1939*. Westport: Praeger, 1992: 105–27.

Faulkner, Marcus. *The Great War at Sea: a Naval Atlas, 1914–19*. Barnsley: Seaforth, 2015.

Faulkner, Marcus. 'The Kriegsmarine and the Aircraft Carrier: the Design and Operational Purpose of the Graf Zeppelin, 1933–1940', *War in History*, 19, 4 (2012): 492–516.

Faulkner, Marcus. 'Kriegsmarine, Signals Intelligence and the Development of the B-Dienst before the Second World War', *Intelligence and National Security*, 25, 4 (2010): 521–546.

Faulkner, Marcus. *War at Sea: a Naval Atlas, 1939–45*. Barnsley: Seaforth, 2012.

Fayle, Charles E. *Seaborne Trade*. New York: Longmans, Green & Co., 1924.

Fernandez-Armesto, Felipe. *The Spanish Armada: the Experience of War in 1588*. Oxford: Oxford University Press, 1989.

Ferris, John. 'The Road to Bletchley Park: the British Experience with Signals Intelligence, 1892–1945', *Intelligence and National Security*, 17, 1 (Spring 2002): 55–84.

Ferris, John, and Evan Mawdsley (eds). *The Second World War. Vol. 1: Fighting the War*. Cambridge: Cambridge University Press, 2015.

Figes, Orlando. *Crimea: the Last Crusade*. London: Allen Lane, 2010.

Filho, João Roberto Martins. *A marinha brasileira na era dos encouraçados, 1895–1910: tecnologia, forças armadas e política*. Rio de Janeiro: FGV Editora, 2010.

Ford, C.J. 'Piracy or Policy: the Crisis in the Channel, 1400–1403', *Transactions of the Royal Historical Society*, 29 (1979): 63–78.

Foreign and Commonwealth Office Historians. *Slavery in Diplomacy: the Foreign Office and the Suppression of the Transatlantic Slave Trade*. London: Foreign and Commonwealth Office, 2007.

Forrest, Alan. 'French Revolutionary and Napoleonic Wars', in Geoff Mortimer (ed.), *Early Modern Military History, 1450–1815*. London: Palgrave, 2004.

Fotakis, Zisis. *Greek Naval Strategy and Policy, 1910–1919*. London: Routledge, 2005.

Franken, Klaus. *Vizeadmiral Karl Galster - Ein Kritiker des Schlachtflottenbaus der Kaiserlichen Marine*. Bochum: Verlag Dr. Dieter Winkler, 2011.

French, David. 'The Nation in Arms II: the Nineteenth Century', in Charles Townshend (ed.), *The Oxford History of Modern War*. Oxford: Oxford University Press, 2000: 74–93.

Freure, Russell. 'When Memory and Reality Clash: the First World War and the Myth of American Neutrality', *Northern Mariner*, 22, 2 (2012): 141–63.

Frost, Robert I. *The Northern Wars: War, State, and Society in Northeastern Europe, 1558–1721*. London: Longman, 2000.

Fulbrook, Mary. *History of Germany, 1918–2008: the Divided Nation*. Oxford: Wiley-Blackwell, 2009: 38–55.

Fuller, Howard J. *Clad in Iron: the American Civil War and the Challenge of British Naval Power*. Westport: Praeger, 2008.

Fuller, Howard J. '"Seagoing Purposes Indispensable to the Defence of this Country": Policy Pitfalls of Great Britain's Early Ironclads', *The Northern Mariner*, 13 (2003): 19–36.

Fusaro, Maria. *Political Economies of Empire in the Early Modern Mediterranean: the Decline of Venice and the Rise of England, 1450–1700*. Cambridge: Cambridge University Press, 2015.

Gabriele, Mariano and Giuliano Friz. *La politica navale italiana dal 1885 al 1915*. Rome: Ufficio Storico della Marina Militare, 1982.

Gallagher, J. 'Fowell Buxton and the New African Policy, 1838–1842', *Cambridge Historical Journal*, 10, 1 (1950): 36–58.

Gannon, Michael. *Operation Drumbeat: the Dramatic Story of Germany's First U-boat Attacks along the American Coast in World War II*. New York: Harper Perennial, 1991.

Gardiner, Robert (ed.). *Conway's All the World's Fighting Ships, 1922–1946*. London: Conway Maritime Press, 1980.

Gardner, W.J.R. (ed.). *The Evacuation from Dunkirk: 'Operation Dynamo'*. London: Frank Cass, 2000.

Garrett, Richard. *Scharnhorst and Gneisenau: the Elusive Sisters*. Newton Abbot: David & Charles, 1978.

Gat, Azar. *A History of Military Thought: from the Enlightenment to the Cold War*. Oxford: Oxford University Press, 2001.

Gatzke, Hans W. *Stresemann and the Rearmament of Germany*. New York: W.W. Norton & Co., 1969.

Gelb, Norman. *Desperate Venture: the Story of Operation Torch, the Allied Invasion of North Africa*. New York: W.W. Morrow, 1992.

Geppert, Dominik and Andreas Rose. 'Machtpolitik und Flottenbau vor 1914. Zur Neuinterpretation britischer Außenpolitik im Zeitalter des Hochimperialismus', *Historische Zeitschrift*, 293 (2011): 401–37.

Getzler, Israel. *Kronstadt, 1917–1921: the Fate of a Soviet Democracy*. Cambridge: Cambridge University Press, 1983.

Gibbs, N.H. *Grand Strategy. Vol. 1: Rearmament Policy*. London: HMSO, 1976.

Gill, G. Hermon. *Royal Australian Navy, 1939–1942*. Sydney: Collins, 1985.

Glasgow, Tom. 'The Navy in the French Wars of Mary and Elizabeth I: Part III. The Navy in the Le Havre Expedition, 1562–1564', *Mariner's Mirror*, 54, 3 (1968): 281–96.

Glete, Jan. *Navies and Nations: Warships, Navies, and State Building in Europe and America, 1500–1860. 2 vols*. Stockholm: Almqvist & Wiksell, 1993.

Glete, Jan. *Swedish Naval Administration, 1521–1721: Resource Flows and Organisational Capabilities*. Leiden: Brill, 2010.

Glete, Jan. *Warfare at Sea, 1500–1650: Maritime Conflicts and the Transformation of Europe*. London: Routledge, 2000.

Glines, Carroll V. *The Doolittle Raid: America's Daring First Strike against Japan.* West Chester: Schiffer Military History, 1991.

Goldman, Stuart D. *Nomonhan 1939: the Red Army's Victory that Shaped World War II.* Annapolis: Naval Institute Press, 2012.

Goldrick, James. *Before Jutland: the Naval War in Northern European Waters, August 1914–February 1915.* Annapolis: Naval Institute Press, 2015.

Goldrick, James, and John B. Hattendorf (eds). *Mahan is not Enough: the Proceedings of a Conference on the Works of Sir Julian Corbett and Admiral Sir Herbert Richmond.* Newport: Naval War College Press, 1993.

González Enciso, A. *War, Power and the Economy: Mercantilism and State Formation in Eighteenth-Century Europe.* London: Routledge, 2016.

Gooch, John. 'The Weary Titan: Strategy and Policy in Great Britain, 1890–1918', in Williamson Murray, MacGregor Knox, and Alvin Bernstein (eds), *The Making of Strategy: Rulers, States, and War.* Cambridge: Cambridge University Press, 1994: 278–306.

Goodman, David. *Spanish Naval Power, 1589–1665: Reconstruction and Defeat.* Cambridge: Cambridge University Press, 1997.

Goodman, Jennifer R. *Chivalry and Exploration, 1298–1630.* Woodbridge: Boydell Press, 1998.

Gough, Barry. *Churchill and Fisher: Titans at the Admiralty.* Barnsley: Seaforth, 2017.

Gough, Barry. *Pax Britannica: Ruling the Waves and Keeping the Peace before Armageddon.* Basingstoke: Palgrave, 2014.

Graham, Gerald S. *The China Station: War and Diplomacy, 1830–1860.* Oxford: Clarendon Press, 1978.

Graham, Gerald S. *The Politics of Naval Supremacy: Studies in British Maritime Ascendancy.* Cambridge: Cambridge University Press, 1965.

Granier, Hubert. 'La Pensée navale française au XVIIIe siècle', in Hervé Coutau-Bégarie (ed.), *L'Évolution de la pensée navale.* Paris: Fondation pour les Études de Défense Nationale, 1993: 33–56.

Grant, Jonathan A. *Rulers, Guns, and Money: the Global Arms Trade in the Age of Imperialism.* Cambridge: Harvard University Press, 2007.

Grau, Lester W. 'River Flotillas in Support of Defensive Ground Operations: the Soviet Experience', *Journal of Slavic Military Studies*, 29, 1 (2016): 73–98.

Gray, Edwyn. *The Devil's Device: the Story of Robert Whitehead, Inventor of the Torpedo.* London: Seeley Service, 1975.

Gray, Randal (ed.). *Conway's All the World's Warships, 1906–1921.* London: Conway Maritime Press, 1985.

Greene, Jack, and Alessandro Massignani. *The Naval War in the Mediterranean, 1940–1943.* London: Chatham Publishing, 1998.

Greene, Molly. *A Shared World: Christians and Muslims in the Early Modern Mediterranean.* Princeton: Princeton University Press, 2000.

Greenhalgh, Elizabeth. *Victory through Coalition: Britain and France during the First World War.* Cambridge: Cambridge University Press, 2005.

Grell, Ole Peter. 'Scandinavia', in Robert Scribner, Roy Porter, and Mikulas Teich (eds), *The Reformation in National Context.* Cambridge: Cambridge University Press, 1994.

Grewe, Wilhelm G. *The Epochs of International Law.* Berlin: Walter de Gruyter, 2000.

Grotius, Hugo. *The Freedom of the Seas.* New York: Oxford University Press, 1916.

Grove, Eric. 'The Memory of the Battle of Jutland in Britain', in Michael Epkenhans, Jörg Hillmann, and Frank Nägler (eds), *Jutland: World War I's Greatest Naval Battle.* Lexington: University Press of Kentucky, 2015.

Grove, Eric. *The Price of Disobedience: the Battle of the River Plate Reconsidered*. Stroud: Sutton, 2000.

Grove, Eric. *The Royal Navy since 1815: a New Short History*. Basingstoke: Palgrave, 2005.

Grove, Eric. *Vanguard to Trident: British Naval Policy since the Second World War*. London: Bodley Head, 1987.

Guilmartin, John F. *Gunpowder and Galleys*. Cambridge: Cambridge University Press, 1974.

Guimerá, Agustín. 'The Offensive Strategy of the Spanish Navy, 1763–1808', in N.A.M. Rodger, J. Ross Dancy, Benjamin Darnell, and Evan Wilson (eds), *Strategy and the Sea: Essays in Honour of John B. Hattendorf*. Woodbridge: Boydell, 2016: 98–108.

Haarr, Geirr H. *The Battle for Norway: April–June 1940*. Barnsley: Seaforth, 2010.

Hagan, Kenneth J. *American Gunboat Diplomacy and the Old Navy, 1877–1889*. Westport: Greenwood Press, 1973.

Halpern, Paul G. '"Handelskrieg mit U-Booten": the German Submarine Offensive in World War I', in Bruce A. Elleman and S.C.M. Paine (eds), *Commerce Raiding: Historical Case Studies, 1755–2009*. Newport: Naval War College Press, 2013.

Halpern, Paul G. *The Mediterranean Naval Situation, 1908–1912*. Cambridge: Harvard University Press, 1971.

Halpern, Paul G. *A Naval History of World War I*. Annapolis: Naval Institute Press, 2012.

Hamer, David. *Bombers versus Battleships*. Annapolis: Naval Institute Press, 1998.

Hamilton, C.I. *Anglo-French Naval Rivalry, 1840–1870*. Oxford: Clarendon Press, 1993.

Hamilton, C.I. 'Anglo-French Seapower and the Declaration of Paris', *International History Review*, 4, 2 (1982): 166–90.

Hamilton, C.I. 'The Diplomatic and Naval Effects of the Prince de Joinville's *Note sur l'état des forces navales de la France* of 1844', *The Historical Journal*, 32 (1989): 675–87.

Hammel, Eric. *Guadalcanal: the Carrier Battles*. New York: Crown Publishers, 1987.

Hammond, Richard. 'An Enduring Influence on Imperial Defence and Grand Strategy: British Perceptions of the Italian Navy, 1935–1943', *International History Review*, 39, 5 (2017): 810–35.

Hannay, David. 'The Battle of Jutland', *Edinburgh Review*, 233, 475 (1921): 29–47.

Hanotaux, Gabriel. *La Guerre des Balkans et l'Europe, 1912–1913*. Paris: Plon-Nourrit et Cie., 1914.

Hardach, Gerd. *The First World War, 1914–1918*. Berkeley: University of California Press, 1977.

Harding, Richard. *The Emergence of Britain's Global Naval Supremacy the War of 1739–1748*. Woodbridge: Boydell, 2010.

Harding, Richard. *Modern Naval History: Debates and Prospects*. London: Bloomsbury, 2016.

Harding, Richard. *Seapower and Naval Warfare, 1650–1830*. Annapolis: Naval Institute Press, 1999.

Harding, Richard, and S. Sobles Ferri (eds). *The Contractor State and its Implications*. Las Palmas: Universidad de las Palmas de Gran Canaria, 2012.

Harmon, J. Scott. 'The United States and the Suppression of the Illegal Slave Trade, 1830–1850', in Craig L. Symmonds (ed.), *New Aspects of Naval History*. Annapolis: Naval Institute Press, 1981: 211–19.

Hart, Jonathan Locke. *Comparing Empires: European Colonialism from Portuguese Expansion to the Spanish-American War*. Basingstoke: Palgrave, 2003.

Harvey, A.D. 'European Attitudes to Britain during the French Revolutionary and Napoleonic Era', *History*, 63 (1978): 356–65.

Hattendorf, John B. *Doing Naval History: Essays toward Improvement*. Newport: Naval War College Press, 1995.

Hattendorf, John B. *England in the War of the Spanish Succession: a Study of the English View and Conduct of Grand Strategy, 1702–1712*. New York: Garland Publishing, 1987.

Hattendorf, John B. 'The Naval War of 1812 in International Perspective', *Mariner's Mirror*, 99, 1 (2013): 5–22.

Hattendorf, John B. *Ubi Sumus?: The State of Naval and Maritime History*. Newport: Naval War College Press, 1994.

Hauner, Milan L. 'Stalin's Big-Fleet Program', *Naval War College Review*, 57, 2 (Spring 2004): 87–120.

Headrick, Daniel. *The Tentacles of Progress: Technology Transfer in the Age of Imperialism, 1850–1940*. New York: Oxford University Press, 1988.

Hendrix, Henry J. *Theodore Roosevelt's Naval Diplomacy: the U.S. Navy and the Birth of the American Century*. Annapolis: Naval Institute Press, 2009.

Herring, George C. *From Colony to Superpower: U.S. Foreign Relations since 1776*. New York: Oxford University Press, 2008.

Herwig, Holger H. 'Strategic Uncertainties of a Nation-state: Prussia-Germany, 1871–1918', in Williamson Murray, MacGregor Knox, and Alvin Bernstein (eds), *The Making of Strategy: Rulers, States, and War*. Cambridge: Cambridge University Press, 1994.

Hess, Andrew C. 'The Battle of Lepanto and its Place in Mediterranean History', *Past & Present*, 57 (1972): 53–73.

Heuser, Beatrice. *Reading Clausewitz*. London: Pimlico, 2002.

Hickey, Des, and Gus Smith. *Operation Avalanche: the Salerno Landings, 1943*. London: Heinemann, 1983.

Hobbs, David. *The British Pacific Fleet: the Royal Navy's Most Powerful Strike Force*. Barnsley: Seaforth, 2011.

Hobsbawm, E.J. *The Age of Empire, 1875–1914*. London: Phoenix Press, 2000.

Hobson, Rolf. *Imperialism at Sea: Naval Strategic Thought, the Ideology of Sea Power and the Tirpitz Plan, 1875–1914*. Leiden: Brill, 2002.

Hobson, Rolf. 'Prussia, Germany and Maritime Law from Armed Neutrality to Unlimited Submarine Warfare, 1780–1917', in Rolf Hobson and Tom Kristiansen (eds), *Navies in Northern Waters, 1721–2000*. London: Frank Cass, 2004: 97–116.

Hocker, Frederick M. *Vasa: a Swedish Ship*. Stockholm: Medstroms Bokforlag, 2011.

Hodge, Carl C. 'The Global Strategist: the Navy as the Nation's Big Stick', in Serge Ricard (ed.), *A Companion to Theodore Roosevelt*. Chichester: Wiley-Blackwell, 2011: 257–73.

Honig, Jan Willem. 'Reappraising Late Medieval Strategy: the Example of the 1415 Agincourt Campaign', *War in History*, 19, 2 (2012): 123–51.

Honig, Jan Willem. 'Warfare in the Middle Ages', in Anja V. Hartmann and Beatrice Heuser (eds), *War, Peace and World Orders in European History*. London: Routledge, 2001: 113–26.

Horn, Daniel (ed.). *The Private War of Seaman Stumpf: the Unique Diaries of a Young German in the Great War*. London: Leslie Frewin, 1969.

Hoste, P. Paul. *L'Art des armées navales, ou traité des évolutions navales*. Lyon: Anisson et Posuel, 1697.

Hovgaard, William. *Modern History of Warships*. London: Conway Maritime Press, 1971.

Howard, Michael. 'The Edwardian Arms Race', in Michael Howard (ed.), *The Lessons of History*. New Haven: Yale University Press, 1991: 81–96.

Howard, Michael. *War in European History*. Oxford: Oxford University Press, 1976.

Howarth, Stephen. 'Admiral of the Fleet, Sir Philip Vian', in Stephen Howarth (ed.), *Men of War*. New York: St. Martin's Press, 1993.

Hoyt, Edwin P. *The Kamikazes*. New York: Arbor House, 1983.

Hsu, C.Y. 'The Great Policy Debate in China, 1874: Maritime Defense vs. Frontier Defense', *Harvard Journal of Asiatic Studies*, 25 (1965): 212–28.

Hubatsch, Walter. 'Die deutsche Reichsflotte 1848 und der Deutsche Bund', in Walter Hubatsch (ed.), *Die erste Deutsche Flotte 1848-1853*. Herford: E.S. Mittler & Sohn, 1981: 29–40.

Hughes, Terry, and John Costello. *The Battle of the Atlantic*. New York: Dial Press, 1977.

Humbert, Jean-Marcel, and Bruno Ponsonnet. *Napoléon et la mer, un rêve d'empire*. Paris: Seuil, 2004.

Humble, Richard. *Fraser of North Cape*. London: Routledge, 1983.

Hutcheon, Wallace S. *Robert Fulton: Pioneer of Undersea Warfare*. Annapolis: Naval Institute Press, 1981.

Hutchins, John G.B. 'History and Development of Shipbuilding, 1776–1944', in F.G. Fassett (ed.), *The Shipbuilding Business in the United States of America*. New York: Society of Naval Architects and Marine Engineers, 1948: 14–60.

Hyam, Ronald. *Britain's Imperial Century, 1815–1914: a Study of Empire and Expansion*. Basingstoke: Palgrave Macmillan, 2002.

Imlah, Albert H. *Economic Elements in the Pax Britannica: Studies in British Foreign Trade in the Nineteenth Century*. Cambridge: Harvard University Press, 1958.

Ingram, Edward. 'Illusions of Victory: the Nile, Copenhagen and Trafalgar Revisited', *Military Affairs*, 48, 3 (1984): 140–43.

Israel, Jonathan I. *Dutch Primacy in World Trade 1585–1740*. Oxford: Clarendon Press, 1989.

Jacobson, Jon. *Locarno Diplomacy: Germany and the West 1925–1929*. Princeton: Princeton University Press, 1972.

James, Alan. 'A French Armada? The Azores Campaigns, 1580–1583', *The Historical Journal*, 55, 1 (2012): 1–20.

James, Alan. 'La Bataille du cap Béveziers (1690): une glorieuse victoire pour Le roi stratège', in Ariane Boltanski, Yann Lagadec, and Frank Mercier (eds), *La Bataille. Du fait d'armes au combat idéologique (XIe – XIXe siècles)*. Rennes: Presses Universitaires de Rennes, 2015: 205–18.

James, Alan. *The Navy and Government in Early Modern France, 1572–1661*. Woodbridge: Boydell, 2004.

James, Alan. 'Raising the Profile of Naval History: an International Perspective on Early Modern Navies', *Mariner's Mirror*, 97, 1 (2011): 193–206.

Jenkins, Ernest Harold. *A History of the French Navy: from its Beginnings to the Present Day*. London: Macdonald and Jane's, 1973.

Jennings, Lawrence C. *French Reaction to British Slave Emancipation*. Baton Rouge: Louisiana State University Press, 1988.

Joinville, François Ferdinand Philippe Louis Marie d'Orléans, Prince de. 'Note sur l'état des forces navales de la France', *Revue des Deux Mondes*, 15 May 1844, 708–46.

Jomini, Antoine Henri. *Histoire critique et militaire des guerres de la Révolution, vol. 1*. Paris: Anselin et Pochard, 1820.

Jones, Colin. *The Great Nation: France from Louis XV to Napoleon 1715–99*. New York: Columbia University Press, 2002.

Jones, D., and A. Rakestraw. *Prologue to Manifest Destiny: Anglo-American Relations in the 1840s*. Wilmington: SR Books, 1997.

Jones, J.R. *The Anglo-Dutch Wars of the Seventeenth Century*. Harlow: Longman, 1996.

Jones, J.R. 'The Dutch Navy and National Survival in the Seventeenth Century', *International History Review*, 10, 1 (1988): 18–32.

Jónsson, Már. 'Denmark-Norway as a Potential World Power in the Early Seventeenth Century', *Itinerario*, 33, 2 (2009): 17–27.

Jordan, John. *Warships after Washington: the Development of the Five Major Fleets, 1922–1930*. Annapolis: Naval Institute Press, 2011.

Jurien de La Gravière, Jean Pierre Edmond. *Souvenirs d'un amiral, vol. 2*. Paris: Hachette, 1860.

Kelly, Patrick J. *Tirpitz and the Imperial German Navy*. Bloomington: Indiana University Press, 2011.

Kemp, Paul. *Friend or Foe: Friendly Fire at Sea, 1939–1945*. London: Leo Cooper, 1995.

Kemp, Paul. *Underwater Warriors*. London: Arms and Armour, 1996.

Kennedy, Greg. 'The 1930 London Naval Conference and Anglo-American Maritime Strength, 1927–1930', in B.J.C. McKercher (ed.), *Arms Limitation and Disarmament*. Westport: Praeger, 1992: 149–71.

Kennedy, Greg (ed.). *British Naval Strategy East of Suez, 1900–2000: Influences and Actions*. London: Frank Cass, 2005.

Kennedy, Greg (ed.). *Imperial Defence: the Old World Order, 1856–1956*. London, Routledge: 2008.

Kennedy, Paul. 'The Influence of Sea Power upon Three Great Global Wars, 1793–1815, 1914–1918, 1939–1945: a Comparative Analysis', in N.A.M. Rodger, J. Ross Dancy, Benjamin Darnell, and Evan Wilson (eds), *Strategy and the Sea: Essays in Honour of John B. Hattendorf*. Woodbridge: Boydell, 2016: 109–137.

Kennedy, Paul. 'Mahan versus Mackinder. Two Interpretations of British Sea Power', *Militärgeschichtliche Mitteilungen*, 2 (1974): 39–66.

Kennedy, Paul. *The Rise and Fall of British Naval Mastery*. London: Penguin Books, 2017.

Kershaw, Ian. *Hitler, 1889–1936: Hubris*. New York: W.W. Norton, 2000.

Kipp, Jacob W. 'The Grand Duke Konstantin Nikolaevic: the Making of a Tsarist Reformer, 1827–1853', *Jahrbücher für die Geschichte Osteuropas*, 34 (1986): 3–18.

Kirk, Thomas Allison. *Genoa and the Sea: Policy and Power in an Early Modern Maritime Republic, 1559–1684*. Baltimore: Johns Hopkins University Press, 2005.

Kissinger, Henry. *A World Restored: Metternich, Castlereagh and the Problem of Peace, 1812–1822*. London: Phoenix Press, 2000.

Kludas, Arnold. 'Die Kriegsschiffe des Deutschen Bundes 1848 bis 1851', in Walter Hubatsch (ed.), *Die erste Deutsche Flotte 1848–1853*. Herford: E.S. Mittler & Sohn, 1981: 51–60.

Klunder, Willard C. *Lewis Cass and the Politics of Moderation*. Kent: Kent State University Press, 1996.

Knecht, R.J. *Renaissance Warrior and Patron: the Reign of Francis I*. Cambridge: Cambridge University Press, 1994.

Knight, Roger, and Martin Wilcox. *Sustaining the Fleet, 1793–1815: War, the British Navy and the Contractor State*. Woodbridge: Boydell, 2010.

Knight, Roger. *Britain against Napoleon: the Organization of Victory, 1793–1815*. London: Allen Lane, 2013.

Kolb, Eberhard. *Gustav Stresemann*. München: C.H. Beck, 2003.

Labayle Couhat, Jean. *French Warships of World War I*. London: Ian Allan, 1974.

Lambert, Andrew (ed.). *21st Century Corbett: Maritime Strategy and Naval Policy for the Modern Era*. Annapolis: US Naval Institute Press, 2017.

Lambert, Andrew. *Battleships in Transition: the Creation of the Steam Battlefleet, 1815–1860*. London: Conway Maritime Press, 1984.

Lambert, Andrew. *The Challenge: America, Britain and the War of 1812*. London: Faber and Faber, 2012.

Lambert, Andrew. 'The Construction of Naval History 1815–1914', *Mariner's Mirror*, 97, 1 (2011): 207–24.

Lambert, Andrew. *The Crimean War: British Grand Strategy, 1853–56*. Manchester: Manchester University Press, 1990.

Lambert, Andrew. 'Duke of Wellington Class Steam Battleships', *Warship*, 32 (1984): 239–343.

Lambert, Andrew. *The Last Sailing Battlefleet: Maintaining Naval Mastery 1815–1850*. London: Conway Maritime Press, 1991.

Lambert, Andrew. *Nelson: Britannia's God of War*. London: Faber and Faber, 2004.

Lambert, Andrew. 'Politics, Technology and Policy-Making, 1859–1865: Palmerston, Gladstone and the Management of the Ironclad Naval Race', *The Northern Mariner*, 8 (1998): 9–38.

Lambert, Andrew. 'Preparing for the Long Peace: the Reconstruction of the Royal Navy 1815–1830', *Mariner's Mirror*, 82 (1996): 41–54.

Lambert, Andrew. *Seapower States: Culture, Identity and Strategy*. New Haven: Yale University Press, 2018.

Lambert, Craig. 'Henry V and the Crossing to France: Reconstructing Naval Operations for the Agincourt Campaign, 1415', *Journal of Medieval History*, 43, 1 (2017): 24–39.

Lambert, Nicholas A. *Planning Armageddon: British Economic Warfare and the First World War*. Cambridge: Harvard University Press, 2012.

Lambert, Nicholas A. *Sir John Fisher's Naval Revolution*. Columbia: University of South Carolina Press, 1999.

Lane, Frederic C. *Ships for Victory: a History of Shipbuilding under the U.S. Maritime Commission in World War II*. Baltimore: Johns Hopkins University Press, 2001.

Lanessan, Jean-Louis de. *Le Bilan de notre marine*. Paris: Félix Alcan, 1909.

Langer, William L. *The Franco-Russian Alliance, 1890–1894*. Cambridge: Harvard University Press, 1929.

Langer, William L. *European Alliances and Alignments, 1871–1890*. New York: A.A. Knopf, 1931.

Laughton, J.K. *State Papers Relating to the Defeat of the Spanish Armada, Anno 1588*. London: Temple Smith, 1987.

Lavery, Brian. 'The Revolution in Naval Tactics', in Martine Acerra, José P. Merino, et al. (eds), *Les Marines de guerre européennes XVIIe-XVIIIe siècles*. Paris: Presses de l'Université de Paris-Sorbonne, 1985.

Le Fevre, Peter. 'Gibraltar, Tangier and the English Mediterranean Fleet, 1680–1690', *Transactions of the Naval Dockyards Society*, 2 (2006): 19–30.

Le Fevre, Peter (ed.). *Guerres Maritimes, 1688–1713*. Vincennes: Service Historique de la Marine, 1996.

Le Mao, Caroline. *Les Villes portuaires maritimes dans la France moderne XVIe-XVIIIe siècle*. Paris: Armand Colin, 2015.

Le Mao, Caroline, and Philippe Meyzie (eds). *L'Approvisionnement des villes portuaires en Europe du XVIe siècle à nos jours*. Paris: Presses de l'Université de Paris-Sorbonne, 2015.

Lemnitzer, Jan Martin. *Power, Law and the End of Privateering*. London: Palgrave, 2014.

Lemnitzer, Jan Martin. 'Woodrow Wilson's Neutrality, the Freedom of the Seas, and the Myth of the "Civil War Precedents"', *Diplomacy & Statecraft*, 27, 4 (2016): 615–38.

Lenman, Bruce. *Britain's Colonial Wars, 1688–1783*. Harlow: Longman, 2001.

Lenman, Bruce. *England's Colonial Wars, 1550–1688: Conflicts, Empire and National Identity*. Harlow: Longman, 2001.

Leroy-Beaulieu, Paul. *De la Colonisation chez les peuples modernes*. Paris: Guillaumin et Cie., 1874.

Lestringant, Frank. *Le Huguenot et le sauvage. L'Amérique et la controverse coloniale, en France, au temps des guerres de religion (1555–1589)*. Genève: Droz, 2004.

Levine, Alan J. *The War against Rommel's Supply Lines, 1942–43*. Westport: Praeger, 1999.

Levy, James P. *The Royal Navy's Home Fleet in World War II*. Basingstoke: Palgrave, 2003.

Lincoln, Margarette. *Representing the Royal Navy: British Sea Power, 1750–1815*. London: Routledge, 2017.

Lind, Lew. *Battle of the Wine Dark Sea: the Aegean Campaign, 1940–45*. Kenthurst: Kangaroo Press, 1994: 165–68.

Link, Arthur S. *Wilson: the Struggle for Neutrality, 1914–1915*. Princeton: Princeton University Press, 1960.

Linklater, Eric. *The Campaign in Italy*. London: HMSO, 1977.

List, Friedrich. *Das nationale System der politischen Ökonomie*. Stuttgart: F.C. Kotta'scher Verlag, 1841.

List, Friedrich. *National System of Political Economy*. Philadelphia: J.B. Lippincott & Co., 1856.

Livermore, Seward W. 'Battleship Diplomacy in South America, 1905–1925', *Journal of Modern History*, 16, 1 (1944): 31–48.

Lloyd, Christopher. *The Navy and the Slave Trade: the Suppression of the African Slave Trade in the Nineteenth Century*. London: Longmans, Green and Co., 1949.

Lloyd George, David. *War Memoirs, vol. 1*. London: Odhams Press Limited, 1938.

Loades, D.M. *The Making of the Elizabethan Navy, 1540–1590: from the Solent to the Armada*. Woodbridge: Boydell, 2009.

Londonderry, Marquis of (ed.). *Correspondence, Despatches, and other Papers, of Viscount Castlereagh*. 12 vols. London: John Murray, 1853.

Louis, Jérôme. *La question d'Orient sous Louis-Philippe*. PhD thesis, École Practique des Hautes Études, Paris, 2004.

Love, Robert W. *History of the U.S. Navy*. Harrisburg: Stackpole Books, 1992.

Love, Robert W., and John Major. *The Year of D-Day: the 1944 Diary of Admiral Sir Bertram Ramsay*. Hull: University of Hull Press, 1994.

Love, Ronald S. 'Monarchs, Merchants, and Missionaries in Early Modern Asia: the *missions étrangères* in Siam, 1662–1684', *International History Review*, 21, 1 (1999): 1–27.

Luraghi, Raimondo. *A History of the Confederate Navy*. London: Chatham, 1996.

Lutun, Bernard. *La Marine de Colbert études d'organisation*. Paris: Economica, 2003.

Lynn, Martin. *Commerce and Economic Change in West Africa: the Palm Oil Trade in the Nineteenth Century*. Cambridge: Cambridge University Press, 1997.

Lyons, Adam. *The Expedition to Quebec: Politics and the Limitations of British Global Strategy*. London: Bloomsbury, 2013.

MacDonald, Callum. *The Lost Battle: Crete 1941*. London: Macmillan, 1993.

Mackinder, H.J. 'The Geographical Pivot of History', *The Geographical Journal*, 23, 4 (1904): 421–37.

Mahan, Alfred T. *The Influence of Sea Power upon History, 1660–1783*. Boston: Little, Brown and Co., 1890.

Mahan, Alfred T. 'Reflections, Historic and Other, Suggested by the Battle of the Japan Sea', *Naval Institute Proceedings*, 32 (1906): 447–71.

Mahan, Alfred T. *Retrospect & Prospect: Studies in International Relations, Naval and Political*. Boston: Little, Brown, and Company, 1902.

Maiolo, Joseph A. 'The Admiralty and the Anglo-German Naval Agreement of 18 June 1935', *Diplomacy & Statecraft*, 10, 1 (1999): 87–126.

Maiolo, Joseph A. *Cry Havoc: the Arms Race and the Second World War, 1931–1941*. London: John Murray, 2010.

Malkin, H.W. 'The Inner History of the Declaration of Paris', *British Yearbook of International Law*, 8 (1927): 1–44.

Mallet, Robert. *The Italian Navy and Fascist Expansionism, 1935–1940*. London: Frank Cass, 1998.

Mallmann-Showell, Jak P. *German Naval Codebreakers*. Annapolis: Naval Institute Press, 2003.

Mansergh, Aubrey (ed.). *With the Red Fleet: the War Memoirs of the Late Admiral Arseni G. Golovko*. London: Putnam, 1965.

Marder, Arthur J. *The Anatomy of British Sea Power: a History of British Naval Policy in the Pre-Dreadnought Era, 1880–1905*. London: Frank Cass, 1972.

Marder, Arthur J. *From the Dreadnought to Scapa Flow*. 5 vols. Barnsley: Seaforth, 2014.

Marienfeld, Wolfgang. *Wissenschaft und Schlachtflottenbau in Deutschland, 1897-1906*. Berlin: E.S. Mittler & Sohn, 1957.

Marks, Sally. *The Illusion of Peace: International Relations in Europe, 1918–1933*. Basingstoke: Macmillan, 2003.

Marks, Sally. 'The Myths of Reparations', *Central European History*, 11, 3, (1978): 231–55.

Marquand, David. *Ramsay MacDonald*. London: Jonathan Cape, 1977.

Martin, Colin, and Geoffrey Parker. *The Spanish Armada*. Manchester: Mandolin, 1999.

Martin, Louis-Aimé (ed.). *Oeuvres complètes de Jean Racine*. Paris: Lefèvre, 1820.

Marzin, Servane. 'La France, l'Anglaterre et la répression de la traite des Noirs sous le ministère Guizot (1840-1848)', in Sylvie Aprile and Fabrice Bensimon (eds), *La France et l'Angleterre au XIXe siècle: échanges, représentations, comparaisons*. Paris: Créaphis, 2006: 237–54.

Mattox, W.C. *Building the Emergency Fleet*. Cleveland: Penton Publishing, 1920.

Matzke, Rebeca B. *Deterrence through Force: British Naval Power and Foreign Policy under Pax Britannica*. Lincoln: University of Nebraska Press, 2011.

Mawdsley, Evan. *World War II: a New History*. Cambridge: Cambridge University Press, 2009.

McKercher, B.J.C. 'Of Horns and Teeth: the Preparatory Commission and the World Disarmament Conference, 1926–1934', in B.J.C. McKercher (ed.), *Arms Limitation and Disarmament: Restraints on War, 1899–1939*. Westport: Praeger, 1992: 173–201.

McLean, David. *War, Diplomacy and Informal Empire: Britain and the Republics of La Plata 1836–1853*. British Academic Press: London, 1995.

McLean, Samuel. *The Westminster Model Navy: Defining the Royal Navy, 1660–1749*. PhD thesis, King's College London, 2017.

McMeekin, Sean. *The Russian Origins of the First World War*. Cambridge: The Belknap Press, 2011.

McNeill, William H. 'The Industrialization of War', *Review of International Studies*, 8, 3 (1982): 203–13.

McPherson, James M. *War on the Waters: the Union and Confederate Navies, 1861–1865*. Chapell Hill: University of North Carolina Press, 2012.

Mead, Walter Russell. *Special Providence: American Foreign Policy and How it Changed the World*. New York: Routledge, 2002.

Melton, George E. *From Versailles to Mers-el-Kébir: the Promise of Anglo-French Naval Cooperation, 1919–40*. Annapolis: Naval Institute Press, 2015.

Mends, B.S. *Life of Admiral Sir William Robert Mends*. London: John Murray, 1899.

Merlin-Chazelas, Anne (ed.). *Documents relatifs au Clos Des Galées de Rouen et aux armées de mer du roi de France de 1293 à 1418, vol. 1*. Paris: Bibliothèque nationale, 1977.

Micali Baratelli, Franco. *La marina militare italiana nella vita nazionale (1860–1914)*. Milano: Mursia, 1983.

Middlebrook, Martin, and Chris Everitt. *The Bomber Command Diaries: an Operational Reference Book, 1939–1945*. London: Penguin Books, 1990.

Middlebrook, Martin, and P. Mahoney. *The Sinking of the Prince of Wales and the Repulse: the End of the Battleship Era*. Barnsley: Leo Cooper, 2004.

Milner, Marc. *Battle of the Atlantic*. Stroud: Tempus, 2003.

Mindell, David A. *War, Technology and Experience aboard the USS Monitor*. Baltimore: Johns Hopkins University Press, 2000.

Modelski, George, and William R. Thompson. *Seapower in Global Politics, 1494–1994*. Basingstoke: Macmillan, 1988.

Mommsen, Wolfgang. *Max Weber and German Politics, 1890–1920*. Chicago: University of Chicago Press, 1984.

Monina, Giancarlo. *La grande Italia marittima: la propaganda navalista e la Lega navale italiana, 1866–1918*. Soveria Mannelli: Rubbettino, 2009.

Monteiro, Armando da Silva Saturnino. *The First World Sea Power, 1139–1521. Portuguese Sea Battles*. Lisbon: Monteiro, 2010.

Morgan-Owen, David. *The Fear of Invasion: Strategy, Politics, and British War Planning, 1880–1914*. Oxford: Oxford University Press, 2017.

Morgan-Owen, David. 'An "Intermediate Blockade"? British North Sea Strategy, 1912–1914', *War in History*, 22, 4 (2015): 478–502.

Morieux, Renaud. *The Channel: England, France and the Construction of a Maritime Border in the Eighteenth Century*. Cambridge: Cambridge University Press, 2016.

Morriss, Roger. *The Foundations of British Maritime Ascendancy: Resources, Logistics and the State, 1755–1815*. Cambridge: Cambridge University Press, 2011.

Motte, Martin. *Les Larmes de nos souverains. La Pensée stratégique navale française*. Paris: Centre d'études stratégiques de la Marine, 2014.

Motte, Martin. 'Théophile Delcassé: marine et diplomatie', *Cahiers du Centre d'Études d'Histoire de la Défense*, 29 (2006): 9–27.

Motte, Martin. *Une Éducation géostratégique. La pensée navale française de la Jeune École à 1914*. Paris: Economica, 2004.

Mulligan, William. *The Origins of the First World War*. Cambridge: Cambridge University Press, 2010.

Mulqueen, Michael, Deborah Sanders, and Ian Speller (eds). *Small Navies: Strategy and Policy for Small Navies in War and Peace*. London: Routledge, 2014.

Murdoch, Steve. *The Terror of the Seas? Scottish Maritime Warfare, 1513–1713*. Leiden: Brill, 2010.

Murfett, Malcolm. 'Casting Doubt on the Inevitability Syndrome', in Malcolm Murfett (ed.), *Imponderable but not Inevitable: Warfare in the 20th Century*. Santa Barbara: Praeger, 2010: 4–8.

Murfett, Malcolm. *Fool-Proof Relations: the Search for Anglo-American Naval Cooperation during the Chamberlain Years, 1937–1940*. Singapore: Singapore University Press, 1984.

Murfett, Malcolm. 'Living in the Past: a Critical Re-examination of the Singapore Naval Strategy, 1918–41', *War & Society*, 11, 1 (1993):73–103.

Murfett, Malcolm. 'Look Back in Anger: the Western Powers and the Washington Conference of 1921–1922', in B.J.C. McKercher (ed.), *Arms Limitation and Disarmament*. Westport: Praeger, 1992: 83–103.

Murfett, Malcolm. *Naval Warfare, 1919–45: an Operational History of the Volatile War at Sea*. London: Routledge, 2013.

Murfett, Malcolm. 'Reflections on an Enduring Theme: the "Singapore Strategy" at Sixty', in Brian Farrell and Sandy Hunter (eds), *Sixty Years On: the Hall of Singapore Revisited*. Singapore: Eastern Universities Press, 2002: 3–28.

Murfett, Malcolm. 'The Sinking of Japan', *History Today*, 66, 12 (2016): 21–27.

Murphy, Elaine. *Ireland and the War at Sea, 1641–1653*. Woodbridge: Boydell, 2012.

Neff, Stephen C. *War and the Law of Nations: a General History*. Cambridge: Cambridge University Press, 2005.

Neillands, Robin. *The Battle of Normandy, 1944*. London: Cassell, 2002.

Neillands, Robin. *The Dieppe Raid: the Story of the Disastrous 1942 Expedition*. London: Aurum Press, 2006.

Neilson, Keith. 'Reinforcements and Supplies from Overseas: British Strategic Sealift in the First World War', in Greg Kennedy (ed.), *The Merchant Marine in International Affairs, 1850–1950*. London: Frank Cass, 2000: 31–58.

Nicholson, Harold. *The Congress of Vienna: a Study in Allied Unity, 1812–1822*. London: Constable & Co., 1946.

O'Brien, Patrick. 'The Nature and Historical Evolution of an Exceptional Fiscal State and its Possible Significance for the Precocious Commercialization and Industrialization of the British Economy from Cromwell to Nelson', *Economic History Review*, 64, 2 (2011): 408–46.

O'Hara, Vincent P. *The German Fleet at War, 1939–1945*. Annapolis: Naval Institute Press, 2011.

O'Hara, Vincent P. *Struggle for the Middle Sea: the Great Navies at War in the Mediterranean Theater, 1940–1945*. Annapolis: Naval Institute Press, 2009.

Offer, Avner. *The First World War: an Agrarian Interpretation*. Oxford: Clarendon Press, 1989.

O'Keefe, Kevin J. *A Thousand Deadlines: the New York City Press and American Neutrality, 1914–17*. The Hague: Martinus Nijhoff, 1972.

Olivier, David H. 'Two Sides of the Same Coin: German and French Maritime Strategies in the Late Nineteenth Century', in Bruce A. Elleman and S.C.M. Paine (eds), *Commerce Raiding: Historical Case Studies, 1755–2009*. Newport: Naval War College Press, 2013: 89–104.

Osbon, G.A. 'The Crimean Gunboats, I', *Mariner's Mirror*, 51 (1965): 103–15.

Padfield, Peter. *War beneath the Sea: Submarine Conflict during World War II*. New York: John Wiley, 1996.

Pagden, A.R., and J.H. Elliott (eds). *Hernán Cortés: Letters from Mexico*. New Haven: Yale University Press, 2001.

Paixhans, Henri-Joseph. *Nouvelle Force Maritime*. Paris: Bachelier, 1822.

Palmer, M.A.J. 'The "Military Revolution" Afloat: the Era of the Anglo-Dutch Wars and the Transition to Modern Warfare at Sea', *War in History*, 4, 2 (1997): 123–49.

Panzac, Daniel. 'Flottes et arsenaux dans l'affrontement turco-égyptien (1830–1840)', *Cahiers de la Mediterranée*, 84 (2012): 367–78.

Panzac, Daniel. *La Marine ottomane de L'apogée à la chute de l'empire, 1572–1923*. Paris: CNRS, 2009.

Papastratigakis, Nicholas. *Russian Imperialism and Naval Power: Military Strategy and the Build-up to the Russo-Japanese War*. London: I.P. Taurus, 2011.

Parillo, Mark P. *The Japanese Merchant Marine in World War II*. Annapolis: Naval Institute Press, 1993.

Parker, Geoffrey. *The Grand Strategy of Philip II*. New Haven: Yale University Press, 1998.

Parker, Geoffrey. *The Military Revolution. Military Innovation and the Rise of the West, 1500–1800*. Cambridge: Cambridge University Press, 1996.

Parkes, Oscar (ed.). *Jane's Fighting Ships 1931*. London: Sampson Low Marston & Co, 1931.

Parrott, David. *The Business of War: Military Enterprise and Military Revolution in Early Modern Europe*. Cambridge: Cambridge University Press, 2012.

Parshall, Jonathan, and Anthony Tully. *Shattered Sword: the Untold Story of the Battle of Midway*. Washington, DC: Potomac Books, 2005.

Partridge, M.S. 'British Naval Power in the 1860's', *Mariner's Mirror*, 75 (1989): 88–90.

Patalano, Alessio. *Post-War Japan as a Sea Power: Imperial Legacy, Wartime Experience and the Making of a Navy*. London: Bloomsbury, 2016.

Peifer, Douglas C. *Choosing War: Presidential Decisions in the* Maine, Lusitania, *and* Panay *Incidents*. New York: Oxford University Press, 2016.

Pérez-Mallaína Bueno, Pablo Emilio. *Política Naval Española en el Atlántico, 1700–1715*. Sevilla: Consejo Superior de Investigaciones Científicas, 1982.

Perras, Arne. *Carl Peters and German Imperialism, 1856–1918: a Political Biography*. Oxford: Clarendon Press, 2004.

Peszke, Michael Alfred. *Poland's Navy 1918–1945*. New York: Hippocrene Books, 1999.

Peters, Gehard, and John T. Woolley. 'The American Presidency Project'. University of California, n.d. www.presidency.ucsb.edu/index.php.

Phillips, E.J. *The Founding of Russia's Navy: Peter the Great and the Azov Fleet, 1688–1714*. Westport: Greenwood Press, 1995.

Picavet, Camille-Georges. *La Diplomatie française au temps de Louis XIV (1661–1715): institutions, moeurs et coutumes*. Paris: F. Alcan, 1930.

Piggott, Francis. *The Declaration of Paris 1856*. London: University of London Press, 1919.

Pincus, Steven C.A. 'Popery, Trade and Universal Monarchy: the Ideological Context of the Outbreak of the Second Anglo-Dutch War', *English Historical Review*, 107, 422 (1992): 1–29.

Pincus, Steven C.A. *Protestantism and Patriotism: Ideologies and the Making of English Foreign Policy, 1650–1668*. Cambridge: Cambridge University Press, 2002.

Pirenne, Jacques-Henri. *La Sainte-Alliance: organisation européenne de la paix mondiale*. 2 vols. Neuchâtel: Éditions de la Baconnière, 1946–49.

Plokhy, Serhii. 'The City of Glory: Sevastopol in Russian Historical Mythology', *Journal of Contemporary History*, 35, 3 (2000): 369–83.

Plouviez, David. *La Marine française et ses réseaux économiques au XVIIIe siècle*. Paris: Rivages des Xantons, 2014.

Polmar, Norman. *Soviet Naval Power: Challenge for the 1970s*. New York: National Strategy Information Center, 1972.

Prados, John. *Combined Fleet Decoded: the Secret History of American Intelligence and the Japanese Navy in World War II*. New York: Random House, 1995.

Pradt, Dominique Dufour de. *Du Congrès de Vienne*. 2 vols. Paris: Delaunay, 1815.

Preneuf, Jean Martinant de. 'Du Rival méprisé à l'adversaire préféré: L'Italie dans la stratégie navale française de 1870 à 1899', *Revue Historique des Armées*, 250 (2008): 34–52.

Preneuf, Jean Martinant de. 'Un vrai-faux déclin? (1870–1914)', *Études Marines*, 4 (2013): 14–37.

Preston, Antony, and John Major. *Send a Gunboat: the Victorian Navy and Supremacy at Sea, 1854–1907*. London: Conway, 2007.

Preston, Paul. *The Politics of Revenge: Fascism and the Military in Twentieth-Century Spain*. London: Routledge, 1995.

Pritchard, James. *Anatomy of a Naval Disaster: the 1746 French Expedition to North America*. Kingston and Montreal: McGill-Queen's Press, 1995.

Pritchard, James. *Louis XV's Navy, 1748–1762: a Study of Organization and Administration*. Kingston and Montreal: McGill-Queens University Press, 1987.

Rahn, Werner. *Reichsmarine und Landesverteidigung 1919–1928: Konception und Führung der Marine in der Weimarer Republik*. Munich: Bernard & Graefe, 1976.

Ratzel, Friedrich. *Politische Geographie*. Munich: Oldenbourg, 1897.

Rawleigh, Sir Walter. 'A Discourse of the Invention of Ships, etc.' in *Judicious and Select Essayes and Observations, etc*. London: Humphrey Moseley, 1650.

Rawlinson, John L. *China's Struggle for Naval Development, 1839–1895*. Cambridge: Harvard University Press, 1967.

Redding, Benjamin W.D. *Divided by La Manche: Naval Enterprise and Maritime Revolution in Early Modern England and France, 1545–1642*. PhD thesis, University of Warwick, 2016.

Redford, Duncan. *The Submarine: a Cultural History from the Great War to Nuclear Combat*. London: I.B. Tauris, 2010.

Reed, Edward J. 'On Long and Short Iron-Clads', *Transactions of the Institution of Naval Architects*, 10 (1869): 59–91.

Reussner, André, and L. Nicholas. *La Puissance navale dans l'historire. Vol. 2: 1815–1914*. Paris: Editions Maritimes et Coloniales, 1961.

Rhys-Jones, Graham. *The Loss of the Bismarck: an Avoidable Disaster*. Annapolis: Naval Institute Press, 1999.

Ricard, Serge. 'The Roosevelt Corollary', *Presidential Studies Quarterly*, 36, 1 (2006): 17–26.

Ringmar, Erik. *Identity, Interest and Action: a Cultural Explanation of Sweden's Intervention in the Thirty Years' War*. Cambridge: Cambridge University Press, 1996.

Robb-Webb, Jon. 'Corbett and the Campaign of Trafalgar: Naval Operations in their Strategic Context', *Defence Studies*, 8, 2 (2008): 157–179.

Roberts, Penny. *Peace and Authority During the French Religious Wars, c.1560–1600*. Basingstoke: Palgrave, 2013.

Roberts, Stephen S. 'The French Transatlantic Steam Packet Programme of 1840', *Mariner's Mirror*, 73 (1987): 273–86.

Roberts, William H. *Civil War Ironclads: the U.S. Navy and Industrial Mobilization*. Baltimore: Johns Hopkins University Press, 2002.

Robiquet, Paul. *Discours et opinions de Jules Ferry, vol. 5*. Paris: Armand Colin, 1897.

Rodger, N.A.M. 'Anglo-German Naval Rivalry, 1860–1914', in Michael Epkenhans, Jörg Hillmann, and Frank Nägler (eds), *Jutland: World War I's Greatest Naval Battle*. Lexington: University Press of Kentucky, 2015: 7–23.

Rodger, N.A.M. *The Command of the Ocean: a Naval History of Great Britain. Vol. 2: 1649–1815*. London: Allen Lane, 2004.

Rodger, N.A.M. 'The Dark Ages of the Admiralty, 1869–1885', *Mariner's Mirror*, 61 (1975): 331–44.

Rodger, N.A.M. 'The Development of Broadside Gunnery, 1450–1650', *Mariner's Mirror*, 82, 3 (1996): 301–24.

Rodger, N.A.M. 'From the "Military Revolution" to the "Fiscal-Naval State"', *Journal for Maritime Research*, 13, 2 (2011): 119–28.

Rodger, N.A.M. 'The Law and Language of Private Naval Warfare', *Mariner's Mirror*, 100, 1 (2014): 5–16.

Rodger, N.A.M. 'The Nature of Victory at Sea', *Journal for Maritime Research*, 7, 1 (2005): 110–122.

Rodger, N.A.M. 'The New Atlantic', in John B. Hattendorf and Richard W. Unger (eds), *War at Sea in the Middle Ages and the Renaissance*. Woodbridge: Boydell, 2003: 233–47.

Rodger, N.A.M. 'Queen Elizabeth and the Myth of Sea-Power in English History', *Transactions of the Royal Historical Society*, 14 (2004): 153–74.

Rodger, N.A.M. *Safeguard of the Sea: a Naval History of Britain. Vol. 1: 660–1649.* London: HarperCollins, 1997.

Rodger, N.A.M. 'Sea-Power and Empire, 1688–1793', in P.J. Marshall (ed.), *The Oxford History of the British Empire. Vol. 2: the Eighteenth Century*. Oxford: Oxford University Press, 1998: 169–183.

Rodger, N.A.M., J. Ross Dancy, Benjamin Darnell, and Evan Wilson (eds), *Strategy and the Sea: Essays in Honour of John B. Hattendorf.* Woodbridge: Boydell, 2016.

Rodríguez González, Agustín Ramón. *Política naval de la Restauración (1875–1898).* Madrid: San Martín, 1988.

Roessler, Eberhard. *Die Unterseeboote der Kaiserlichen Marine.* Bonn: Bernard & Graefe, 1997.

Rogers, H.C.B. *Troopships and their History.* London: Seely Service, 1963.

Röhl, John C.G. *Wilhelm II: into the Abyss of War and Exile 1900–1941.* Cambridge: Cambridge University Press, 2014.

Rohwer, Jürgen. *Chronology of the War at Sea, 1939–1945: the Naval History of World War Two.* London: Chatham Publishing, 2005.

Rohwer, Jürgen, and G. Hummelchen. *Chronology of the War at Sea, 1939–1945: the Naval History of World War Two.* Annapolis: Naval Institute Press, 1992.

Rohwer, Jürgen, and Mikhail S. Monokov, *Stalin's Ocean-Going Fleet: Soviet Naval Strategy and Shipbuilding Programmes, 1935–1953.* London: Frank Cass, 2001.

Roksund, Arne. *The Jeune École: the Strategy of the Weak.* Leiden: Brill, 2007.

Rommelse, Gijs. 'Introduction: the Military Revolution at Sea', *Journal for Maritime Research*, 13, 2 (2011): 117–18.

Rommelse, Gijs. *The Second Anglo-Dutch War (1665–1667): raison d'état, Mercantilism and Maritime Strife.* Hilversum: Verloren, 2006.

Rommelse, Gijs, and Roger Downing. 'The Fleet as an Ideological Pillar of Dutch Radical Republicanism, 1650–1672', *International Journal of Maritime History*, 27, 3 (2015): 387–410.

Ropp, Theodore. *The Development of a Modern Navy: French Naval Policy, 1871–1904.* Annapolis: Naval Institute Press, 1987.

Rose, Gideon. *How Wars End: Why We Always Fight the Last Battle.* New York: Simon & Schuster, 2011.

Rose, Susan. *England's Medieval Navy: Ships, Men and Warfare.* Barnsley: Seaforth, 2013.

Rose, Susan. *Medieval Naval Warfare, 1000–1500.* London: Routledge, 2002.

Rosenberger, Bernard. 'La Croisade africaine et le pouvoir royal au Portugal au XVe siècle', in Bernard Rosenberger et al. (eds), *Genèse de l'état moderne en Méditerranée*. Rome: École Française de Rome, 1993.

Rowlands, Guy. *The Dynastic State and the Army under Louis XIV: Royal Service and Private Interest, 1661–1701.* Cambridge: Cambridge University Press, 2002.

Rowlands, Guy. *The Financial Decline of a Great Power: War, Influence, and Money in Louis XIV's France.* Oxford: Oxford University Press, 2012.

Ruge, Friedrich. *The Soviets as Naval Opponents, 1941–1945.* Cambridge: Patrick Stephens, 1979.

Rüger, Jan. *The Great Naval Game: Britain and Germany in the Age of Empire.* Cambridge: Cambridge University Press, 2007.

Rüger, Jan. 'Revisiting the Anglo-German Antagonism', *Journal of Modern History*, 83, 3 (2011): 579–617.

Sadkovich, James J. *The Italian Navy in World War II.* Westport: Greenwood Press, 1994.

Salewski, Michael. *Deutschland und der Zweite Weldkrieg.* Paderborn: Ferdinance Schoningh Verlag, 2005.

Salewski, Michael. *Die Deutschen und die See.* Stuttgart: Franz Steiner Verlag, 1998.

Sandberg, Brian. *War and Conflict in the Early Modern World, 1500–1700.* Cambridge: Polity Press, 2016.

Sandler, Stanley. *The Emergence of the Modern Capital Ship.* Newark: University of Delaware Press, 1979.

Satsuma, Shinsuke. *Britain and Colonial Maritime War in the Early Eighteenth Century: Silver, Seapower and the Atlantic.* Woodbridge: Boydell, 2013.

Scammell, G.V. *The First Imperial Age: European Overseas Expansion, c.1400–1715.* London: Routledge, 1992.

Schenking, J. Charles. *Making Waves: Politics, Propaganda and the Emergence of the Imperial Japanese Navy, 1868–1922.* Stanford: Stanford University Press, 2005.

Scheybeler, Catherine. *A Study of Spanish Naval Policy During the Reign of Ferdinand VI.* PhD thesis, King's College London, 2014.

Schofield, B.B. *The Arctic Convoys.* London: Macdonald & Janes, 1977.

Schroeder, Joachim. *Die U-Boote des Kaisers.* Bonn: Bernard & Graefe, 2002.

Schroeder, Paul W. *The Transformation of European Politics, 1763–1848.* Oxford: Clarendon Press, 1994.

Scott, Hamish. *The Birth of a Great Power System, 1740–1815.* London: Routledge, 2013.

Scott, Hamish. *British Foreign Policy in the Age of the American Revolution.* Oxford: Oxford University Press, 1990.

Scott, Hamish. 'The Importance of Bourbon Naval Reconstruction to the Strategy of Choiseul after the Seven Years' War', *International History Review*, 1 (1979): 20–35.

Sebag-Montefiore, Hugh. *Enigma: the Battle for the Code.* London: Phoenix, 2001.

Seeley, John. *The Expansion of England.* London: Macmillan, 1883.

Seligmann, Matthew S. 'Naval History by Conspiracy Theory: the British Admiralty before the First World War and the Methodology of Revisionism', *Journal of Strategic Studies*, 38, 7 (2015): 966–84.

Seligmann, Matthew S., and David Morgan-Owen. 'Evolution or Revolution? British Naval Policy in the Fisher Era', *Journal of Strategic Studies*, 38, 7 (2015): 937–943.

Semmel, Bernard. *Liberalism and Naval Strategy: Ideology, Interest and Sea Power during Pax Britannica.* London: Allen & Unwin, 1986.

Semmes, Raphael. *Croisières de l'Alabama et du Sumter.* Paris: E. Dentu, 1864.

Sharp, Alan. *The Versailles Settlement: Peacemaking after the First World War, 1919–1923.* Basingstoke: Palgrave, 2008.

Shaw, Stanford J., and Ezel K. Shaw. *History of the Ottoman Empire and Modern Turkey, vol. 2.* Cambridge: Cambridge University Press, 1977.

Sherwood, Marika. *After Abolition: Britain and the Slave Trade since 1807.* London: I.B. Tauris, 2007.

Shulman, Mark Russell. *Navalism and the Emergence of American Sea Power, 1882–1893.* Annapolis: Naval Institute Press, 1995.

Sicking, Louis. *Neptune and the Netherlands: State, Economy and War at Sea in the Renaissance.* Leiden: Brill, 2004.

Sicking, Louis. 'Selling and Buying Protection: Dutch War Fleets at the Service of Venice (1617–1667)', *Studi Veneziani,* 67 (2013): 89–106.

Silverstone, Paul H. *U.S. Warships of World War I.* London: Ian Allan, 1970.

Simms, Brendan. *Europe: the Struggle for Supremacy, 1453 to the Present.* London: Allen Lane, 2013.

Simms, Brendan. *Three Victories and a Defeat: the Rise and Fall of the First British Empire, 1714–1783.* London: Allen Lane, 2007.

Simpson, Michael (ed.). *The Cunningham Papers. Vol. 1: the Mediterranean Fleet, 1939–1942.* Aldershot: Ashgate, 1999.

Smith, Denis Mack. *Mussolini: a Biography.* New York: Alfred A. Knopf, 1982.

Smith, Michael. *Station X: the Codebreakers of Bletchley Park.* London: Channel 4 Books, 1998.

Sondhaus, Lawrence. *The Great War at Sea: a Naval History of the First World War.* Cambridge: Cambridge University Press, 2014.

Sondhaus, Lawrence. *The Habsburg Empire and the Sea: Austrian Naval Policy, 1797–1866.* West Lafayette: Purdue University Press, 1989.

Sondhaus, Lawrence. *The Naval Policy of Austria-Hungary, 1867–1918: Navalism, Industrial Development and the Politics of Dualism.* West Lafayette: Purdue University Press, 1994.

Sondhaus, Lawrence. *Naval Warfare, 1815–1914.* London: Routledge, 2001.

Sondhaus, Lawrence. *Preparing for Weltpolitik: German Sea Power before the Tirpitz Era.* Annapolis: Naval Institute Press, 1997.

Soulsby, Hugh G. *The Right of Search and the Slave Trade in Anglo-American Relations, 1814–1862.* Baltimore: Johns Hopkins University Press, 1933.

Speller, Ian (ed.). *The Royal Navy and Maritime Power in the Twentieth Century.* London: Frank Cass, 2005.

Spiers, Edward M. *The Army and Society 1815–1914.* London: Longman, 1980.

Sprout, Harold, and Margaret Sprout. *The Rise of American Naval Power, 1776–1918.* Annapolis: Naval Institute Press, 1980.

Spruyt, Hendrik. *The Sovereign State and its Competitors: an Analysis of Systems Change.* Princeton: Princeton University Press, 1994.

Stapelbroek, Koen. 'The Rights of Neutral Trade and its Forgotten History', in Koen Stapelbroek (ed.), *Trade and War: the Neutrality of Commerce in the Inter-State System.* Helsinki: Helsinki Collegium for Advanced Studies, 2011: 3–13.

Stead, W.T. 'What is the Truth about the Navy?', *Pall Mall Gazette,* 15 September 1884, p.1.

Steffen, Dirk. 'The Holtzendorff Memorandum of 22 December 1916 and Germany's Declaration of Unrestricted U-boat Warfare', *Journal of Military History,* 68, 1 (2004): 215–24.

Steiner, Zara. *The Lights that Failed: European International History, 1919–1933.* Oxford: Oxford University Press, 2005.

Steiner, Zara. *The Triumph of the Dark: European International History, 1933–1939.* Oxford: Oxford University Press, 2011.

Stevenson, David. *1914–1918: the History of the First World War.* London: Penguin Books, 2004.

Stevenson, David. *Armaments and the Coming of War: Europe, 1904–1914.* Oxford: Clarendon Press, 1996.

Stevenson, David. *With Our Backs to the Wall: Victory and Defeat in 1918.* London: Allen Lane, 2011.

Stibbe, Matthew. *German Anglophobia and the Great War, 1914–1918.* Cambridge: Cambridge University Press, 2001.

Still, William N. *Crisis at Sea: the US Navy in European Waters in World War I.* Gainesville: University Press of Florida, 2006.

Still, William N. *Iron Afloat: the Story of the Confederate Armorclads.* Columbia: University of South Carolina Press, 1985.

Stone, John. *Military Strategy: the Politics and Technique of War.* London: Continuum, 2011.

Storrs, Christopher. *The Resilience of the Spanish Monarchy, 1665–1700.* Oxford: Oxford University Press, 2006.

Strachan, Hew. *European Armies and the Conduct of War.* London: Routledge, 1983.

Stradling, R.A. *The Armada of Flanders: Spanish Maritime Policy and European War, 1568–1668.* Cambridge: Cambridge University Press, 1992.

Sullivan, Brian R. 'The Strategy of the Decisive Weight: Italy, 1882–1922', in Williamson Murray, MacGregor Knox, and Alvin Bernstein (eds), *The Making of Strategy: Rulers, States, and War.* Cambridge: Cambridge University Press, 1994: 307–51.

Sumida, Jon T. *In Defence of Naval Supremacy: Finance, Technology and British Naval Policy, 1889–1914.* Boston: Unwin Hyman, 1989.

Sumida, Jon T. *Inventing Grand Strategy and Teaching Command: the Classic Works of Alfred Thayer Mahan Reconsidered.* Baltimore: Johns Hopkins University Press, 2000.

Suny, Ronald Grigor. *The Soviet Experiment: Russia, the USSR and the Successor States.* Oxford: Oxford University Press, 2010.

Swann, Julian, and Joël Félix (eds), *The Crisis of the Absolute Monarchy: France from Old Regime to Revolution.* Oxford: Oxford University Press, 2013.

Symcox, Geoffrey Walter. *The Crisis of French Sea Power, 1688–1697: from the guerre d'escadre to the guerre de course.* The Hague: Martinus Nijhoff, 1974.

Symonds, Craig L. *The Civil War at Sea.* Santa Barbara: Praeger, 2009.

Symonds, Craig L. *Lincoln and his Admirals: Abraham Lincoln, the U.S. Navy and the Civil War.* New York: Oxford University Press, 2008.

Syrett, David. *The Defeat of the German U-boats: the Battle of the Atlantic.* Columbia: University of South Carolina Press, 1994.

Syrett, David. 'Home Waters or America? The Dilemma of British Naval Strategy in 1778', *Mariner's Mirror*, 77, 4 (1991): 365–77.

Syrett, David. *The Royal Navy in American Waters, 1775–1783.* Aldershot: Scolar Press, 1989.

Szabo, Franz A.J. *The Seven Years War in Europe, 1756–1763.* London: Routledge, 2015.

Taillemite, Etienne. 'L'Opinion française et la Jeune École', *Marine et technique au XIXe siècle.* Paris: Service Historique de la Marine, 1988: 477–93.

Tarrant, V.E. *The Last Year of the Kriegsmarine: May 1944–May 1945.* London: Arms and Armour, 1995.

Tarrant, V.E. *The U-boat Offensive 1914–1945.* London: Arms and Armour, 1989.

Taylor, A.J.P. *The Struggle for Mastery in Europe, 1848–1918.* Oxford: Oxford University Press, 1971.

Taylor, Theodore. *Battle in the Arctic Seas: the Story of Convoy PQ17.* New York: Thomas Crowell, 1976.

Terraine, John. *Business in Great Waters: the U-boat Wars, 1916–1945.* London: Leo Cooper, 1989.

Thomas, Hugh. *The Spanish Civil War.* New York: Modern Library Paperbacks, 2001.

Thomas, R.T. *Britain and Vichy: the Dilemma of Anglo-French Relations, 1940–42.* London: Macmillan, 1979.

Thompson, I.A.A. *War and Government in Habsburg Spain, 1560–1620.* London: Athlone, 1976.

Till, Geoffrey. *Seapower: a Guide for the Twenty-First Century.* London: Routledge, 2018.

Till, Geoffrey. 'Trafalgar and the Decisive Battles of the Twenty-First Century', *Cambridge Review of International Affairs,* 18, 3 (2005): 455–70.

Tillotson, H.M. *Finland at Peace and War, 1918–1993.* Norwich: Michael Russell, 1993.

Tocqueville, Alexis de. *Oeuvres complètes, vol. 9.* Paris: Michel Lèvy Frères, 1866.

Torres Sánchez, Rafael. *Military Entrepreneurs and the Spanish Contractor State in the Eighteenth Century.* Oxford: Oxford University Press, 2016.

Torres Sánchez, Rafael (ed.). *War, State and Development: Fiscal-Military States in the Eighteenth Century.* Pamplona: Ediciones Universidad de Navarra, 2007.

Tracy, Nicholas. *Attack on Maritime Trade.* London: Macmillan, 1991.

Tracy, Nicholas. 'The Falklands Crisis of 1770: Use of Naval Force', *English Historical Review,* 90, 354 (1975): 40–75.

Tracy, Nicholas. *Manila Ransomed: the British Assault on Manila in the Seven Years War.* Exeter: University of Exeter Press, 1995.

Tracy, Nicholas. *Navies, Deterrence and American Independence Britain and Sea Power in the 1760s and 1770s.* Vancouver: University of British Columbia Press, 1988.

Tracy, Nicholas (ed.). *Sea Power and the Control of Trade: Belligerent Rights from the Russian War to the Beira Patrol, 1854–1970.* London: Ashgate, 2005.

Trim, D.J.B. 'Early-Modern Colonial Warfare and the Campaign of Alcazarquivir, 1578', *Small Wars and Insurgencies,* 8, 1 (1997): 1–34.

Trim, D.J.B. 'Transnational Calvinist Cooperation and "Mastery of the Sea" in the Late Sixteenth Century', in David Davies, Alan James, and Gijs Rommelse (eds), *Ideologies of Western Naval Power, c.1500–1815.* Aldershot: Ashgate, 2018.

Trim, D.J.B., and Mark Charles Fissel (eds). *Amphibious Warfare, 1000–1700: Commerce, State Formation and European Expansion.* Leiden: Brill, 2006.

Trommler, Frank. 'The *Lusitania* Effect: America's Mobilization against Germany in World War I', *German Studies Review,* 32, 2 (2009): 241–66.

Tucker, Spencer C. (ed.). *World War I: the Definitive Encyclopedia and Document Collection.* 5 vols. Santa Barbara: ABC-CLIO, 2014.

Tute, Warren, John Costello, and Terry Hughes. *D-Day.* London: Sidgwick & Jackson, 1974.

Tyler, David B. *Steam Conquers the Atlantic.* New York: D. Appleton-Century Company, 1939.

Van der Vat, Dan. *The Atlantic Campaign: the Great Struggle at Sea, 1939–1945.* London: Hodder & Stoughton, 1988.

Van der Vat, Dan. *The Grand Scuttle: the Sinking of the German Fleet at Scapa Flow in 1919.* Edinburgh: Birlinn, 2007.

Van Dyke, Carl. *The Soviet Invasion of Finland, 1939–40.* London: Frank Cass, 1997.

Van Loo, Ivo. 'For Freedom and Fortune: the Rise of Dutch Privateering in the First Half of the Dutch Revolt, 1568–1609', in Marco Van der Hoeven (ed.), *Exercise of Arms: Warfare in the Netherlands 1568–1648.* Leiden: Brill, 1997.

Vergé-Franceschi, Michel. *La Marine française au XVIIIe siècle.* Paris: SEDES, 1996.

Villa, Brian L. *Unauthorized Action: Mountbatten and the Dieppe Raid*. Toronto: Oxford University Press, 1989.

Villiers, Patrick. 'Et Si Trafalgar n'avait jamais existé? Ou le mythe de la victoire décisive', *La Revue Maritime*, 472 (2005): 38–49.

Villiers, Patrick. 'La Chesapeake, la bataille qui a gagné la guerre d'indépendence', in *La France sur mer: de Louis XIII à Napoléon Ier*. Paris: Pluriel, 2015: 231–40.

Villiers, Patrick. 'Le Commerce colonial au fondement du financement de la guerre d'indépendence américaine', in *La France sur mer*. Paris: Pluriel, 2015: 195–204.

Viner, Jacob. 'Power versus Plenty as Objectives of Foreign Policy in the Seventeenth and Eighteenth Centuries', *World Politics*, 1, 1 (1948): 1–29.

Wanner, Michal. 'Albrecht of Wallenstein as "General of the Ocean and the Baltic Seas" and the Northern Maritime Plan', *Forum Navale*, 64 (2008): 8–33.

Watson, Bruce Allen. *Exit Rommel: the Tunisian Campaign, 1942–43*. Westport: Praeger, 1999.

Webster, Charles K. *The Foreign Policy of Castlereagh, 1815–1822: Britain and the European Alliance*. London: G. Bell and Sons, 1934.

Weinberg, Gerhard. *Hitler's Foreign Policy, 1933–1939: the Road to World War II*. New York: Enigma Books, 2010.

Widén, Jerker. *Theorist of Maritime Strategy: Sir Julian Corbett and His Contribution to Military and Naval Thought*. Burlington: Ashgate, 2012.

Wiggan, Richard. *Hunt the Altmark*. London: Robert Hale, 1982.

Willis, Sam. *Fighting at Sea in the Eighteenth Century: the Art of Sailing Warfare*. Woodbridge: Boydell, 2008.

Willis, Sam. *In the Hour of Victory: the Royal Navy at War in the Age of Nelson*. London: Atlantic Books, 2013.

Willis, Sam. *The Struggle for Sea Power: a Naval History of American Independence*. London: Atlantic Books, 2015.

Willmott, H.P. *The Barrier and the Javelin: Japanese and Allied Pacific Strategies, February to June 1942*. Annapolis: Naval Institute Press, 1983.

Willmott, H.P. *Grave of a Dozen Schemes: British Naval Planning and the War against Japan*. Annapolis: Naval Institute Press, 1996.

Willmott, H.P., Haruo Tohmatsu, and W. Spencer Johnson. *Pearl Harbor*. London: Cassell, 2001.

Wilson, Evan. *A Social History of British Naval Officers, 1775–1815*. Woodbridge: Boydell, 2017.

Wilson, Kathleen. 'Empire, Trade and Popular Politics in Mid-Hanoverian Britain: the Case of Admiral Vernon', *Past & Present*, 121 (1988): 74–109.

Wilson-Bareau, Juliet, and David C. Degener. *Manet and the American Civil War: the Battle of U.S.S. Kearsage and C.S.S. Alabama*. New Haven: Yale University Press, 2003.

Winton, John. *The Forgotten Fleet: the British Navy in the Pacific, 1944–1945*. New York: Coward McCann, 1969.

Wong, J.Y. *Deadly Dreams: Opium, Imperialism and the Arrow War (1856–1860) in China*. Cambridge: Cambridge University Press, 1998.

Woodfine, Philip. 'Ideas of Naval Power and the Conflict with Spain, 1737–1742', in Jeremy Black and Philip Woodfine (eds). *The British Navy and the Use of Naval Power in the Eighteenth Century*. Leicester: Leicester University Press, 1988: 71–90.

Woodman, Richard. *The Arctic Convoys, 1941–1945*. London: John Murray, 1994.

Wragg, David. *Carrier Combat*. Stroud: Sutton Publishing, 1997.

Wragg, David. *Swordfish: the Story of the Taranto Raid*. London: Weidenfeld & Nicolson, 2003.

Yagi, George. *The Struggle for North America, 1754–1758: Britannia's Tarnished Laurels*. London: Bloomsbury, 2016.

Index